Aisha Franz
Earthling

AISHA FRANZ

Earthling

TRANSLATED BY HELGE DASCHER

DRAWN & QUARTERLY

drawnandquarterly.com

First paperback edition: October 2014
Printed in Malaysia
10 9 8 7 6 5 4 3 2 1

Library and Archives Canada Cataloguing in Publication
Franz, Aisha, 1984 -
[Alien. English]
Earthling / Aisha Franz; translated by Helge Dascher.
Originally published: Alien/Aisha Franz. --Berlin: Reprodukt, 2011.
Translation of: Alien.
ISBN 978-1-77046-166-6 (pbk.)
1. Graphic Novels. I. Dascher, Helge, 1965-, translator
II. Title. III. Title: Alien. English.
PN6757.F73A5513 2014 741.5'943 C2013-908539-4

Published in the USA by Drawn & Quarterly,
a client publisher of Farrar, Straus and Giroux
Orders: 888.330.8477

Published in Canada by Drawn & Quarterly,
a client publisher of Raincoast Books
Orders: 800.663.5714

Published in the United Kingdom by Drawn & Quarterly,
a client publisher of Publishers Group UK
Orders: info@pguk.co.uk

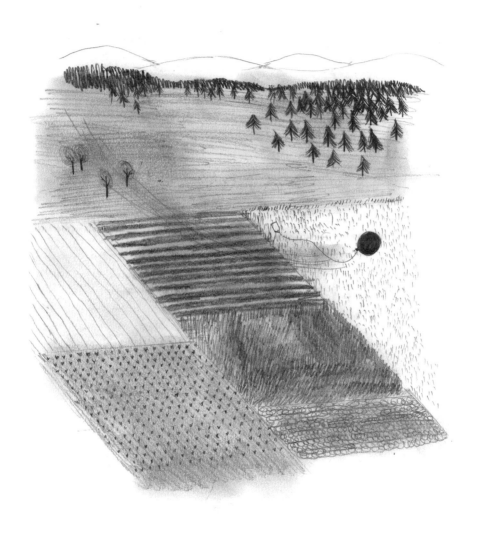

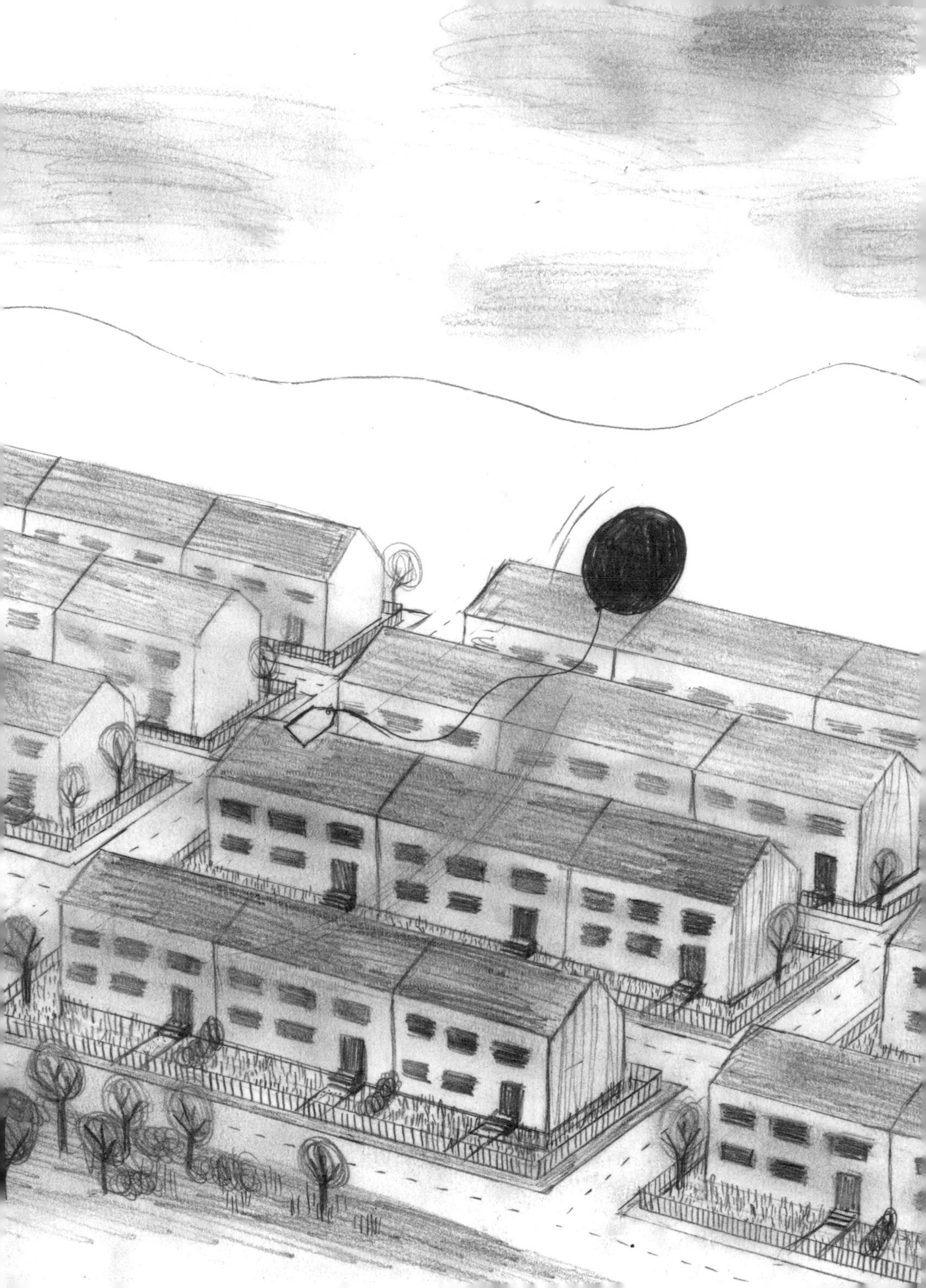

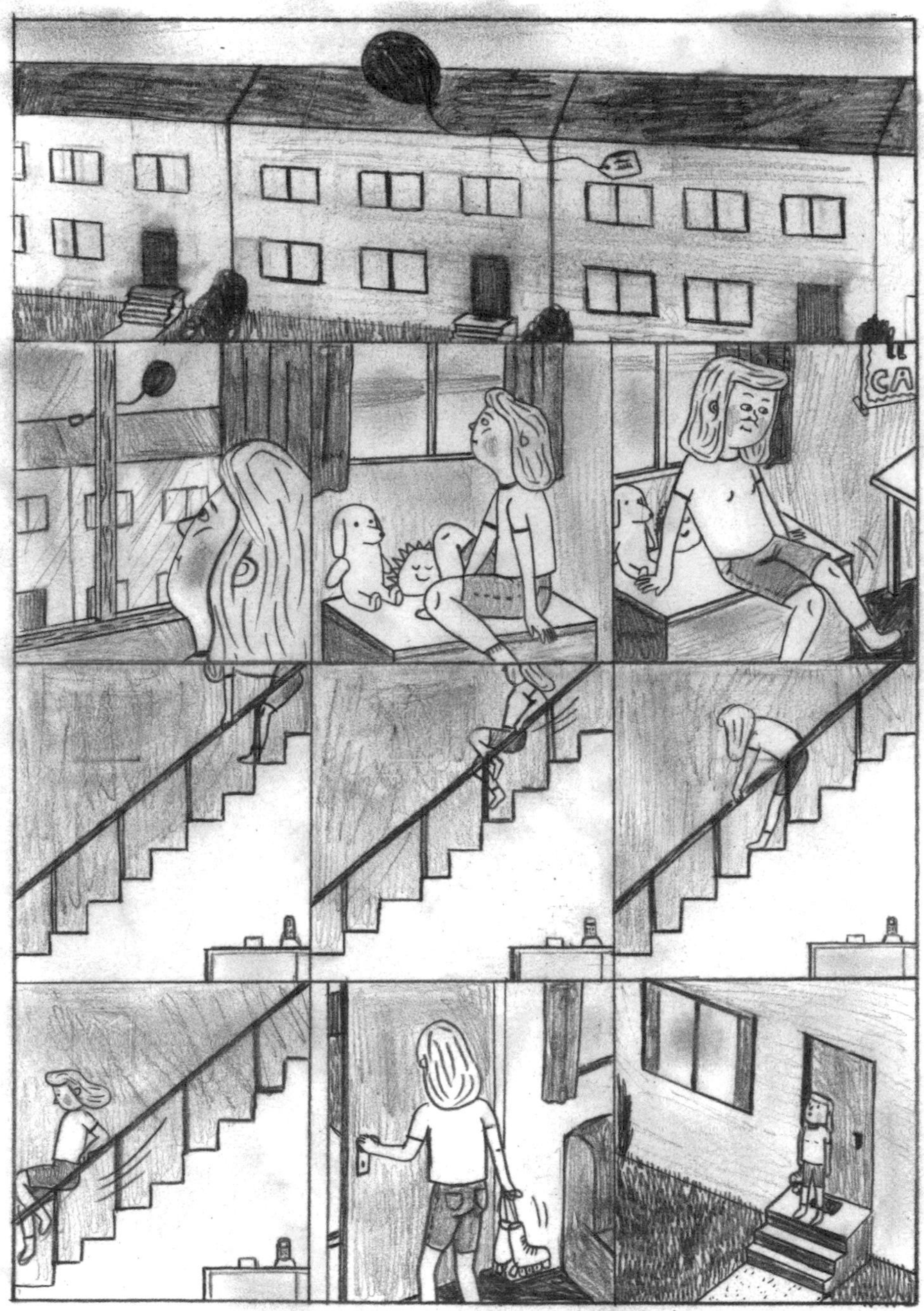
CA

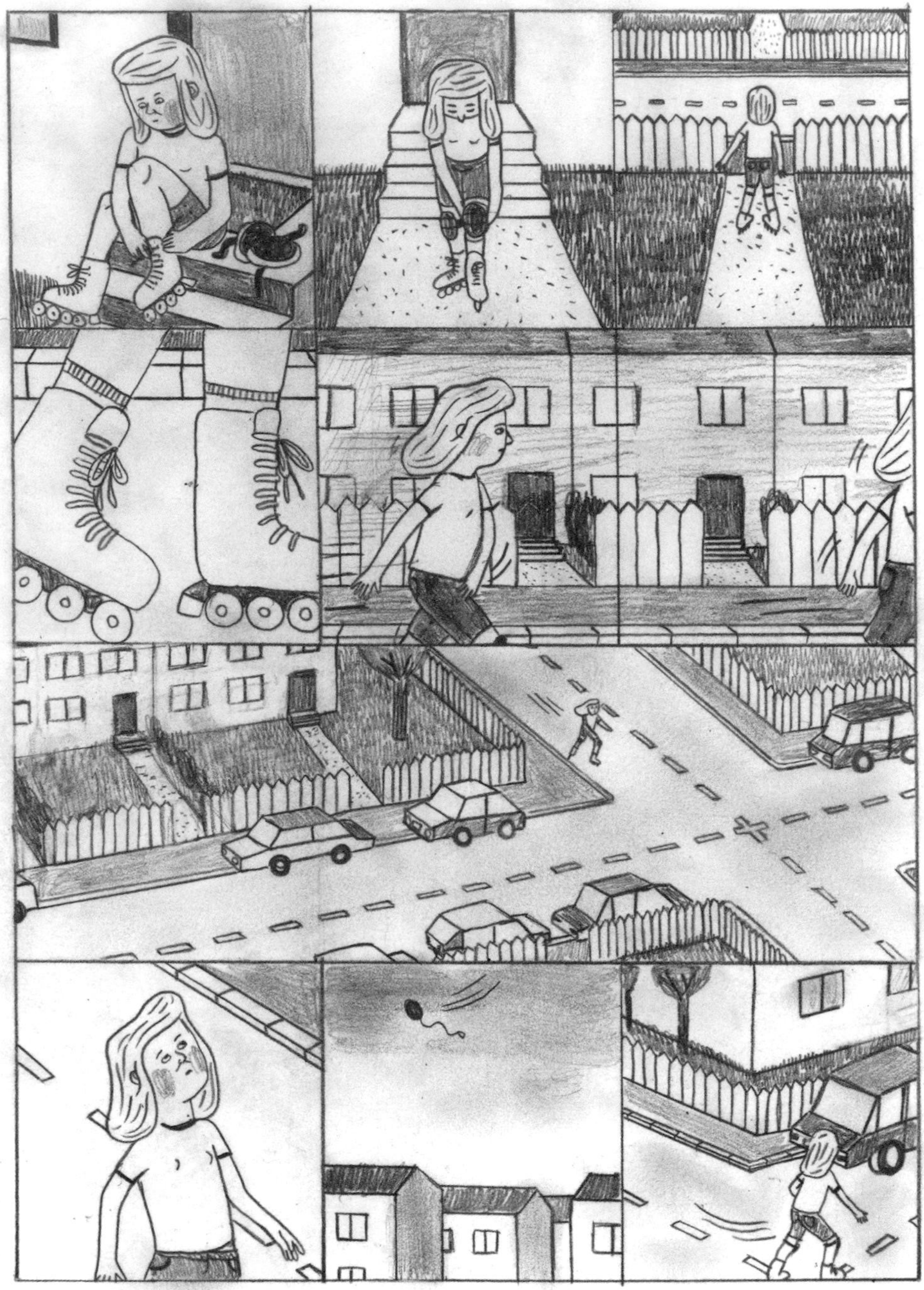

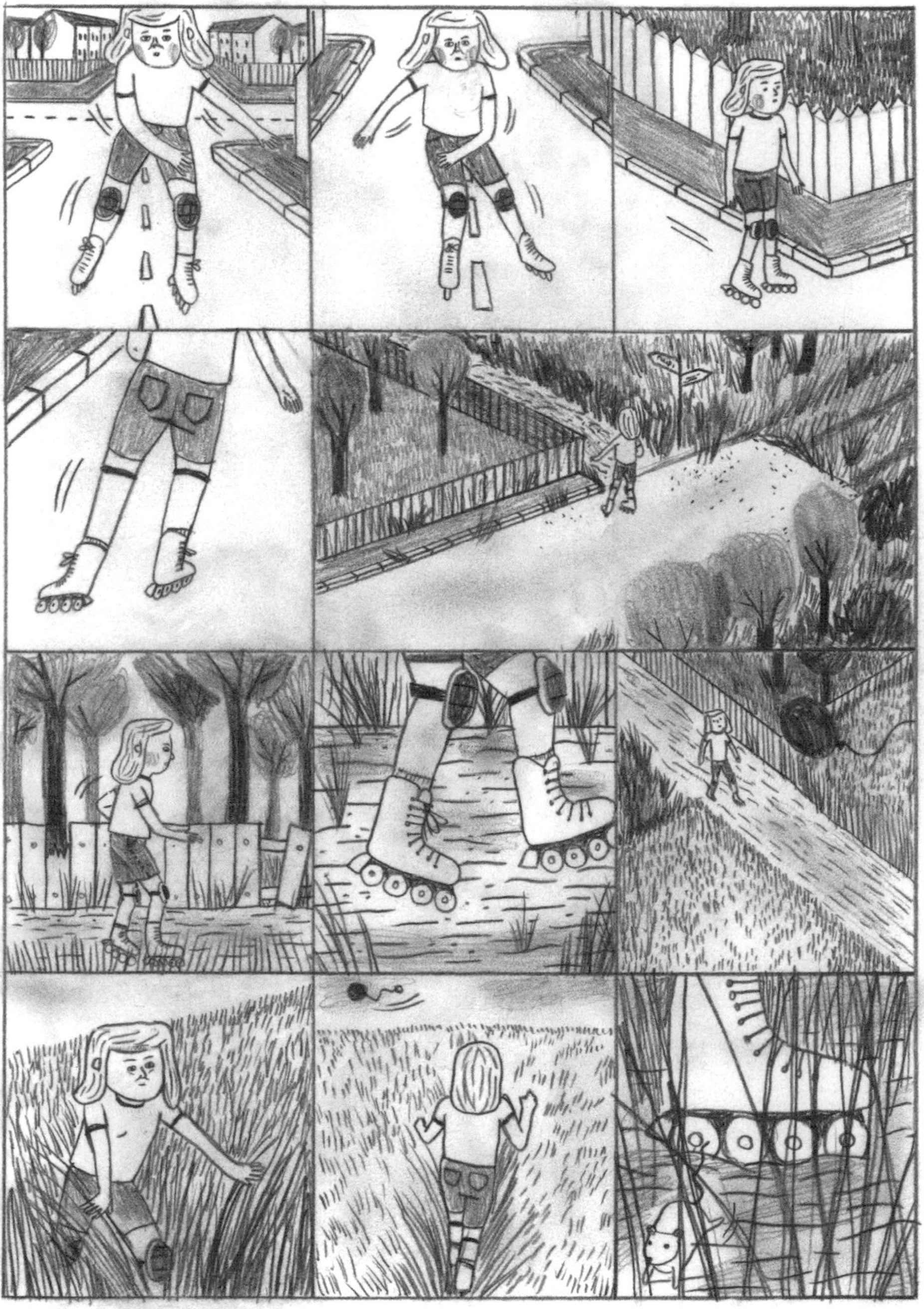

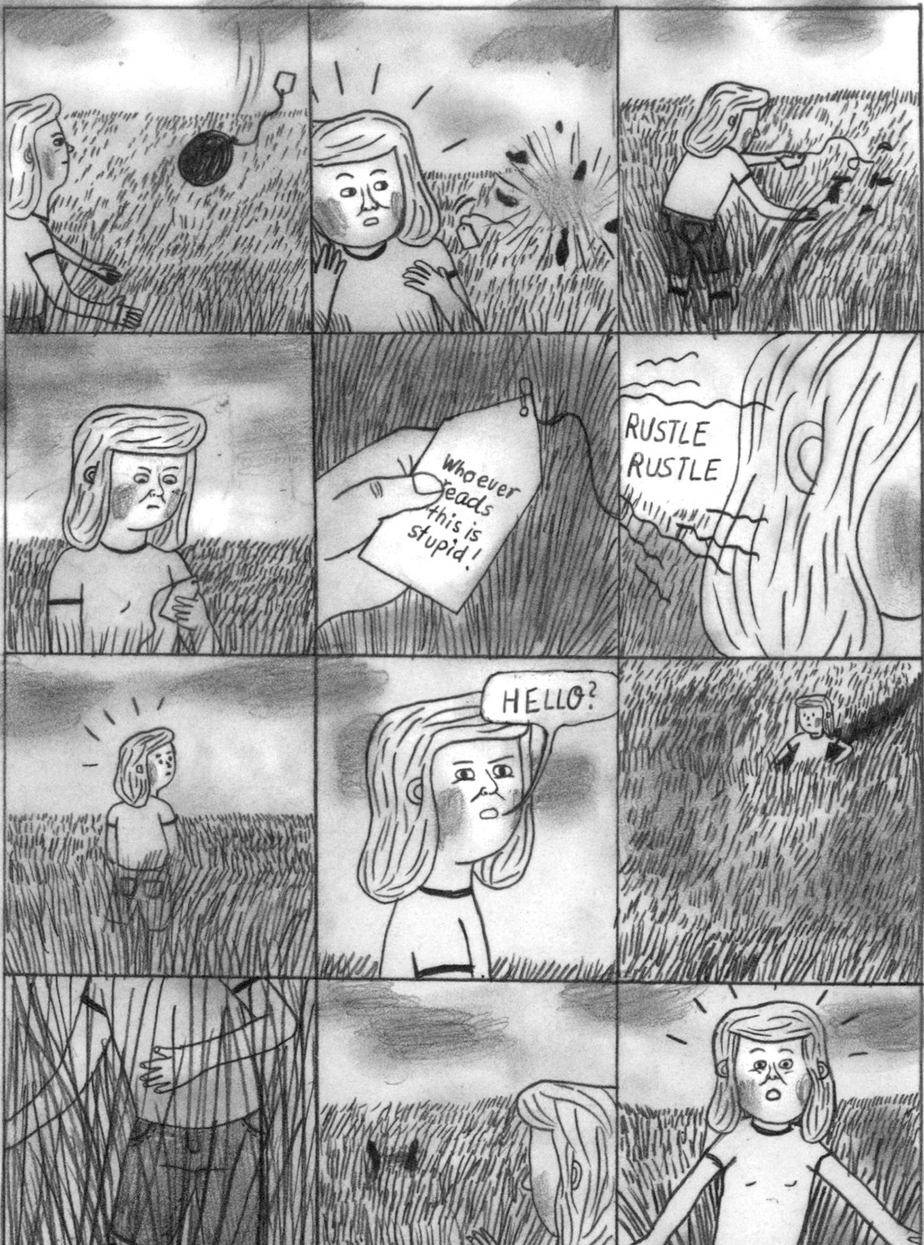
Whoever reads this is stupid!
RUSTLE RUSTLE
HELLO?

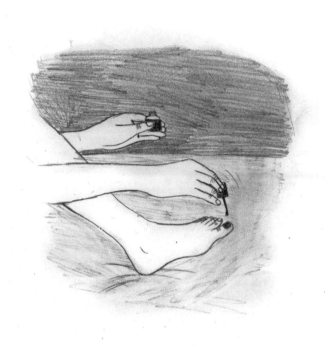

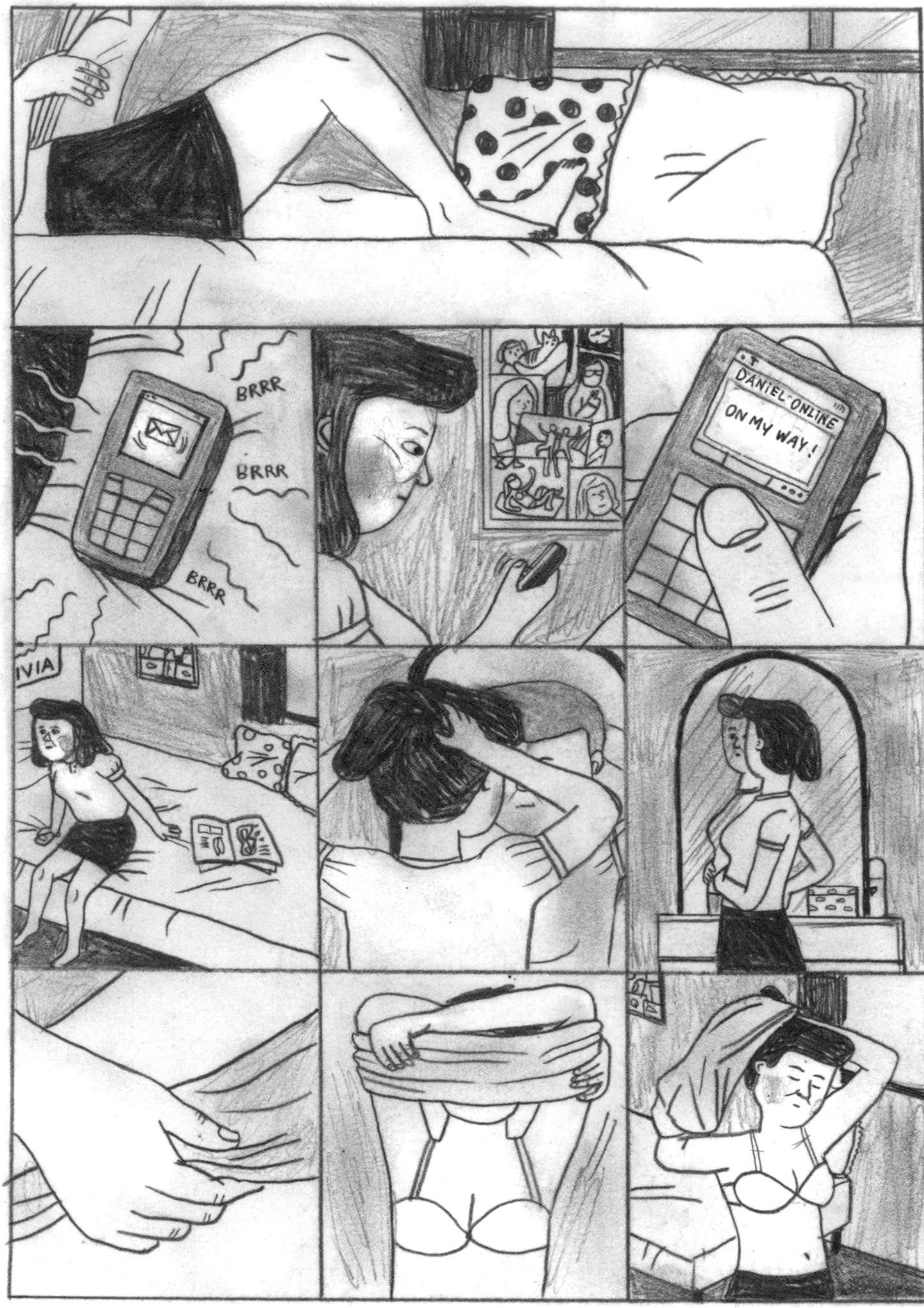
BRRR
BRRR
BRRR
DANIEL-ONLINE
ON MY WAY!
IVIA

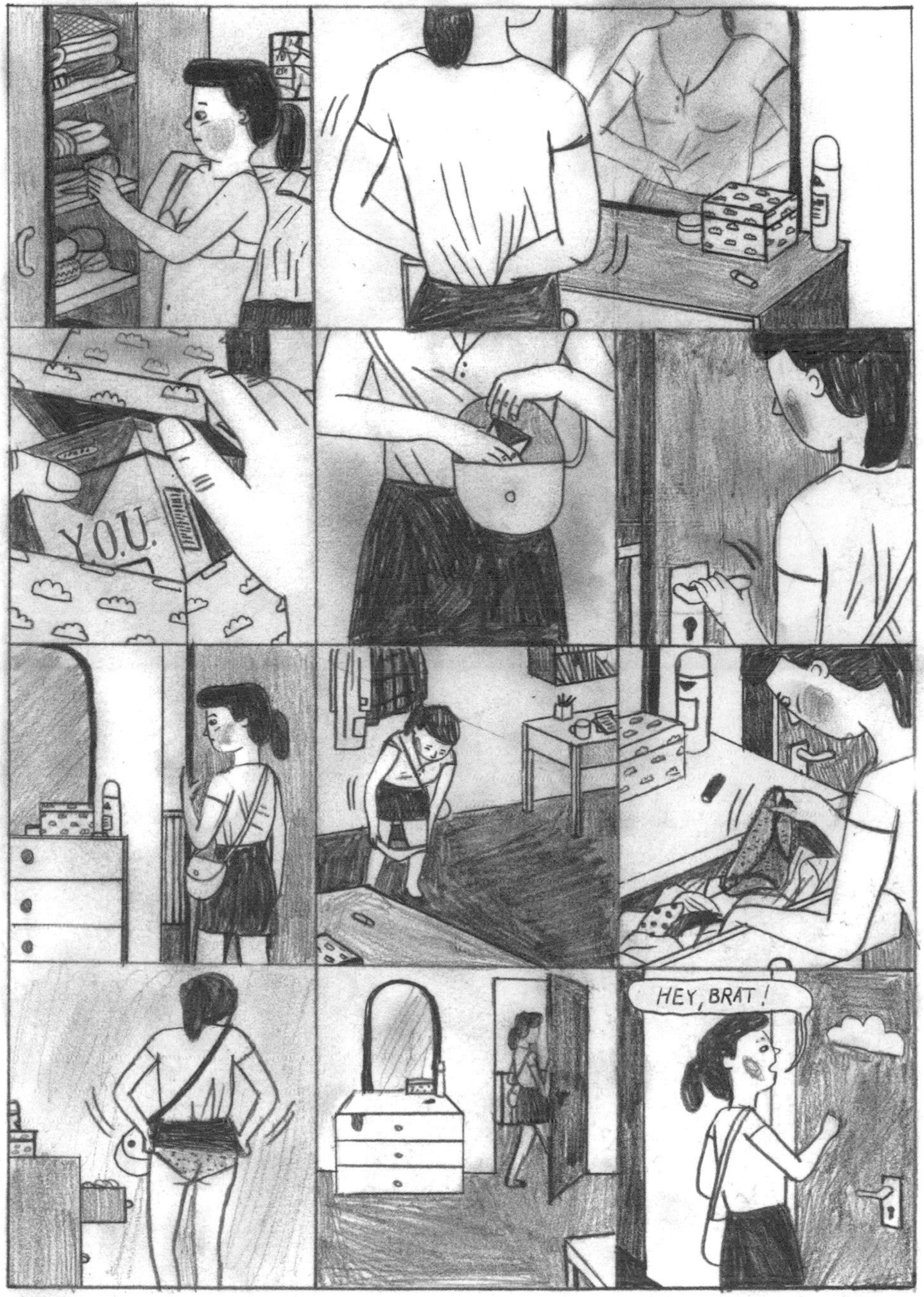
Y.O.U.
HEY, BRAT!

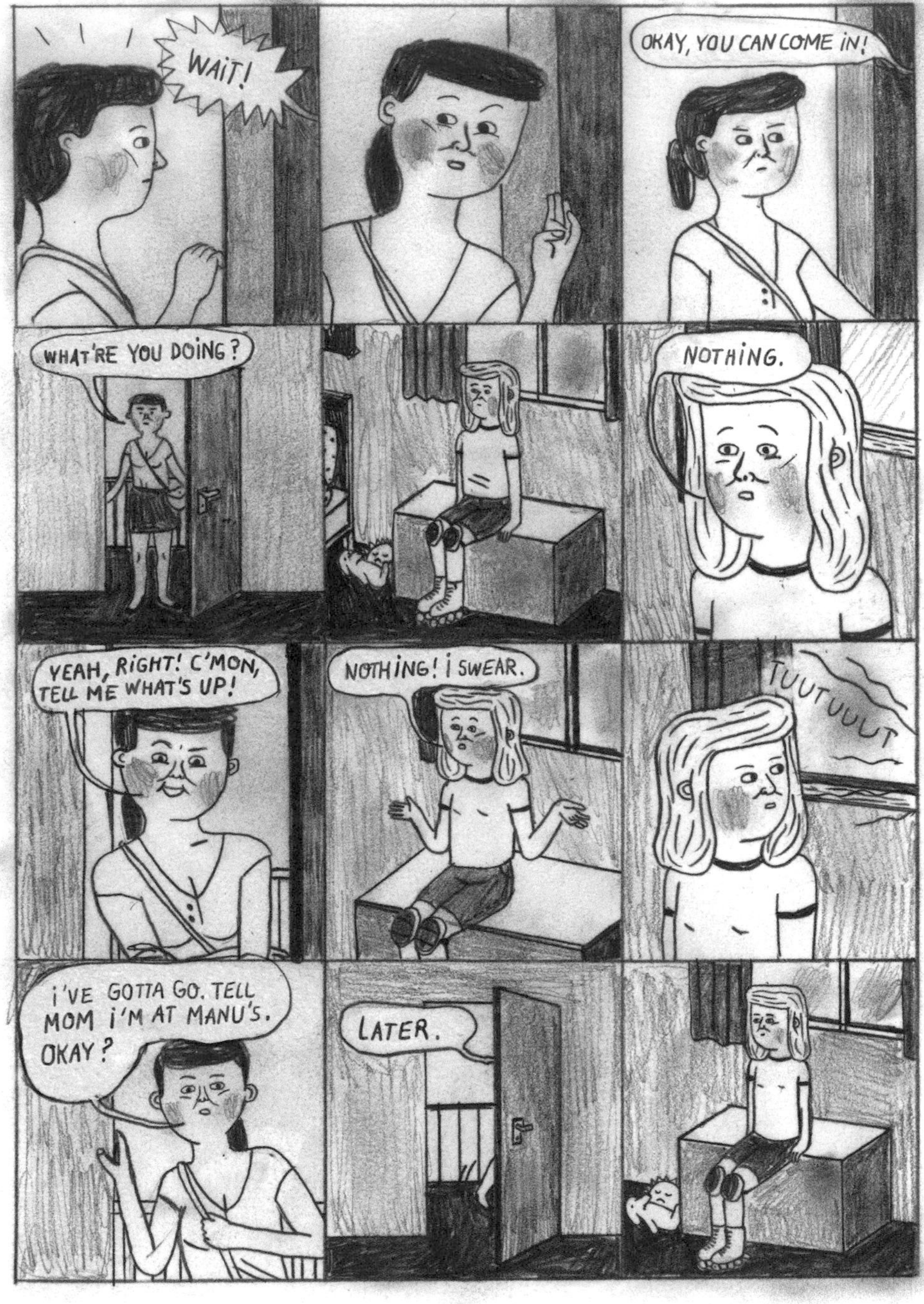
WAIT!
OKAY, YOU CAN COME IN!
WHAT'RE YOU DOING?
NOTHING.
YEAH, RIGHT! C'MON, TELL ME WHAT'S UP!
NOTHING! I SWEAR.
TUUTUUUT
I'VE GOTTA GO. TELL MOM I'M AT MANU'S. OKAY?
LATER.

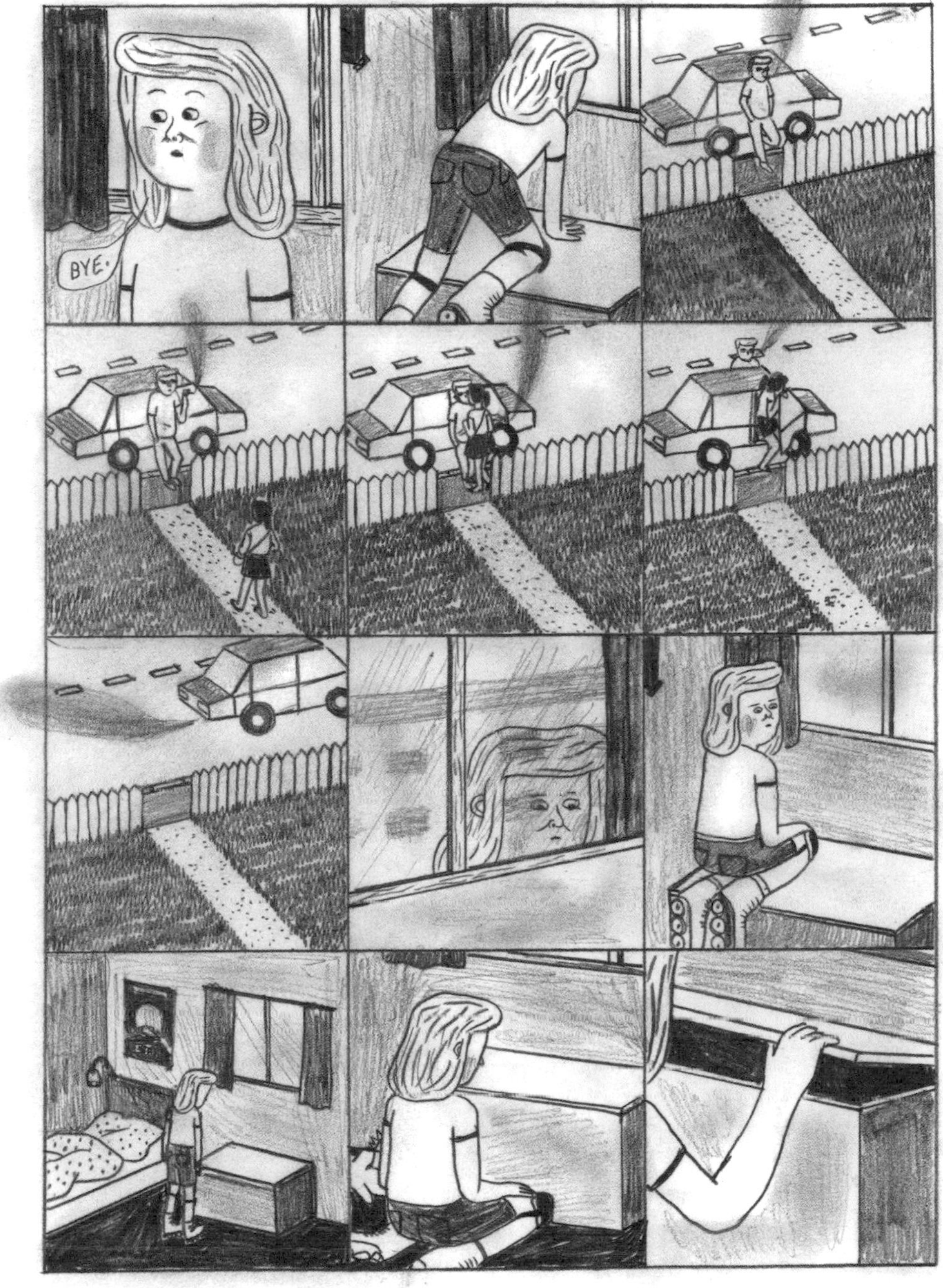
BYE.

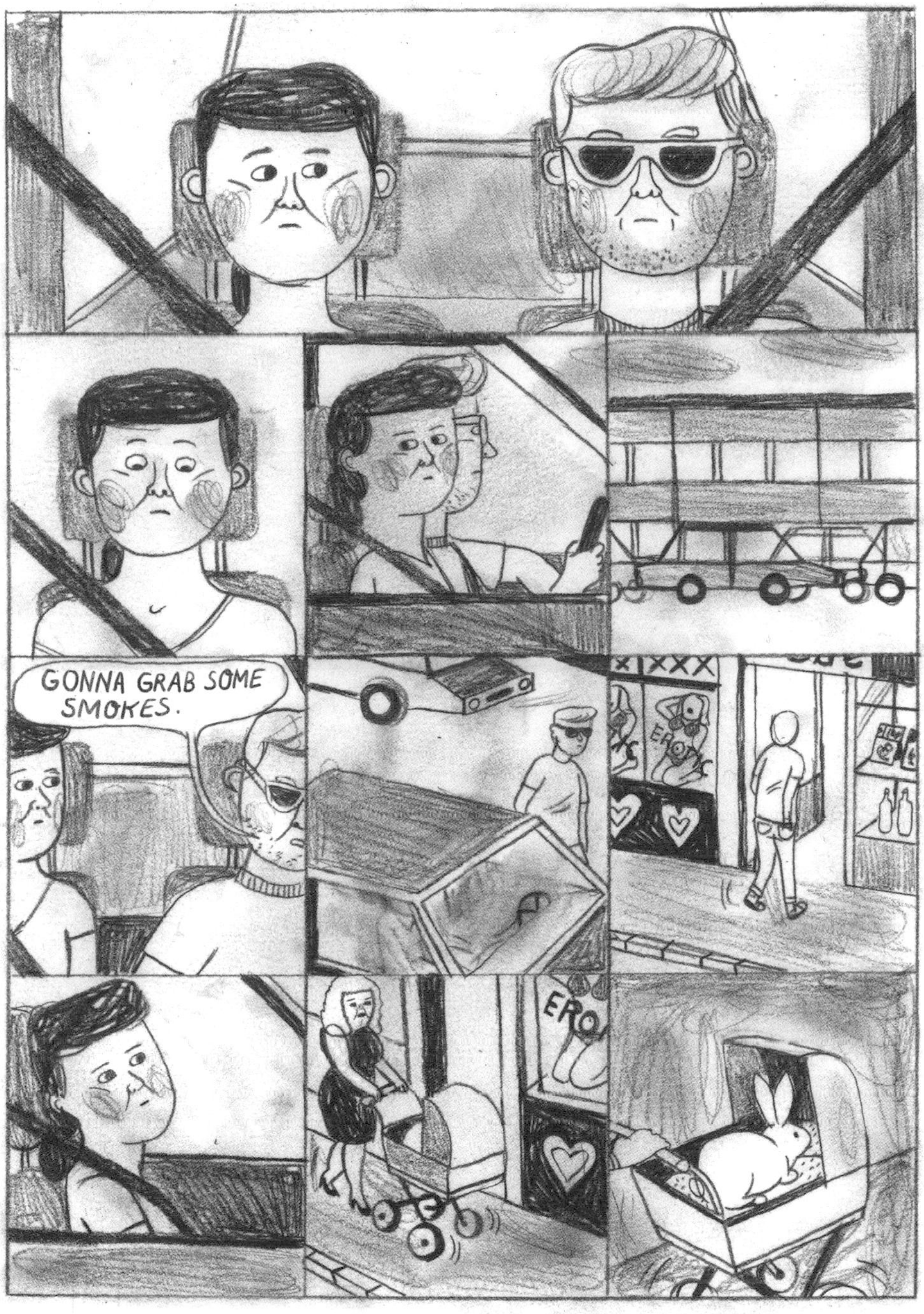
GONNA GRAB SOME SMOKES.
XXXX
EROTIC
ERO

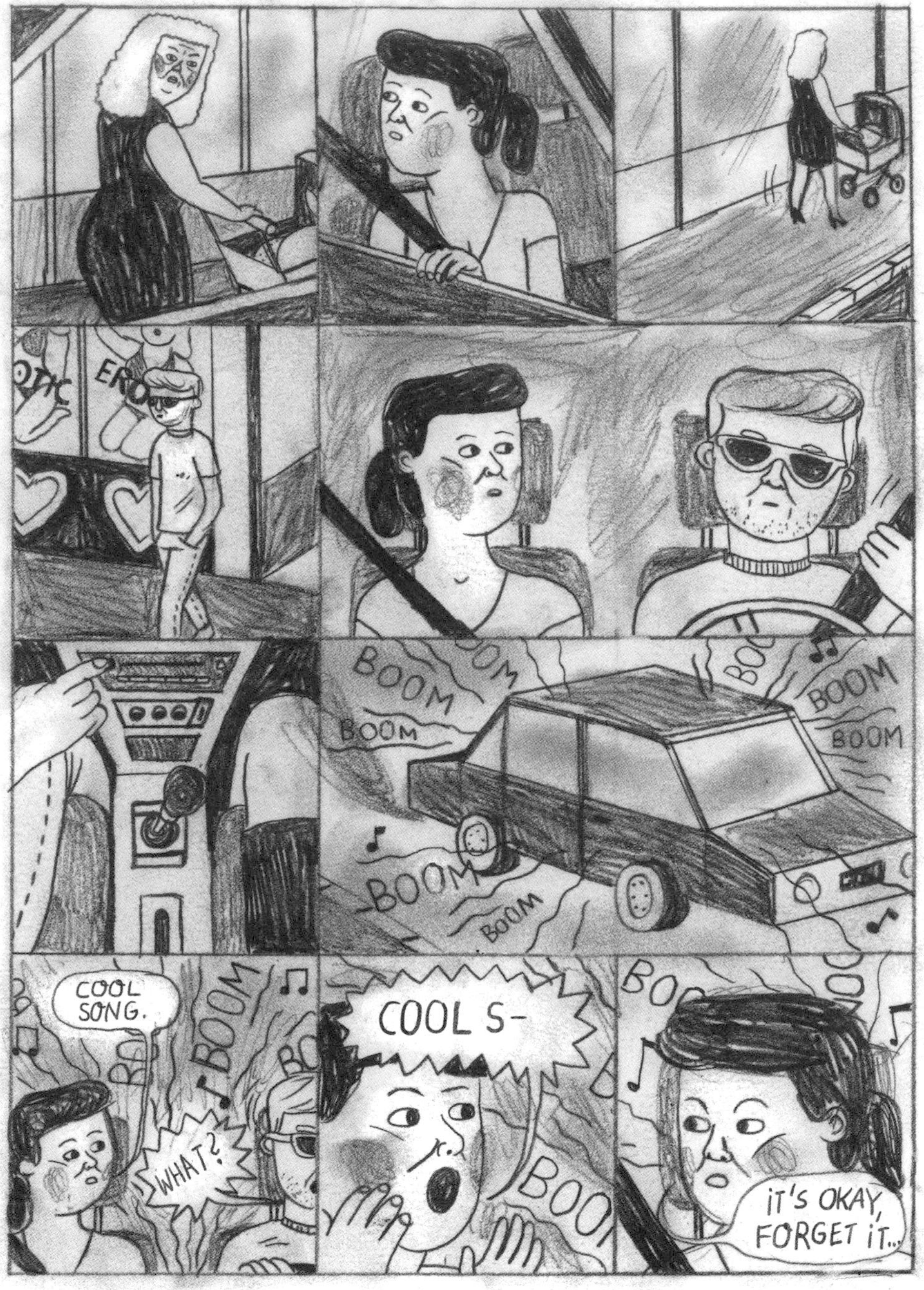
EROTIC
ERO
BOOM
BOOM
BOOM
BOOM
BOOM
BOOM
BOOM
BOOM
COOL SONG.
BOOM
WHAT?
COOL S-
BOO
IT'S OKAY, FORGET IT...

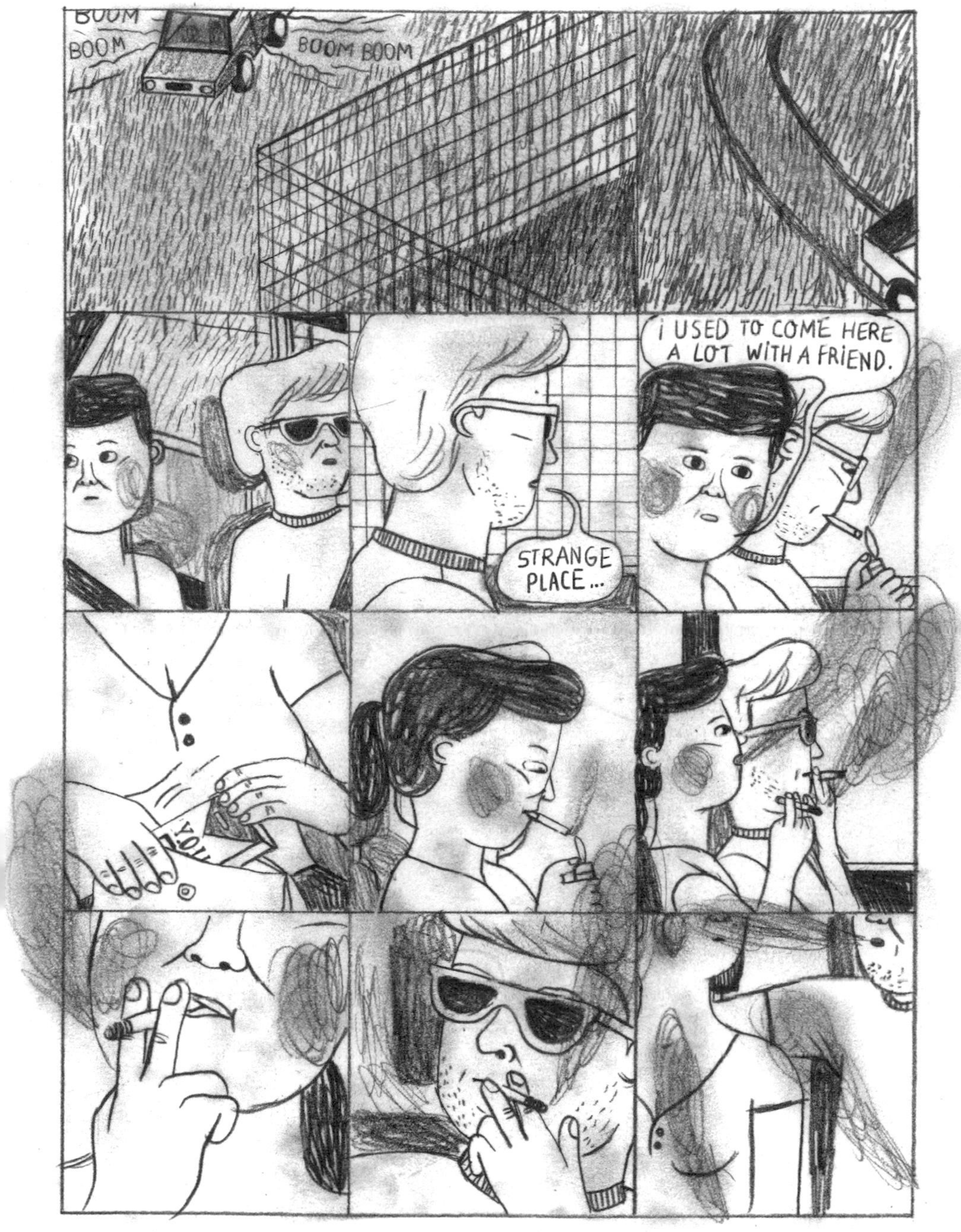
BOOM
BOOM
BOOM BOOM
STRANGE PLACE...
I USED TO COME HERE A LOT WITH A FRIEND.

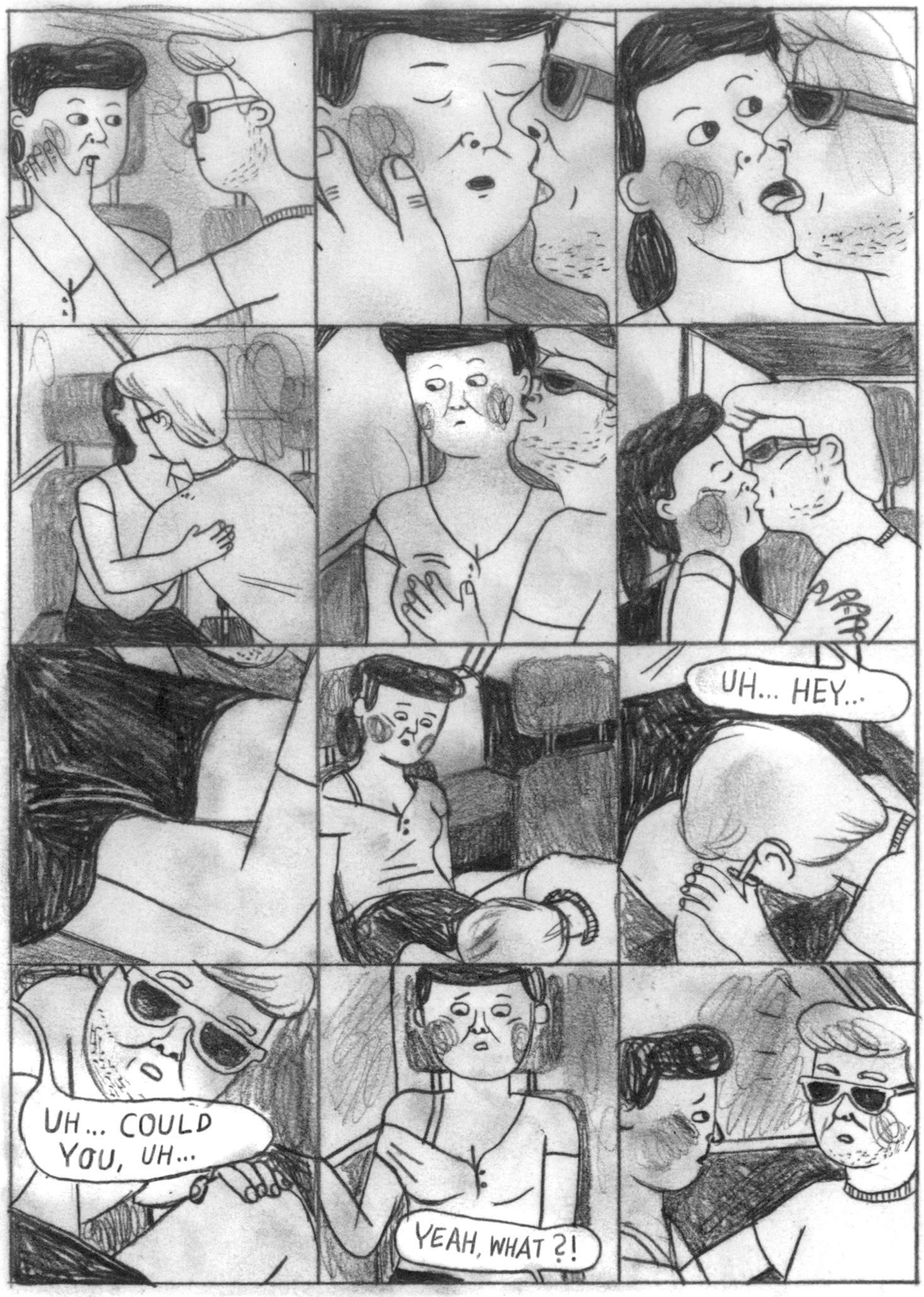
UH... HEY...
UH... COULD YOU, UH...
YEAH, WHAT?!

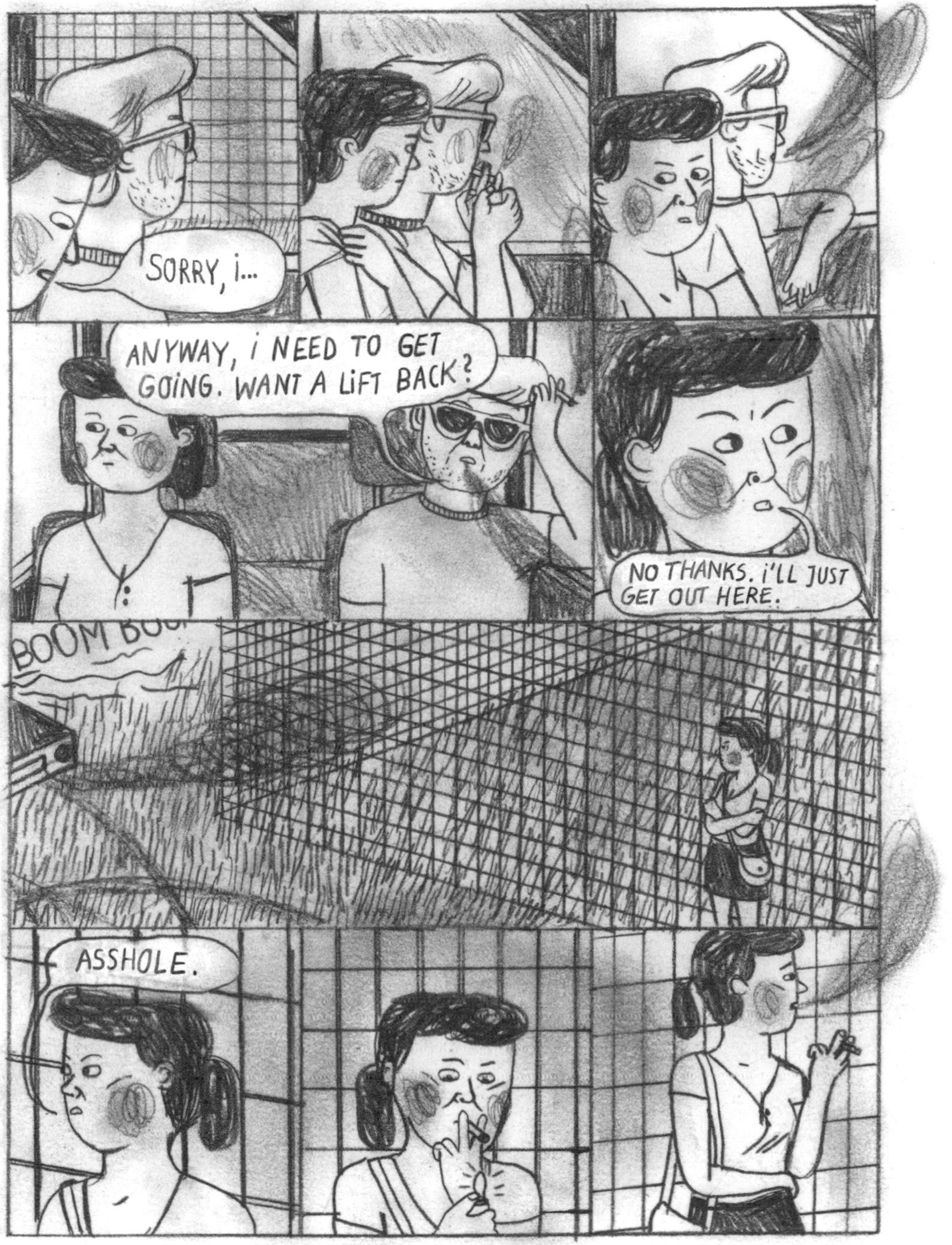
SORRY, i...
ANYWAY, i NEED TO GET GOING. WANT A LiFT BACK?
NO THANKS. i'LL JUST GET OUT HERE.
ASSHOLE.

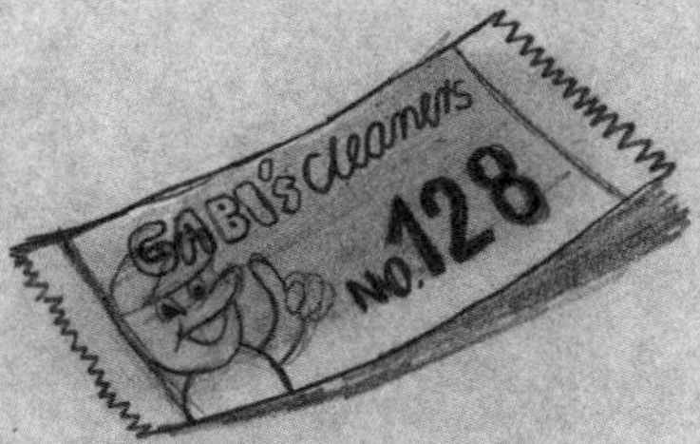
GABI's Cleaners
NO. 128

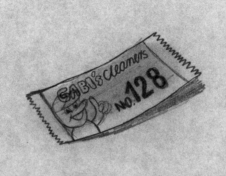

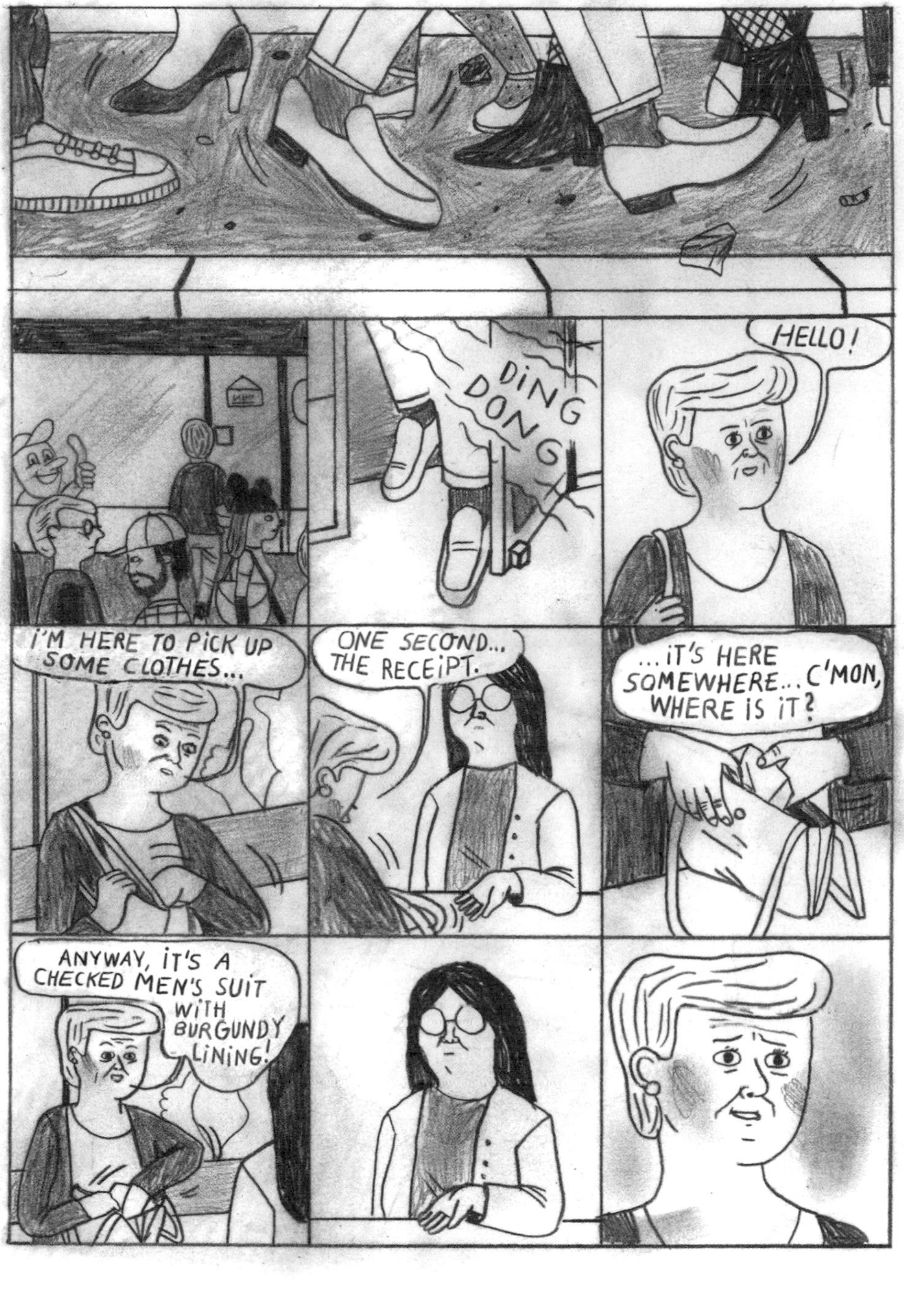
DING
DONG
HELLO!
I'M HERE TO PICK UP SOME CLOTHES...
ONE SECOND... THE RECEIPT.
...IT'S HERE SOMEWHERE... C'MON, WHERE IS IT?
ANYWAY, IT'S A CHECKED MEN'S SUIT WITH BURGUNDY LINING!

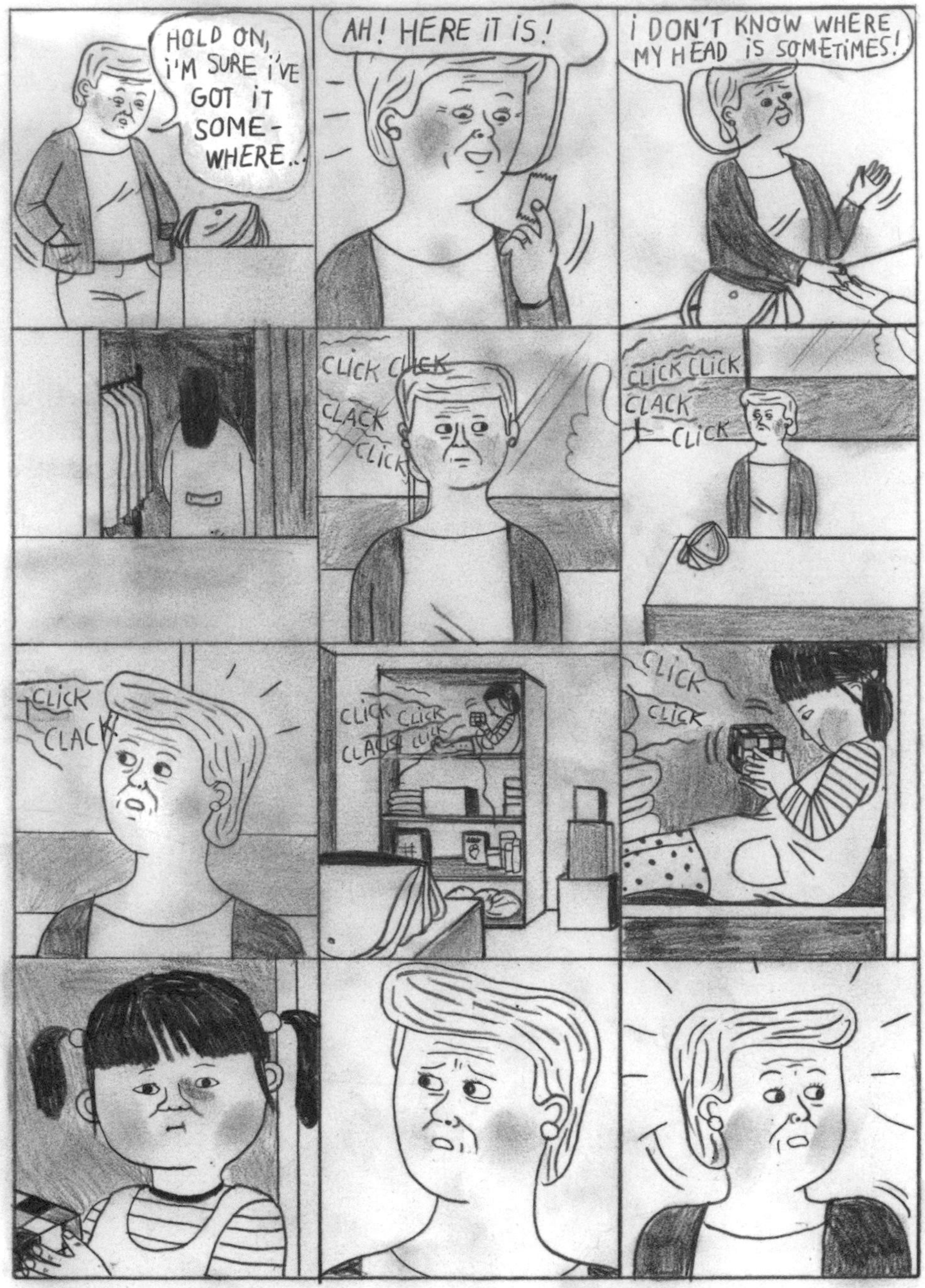
HOLD ON, I'M SURE I'VE GOT IT SOME-WHERE...
AH! HERE IT IS!
I DON'T KNOW WHERE MY HEAD IS SOMETIMES!
CLICK CLICK
CLACK
CLICK
CLICK CLICK
CLACK
CLICK
CLICK
CLACK
CLICK CLICK
CLACK CLICK
CLICK
CLICK

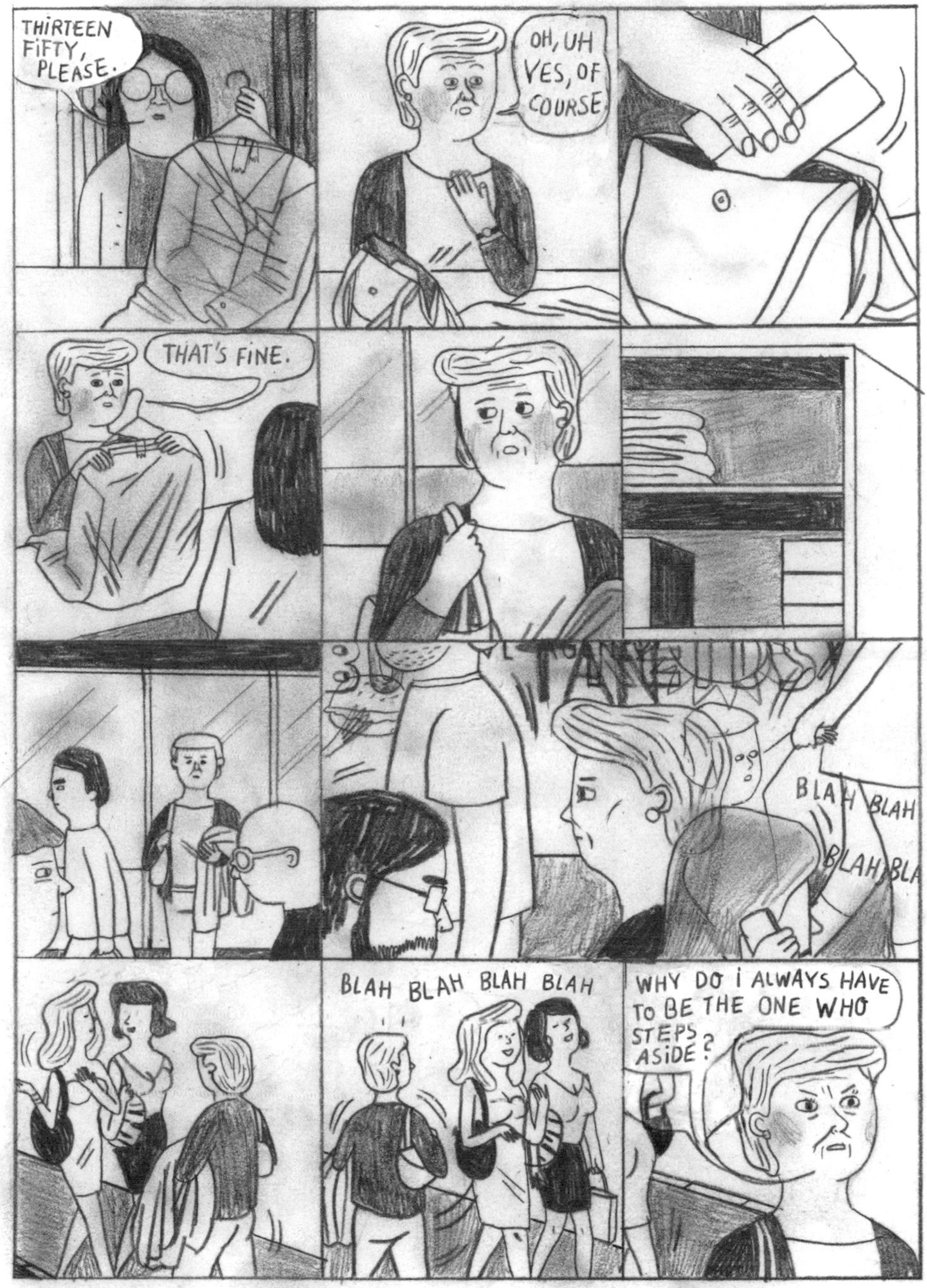
THIRTEEN FIFTY, PLEASE.
OH, UH YES, OF COURSE
THAT'S FINE.
BLAH BLAH
BLAH BLA
BLAH BLAH BLAH BLAH
WHY DO I ALWAYS HAVE TO BE THE ONE WHO STEPS ASIDE?

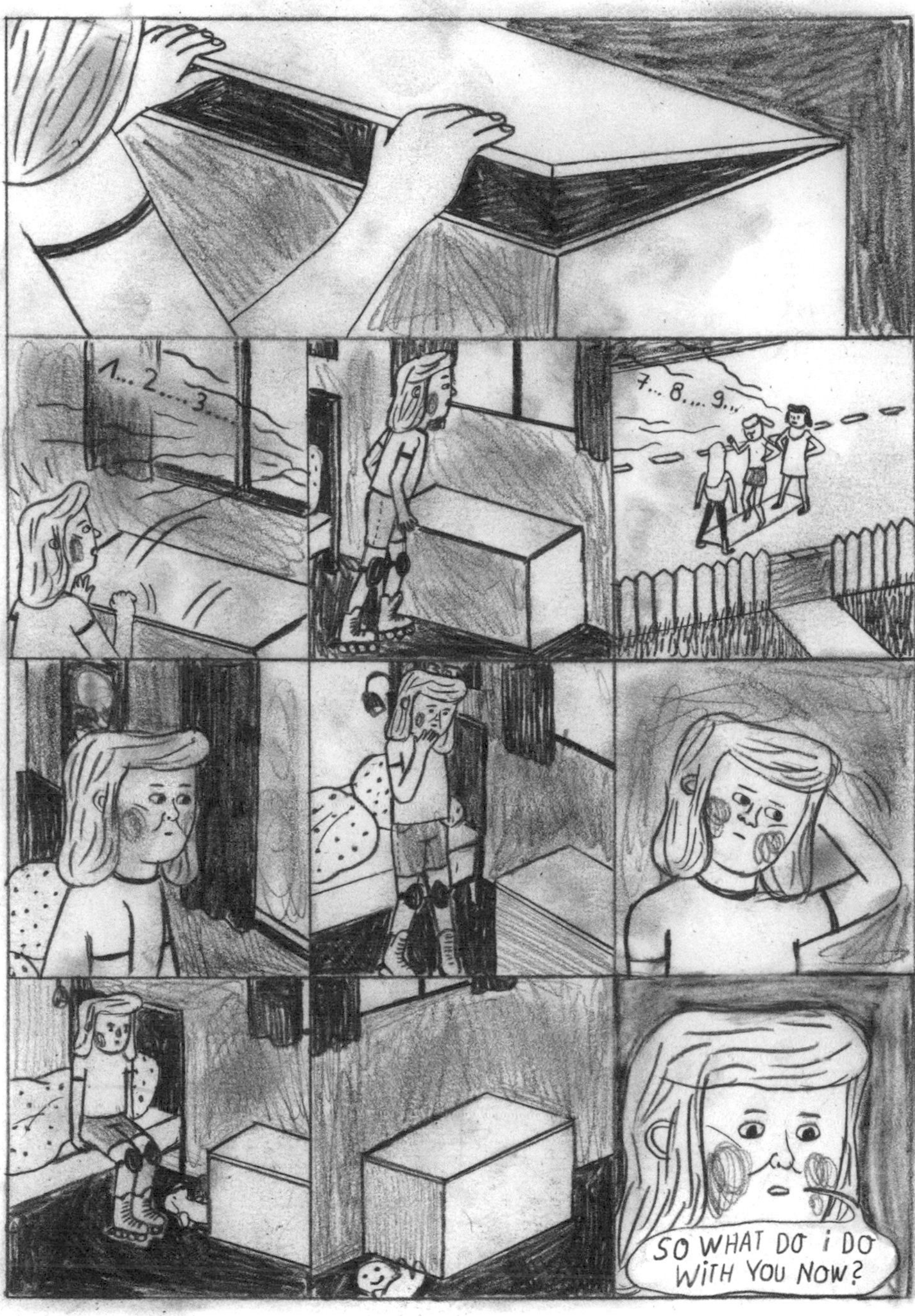
1... 2... 3...
7... 8... 9...
SO WHAT DO i DO WITH YOU NOW?

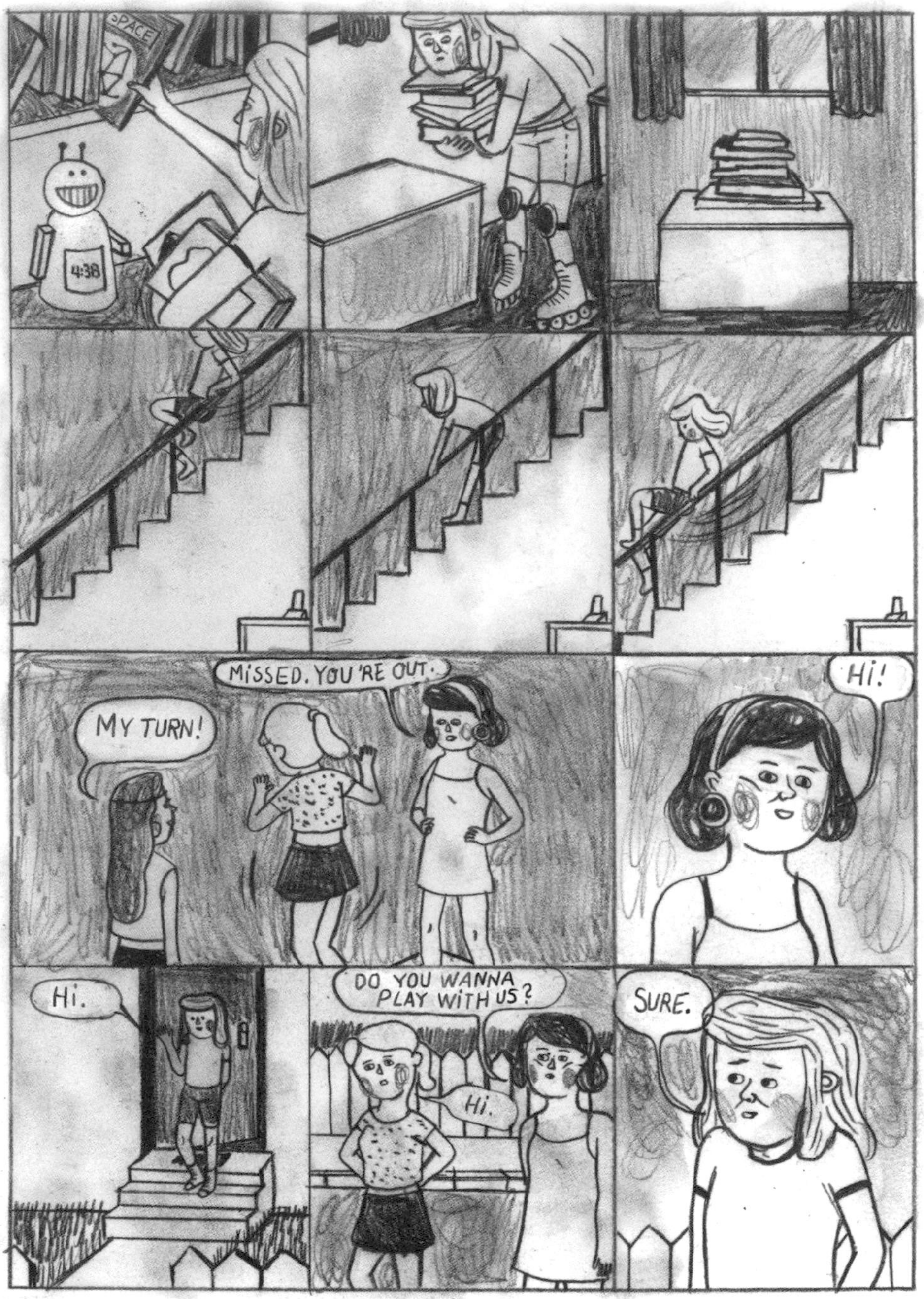
SPACE
4:38
MY TURN!
MISSED. YOU'RE OUT.
Hi!
Hi.
DO YOU WANNA PLAY WITH US?
Hi.
SURE.

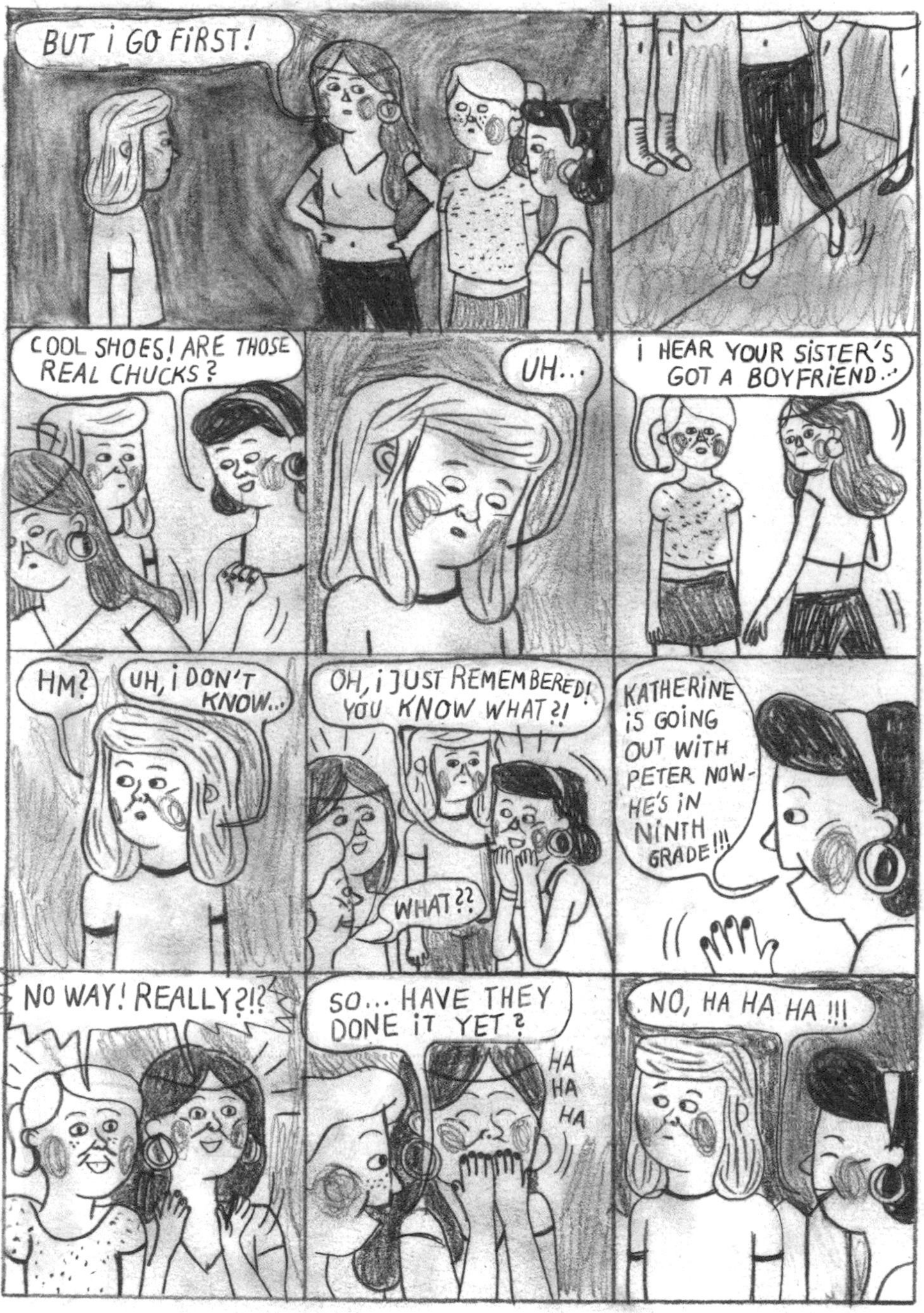
BUT I GO FIRST!
COOL SHOES! ARE THOSE REAL CHUCKS?
UH...
I HEAR YOUR SISTER'S GOT A BOYFRIEND...
HM?
UH, I DON'T KNOW...
OH, I JUST REMEMBERED! YOU KNOW WHAT?!
WHAT??
KATHERINE IS GOING OUT WITH PETER NOW- HE'S IN NINTH GRADE!!!
NO WAY! REALLY?!?
SO... HAVE THEY DONE IT YET?
HA HA HA
NO, HA HA HA !!!

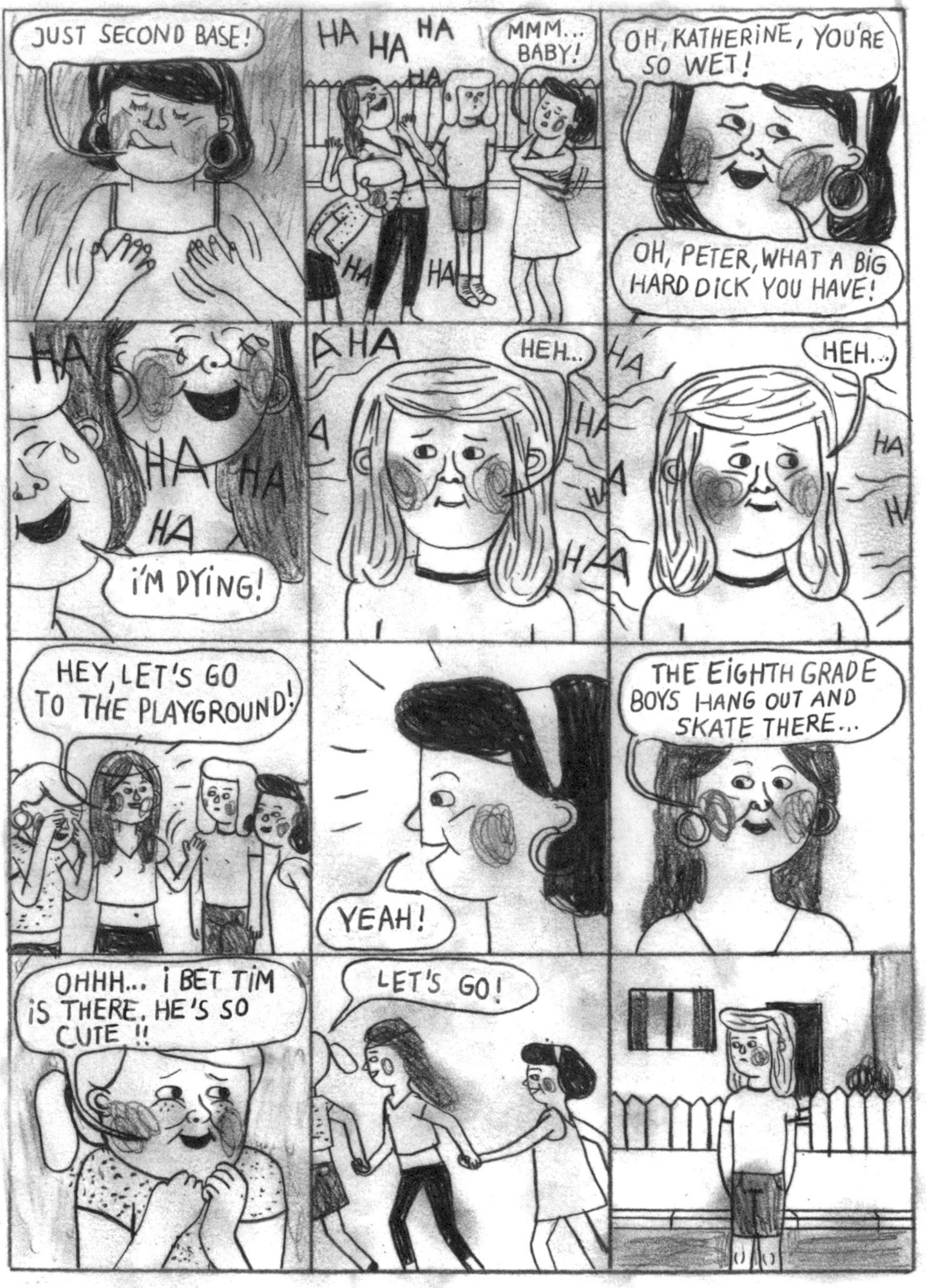
JUST SECOND BASE!
HA HA HA HA
MMM... BABY!
HA HA
OH, KATHERINE, YOU'RE SO WET!
OH, PETER, WHAT A BIG HARD DICK YOU HAVE!
HA HA HA HA
I'M DYING!
HA HA
HEH...
HEH...
HEY, LET'S GO TO THE PLAYGROUND!
YEAH!
THE EIGHTH GRADE BOYS HANG OUT AND SKATE THERE...
OHHH... I BET TIM IS THERE. HE'S SO CUTE !!
LET'S GO!

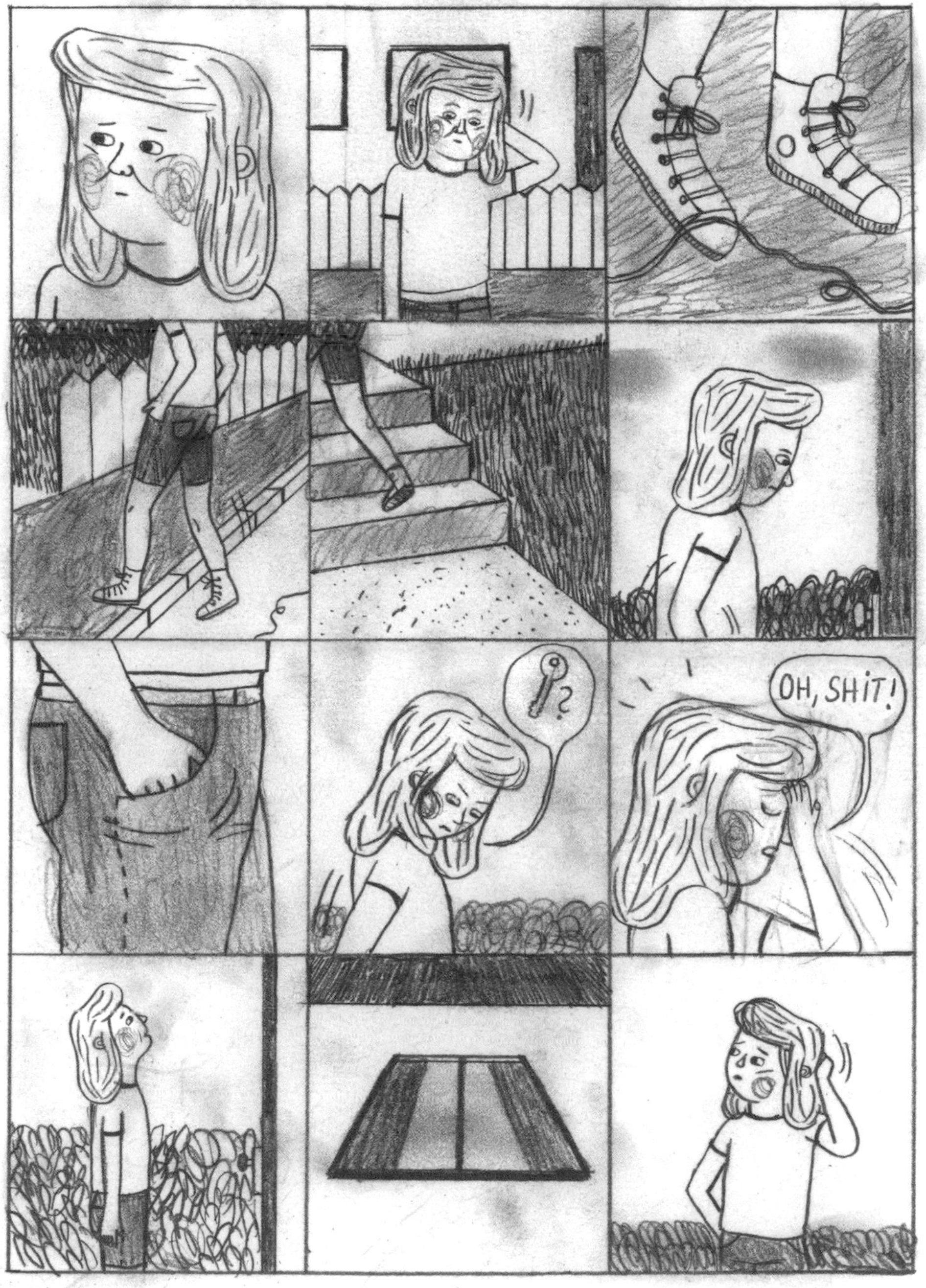
OH, SHIT!

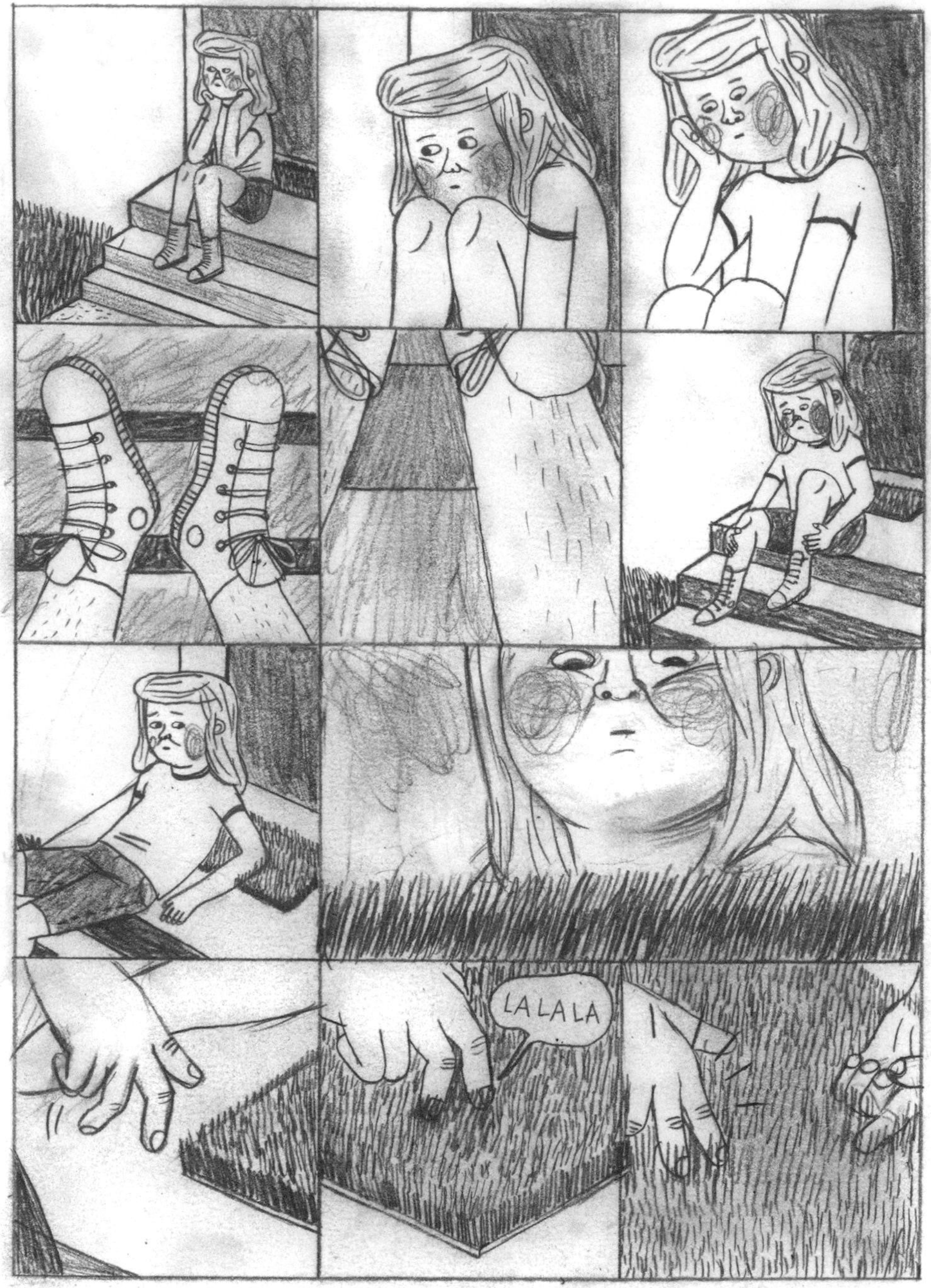
LA LA LA

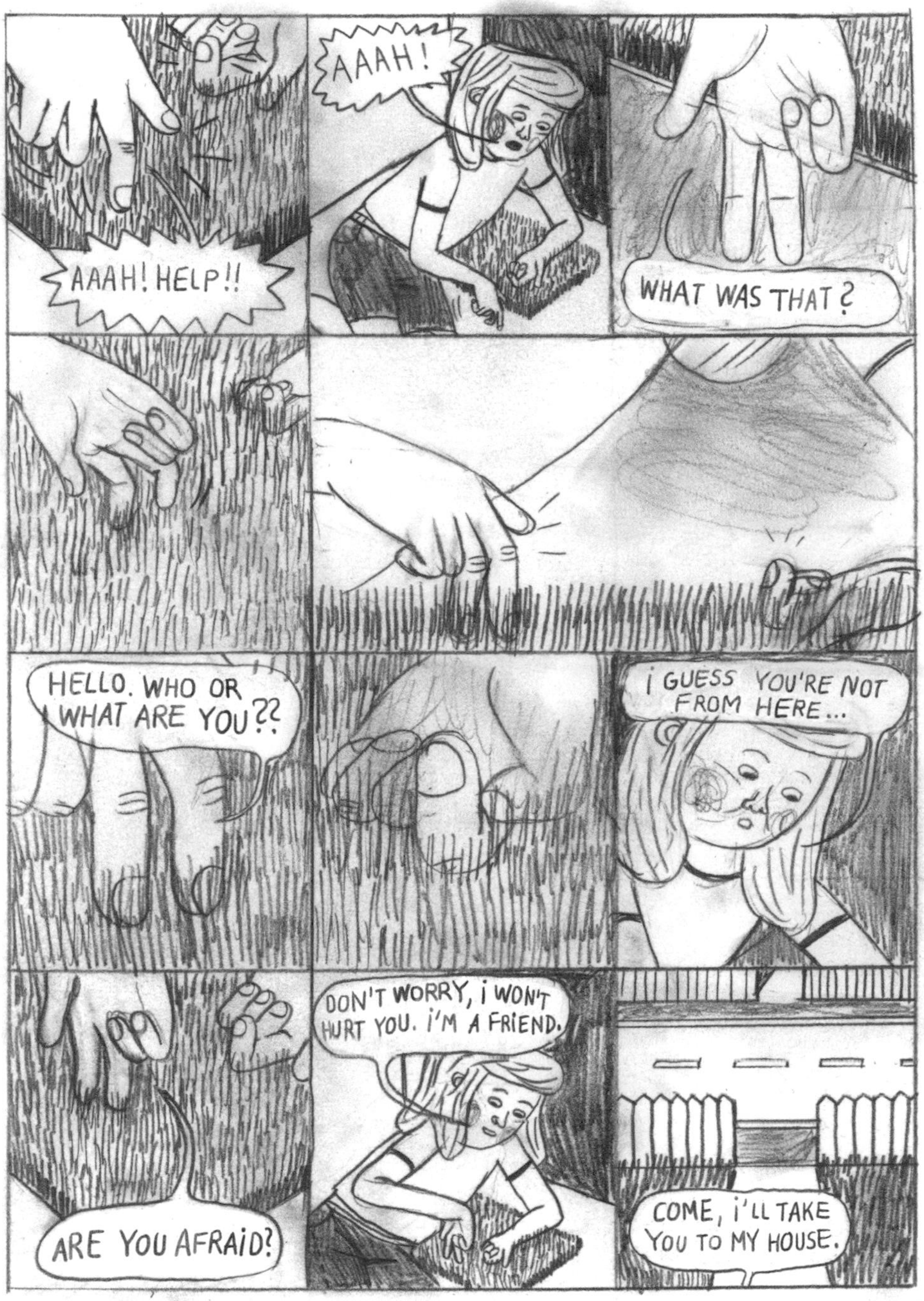
AAAH! HELP!!
AAAH!
WHAT WAS THAT?
HELLO. WHO OR WHAT ARE YOU??
I GUESS YOU'RE NOT FROM HERE...
ARE YOU AFRAID?
DON'T WORRY, I WON'T HURT YOU. I'M A FRIEND.
COME, I'LL TAKE YOU TO MY HOUSE.

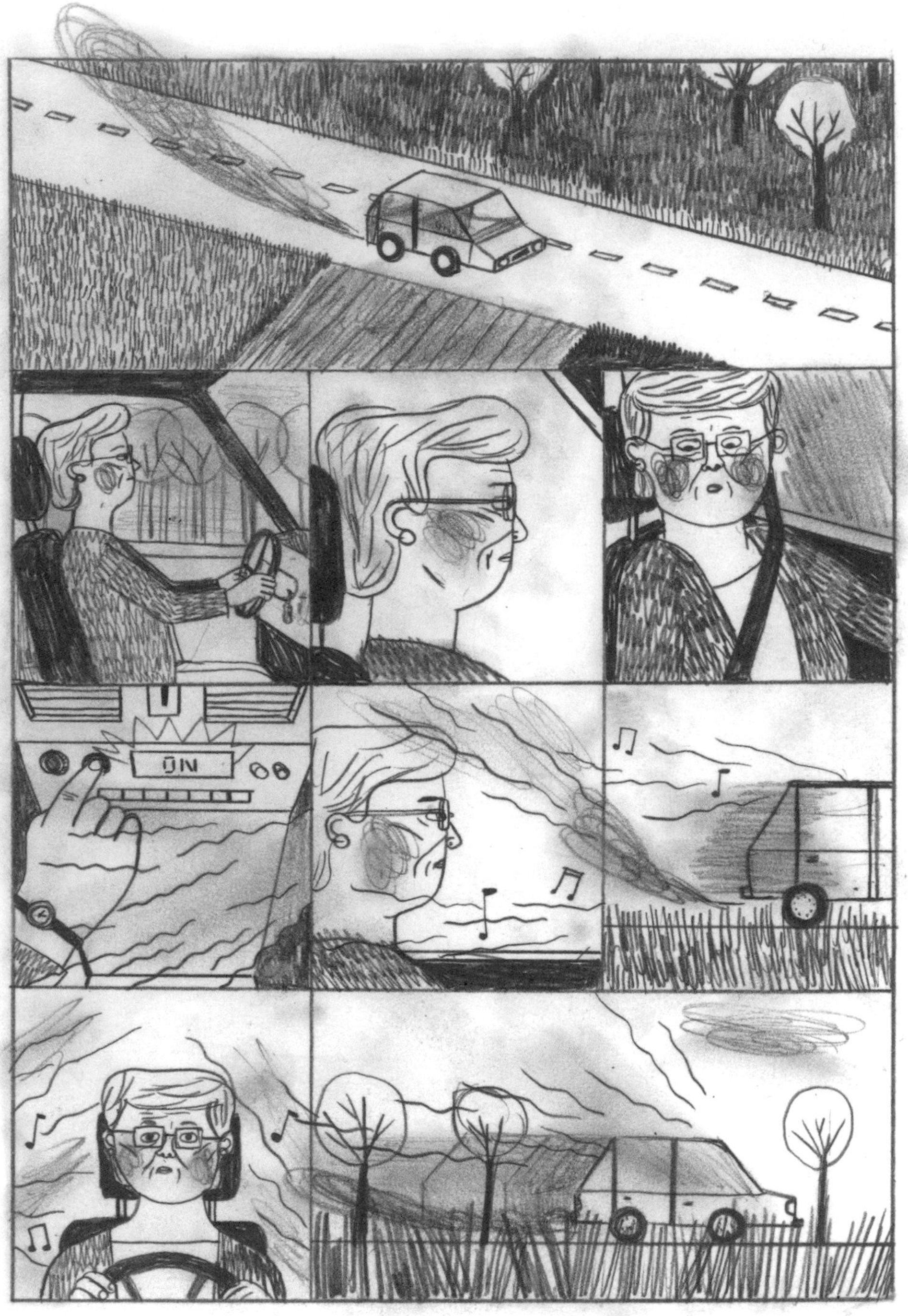
ON

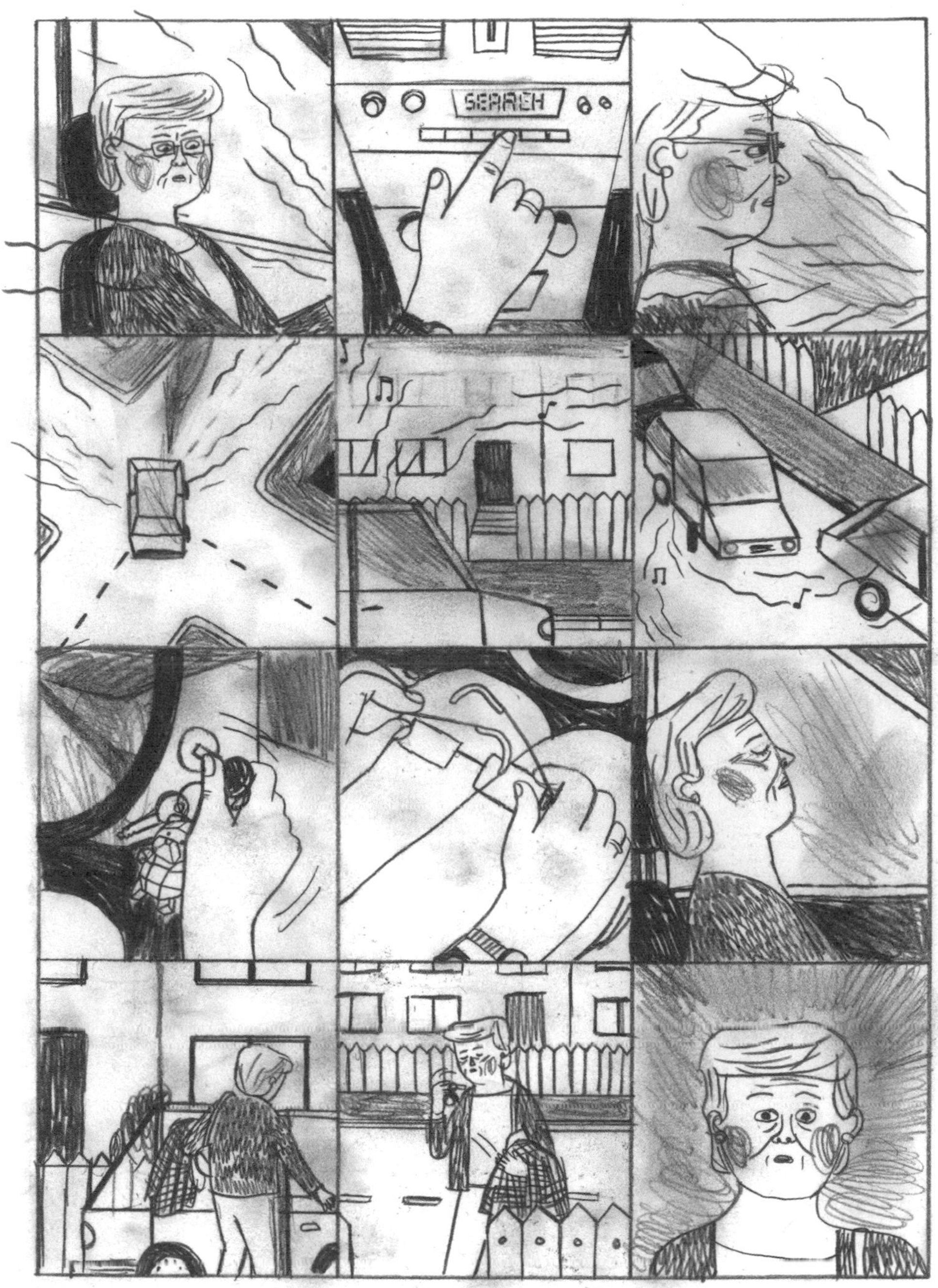
SEARCH

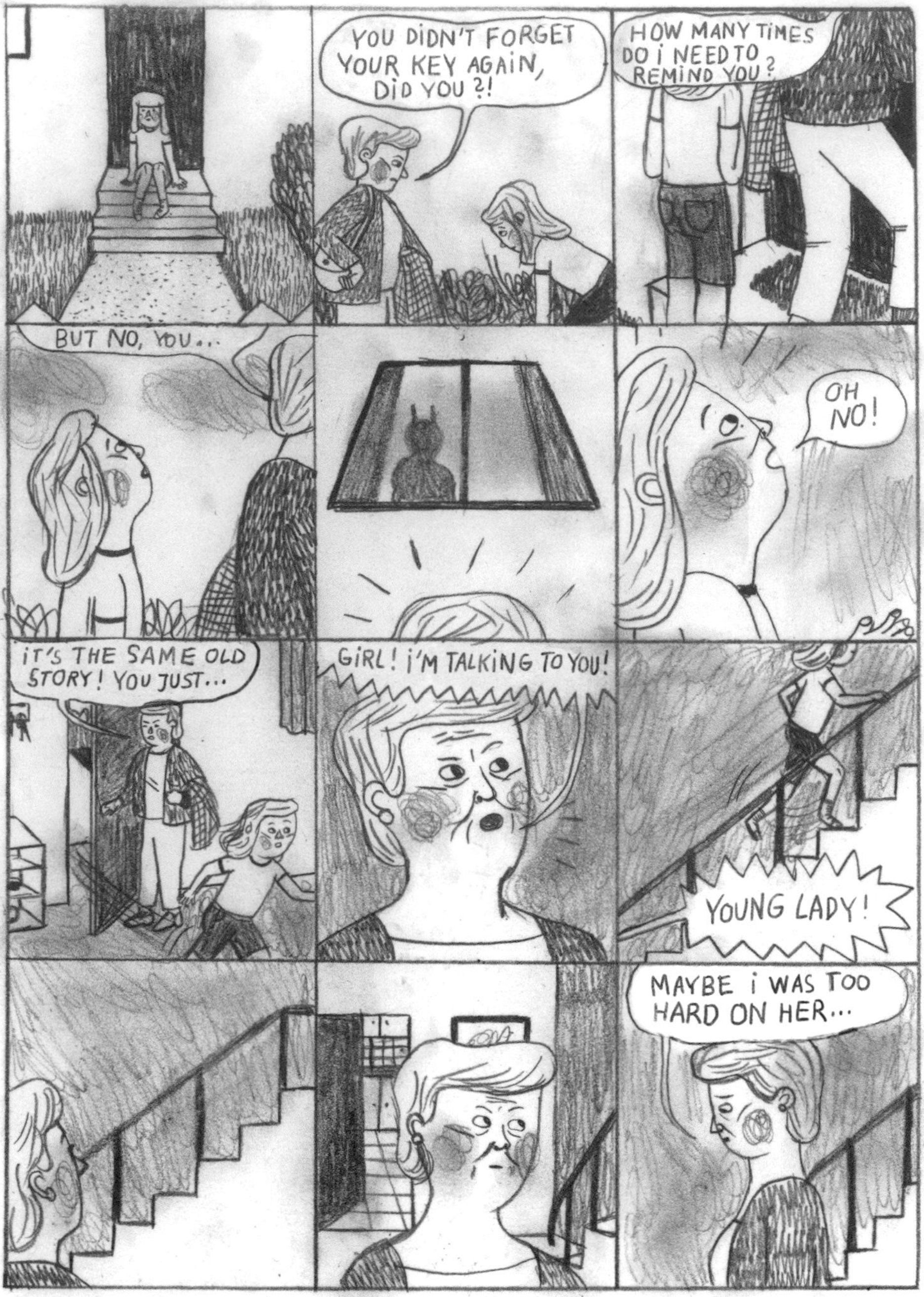
YOU DIDN'T FORGET YOUR KEY AGAIN, DID YOU ?!
HOW MANY TIMES DO I NEED TO REMIND YOU ?
BUT NO, YOU...
OH NO!
IT'S THE SAME OLD STORY! YOU JUST...
GIRL! I'M TALKING TO YOU!
YOUNG LADY!
MAYBE I WAS TOO HARD ON HER...

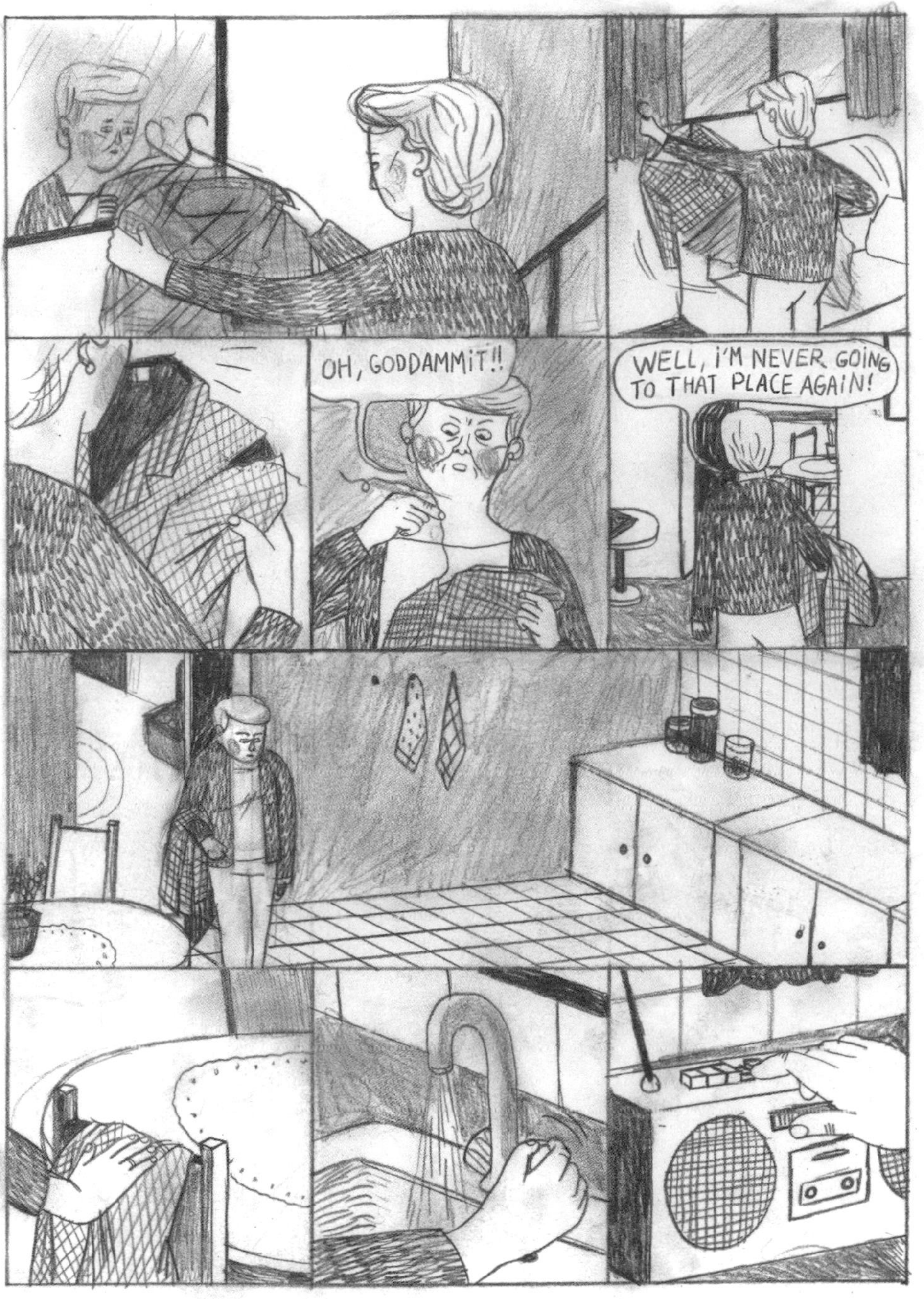
OH, GODDAMMIT!!
WELL, I'M NEVER GOING TO THAT PLACE AGAIN!

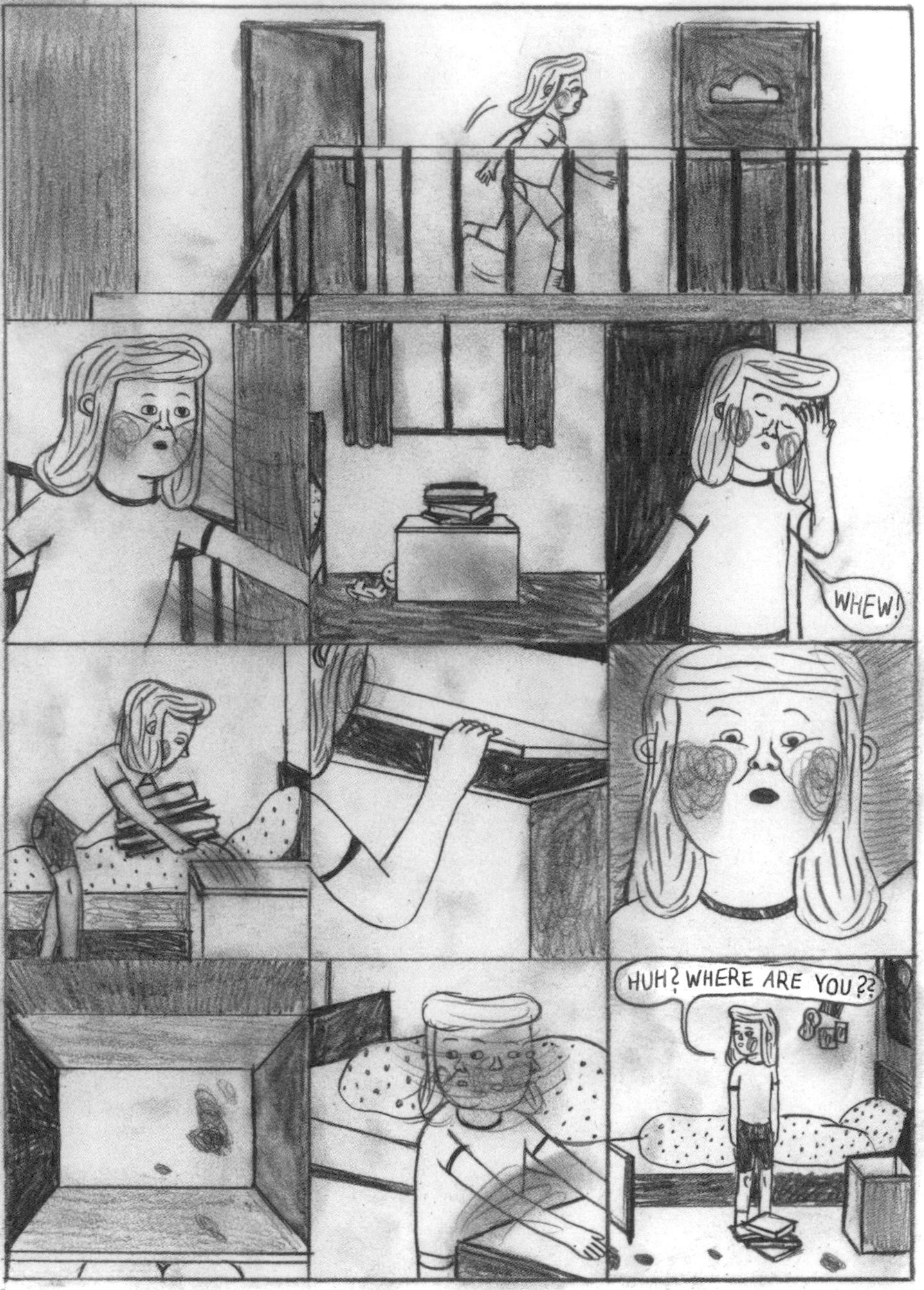
WHEW!
HUH? WHERE ARE YOU??

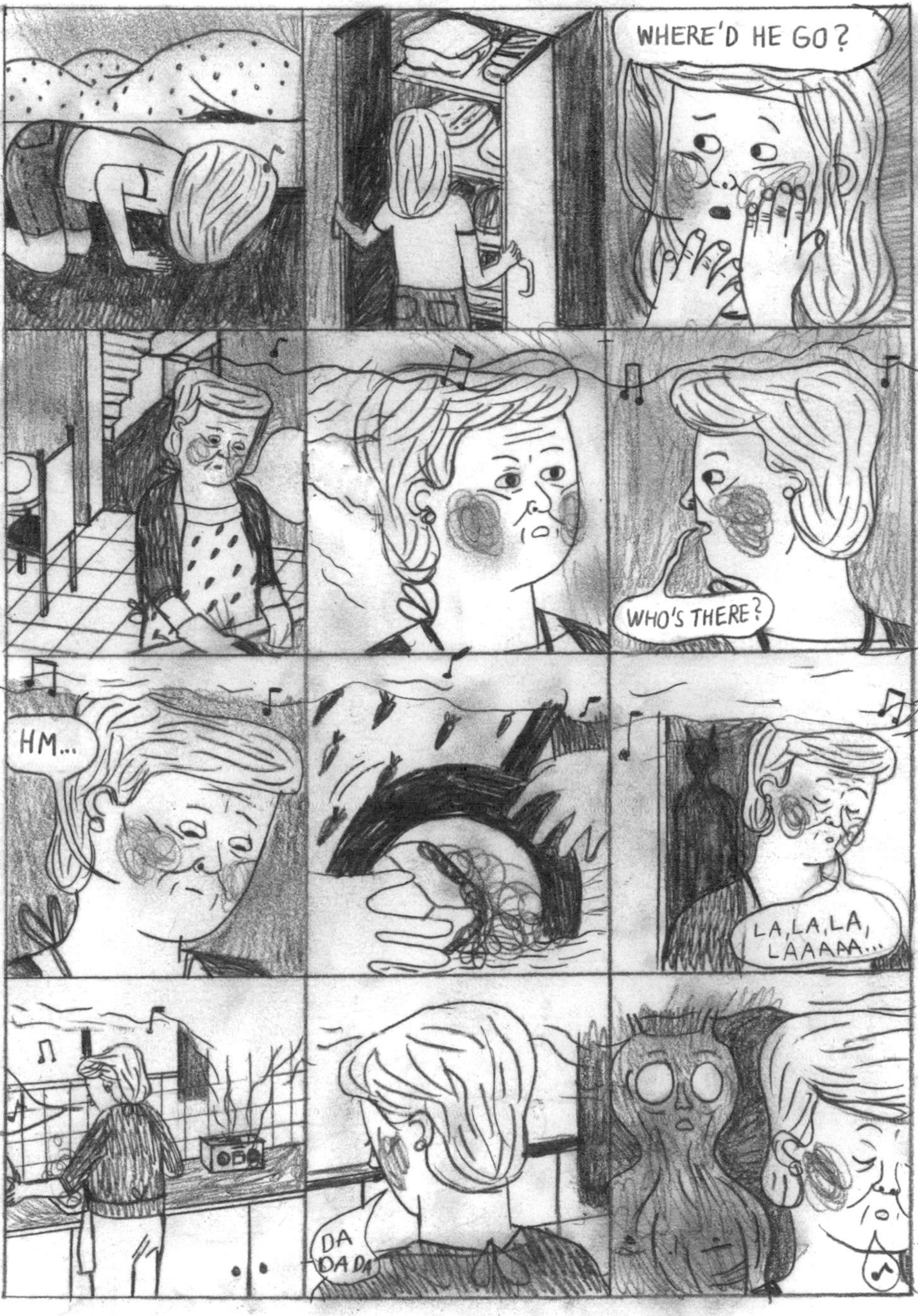
WHERE'D HE GO?
WHO'S THERE?
HM...
LA, LA, LA, LAAAAA...
DA DA DA

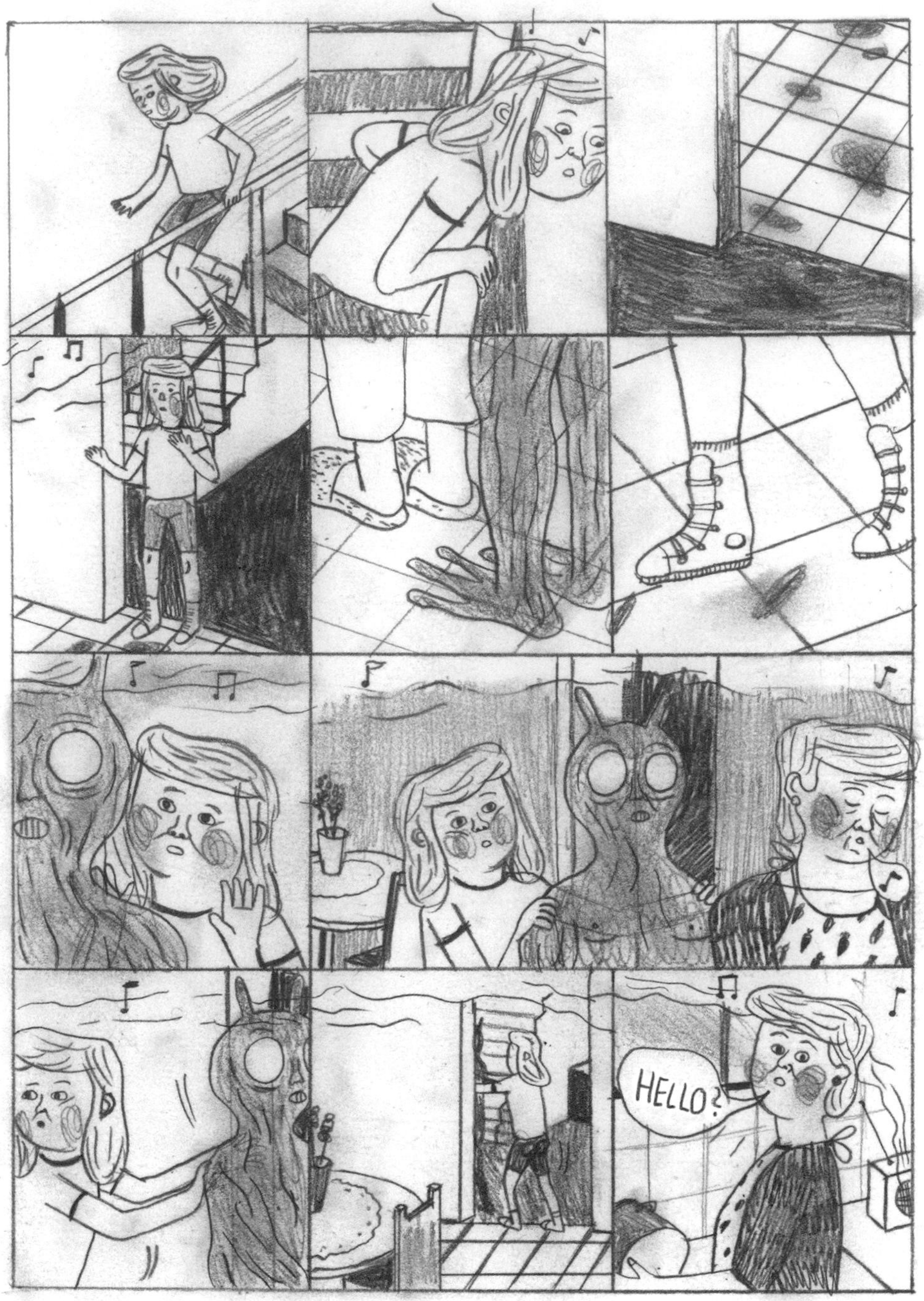
HELLO?

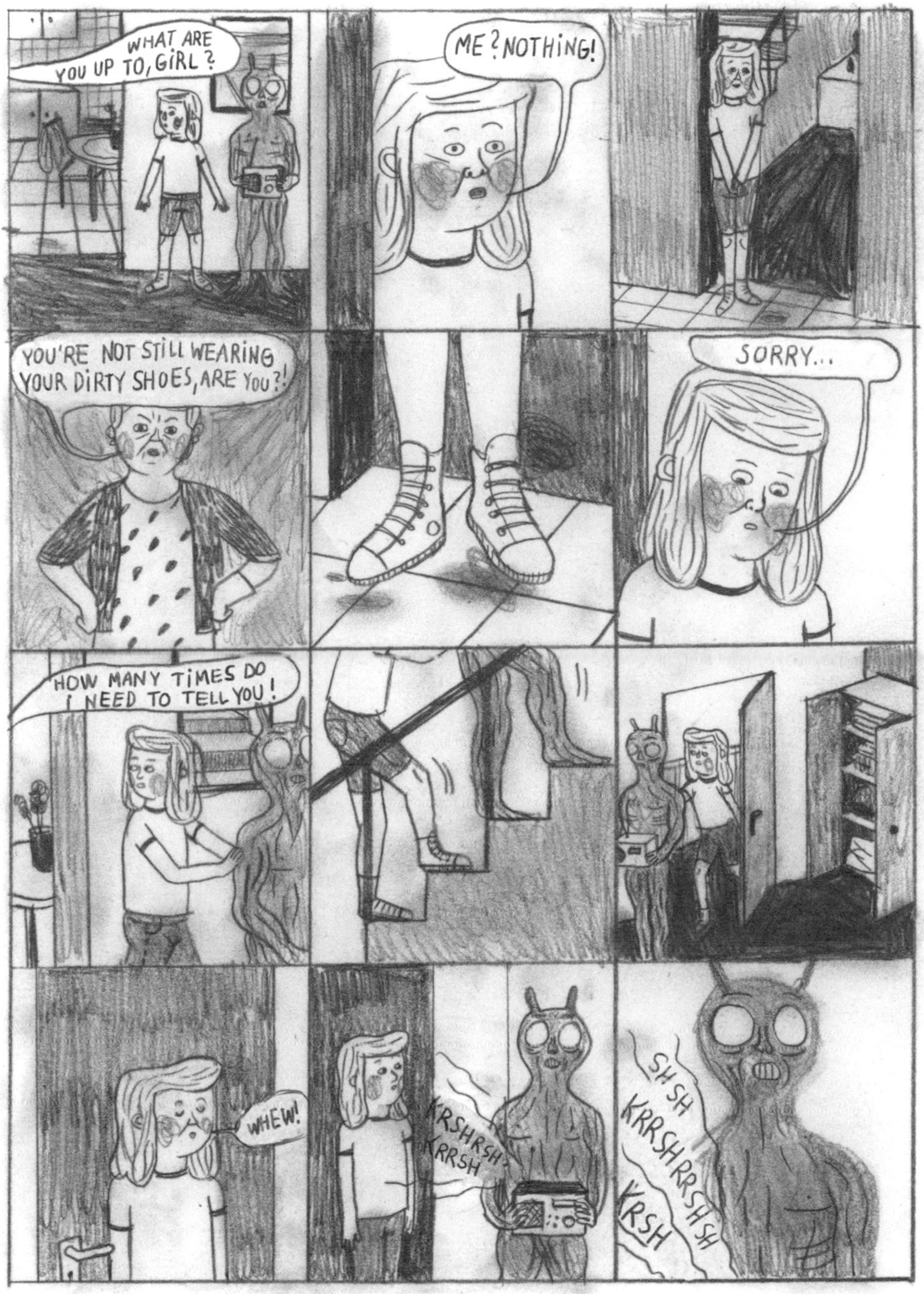
WHAT ARE YOU UP TO, GIRL?
ME? NOTHING!
YOU'RE NOT STILL WEARING YOUR DIRTY SHOES, ARE YOU?!
SORRY...
HOW MANY TIMES DO I NEED TO TELL YOU!
WHEW!
KRSHRSH KRRSH
SH SH KRRSHRRSHSH KRSH

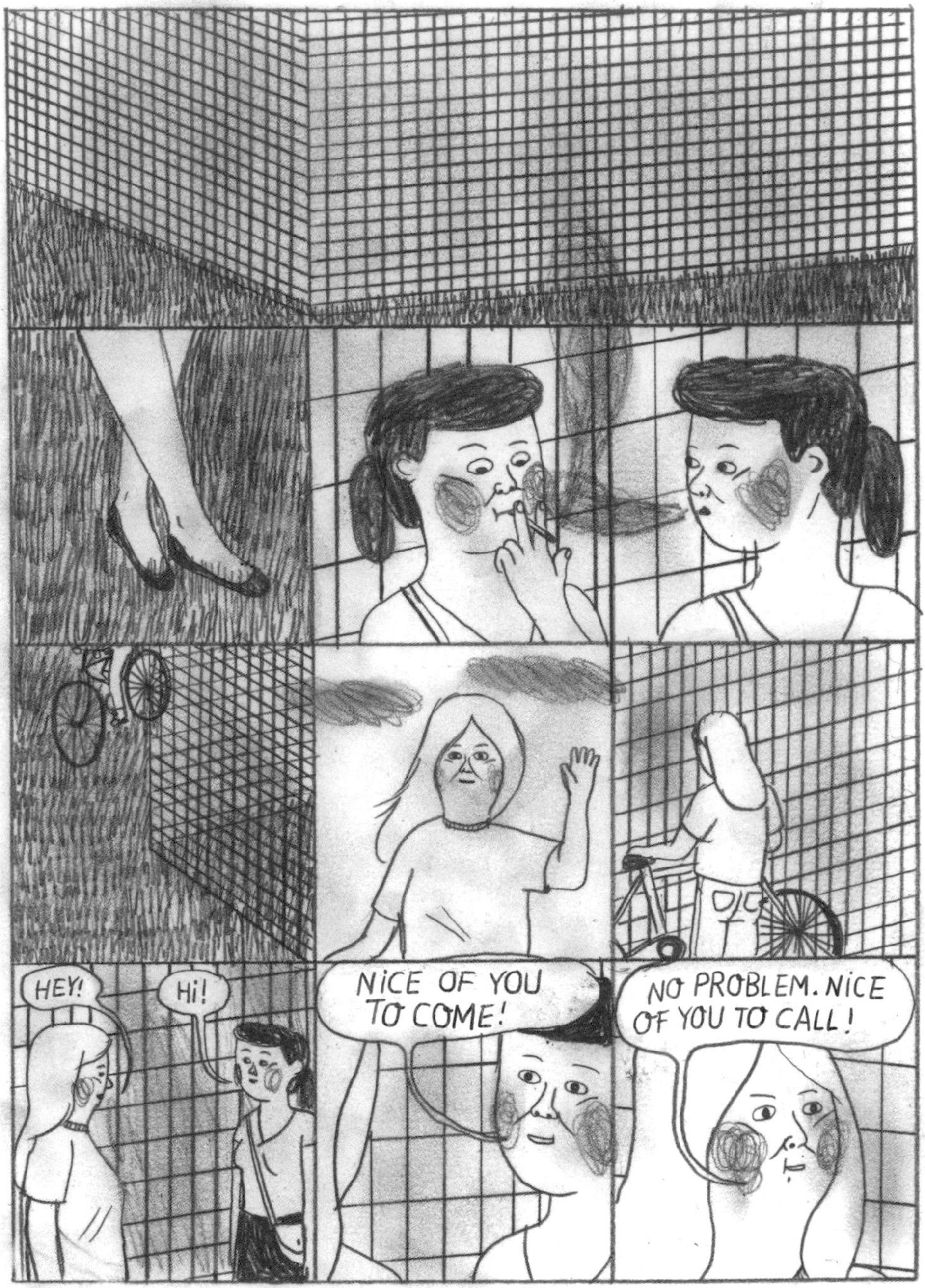
HEY!
Hi!
NICE OF YOU TO COME!
NO PROBLEM. NICE OF YOU TO CALL!

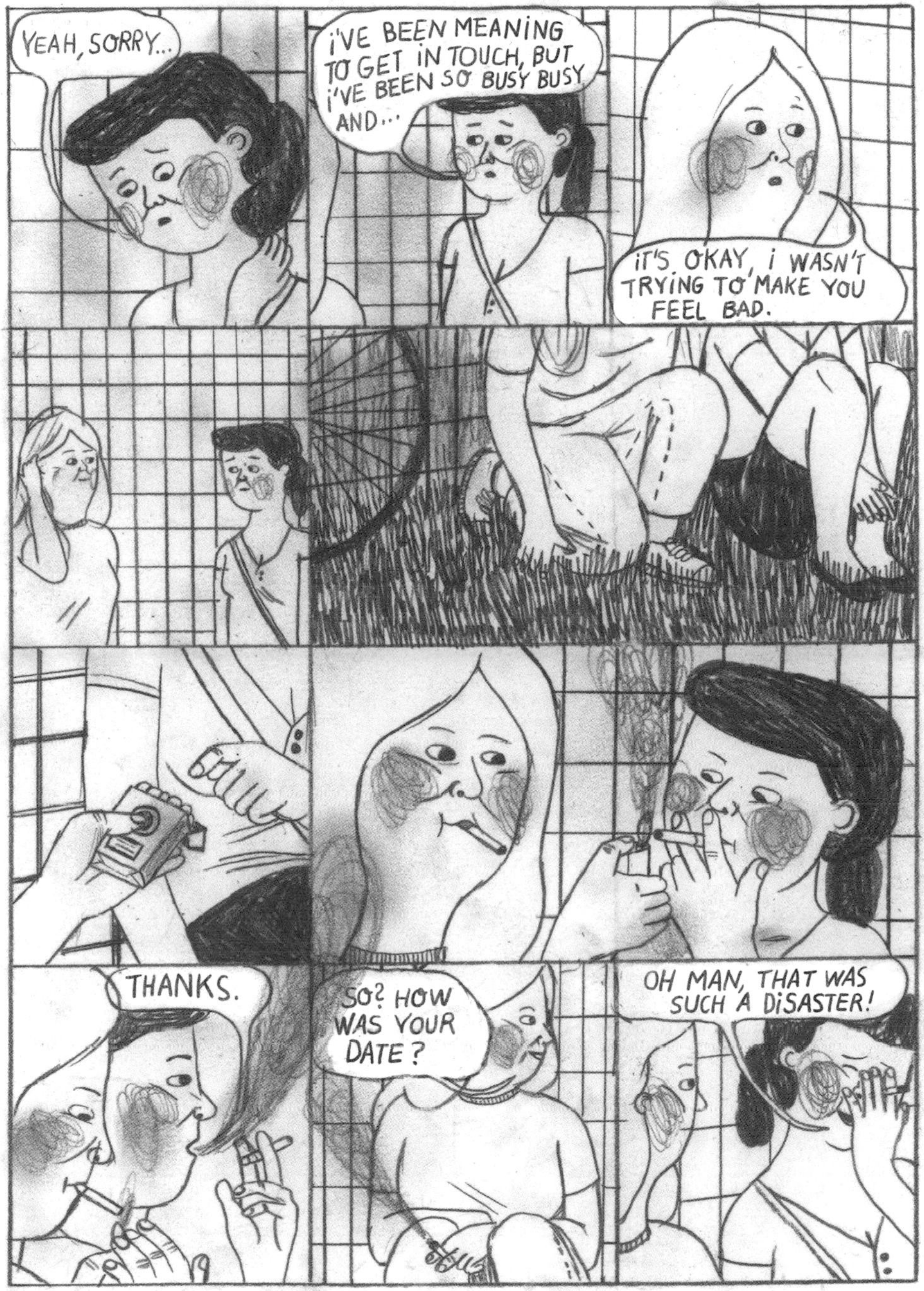
YEAH, SORRY...
i'VE BEEN MEANiNG TO GET iN TOUCH, BUT i'VE BEEN SO BUSY BUSY AND...
iT'S OKAY, i WASN'T TRYiNG TO MAKE YOU FEEL BAD.
THANKS.
SO? HOW WAS YOUR DATE?
OH MAN, THAT WAS SUCH A DiSASTER!

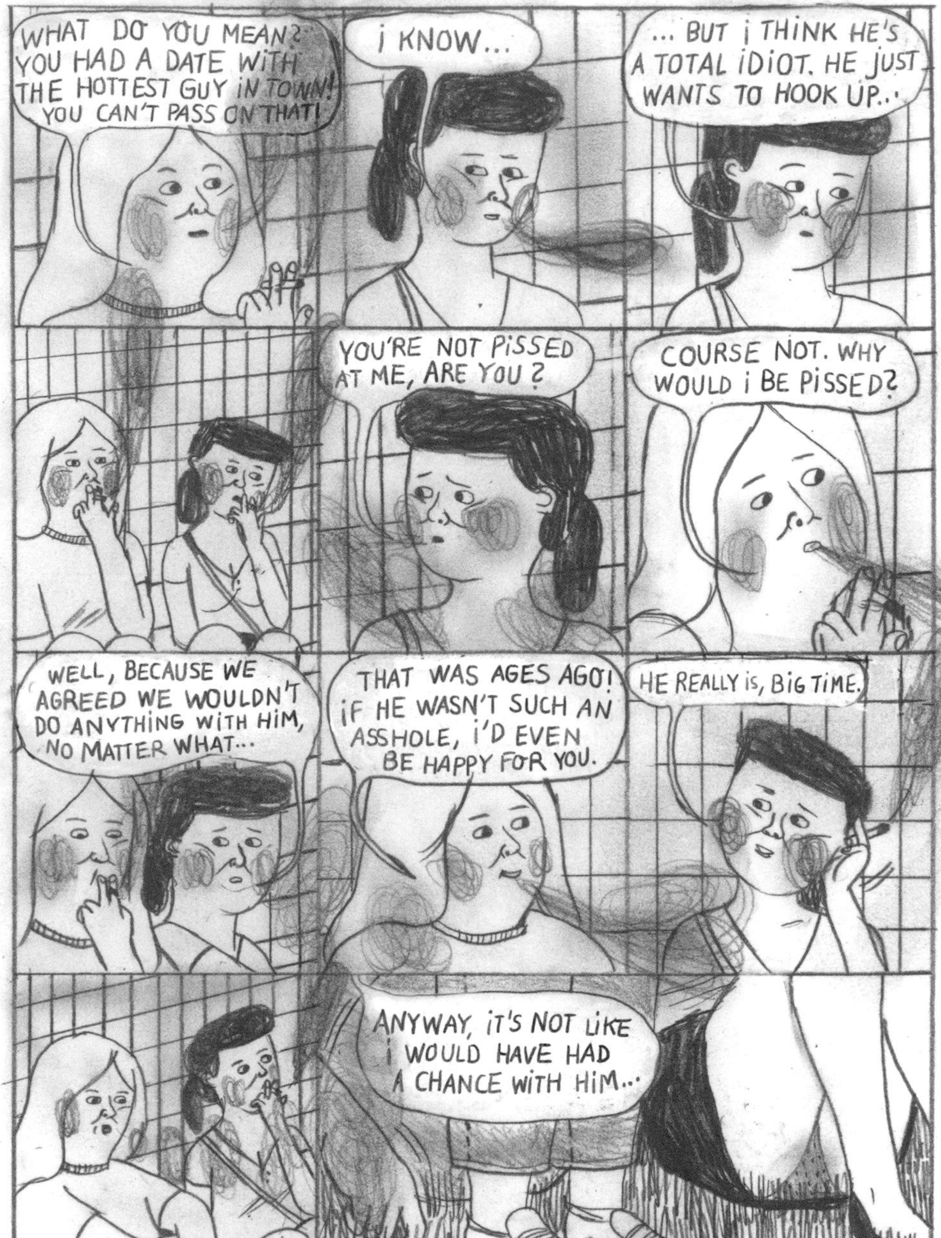
WHAT DO YOU MEAN? YOU HAD A DATE WITH THE HOTTEST GUY IN TOWN! YOU CAN'T PASS ON THAT!
i KNOW...
... BUT i THINK HE'S A TOTAL iDiOT. HE JUST WANTS TO HOOK UP...
YOU'RE NOT PiSSED AT ME, ARE YOU?
COURSE NOT. WHY WOULD i BE PiSSED?
WELL, BECAUSE WE AGREED WE WOULDN'T DO ANYTHING WiTH HiM, NO MATTER WHAT...
THAT WAS AGES AGO! iF HE WASN'T SUCH AN ASSHOLE, i'D EVEN BE HAPPY FOR YOU.
HE REALLY iS, BiG TiME.
ANYWAY, iT'S NOT LiKE i WOULD HAVE HAD A CHANCE WiTH HiM...

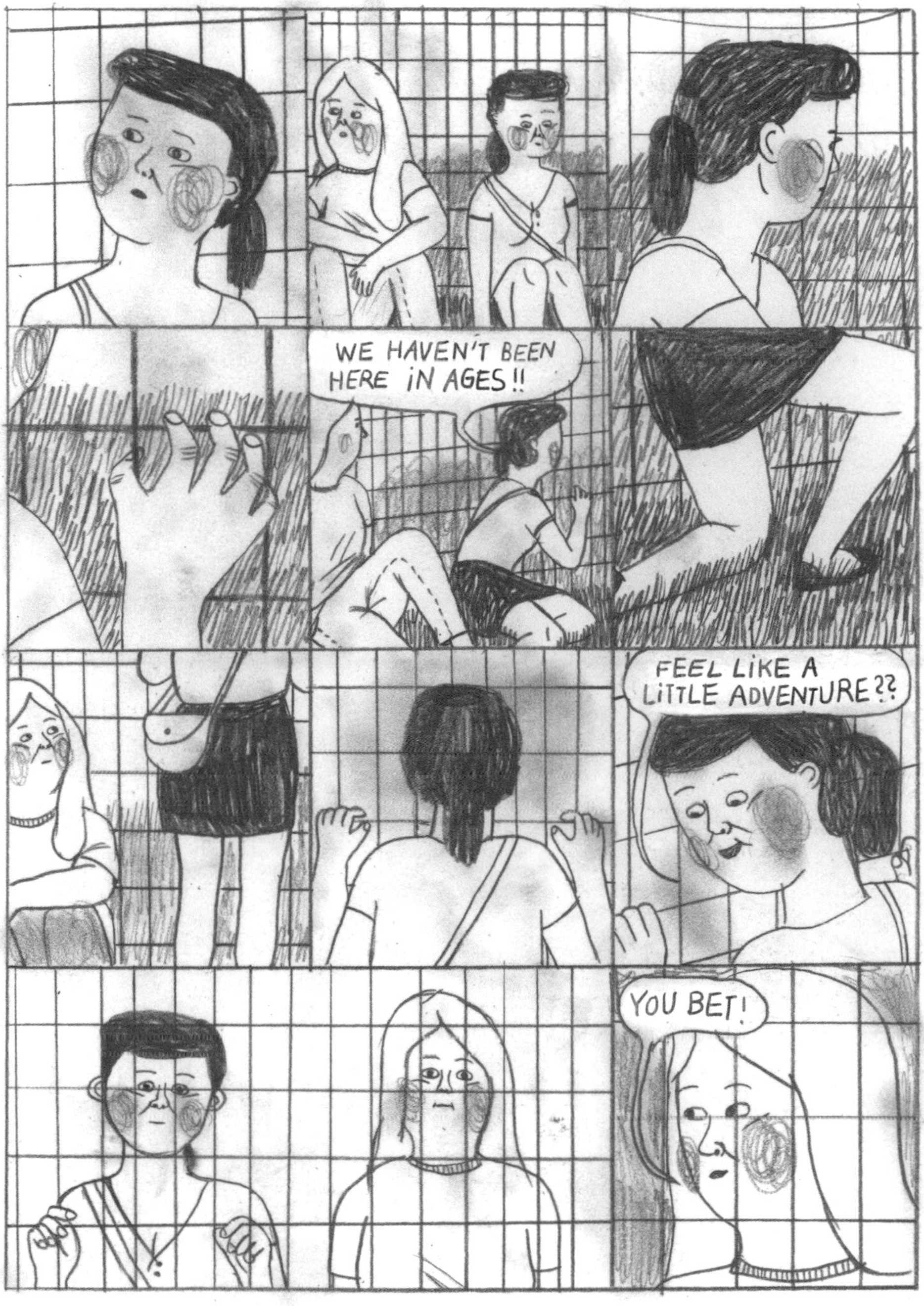
WE HAVEN'T BEEN HERE IN AGES!!
FEEL LIKE A LITTLE ADVENTURE??
YOU BET!

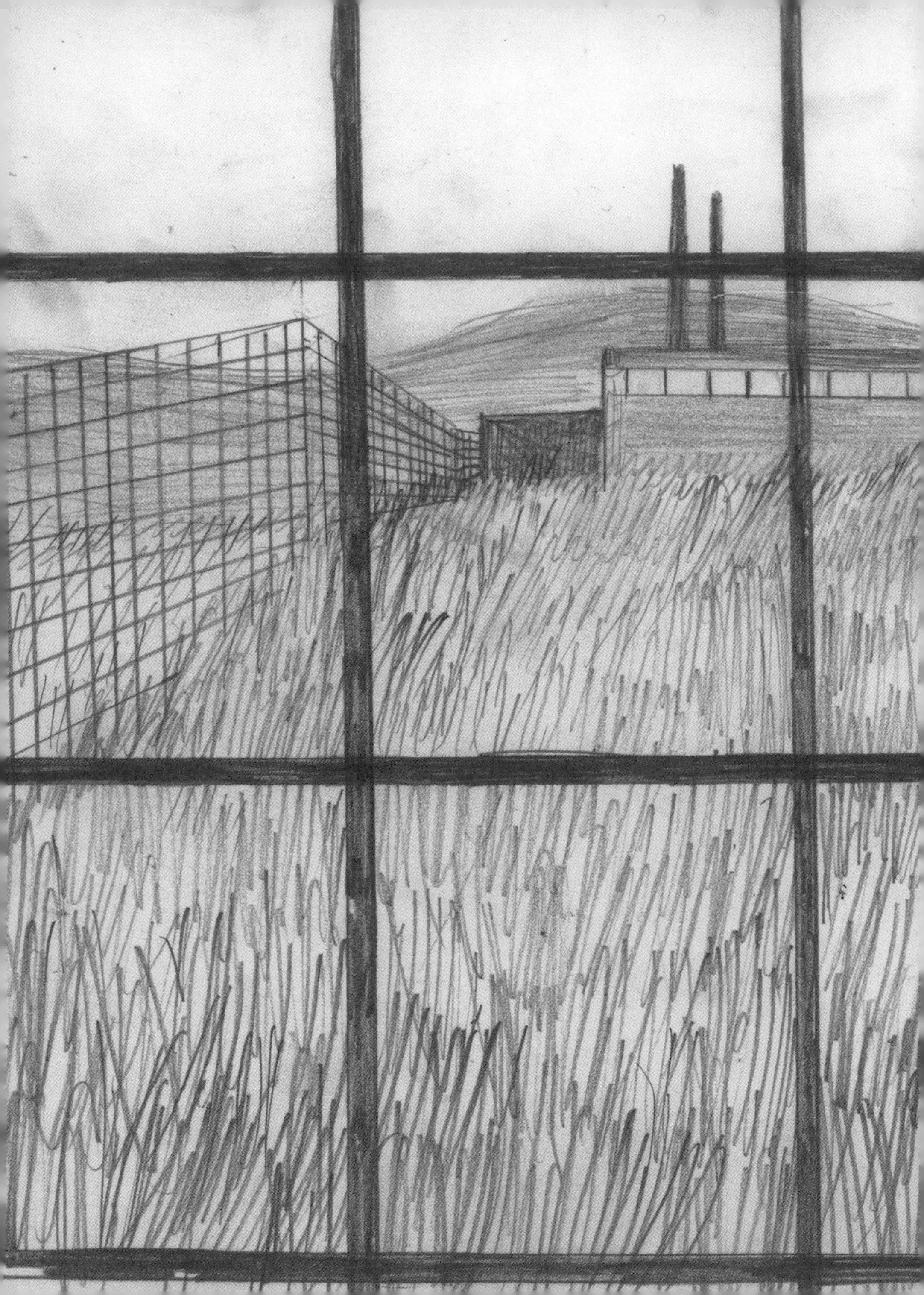

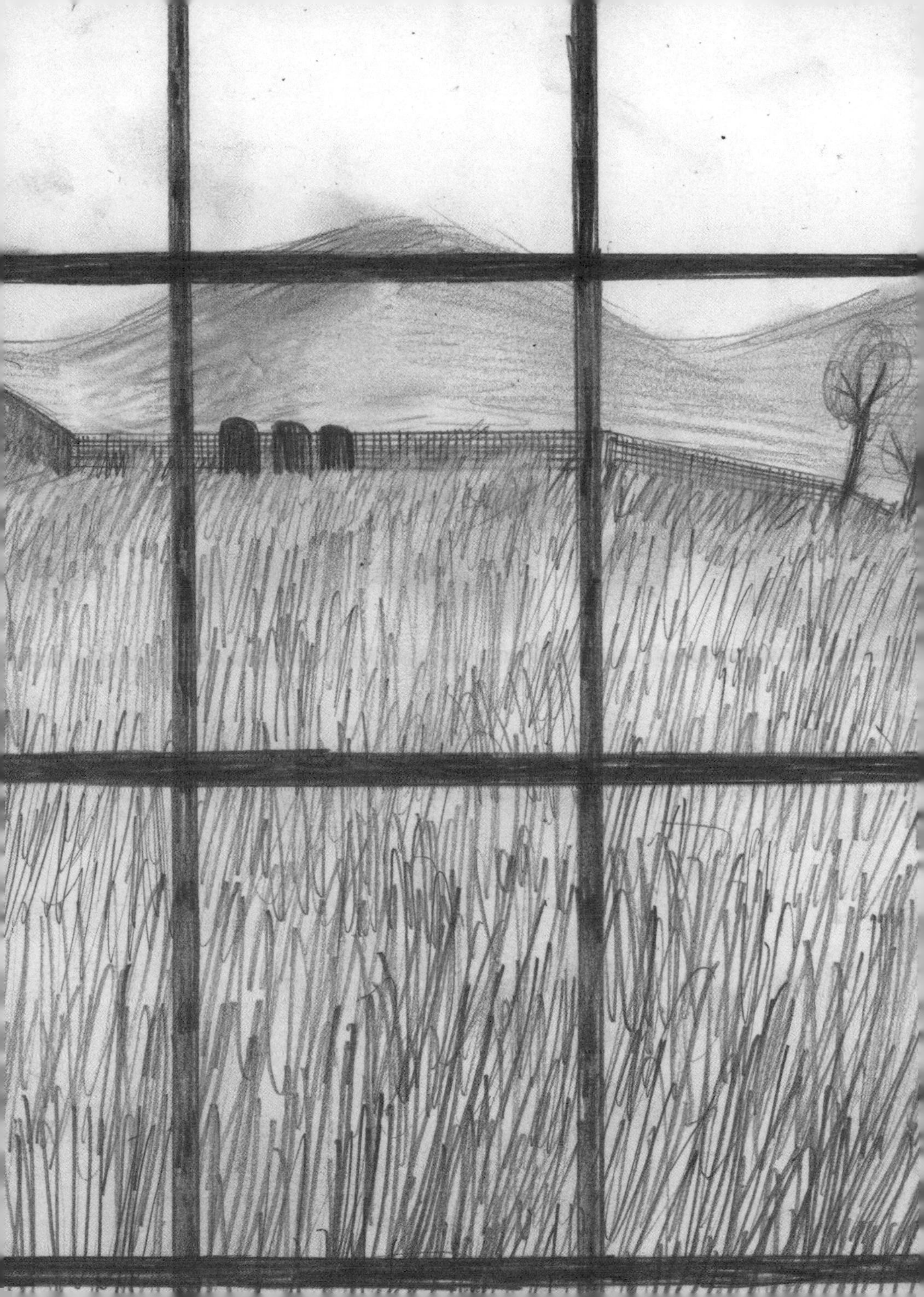

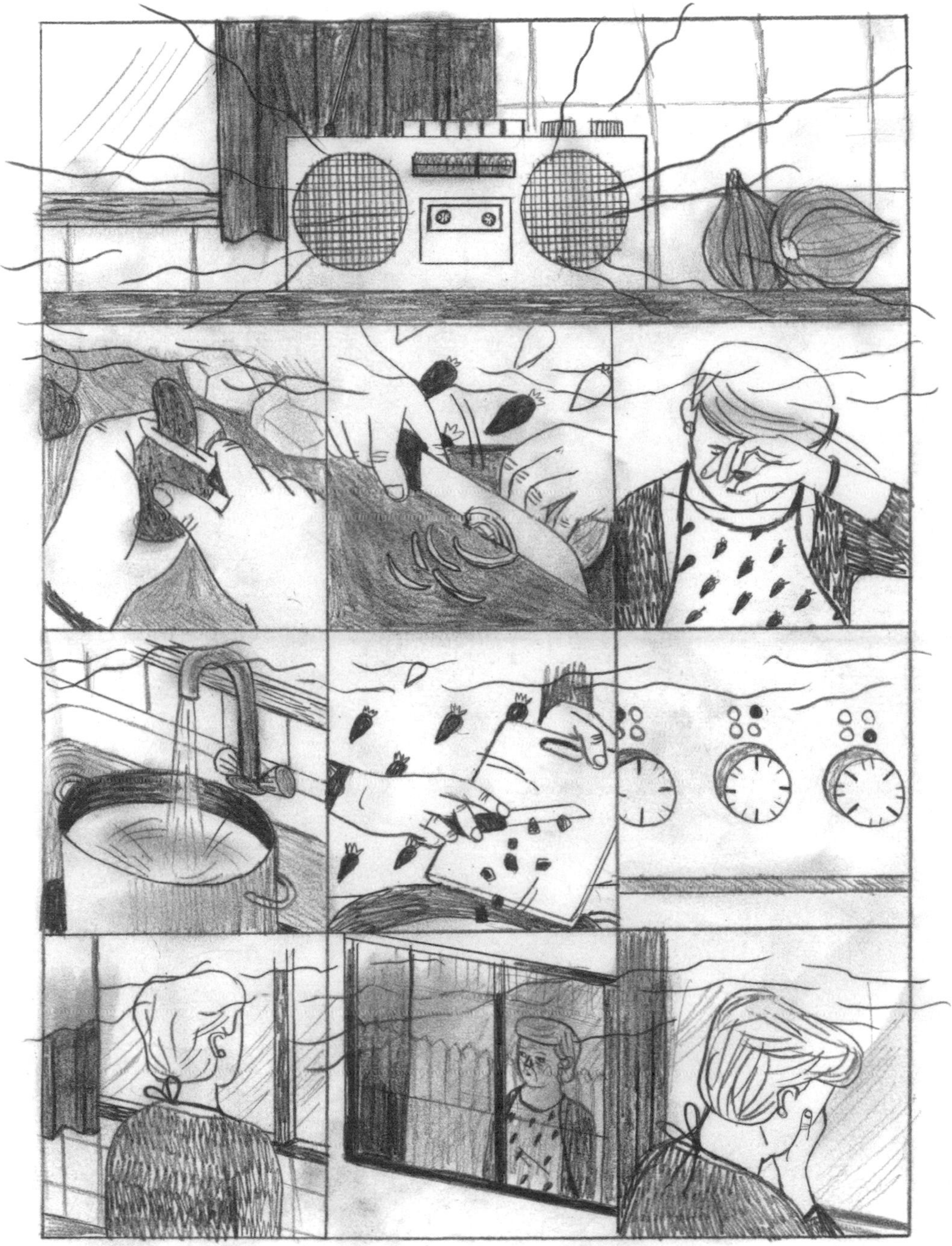

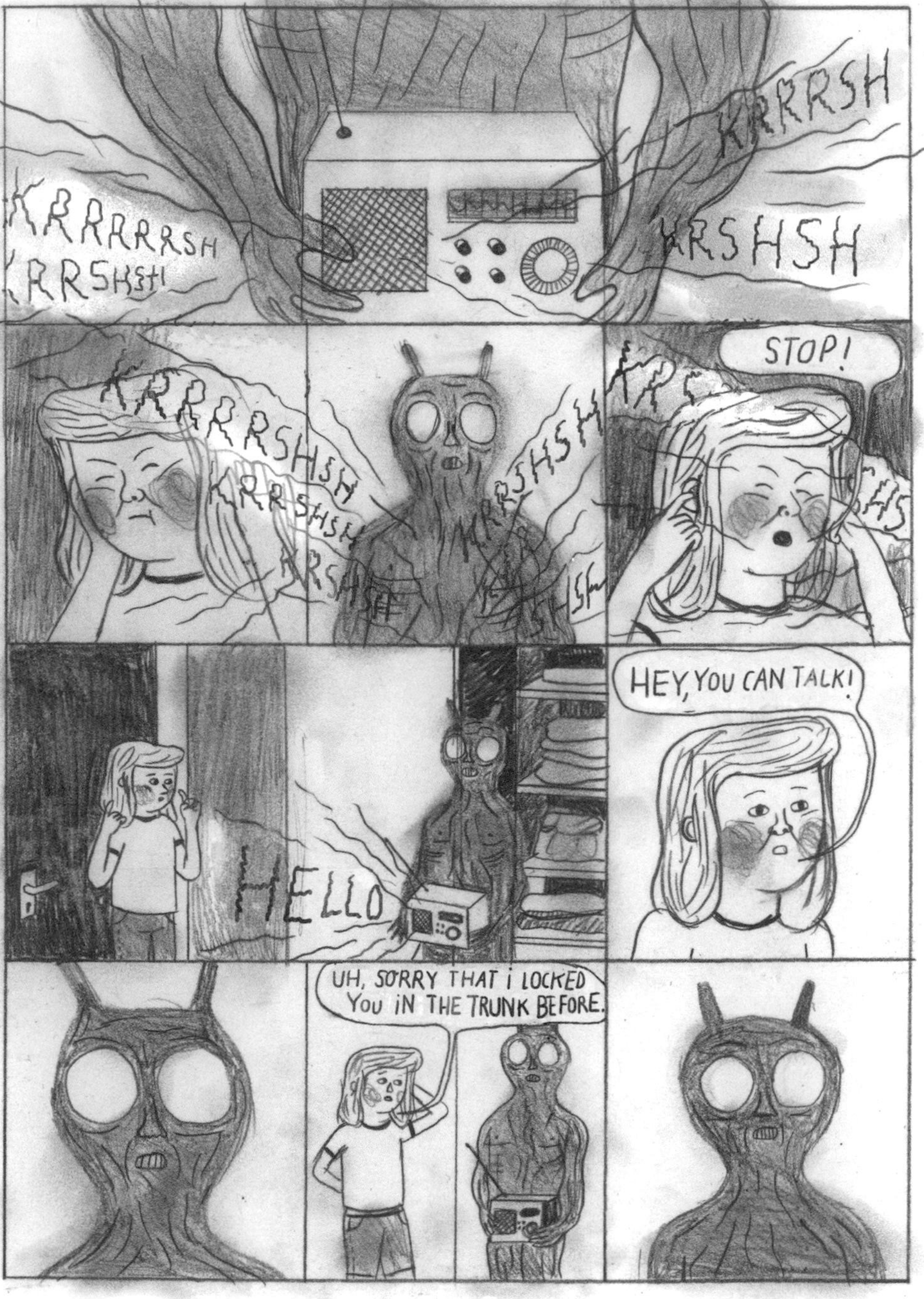
KRRRSH
KRSHSH
KRRRRRSHSH
STOP!
HELLO
HEY, YOU CAN TALK!
UH, SORRY THAT I LOCKED YOU IN THE TRUNK BEFORE.

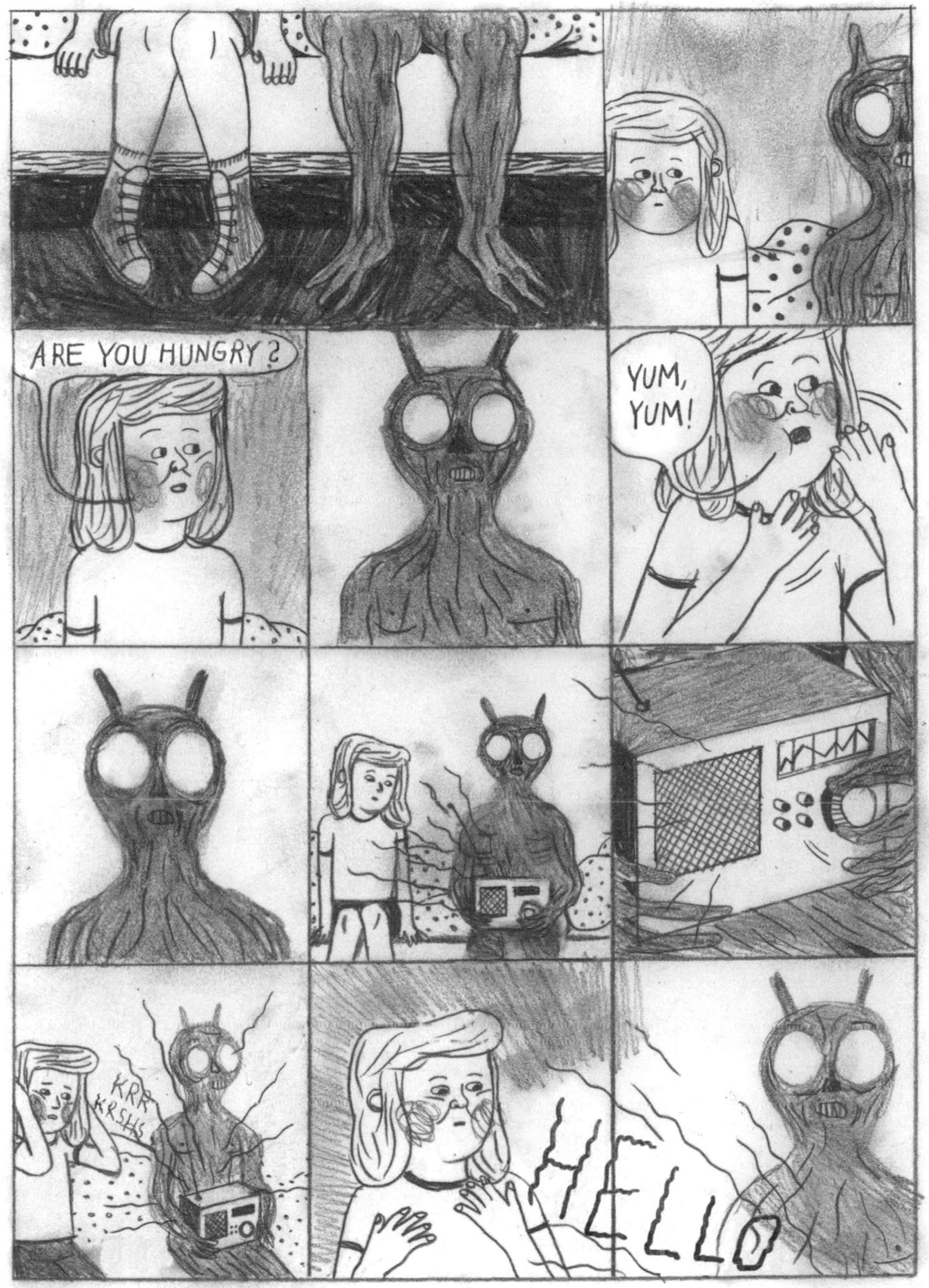
ARE YOU HUNGRY?
YUM, YUM!
KRR KRSHS
HELLO

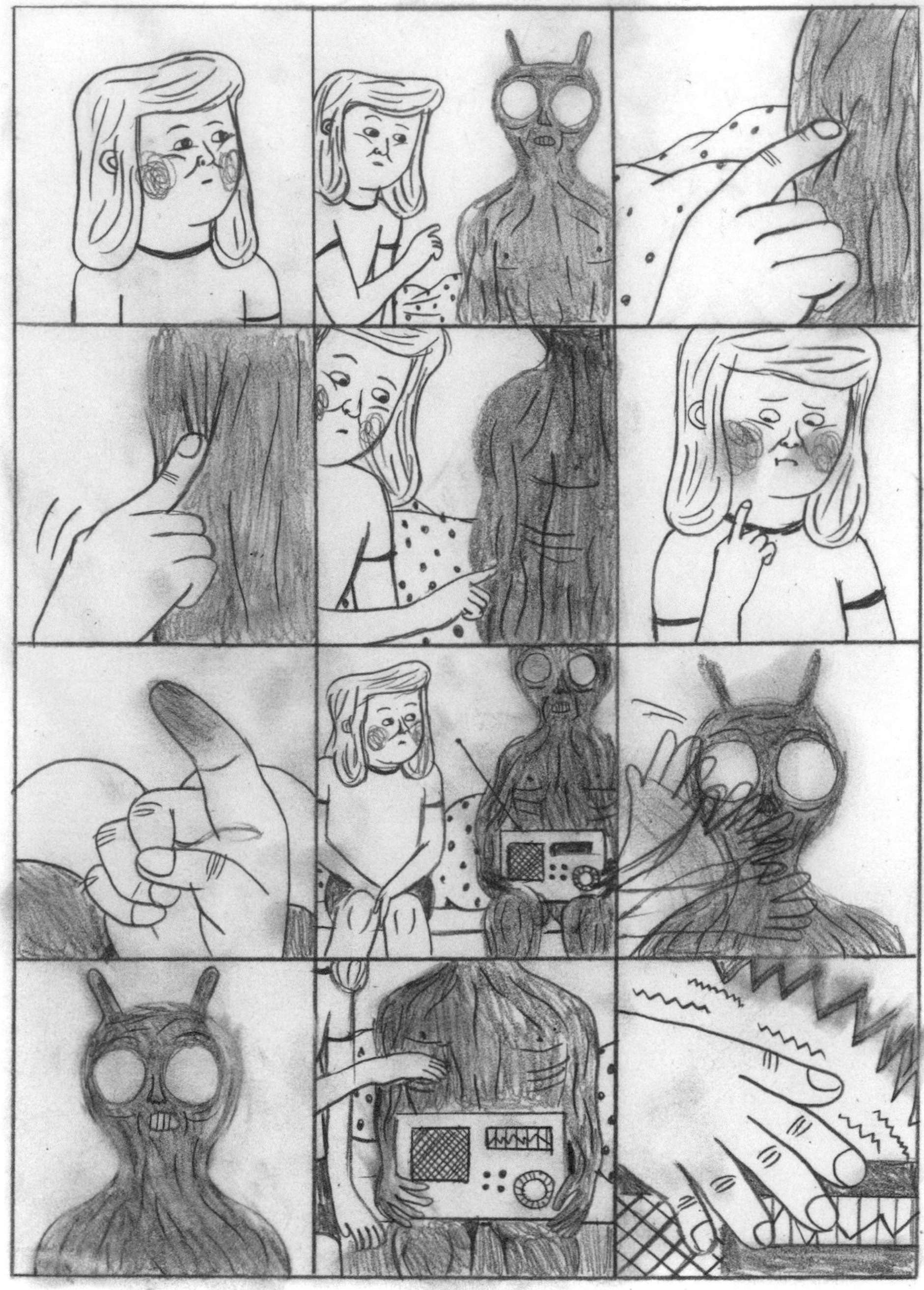

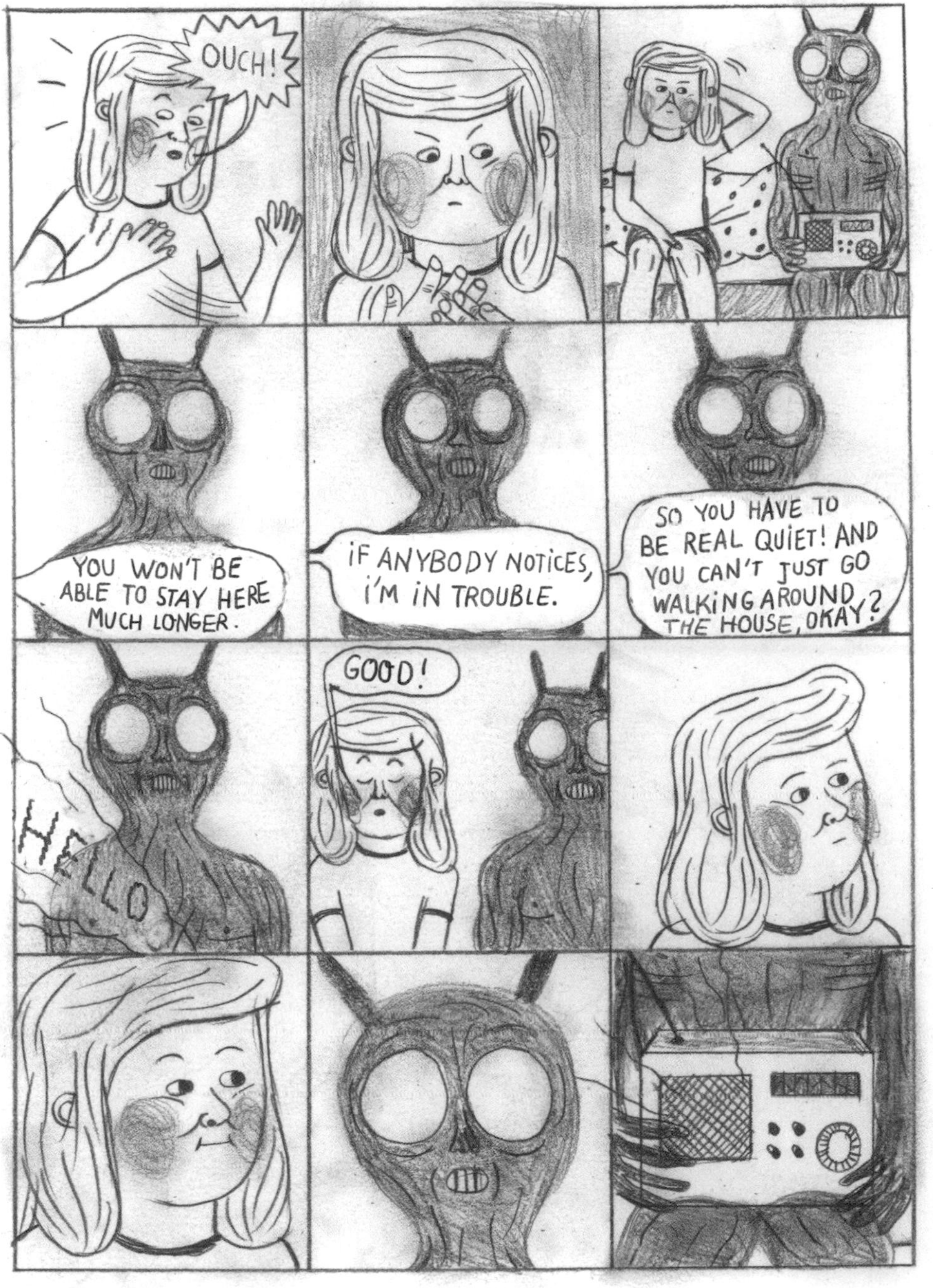
OUCH!
YOU WON'T BE ABLE TO STAY HERE MUCH LONGER.
IF ANYBODY NOTICES, I'M IN TROUBLE.
SO YOU HAVE TO BE REAL QUIET! AND YOU CAN'T JUST GO WALKING AROUND THE HOUSE, OKAY?
HELLO
GOOD!

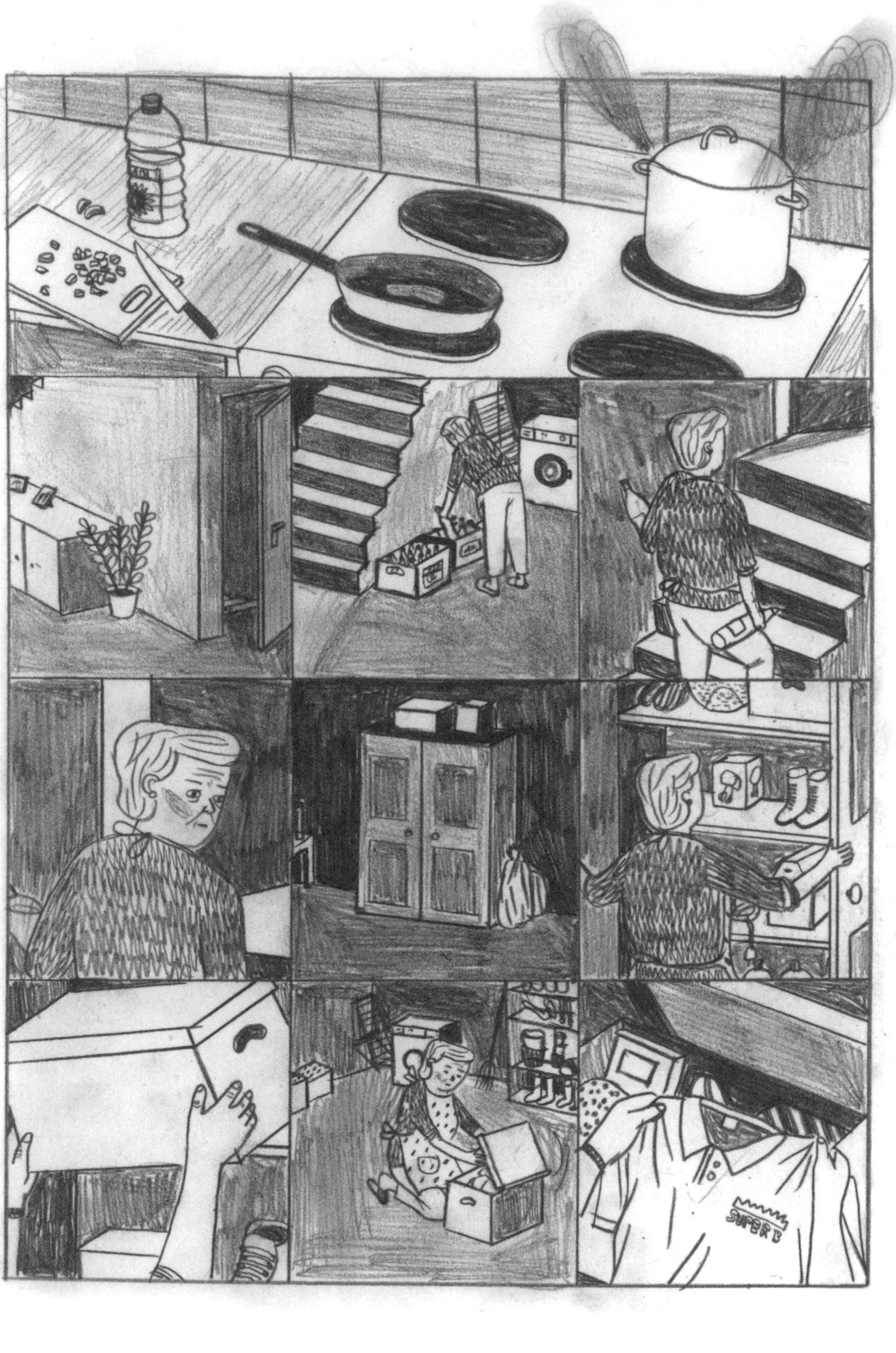
SUPER B

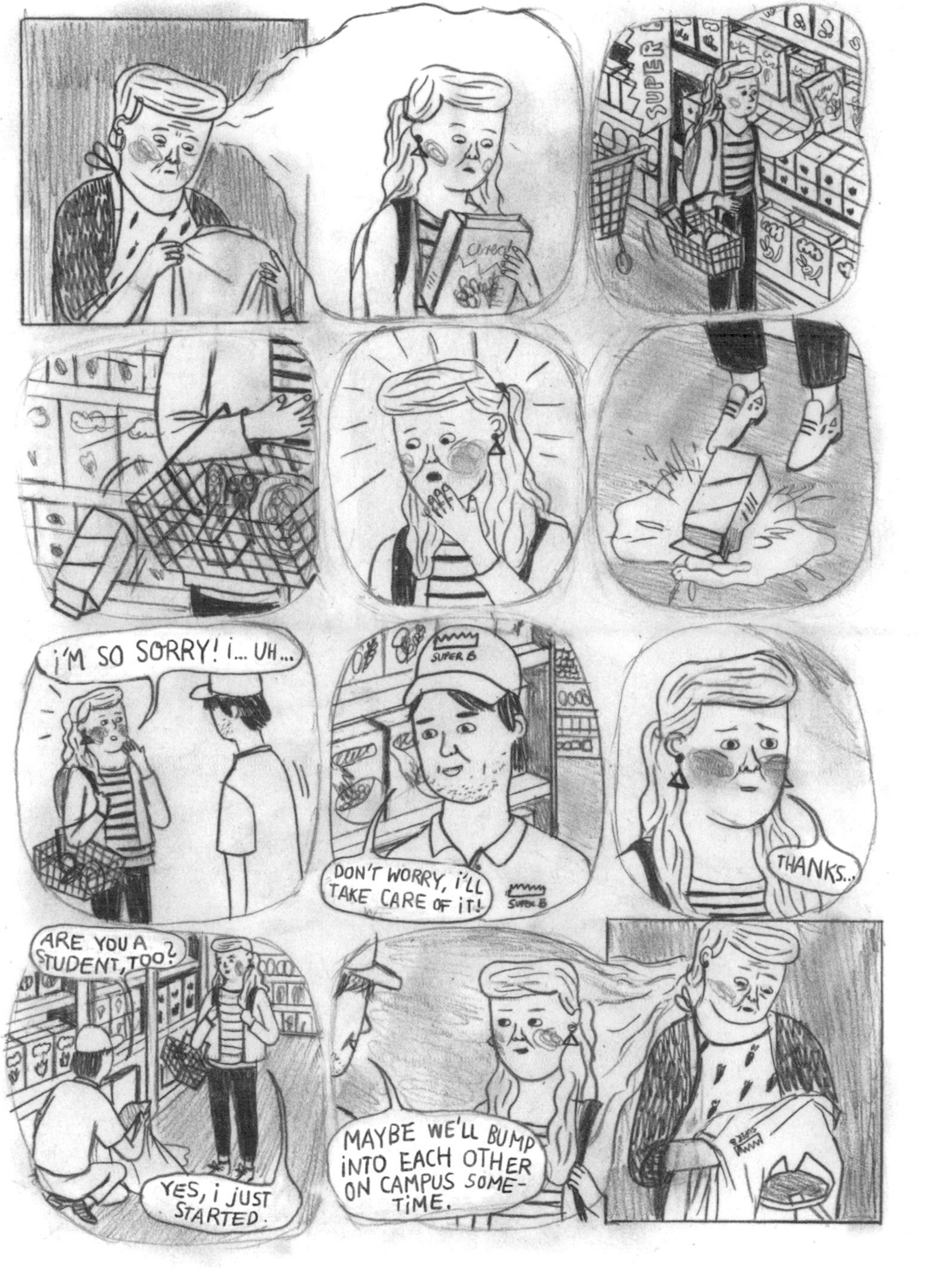

Cereal
SUPER B
¡'M SO SORRY! i... UH...
SUPER B
DON'T WORRY, i'LL TAKE CARE OF iT!
SUPER B
THANKS...
ARE YOU A STUDENT, TOO?
YES, i JUST STARTED.
MAYBE WE'LL BUMP iNTO EACH OTHER ON CAMPUS SOME-TiME.

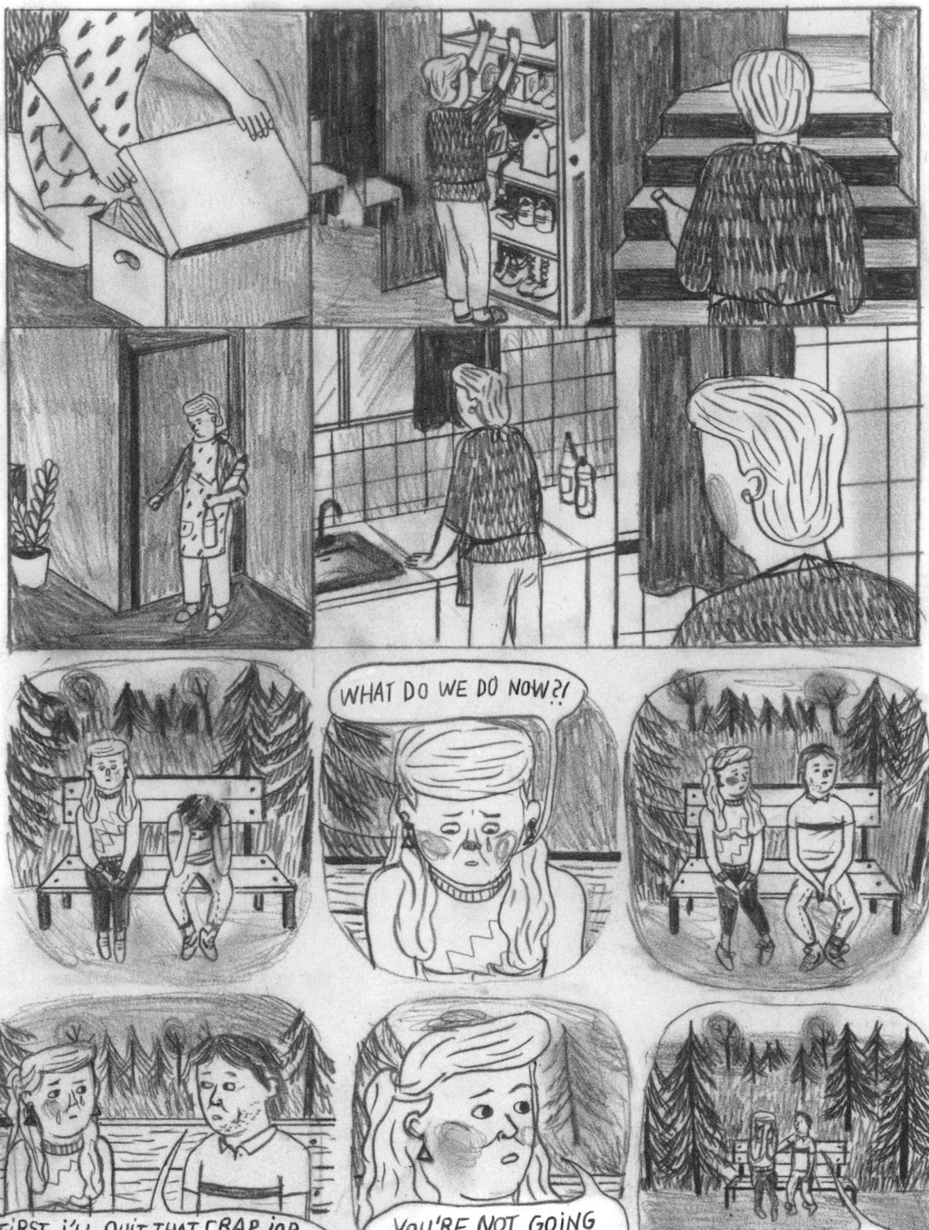
WHAT DO WE DO NOW?!
FIRST I'LL QUIT THAT CRAP JOB AT SUPER B AND GET SOMETHING DECENT. WE CAN MOVE INTO THE TOP FLOOR OF MY PARENTS'...
YOU'RE NOT GOING TO DROP OUT OF SCHOOL, ARE YOU?
DON'T WORRY ABOUT ME. WE'LL FIGURE IT OUT!

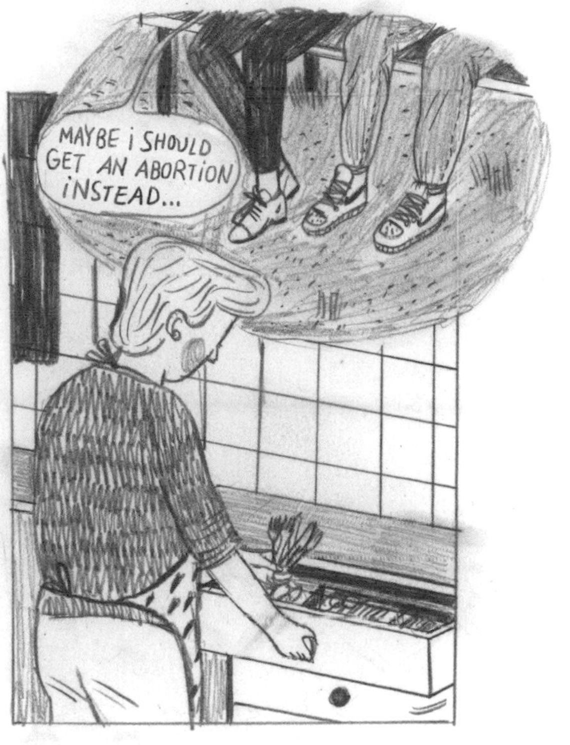
MAYBE i SHOULD GET AN ABORTION iNSTEAD...

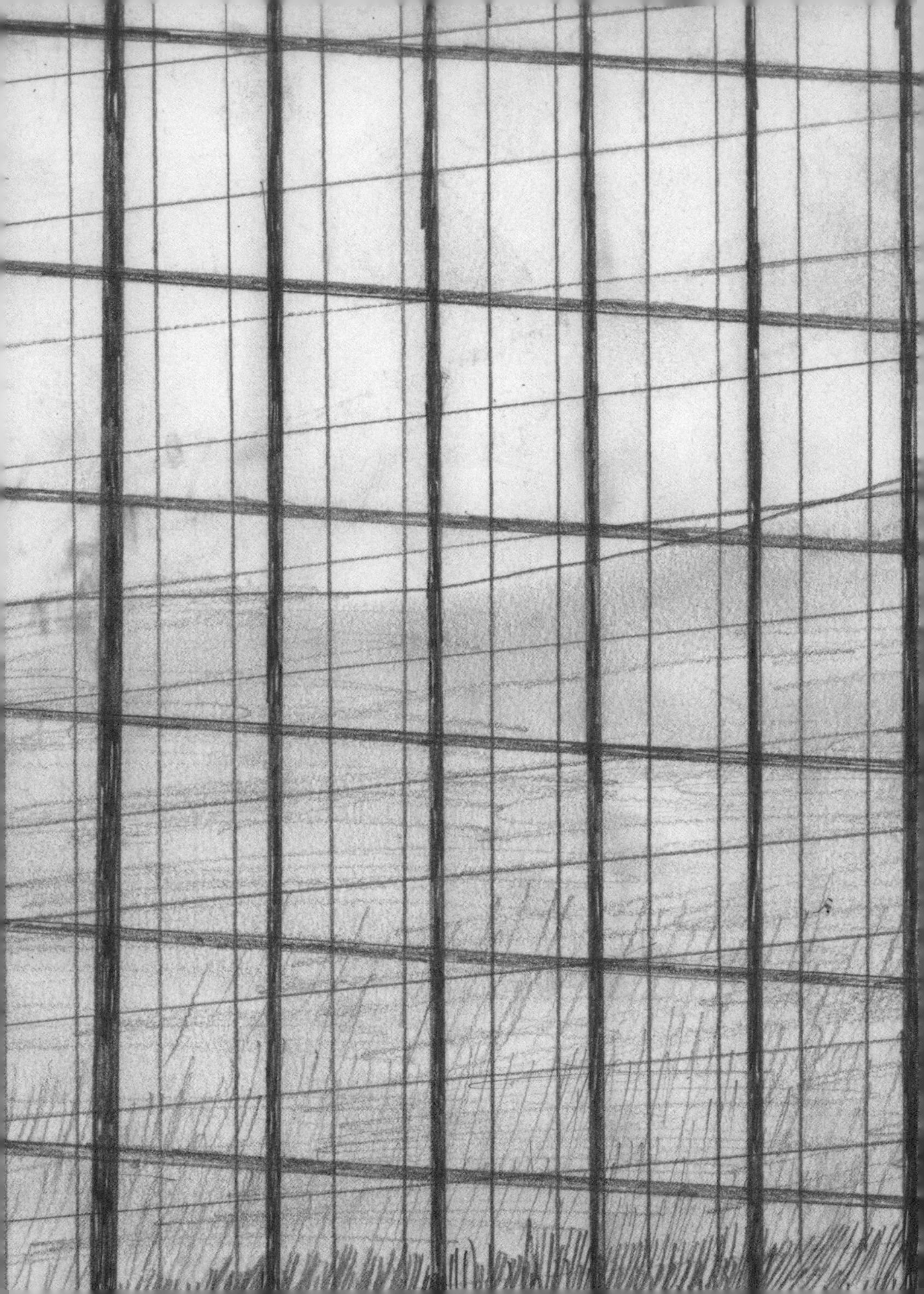

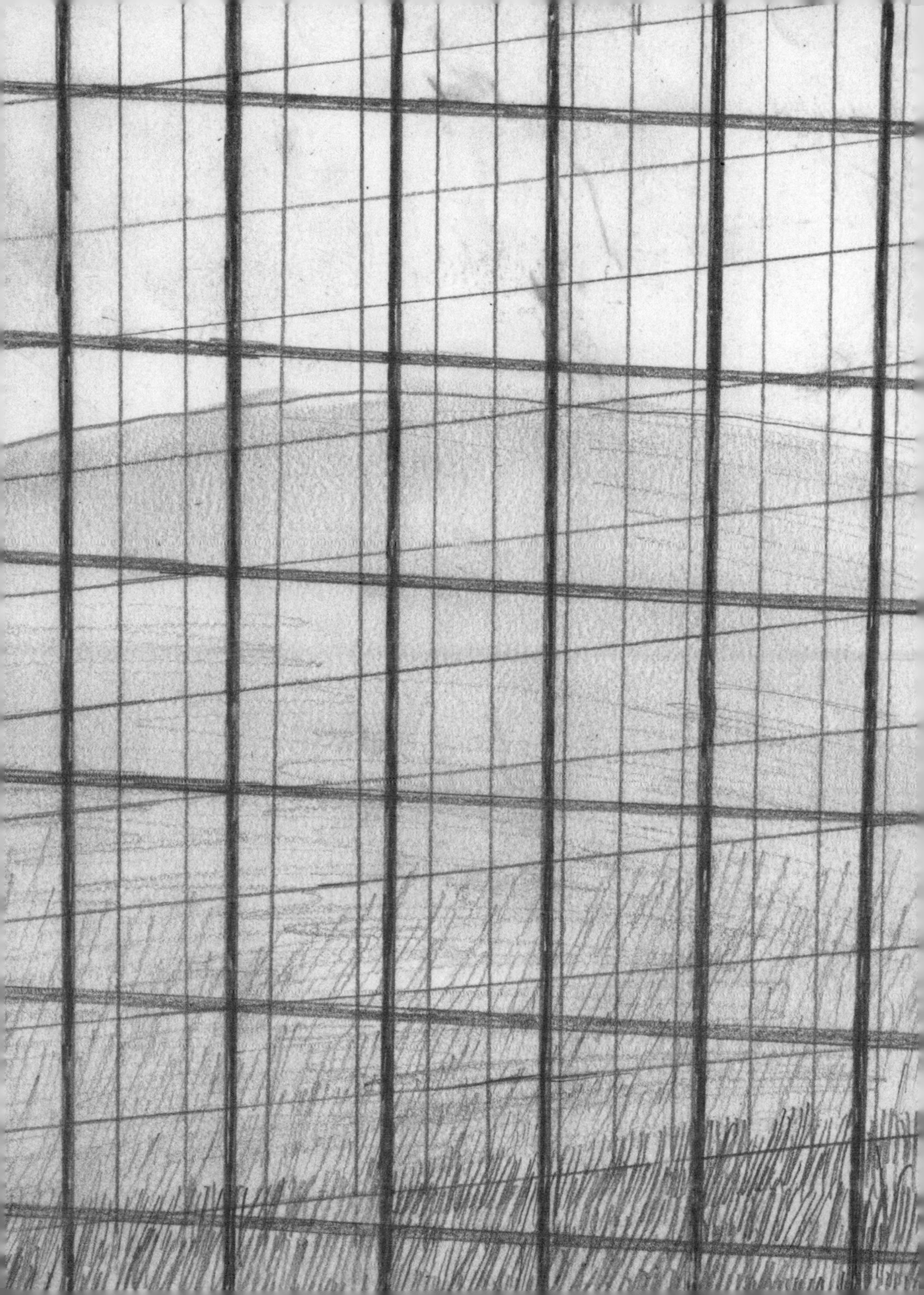

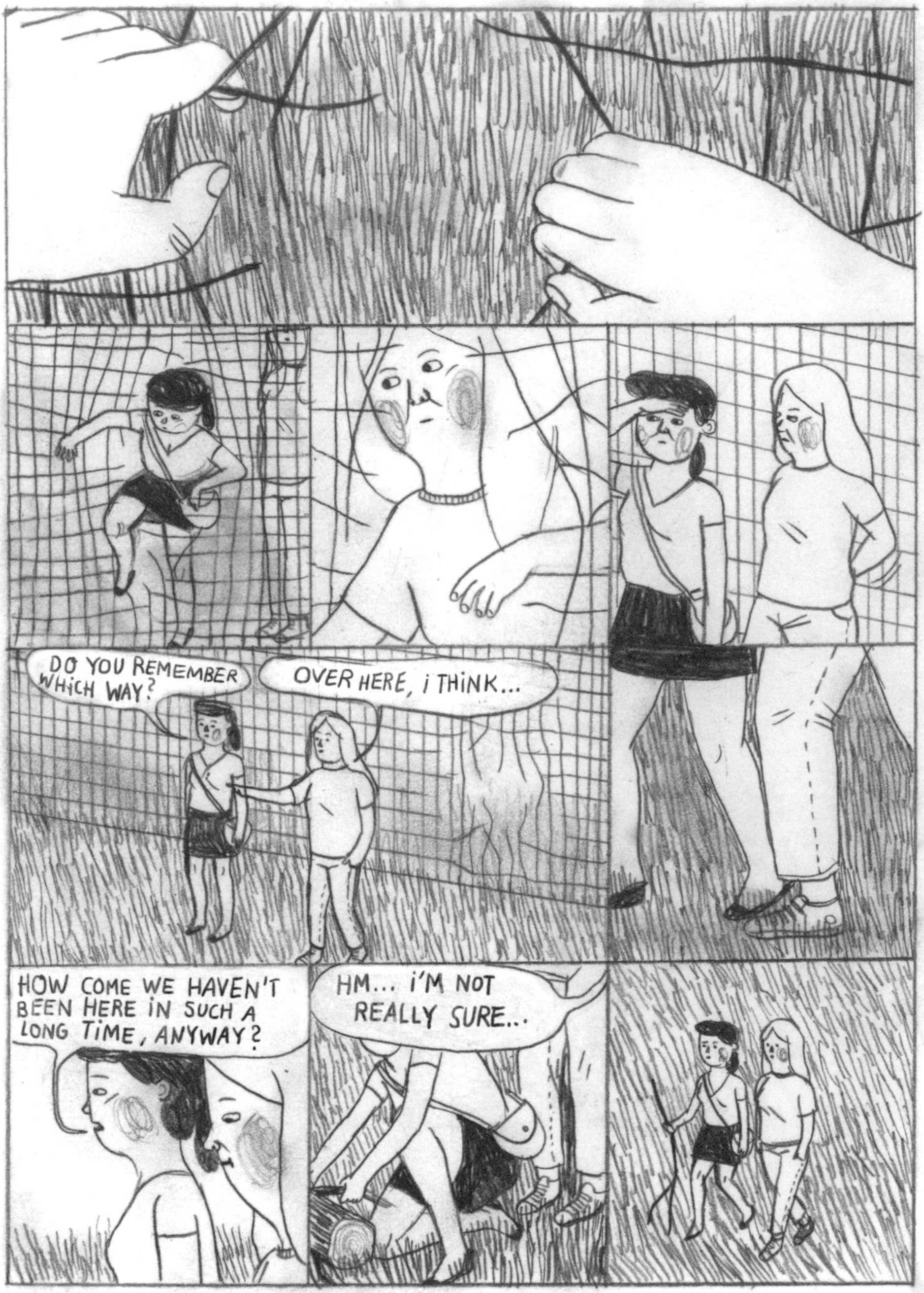
DO YOU REMEMBER WHICH WAY?
OVER HERE, I THINK...
HOW COME WE HAVEN'T BEEN HERE IN SUCH A LONG TIME, ANYWAY?
HM... I'M NOT REALLY SURE...

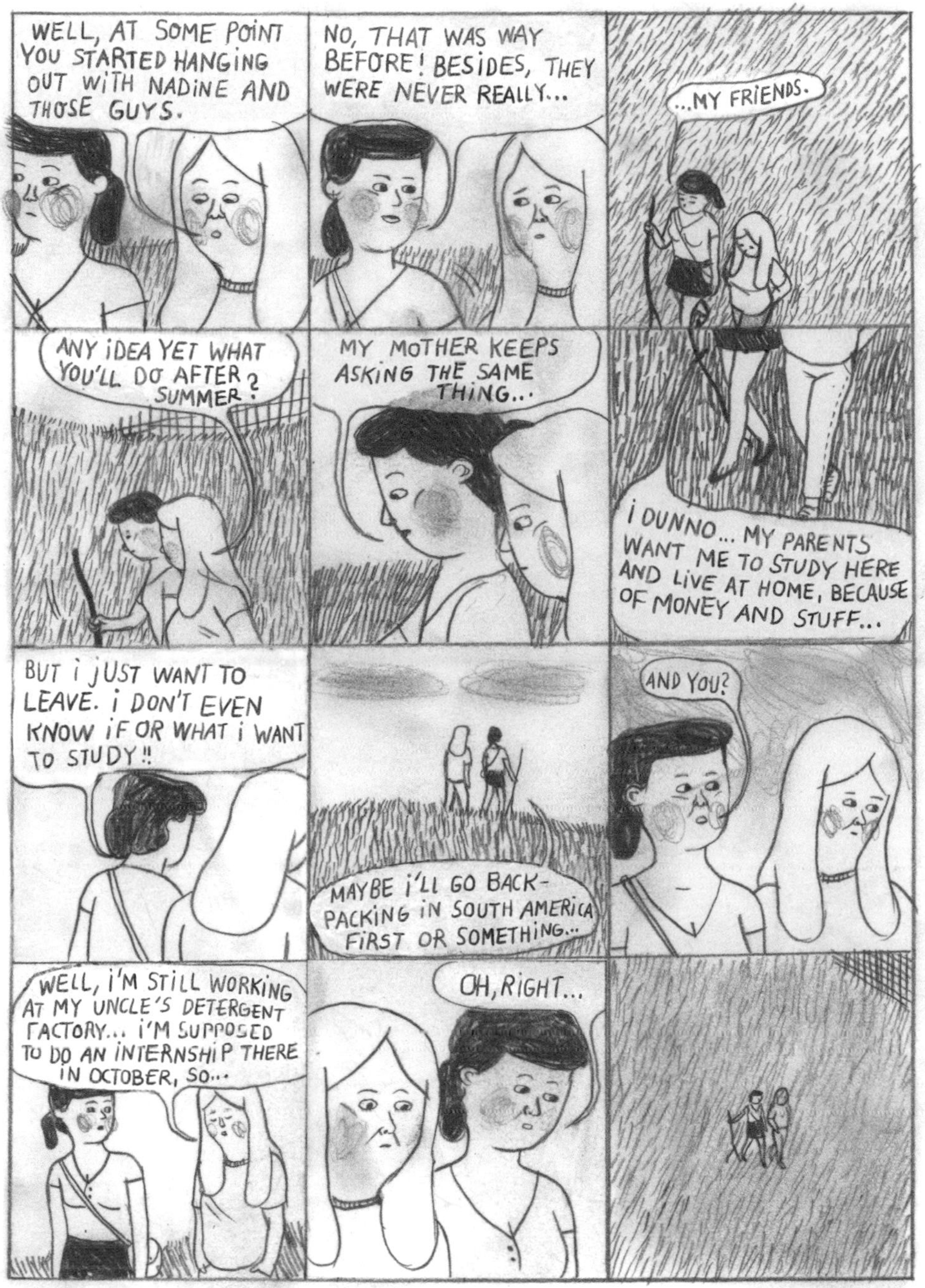
WELL, AT SOME POINT YOU STARTED HANGING OUT WITH NADINE AND THOSE GUYS.
NO, THAT WAS WAY BEFORE! BESIDES, THEY WERE NEVER REALLY...
...MY FRIENDS.
ANY IDEA YET WHAT YOU'LL DO AFTER SUMMER?
MY MOTHER KEEPS ASKING THE SAME THING...
I DUNNO... MY PARENTS WANT ME TO STUDY HERE AND LIVE AT HOME, BECAUSE OF MONEY AND STUFF...
BUT I JUST WANT TO LEAVE. I DON'T EVEN KNOW IF OR WHAT I WANT TO STUDY!!
MAYBE I'LL GO BACK-PACKING IN SOUTH AMERICA FIRST OR SOMETHING...
AND YOU?
WELL, I'M STILL WORKING AT MY UNCLE'S DETERGENT FACTORY... I'M SUPPOSED TO DO AN INTERNSHIP THERE IN OCTOBER, SO...
OH, RIGHT...

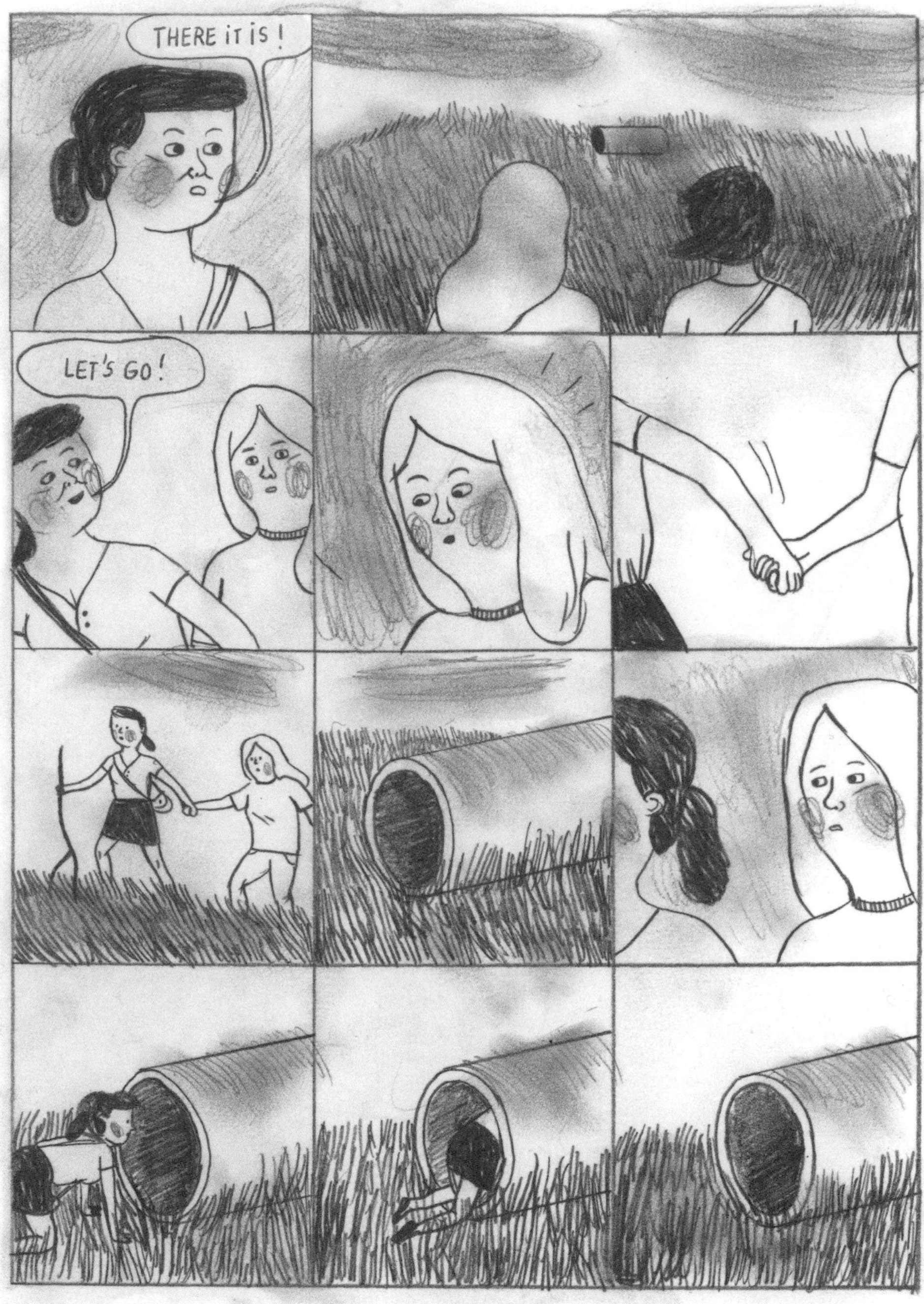
THERE it is!
LET'S GO!

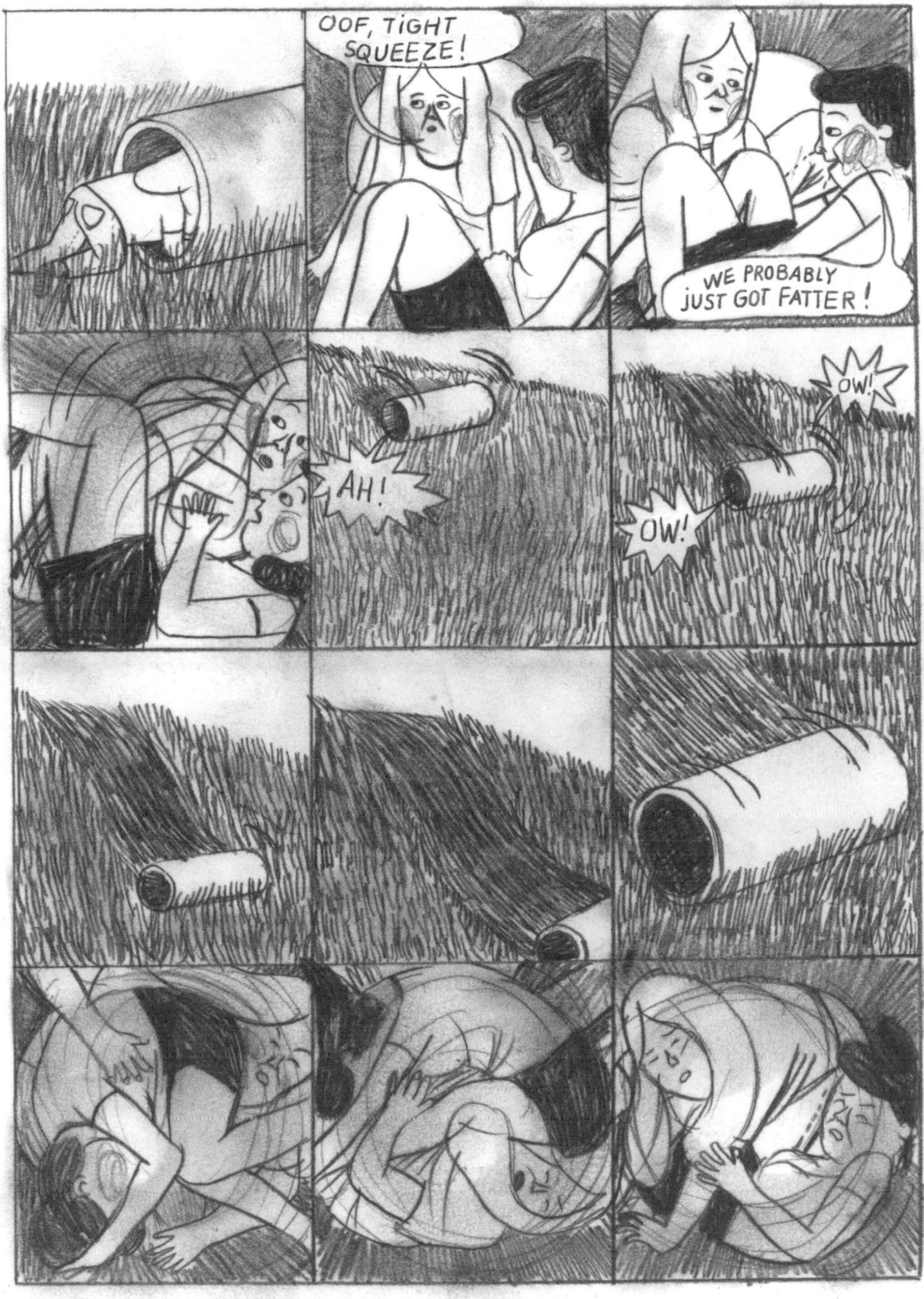
OOF, TIGHT SQUEEZE!
WE PROBABLY JUST GOT FATTER!
AH!
OW!
OW!

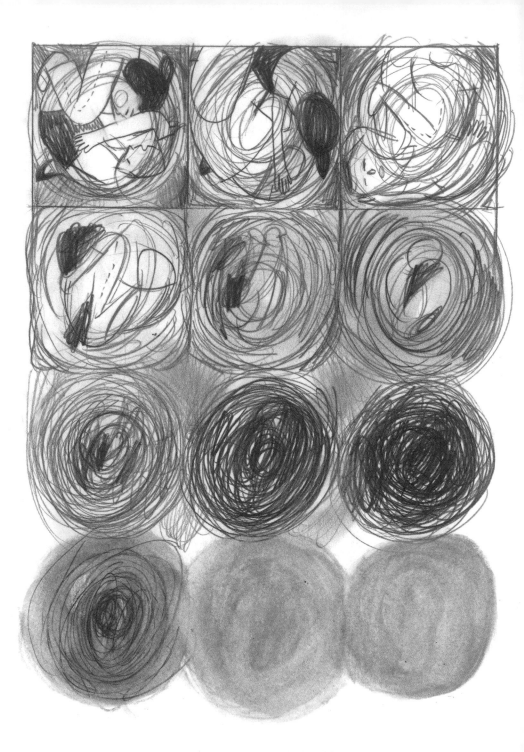

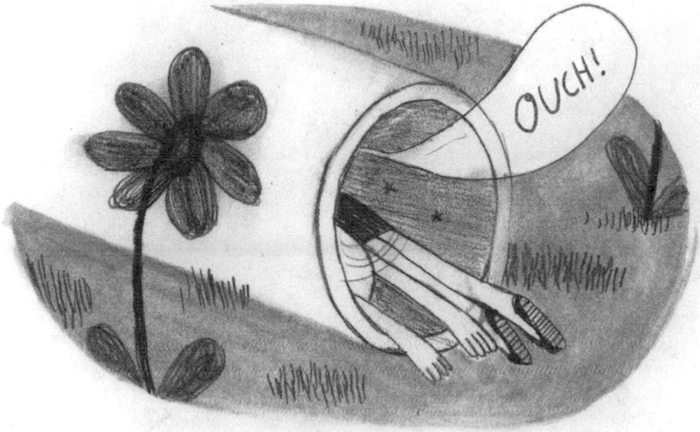
OUCH!

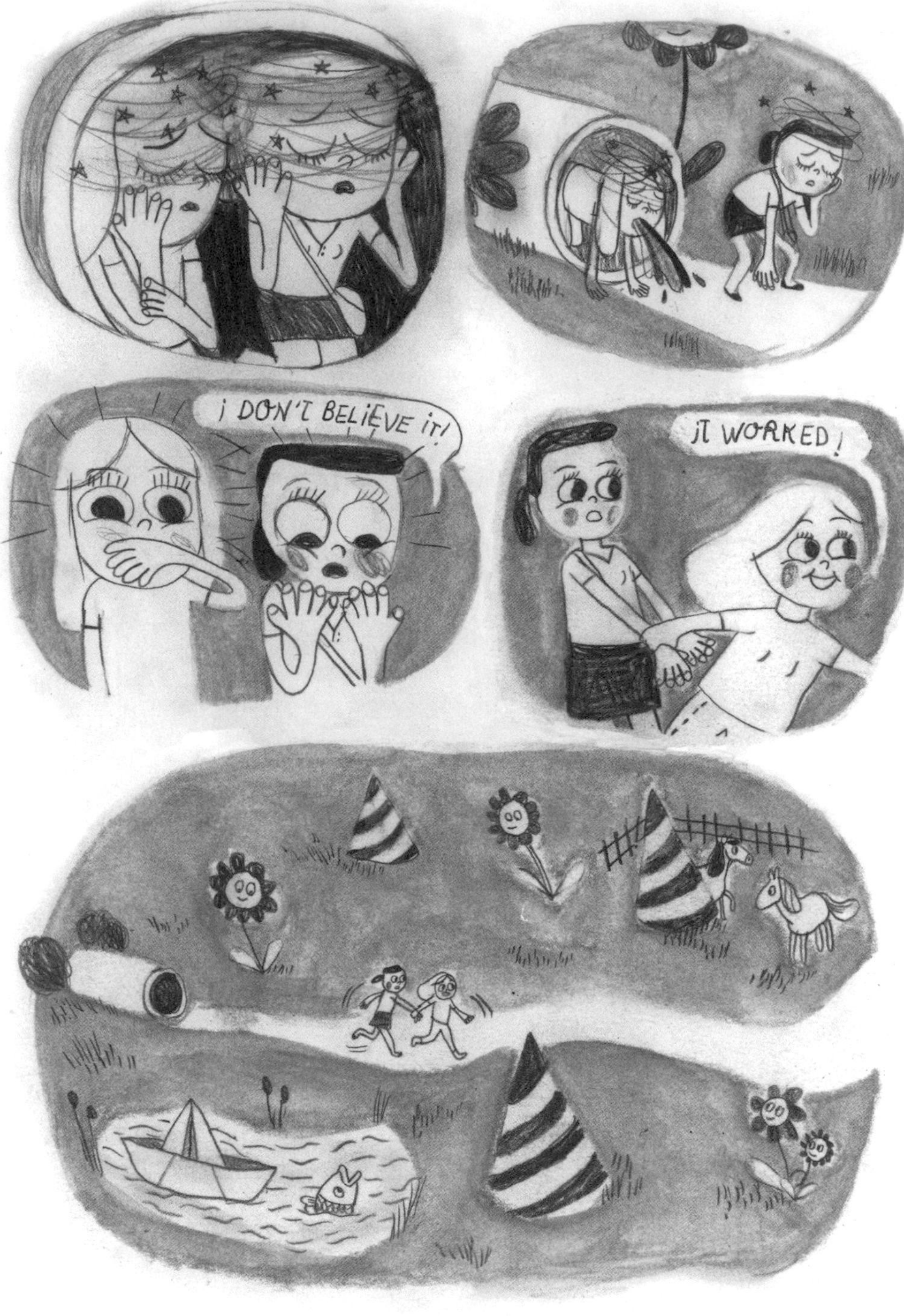

i DON'T BELIEVE it!
iT WORKED!

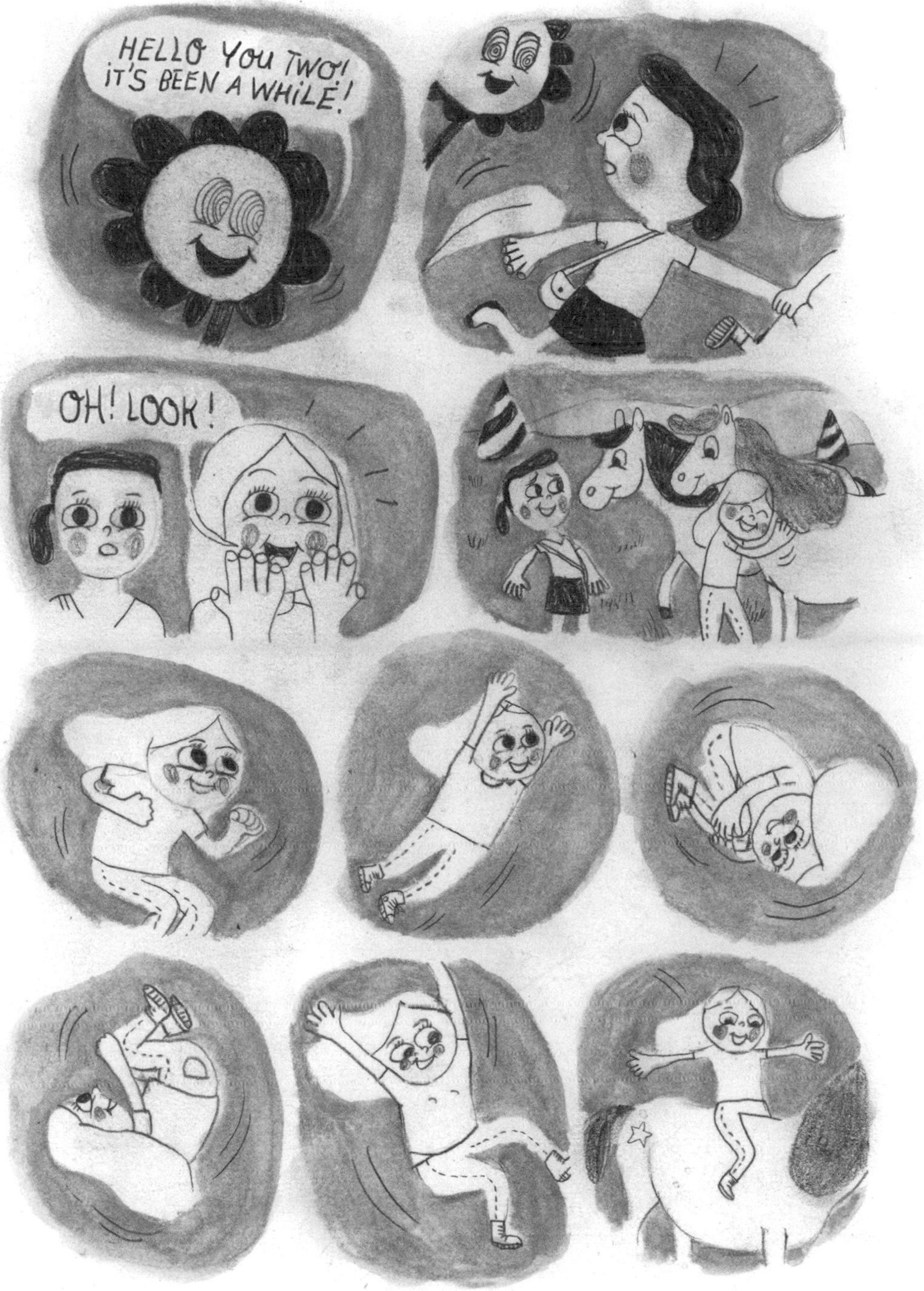
HELLO YOU TWO! IT'S BEEN A WHILE!
OH! LOOK!

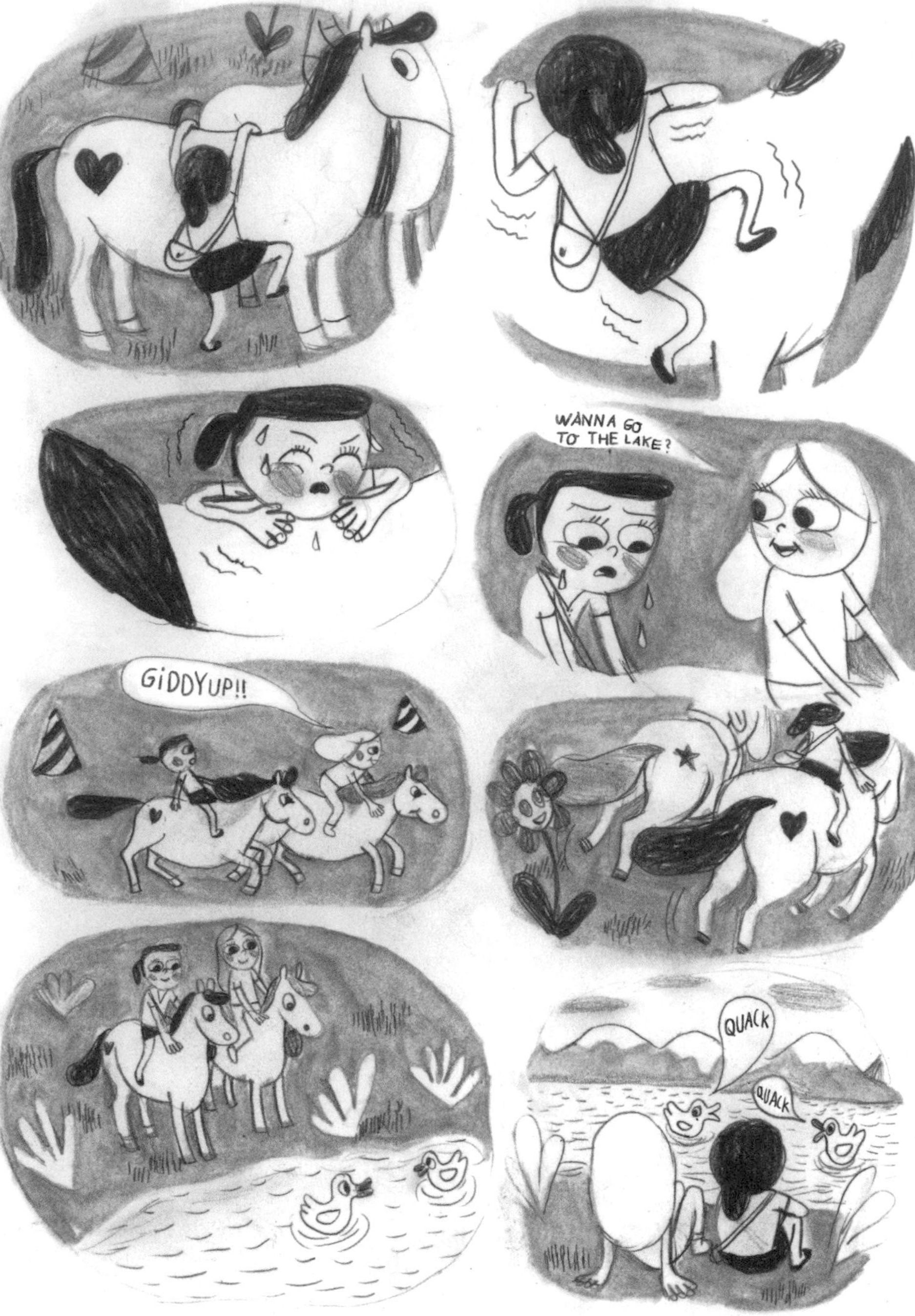
WANNA GO TO THE LAKE?
GIDDYUP!!
QUACK
QUACK

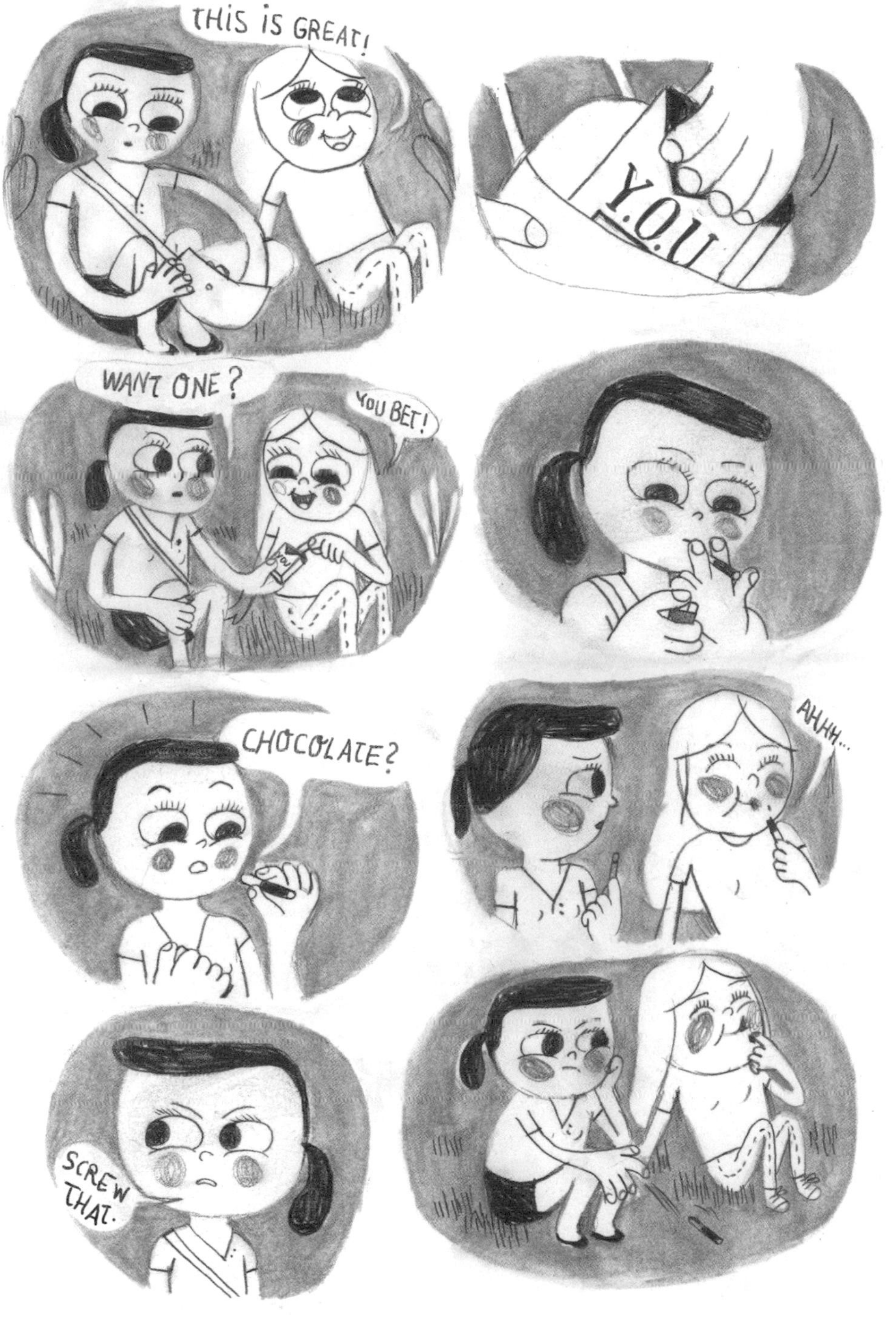
THIS IS GREAT!
Y.O.U
WANT ONE?
YOU BET!
CHOCOLATE?
AHHH...
SCREW THAT.

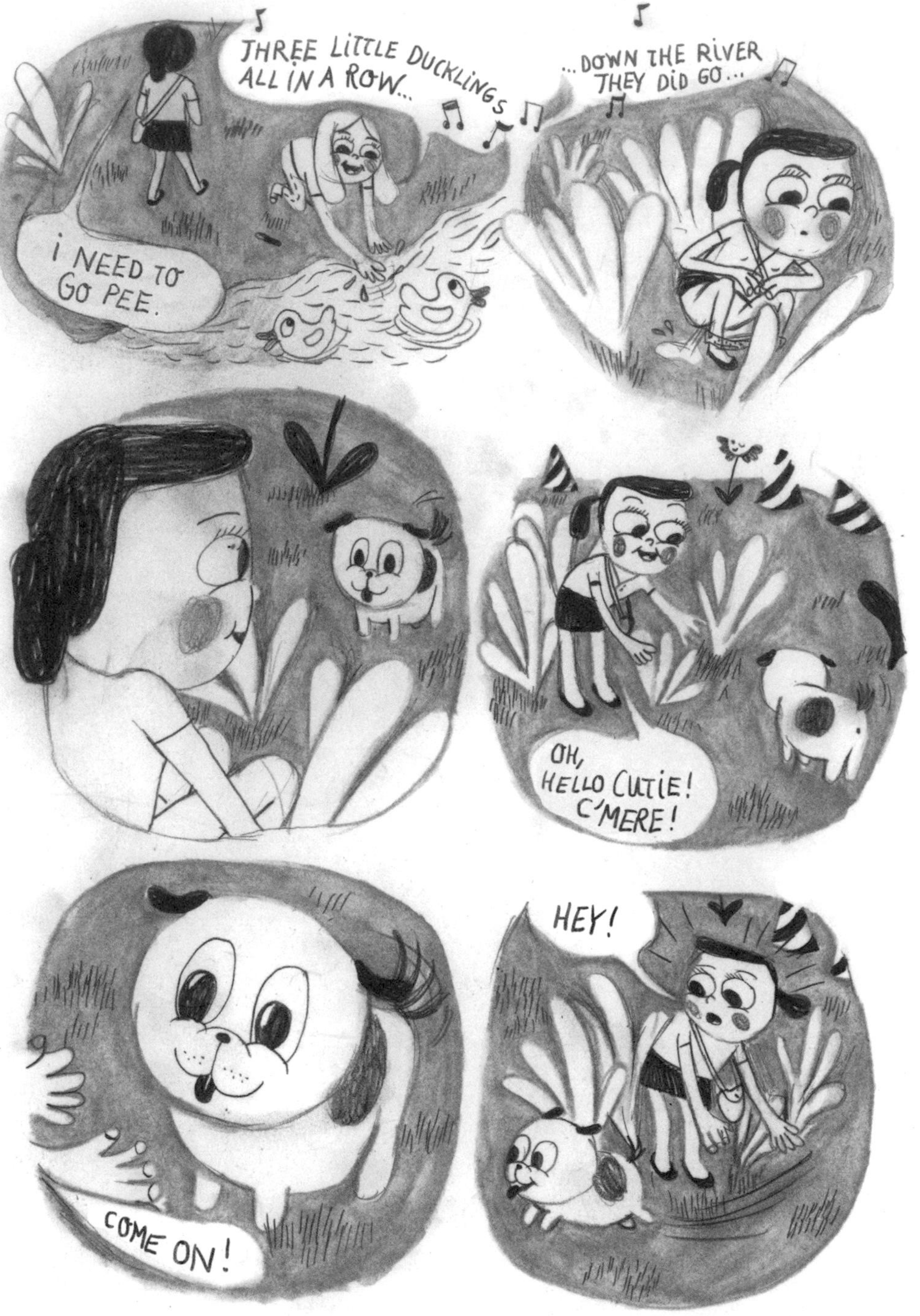
THREE LITTLE DUCKLINGS ALL IN A ROW...
I NEED TO GO PEE.
...DOWN THE RIVER THEY DID GO...
OH, HELLO CUTIE! C'MERE!
COME ON!
HEY!

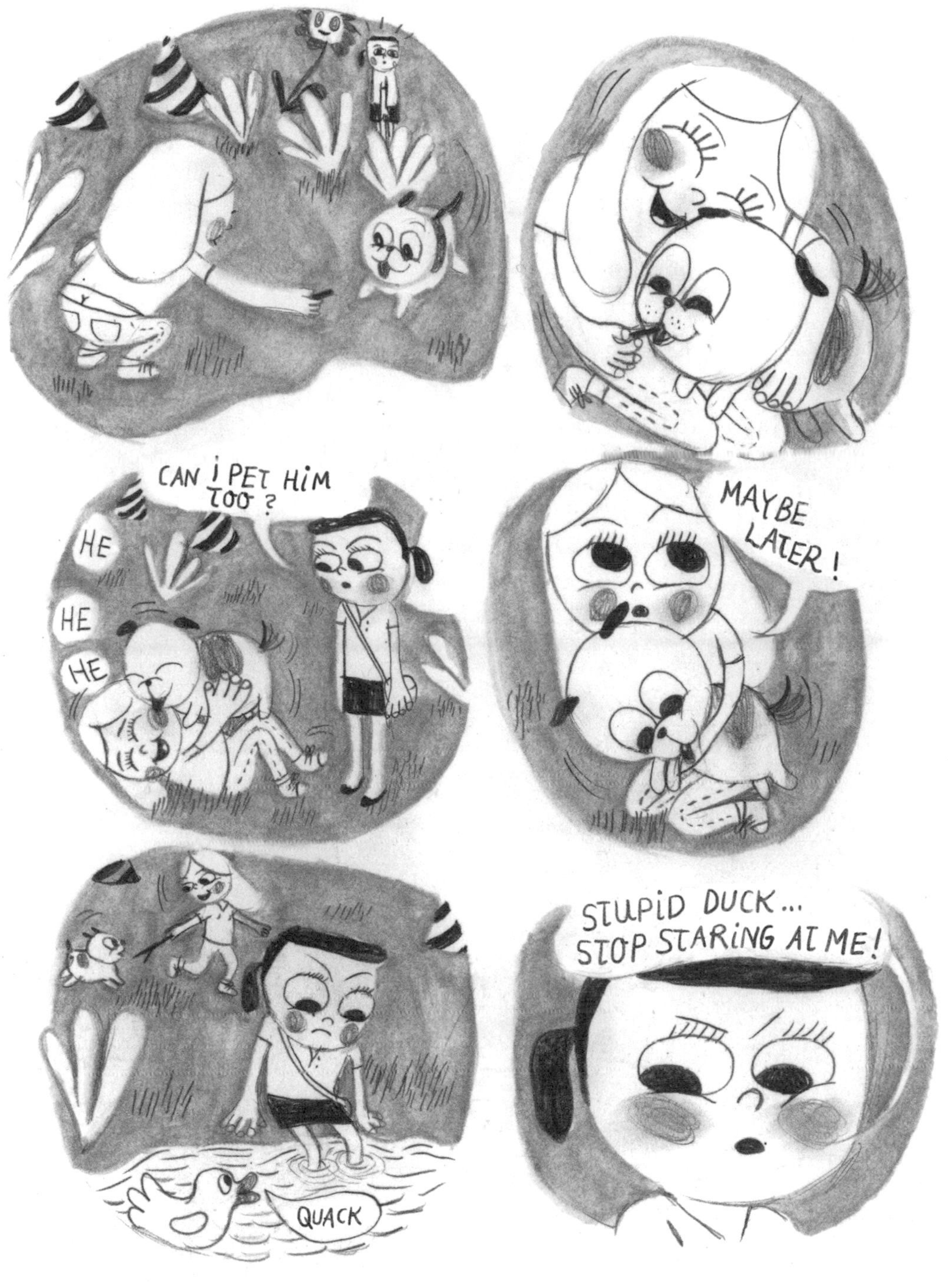
CAN i PET HiM TOO?
HE
HE
HE
MAYBE LATER!
QUACK
STUPiD DUCK...
STOP STARiNG AT ME!

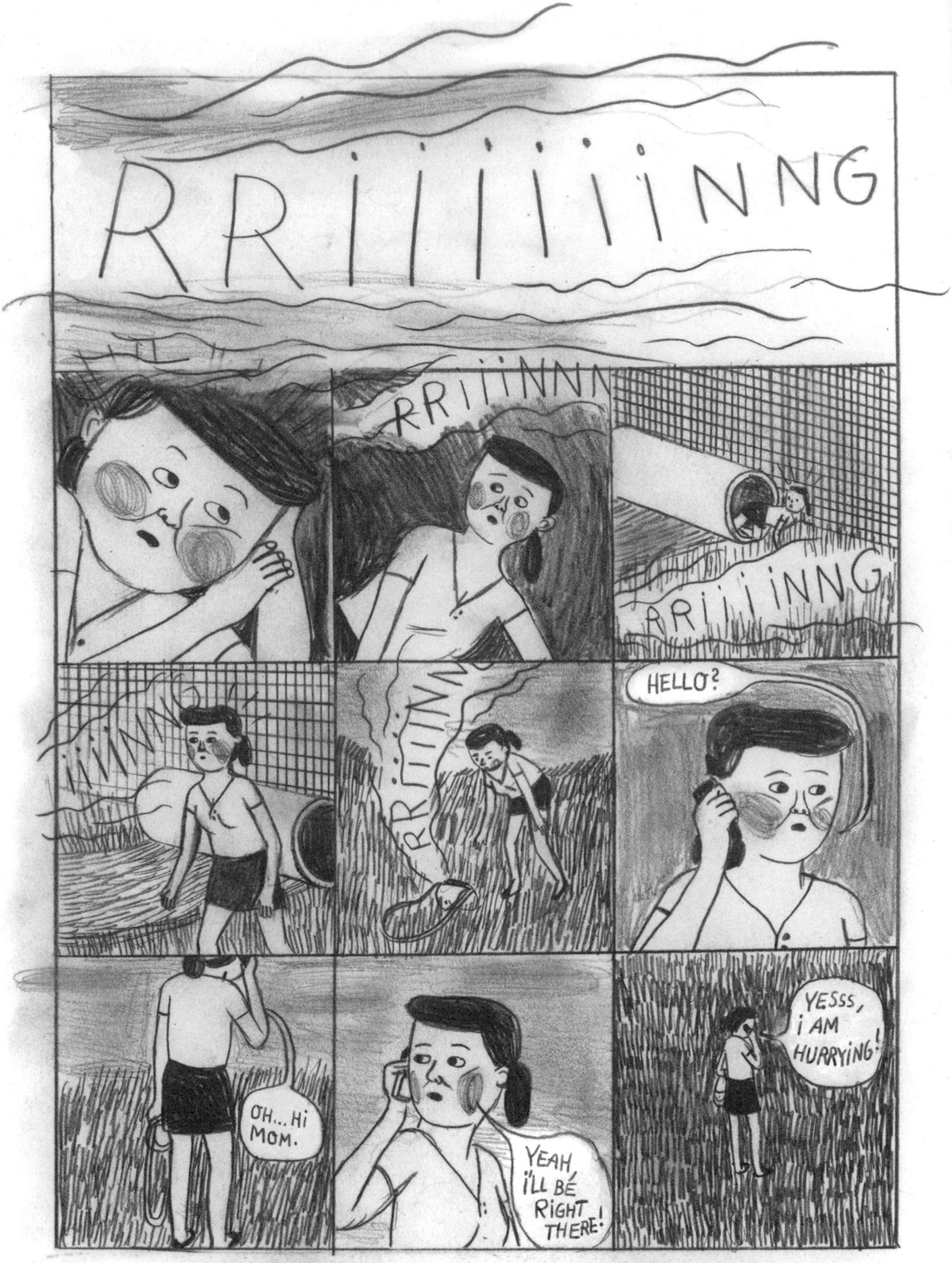
RRIIIIIINNG
RRIIIINNN
RRIIIINNG
IIIINNG
RRIIIIINNG
HELLO?
OH... HI MOM.
YEAH, I'LL BE RIGHT THERE!
YESSS, I AM HURRYING!

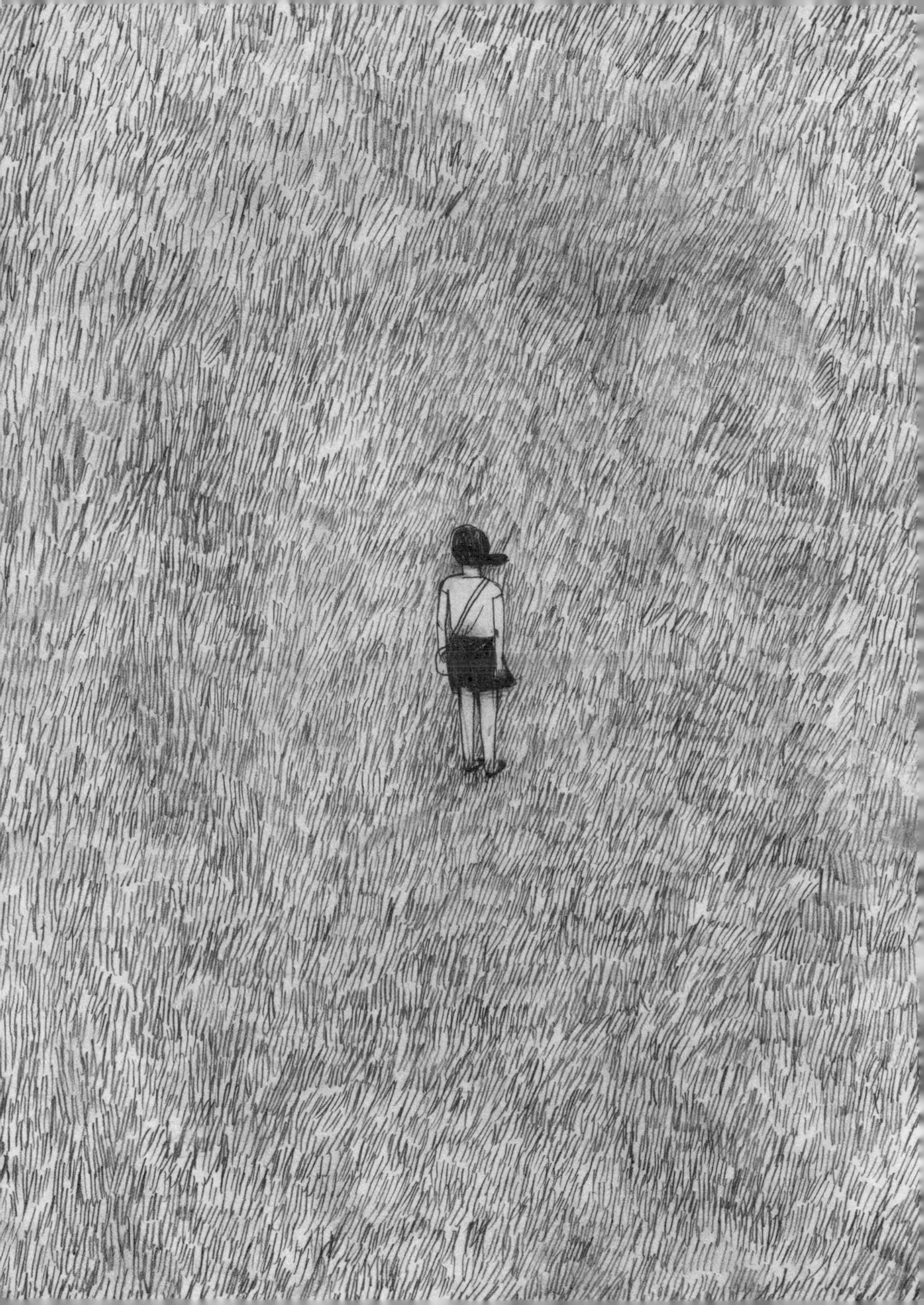

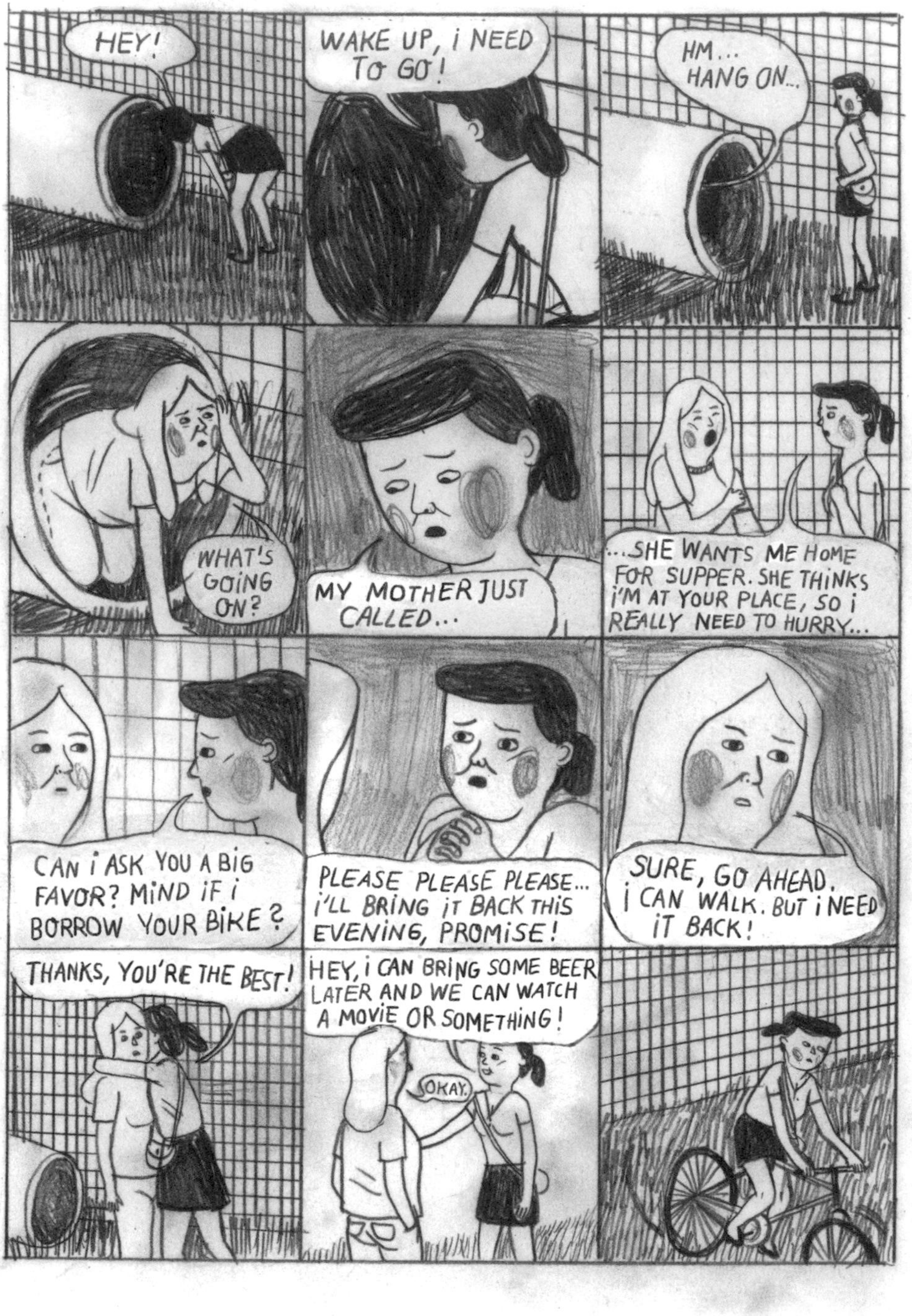
HEY!
WAKE UP, i NEED TO GO!
HM... HANG ON...
WHAT'S GOING ON?
MY MOTHER JUST CALLED...
...SHE WANTS ME HOME FOR SUPPER. SHE THINKS i'M AT YOUR PLACE, SO i REALLY NEED TO HURRY...
CAN i ASK YOU A BIG FAVOR? MIND IF i BORROW YOUR BIKE?
PLEASE PLEASE PLEASE... i'LL BRING iT BACK THIS EVENING, PROMISE!
SURE, GO AHEAD. i CAN WALK. BUT i NEED iT BACK!
THANKS, YOU'RE THE BEST!
HEY, i CAN BRING SOME BEER LATER AND WE CAN WATCH A MOVIE OR SOMETHING!
OKAY.

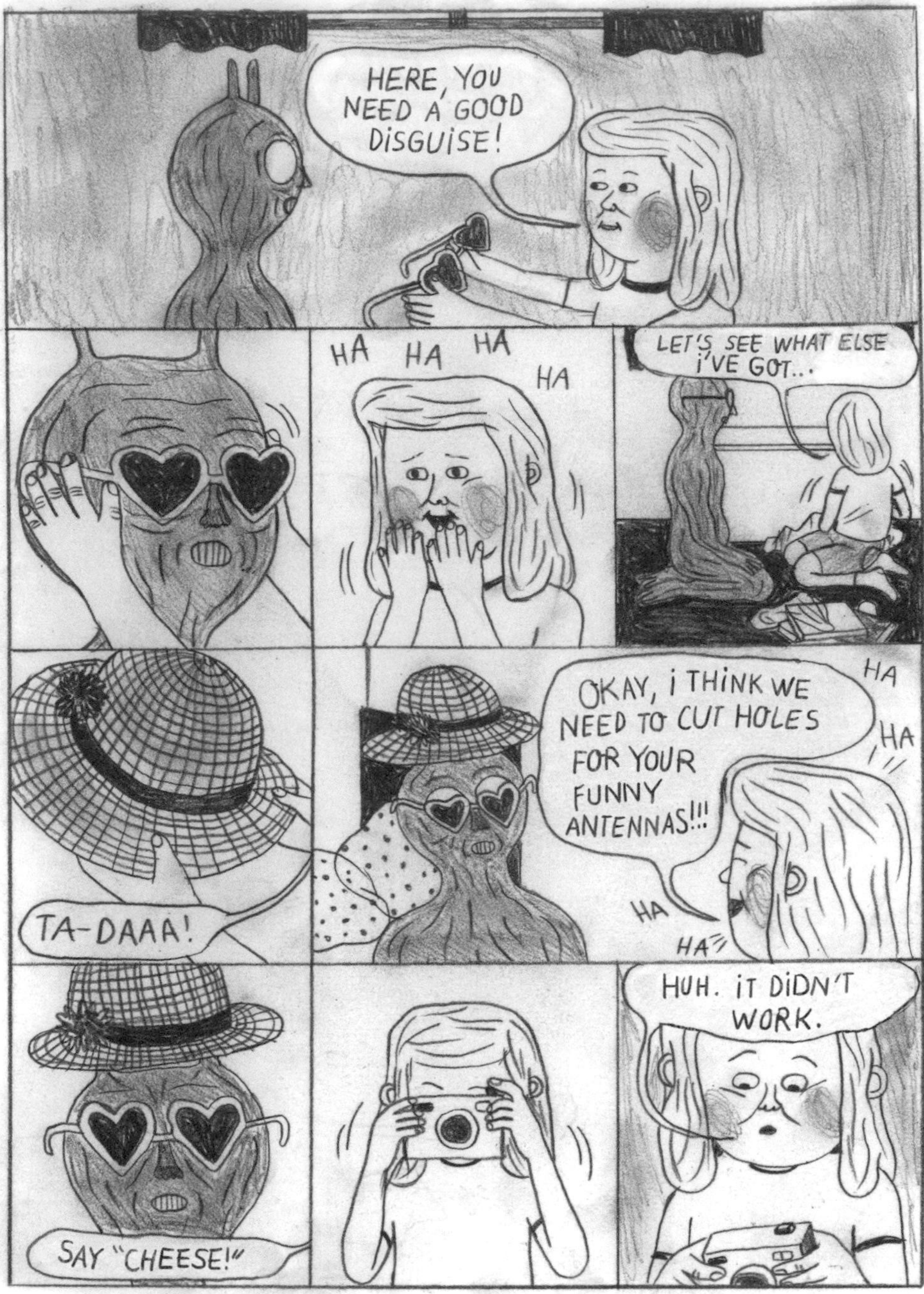
HERE, YOU NEED A GOOD DISGUISE!
HA HA HA HA
LET'S SEE WHAT ELSE I'VE GOT...
TA-DAAA!
OKAY, I THINK WE NEED TO CUT HOLES FOR YOUR FUNNY ANTENNAS!!!
HA HA HA HA
SAY "CHEESE!"
HUH. IT DIDN'T WORK.

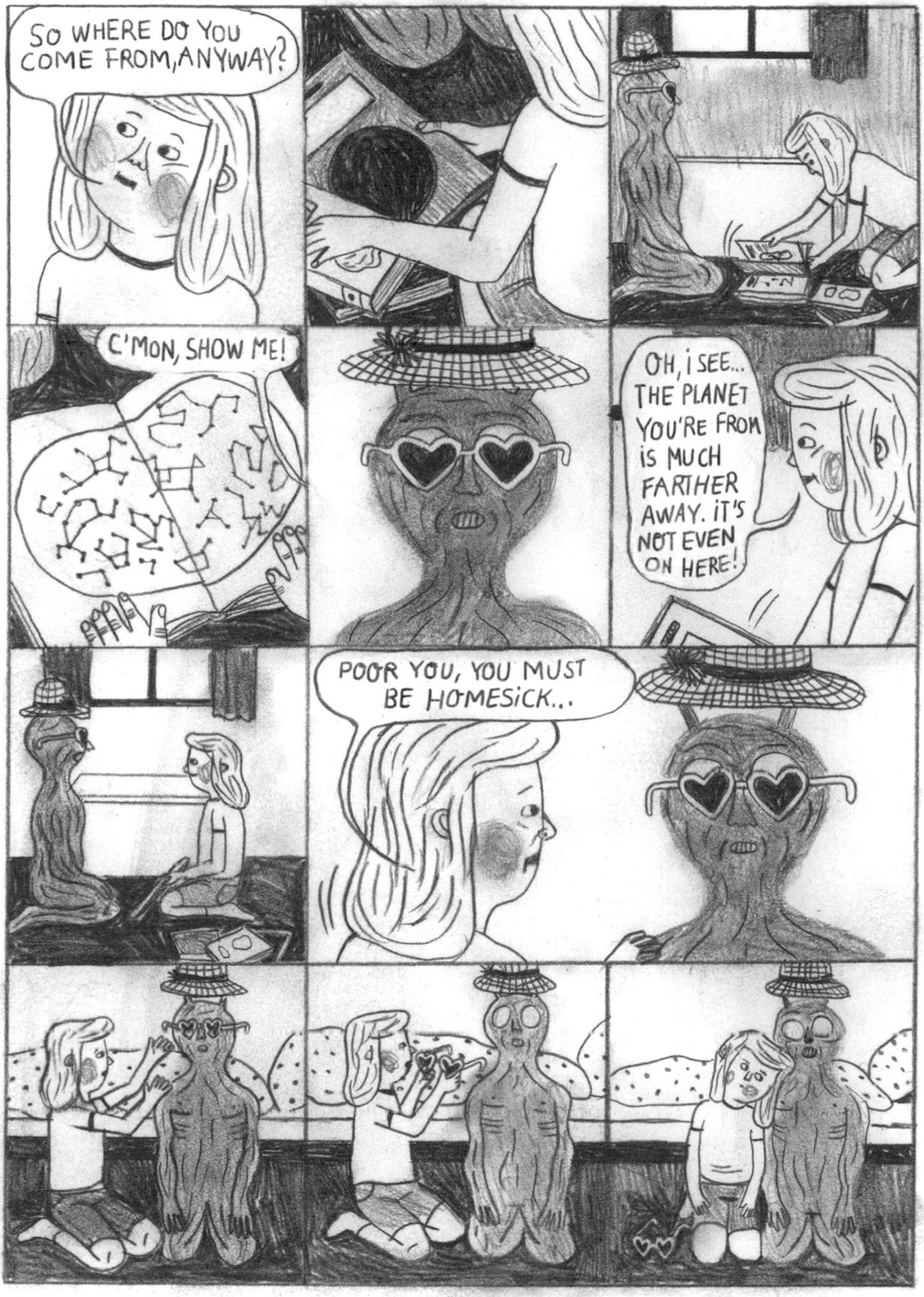
SO WHERE DO YOU COME FROM, ANYWAY?
C'MON, SHOW ME!
OH, I SEE... THE PLANET YOU'RE FROM IS MUCH FARTHER AWAY. IT'S NOT EVEN ON HERE!
POOR YOU, YOU MUST BE HOMESICK...

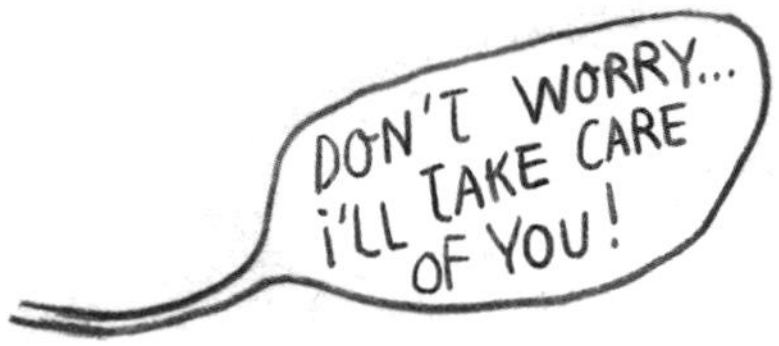
DON'T WORRY... I'LL TAKE CARE OF YOU!

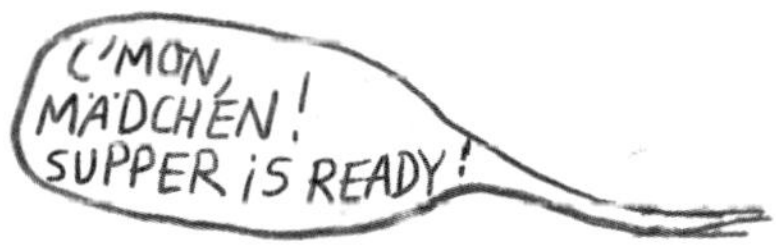
C'MON, MÄDCHEN! SUPPER IS READY!

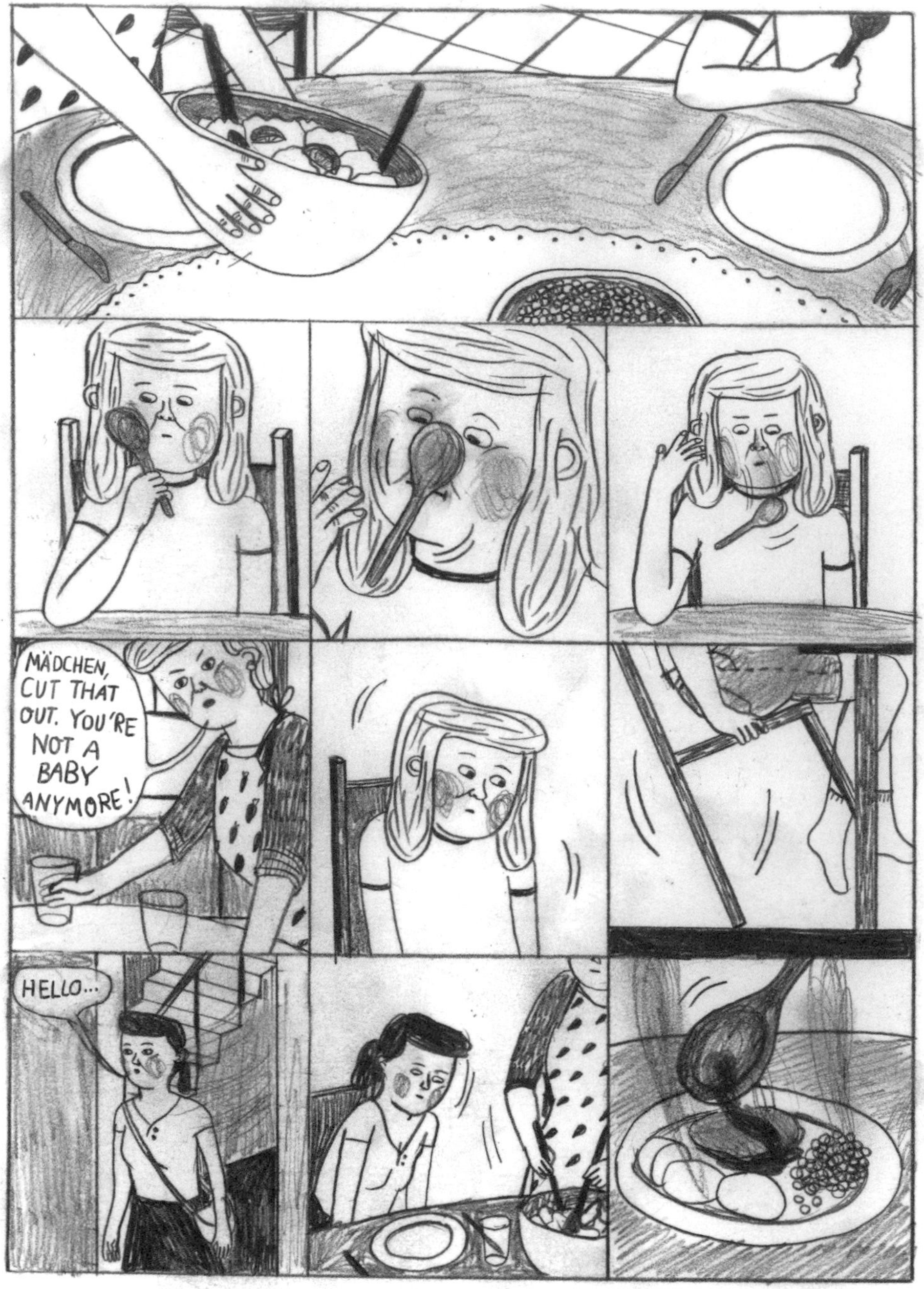
MÄDCHEN, CUT THAT OUT. YOU'RE NOT A BABY ANYMORE!
HELLO...

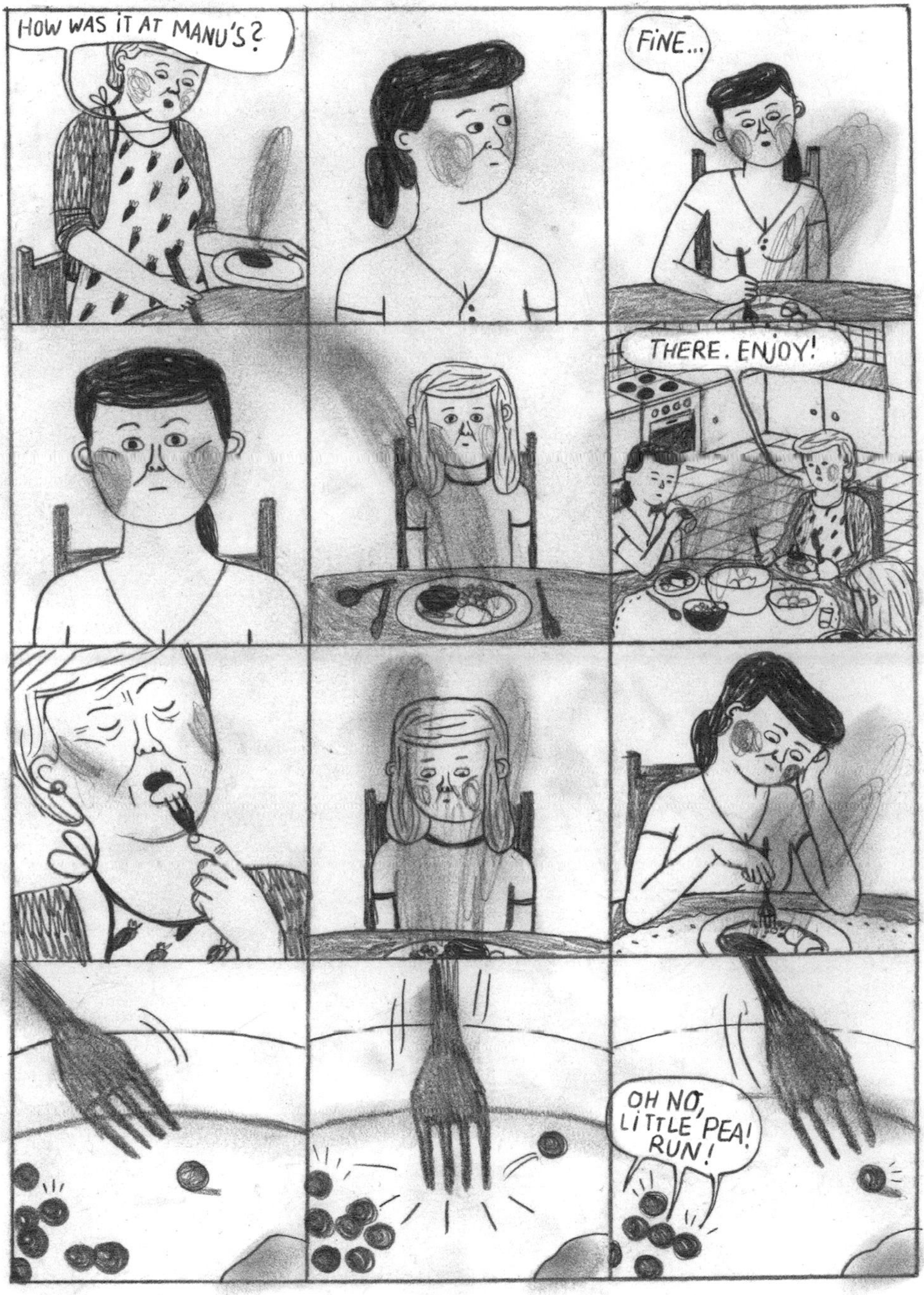
HOW WAS IT AT MANU'S?
FINE...
THERE. ENJOY!
OH NO, LITTLE PEA! RUN!

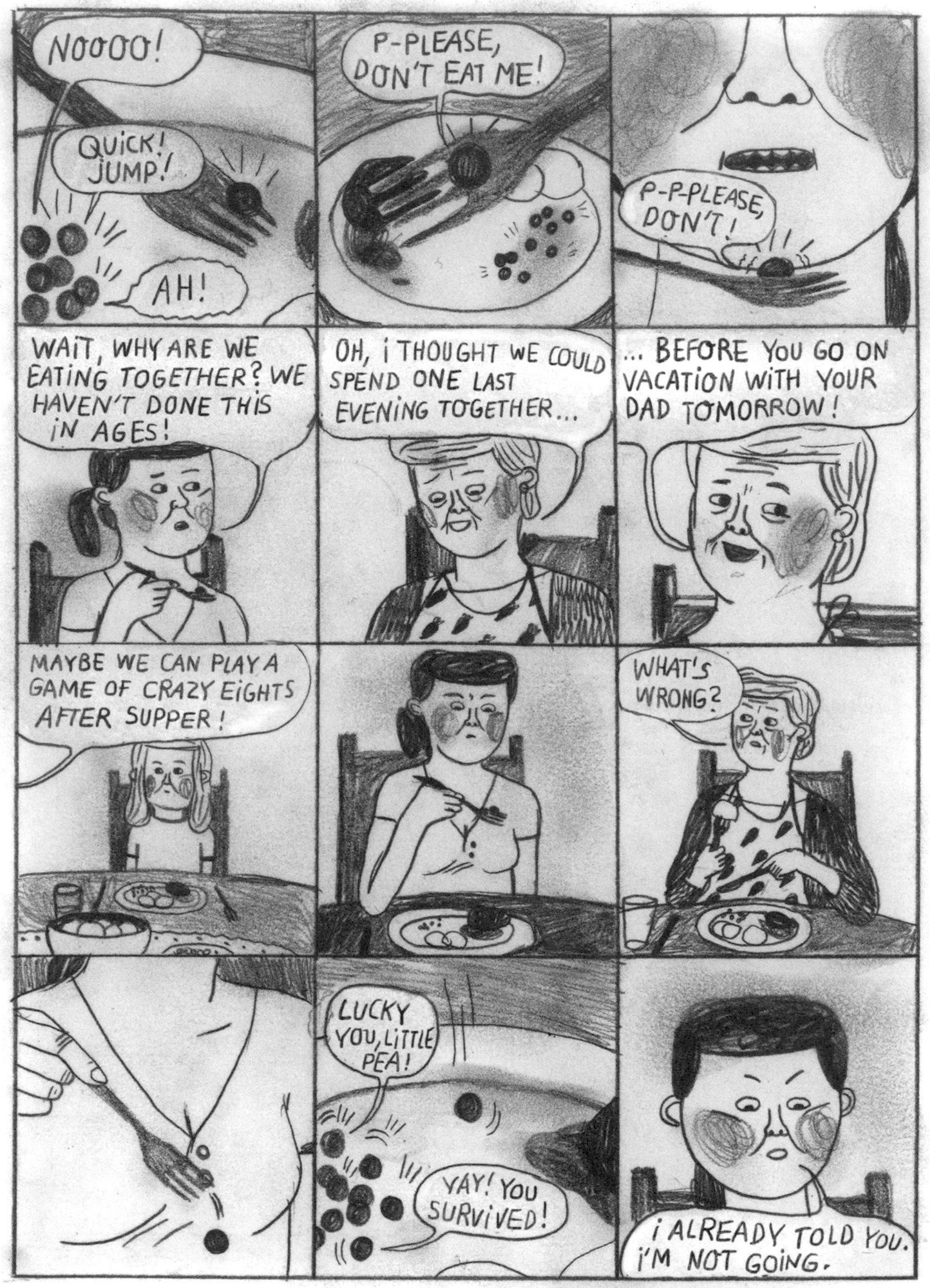
NOOOO!
QUICK! JUMP!
AH!
P-PLEASE, DON'T EAT ME!
P-P-PLEASE, DON'T!
WAIT, WHY ARE WE EATING TOGETHER? WE HAVEN'T DONE THIS IN AGES!
OH, I THOUGHT WE COULD SPEND ONE LAST EVENING TOGETHER...
... BEFORE YOU GO ON VACATION WITH YOUR DAD TOMORROW!
MAYBE WE CAN PLAY A GAME OF CRAZY EIGHTS AFTER SUPPER!
WHAT'S WRONG?
LUCKY YOU, LITTLE PEA!
YAY! YOU SURVIVED!
I ALREADY TOLD YOU. I'M NOT GOING.

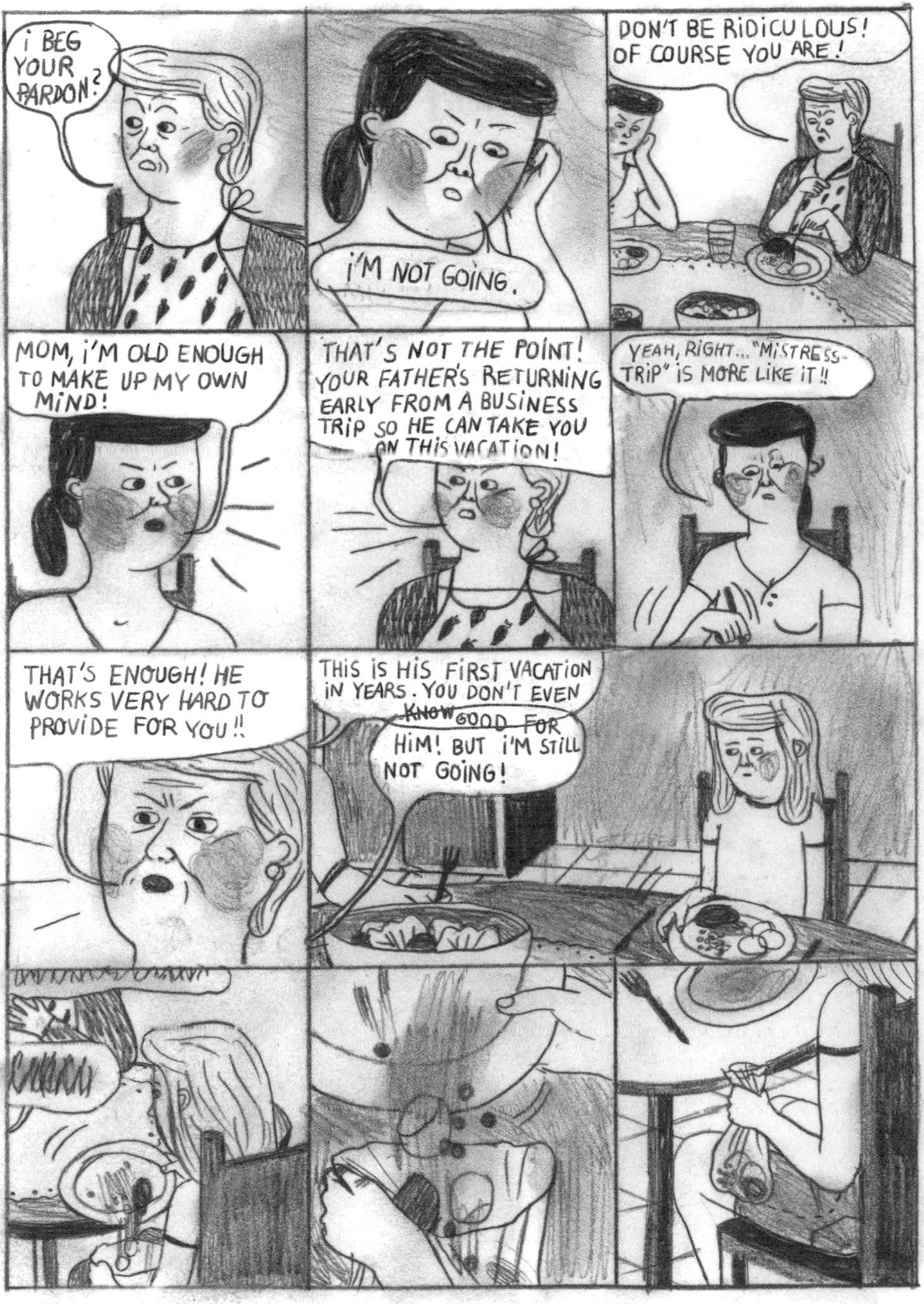
I BEG YOUR PARDON?
I'M NOT GOING.
DON'T BE RIDICULOUS! OF COURSE YOU ARE!
MOM, I'M OLD ENOUGH TO MAKE UP MY OWN MIND!
THAT'S NOT THE POINT! YOUR FATHER'S RETURNING EARLY FROM A BUSINESS TRIP SO HE CAN TAKE YOU ON THIS VACATION!
YEAH, RIGHT... "MISTRESS-TRIP" IS MORE LIKE IT!!
THAT'S ENOUGH! HE WORKS VERY HARD TO PROVIDE FOR YOU!!
THIS IS HIS FIRST VACATION IN YEARS. YOU DON'T EVEN KNOW GOOD FOR
HIM! BUT I'M STILL NOT GOING!

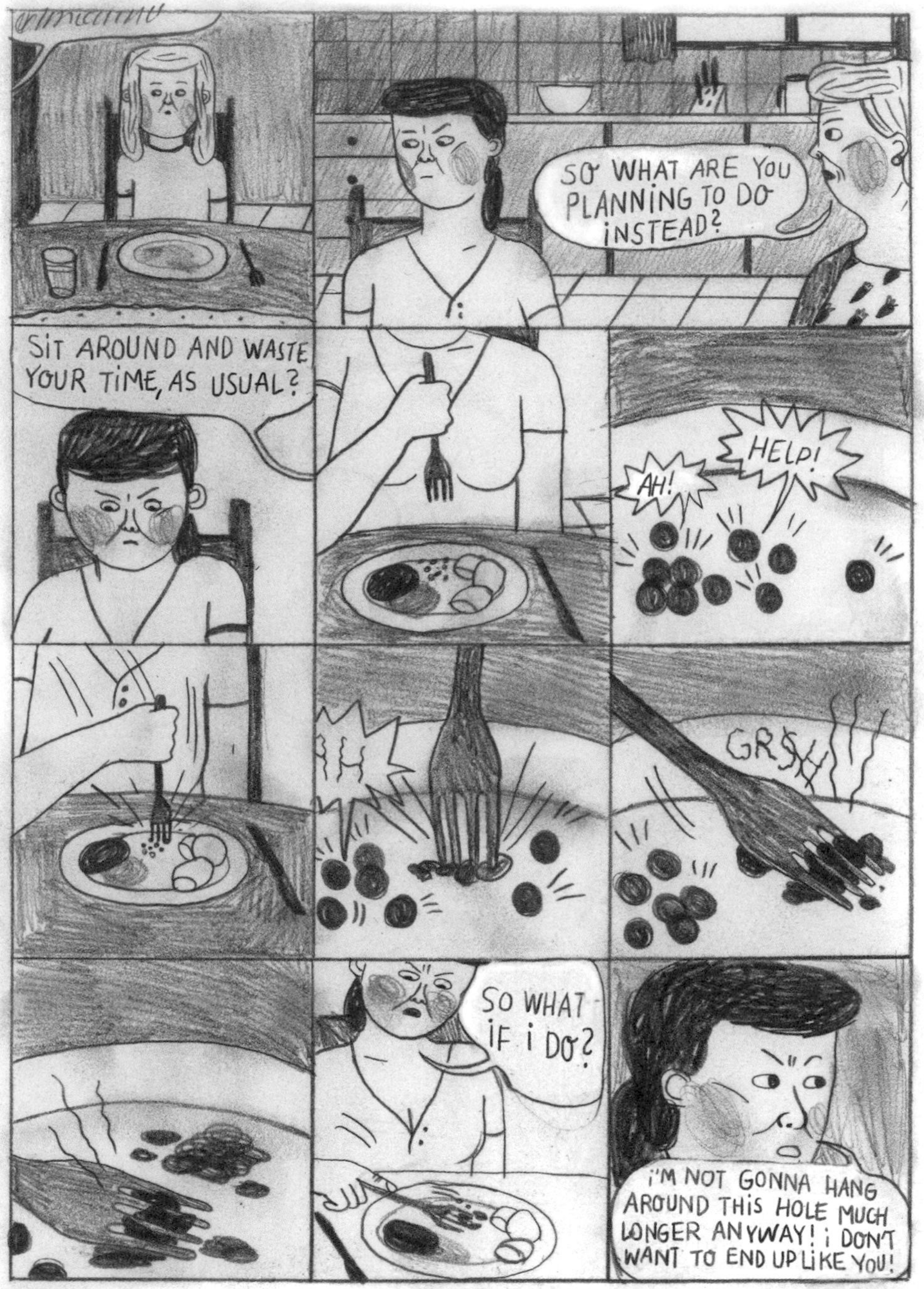
SO WHAT ARE YOU PLANNING TO DO INSTEAD?
SIT AROUND AND WASTE YOUR TIME, AS USUAL?
AH!
HELP!
AH
GRSH
SO WHAT IF I DO?
I'M NOT GONNA HANG AROUND THIS HOLE MUCH LONGER ANYWAY! I DON'T WANT TO END UP LIKE YOU!

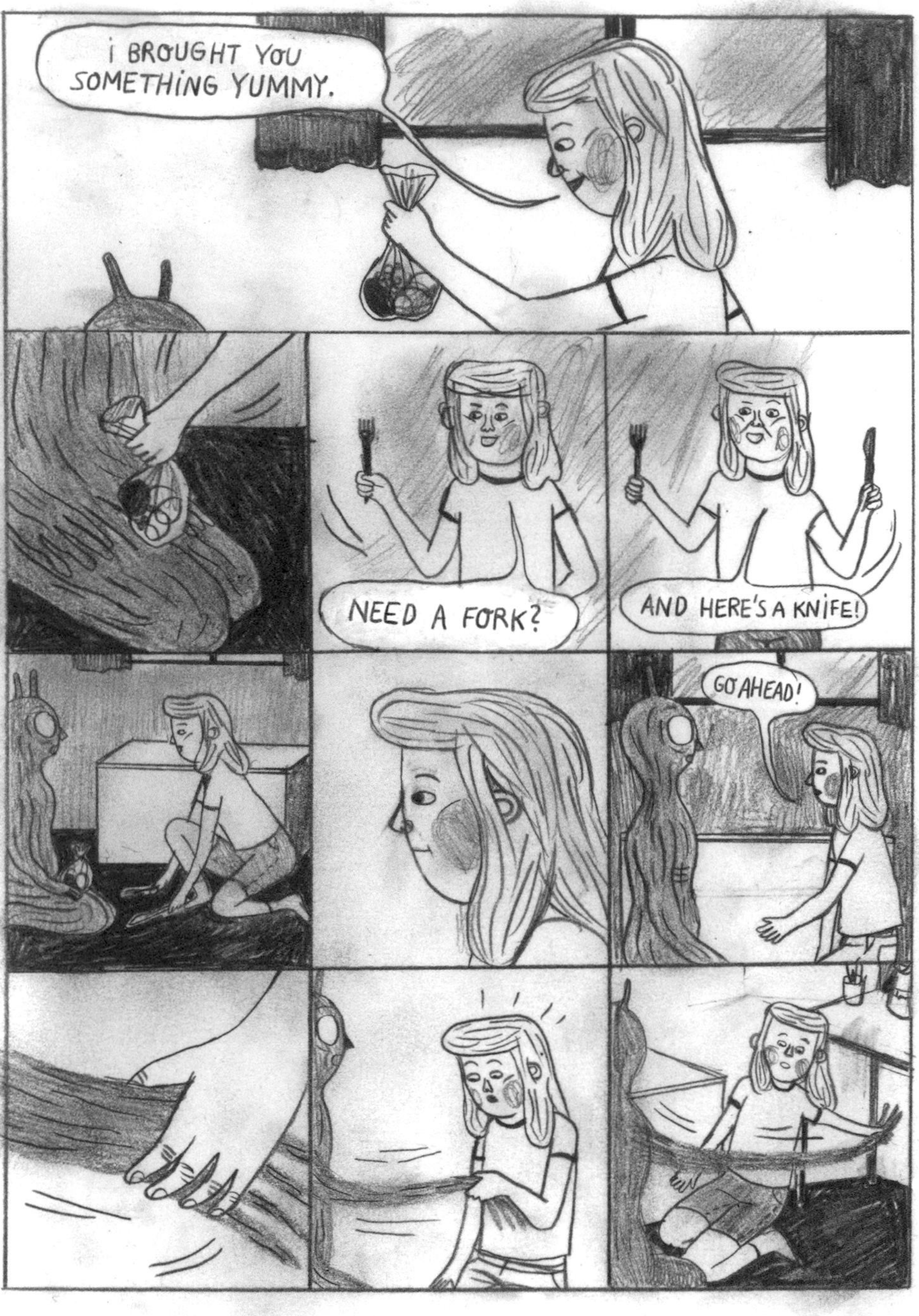
I BROUGHT YOU SOMETHING YUMMY.
NEED A FORK?
AND HERE'S A KNIFE!
GO AHEAD!

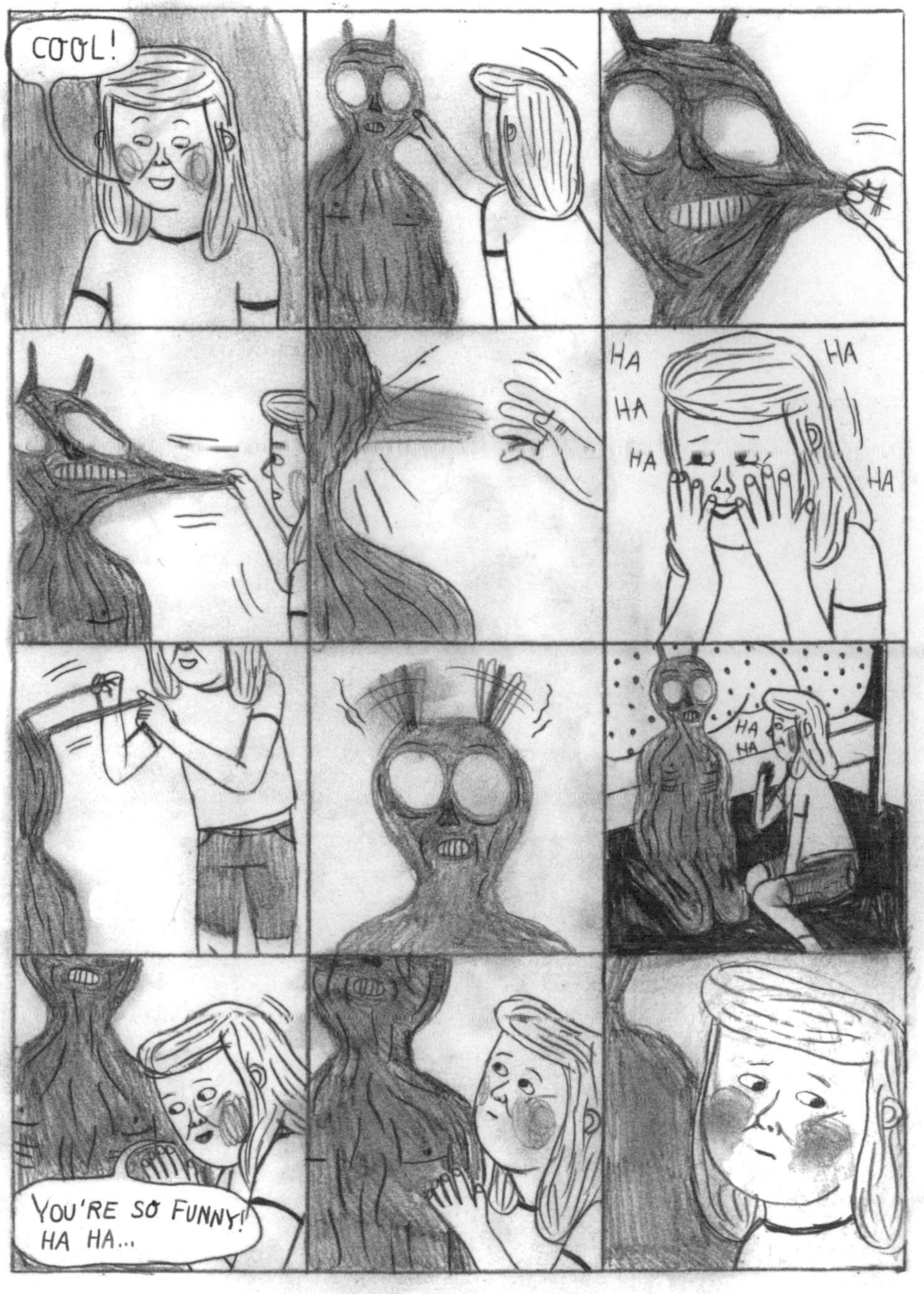
COOL!
HA
HA
HA
HA
HA
HA
HA
YOU'RE SO FUNNY! HA HA...

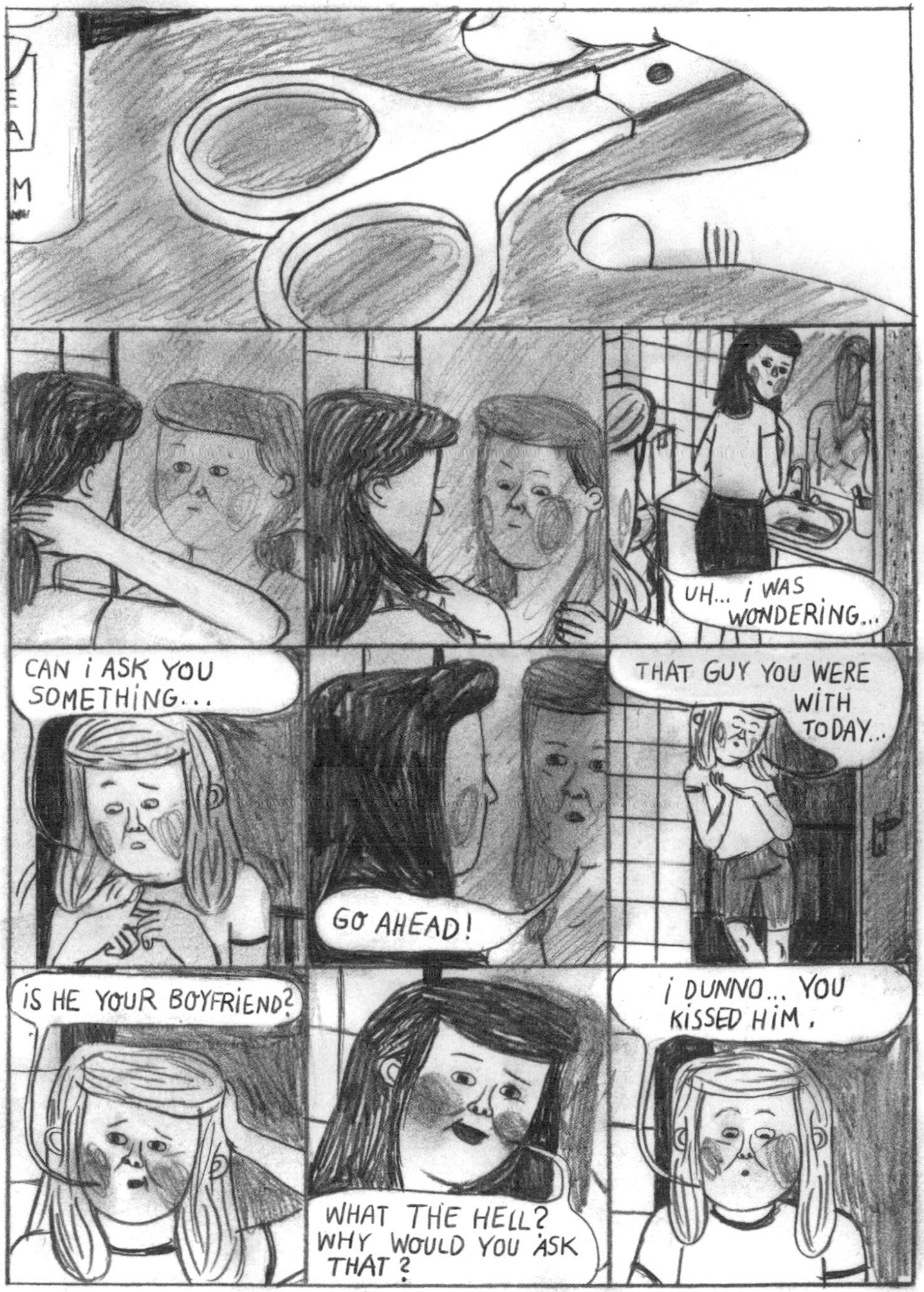
UH... i WAS WONDERING...
CAN i ASK YOU SOMETHING...
GO AHEAD!
THAT GUY YOU WERE WITH TODAY...
iS HE YOUR BOYFRIEND?
WHAT THE HELL? WHY WOULD YOU ASK THAT?
i DUNNO... YOU KISSED HIM.

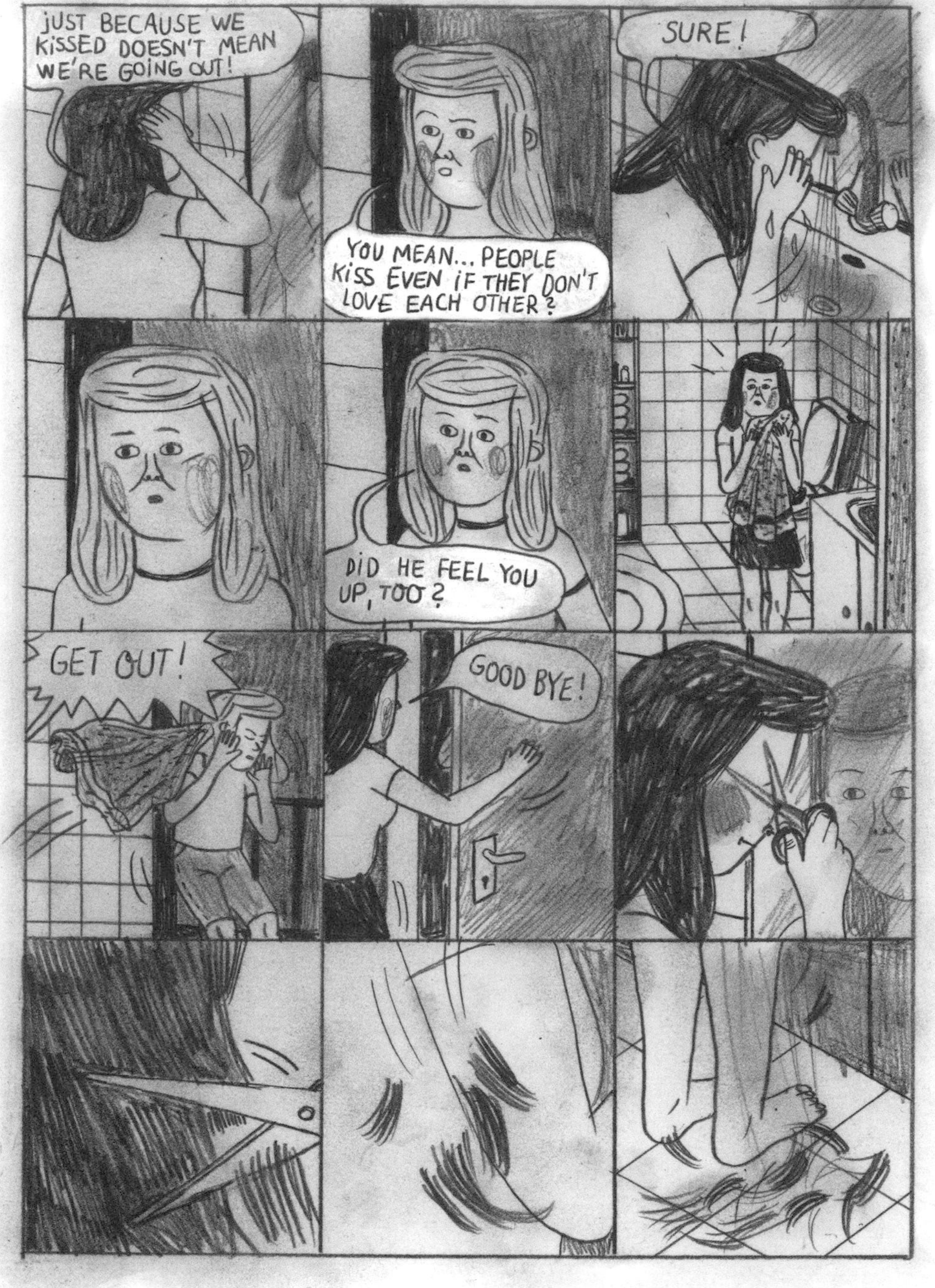
JUST BECAUSE WE KISSED DOESN'T MEAN WE'RE GOING OUT!
YOU MEAN... PEOPLE KISS EVEN IF THEY DON'T LOVE EACH OTHER?
SURE!
DID HE FEEL YOU UP, TOO?
GET OUT!
GOOD BYE!

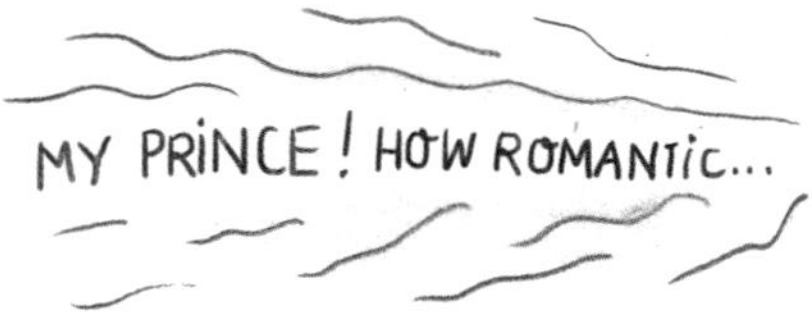
MY PRINCE! HOW ROMANTIC...

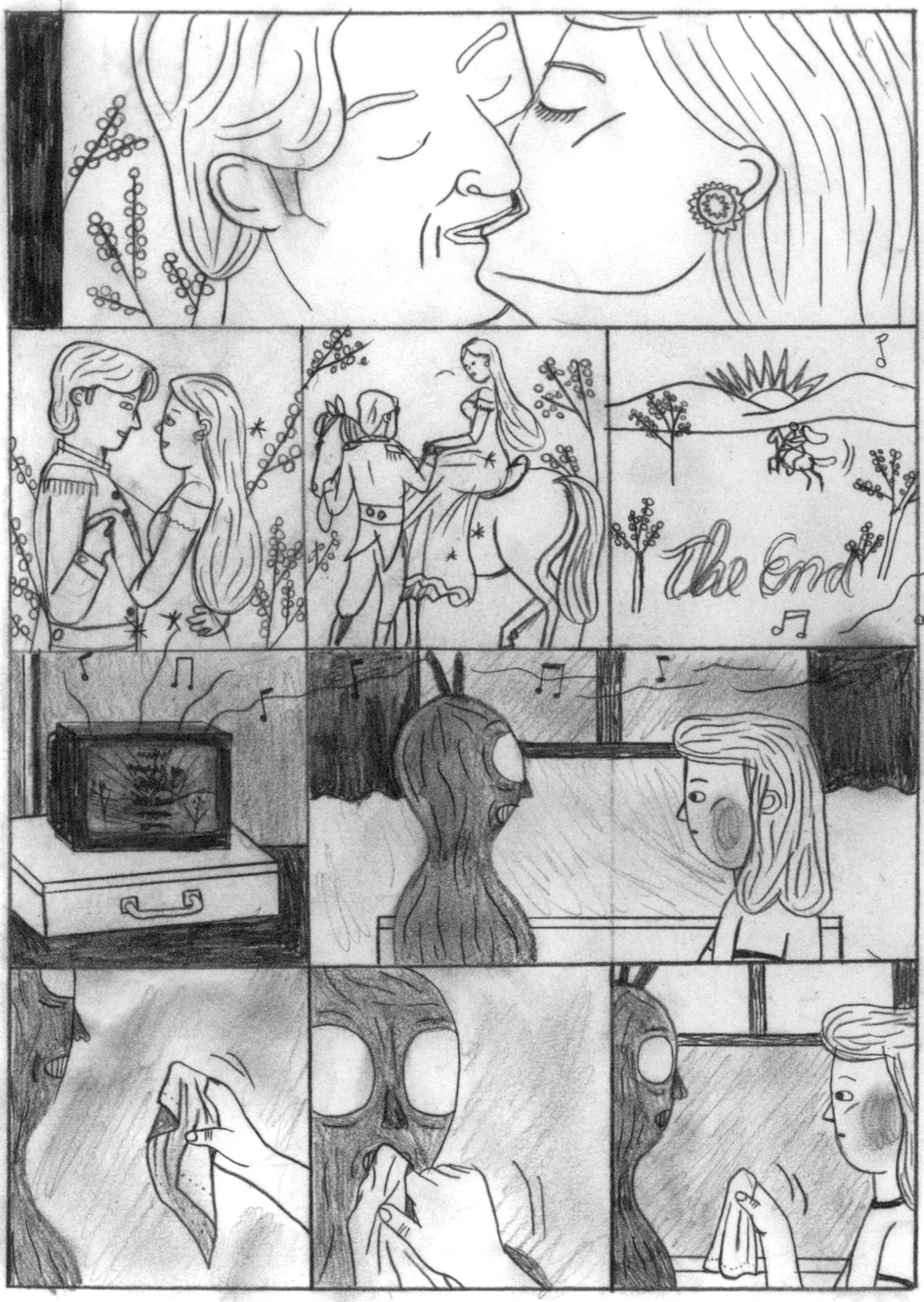
The End

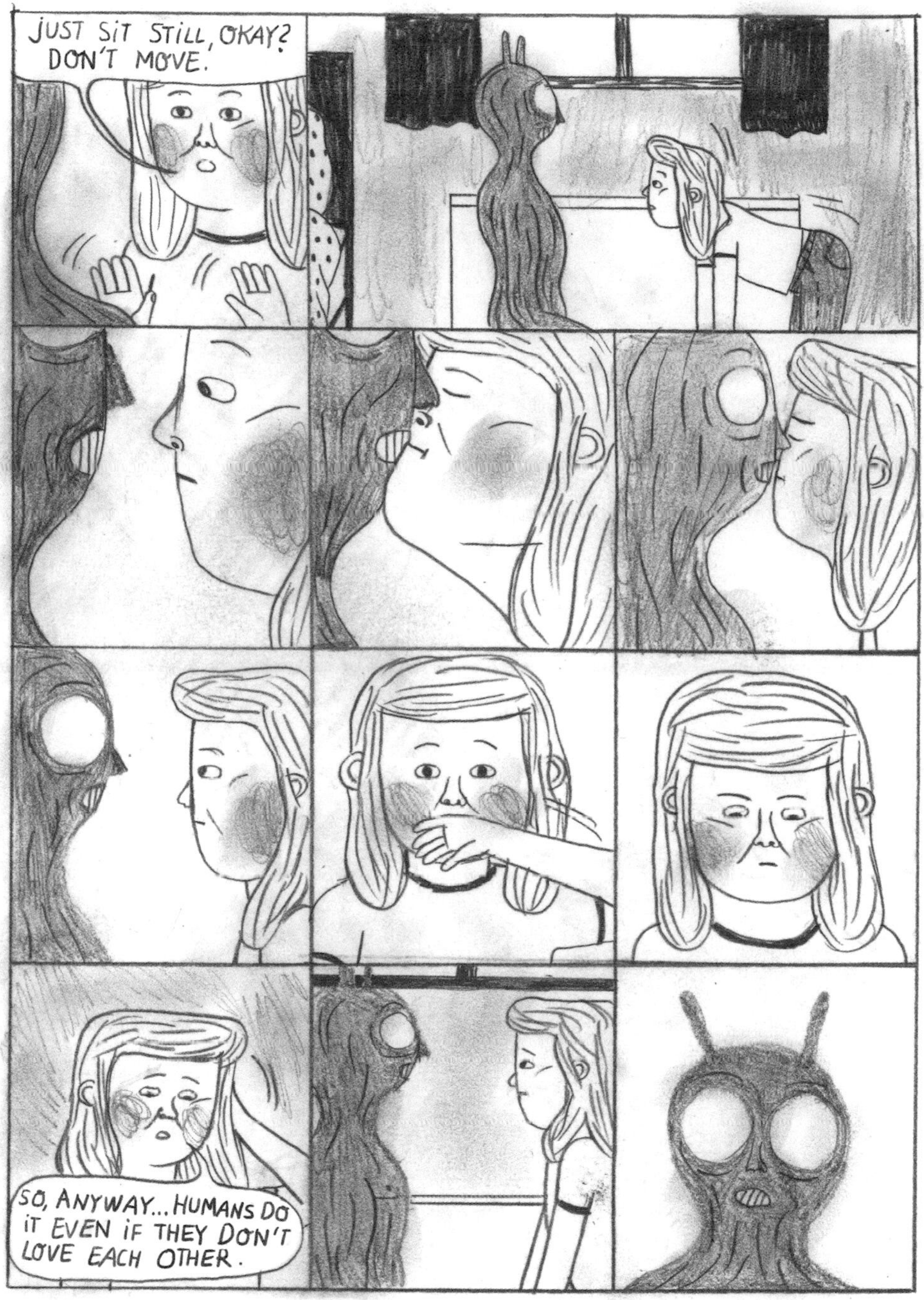
JUST SIT STILL, OKAY? DON'T MOVE.
SO, ANYWAY... HUMANS DO IT EVEN IF THEY DON'T LOVE EACH OTHER.

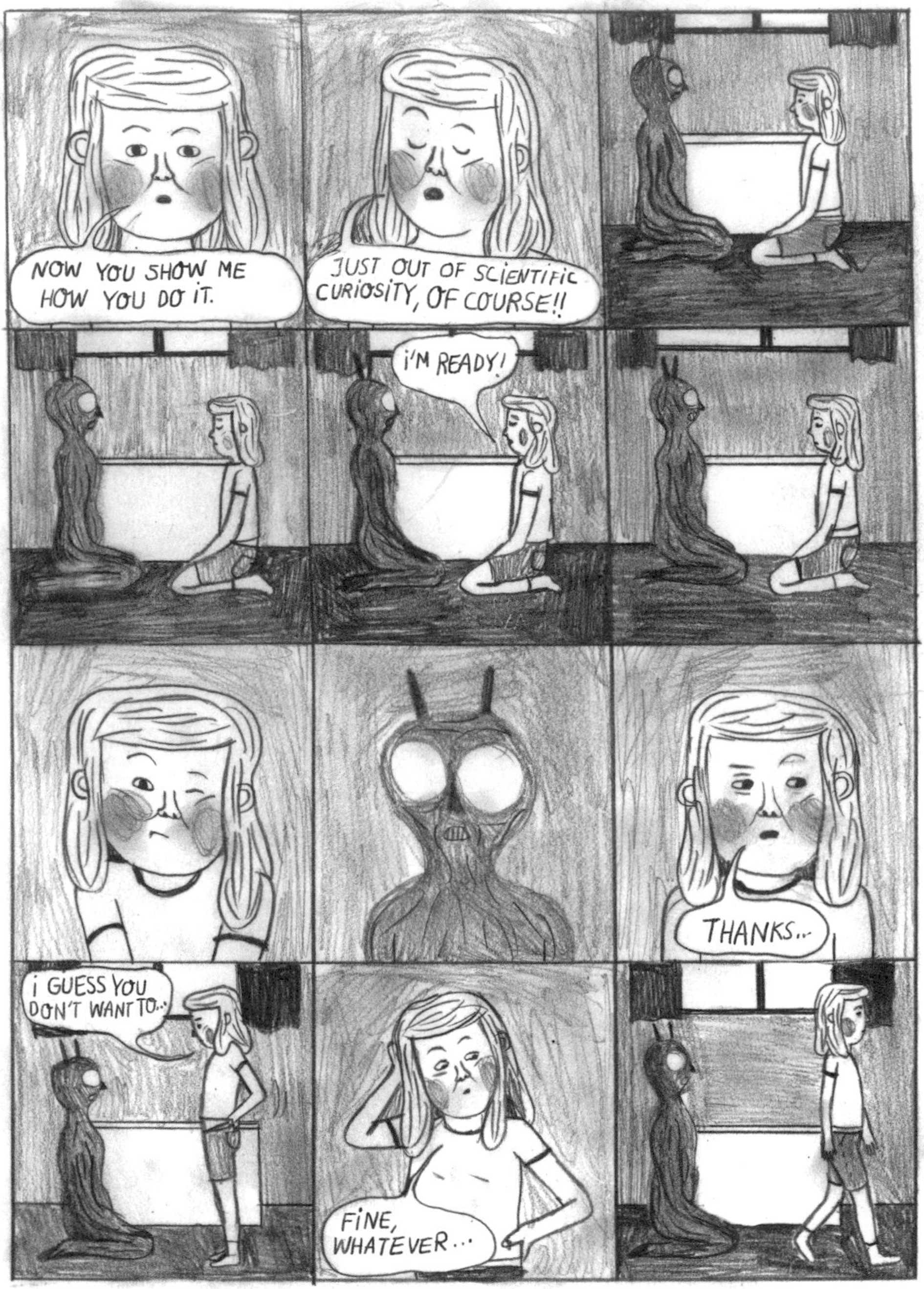
NOW YOU SHOW ME HOW YOU DO IT.
JUST OUT OF SCIENTIFIC CURIOSITY, OF COURSE!!
I'M READY!
THANKS...
I GUESS YOU DON'T WANT TO...
FINE, WHATEVER...

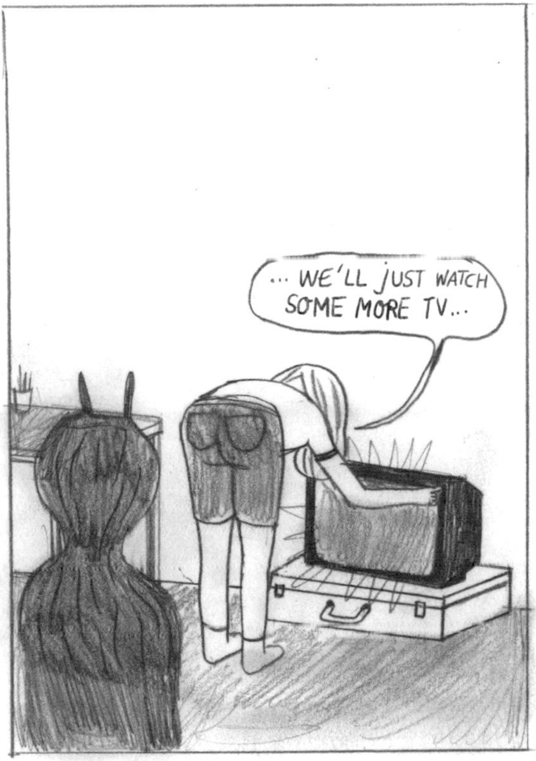
... WE'LL JUST WATCH SOME MORE TV...

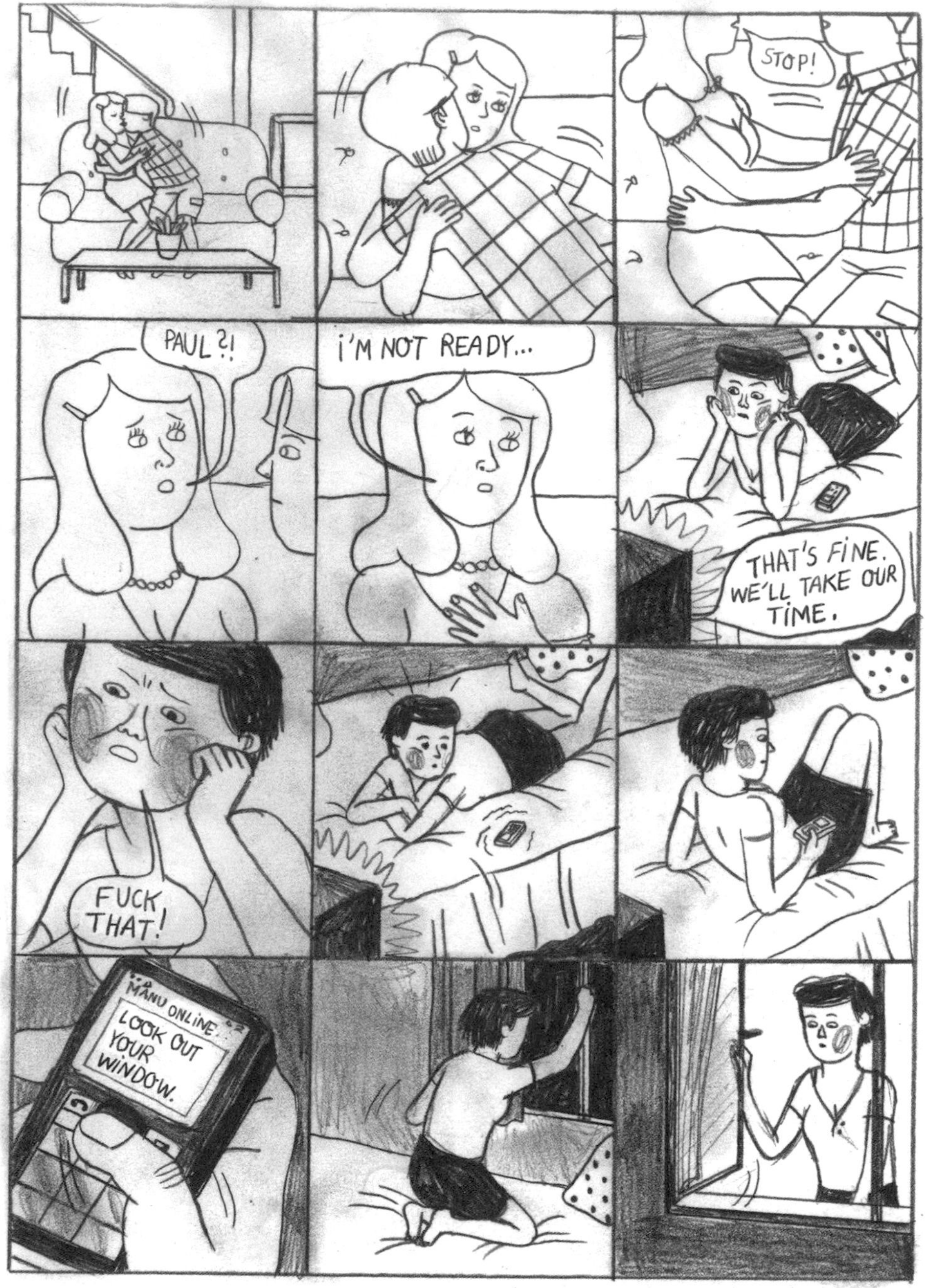
STOP!
PAUL?!
I'M NOT READY...
THAT'S FINE. WE'LL TAKE OUR TIME.
FUCK THAT!
MANU ONLINE...
LOOK OUT YOUR WINDOW.

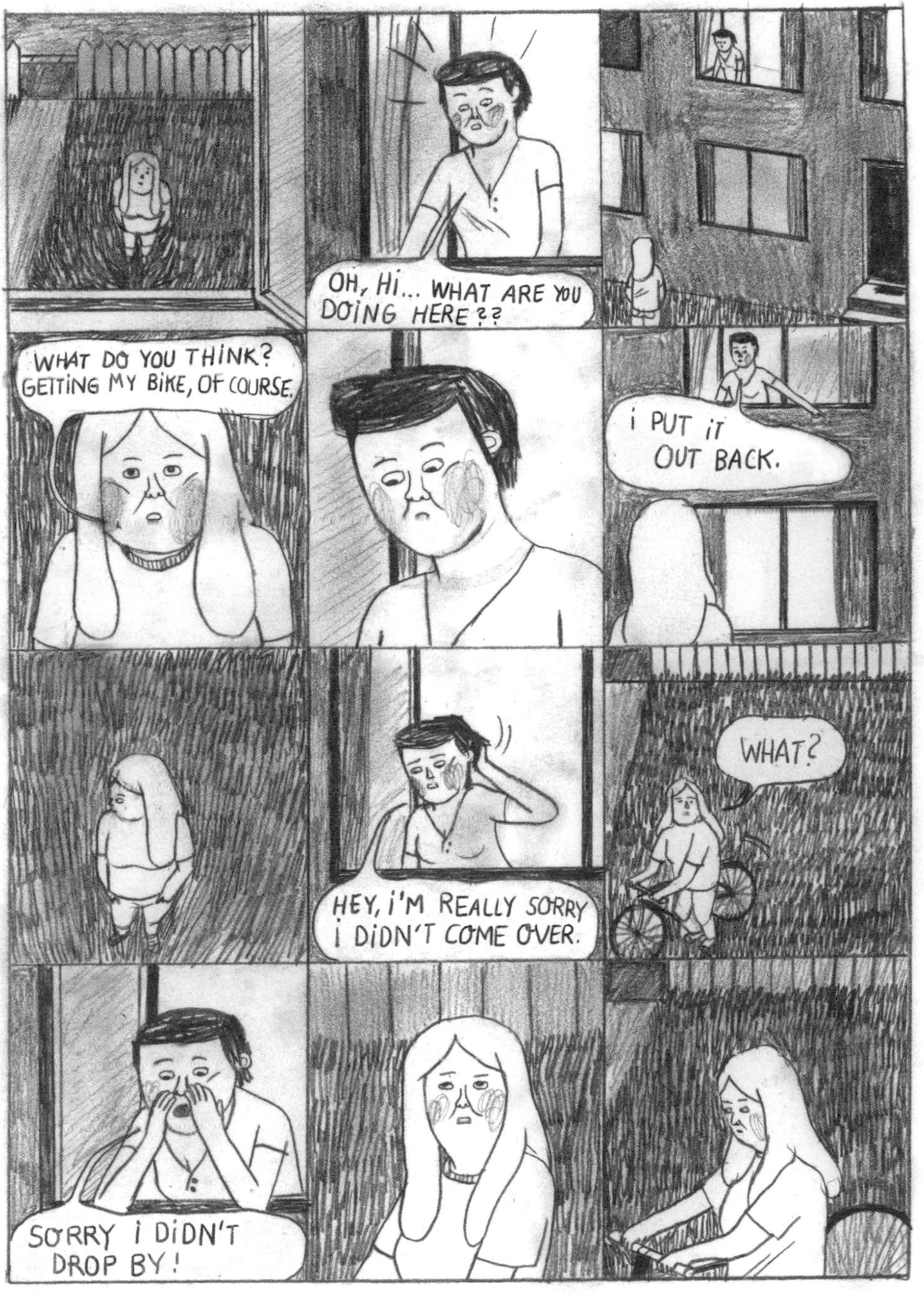
OH, HI... WHAT ARE YOU DOING HERE??
WHAT DO YOU THINK? GETTING MY BIKE, OF COURSE.
I PUT IT OUT BACK.
HEY, I'M REALLY SORRY I DIDN'T COME OVER.
WHAT?
SORRY I DIDN'T DROP BY!

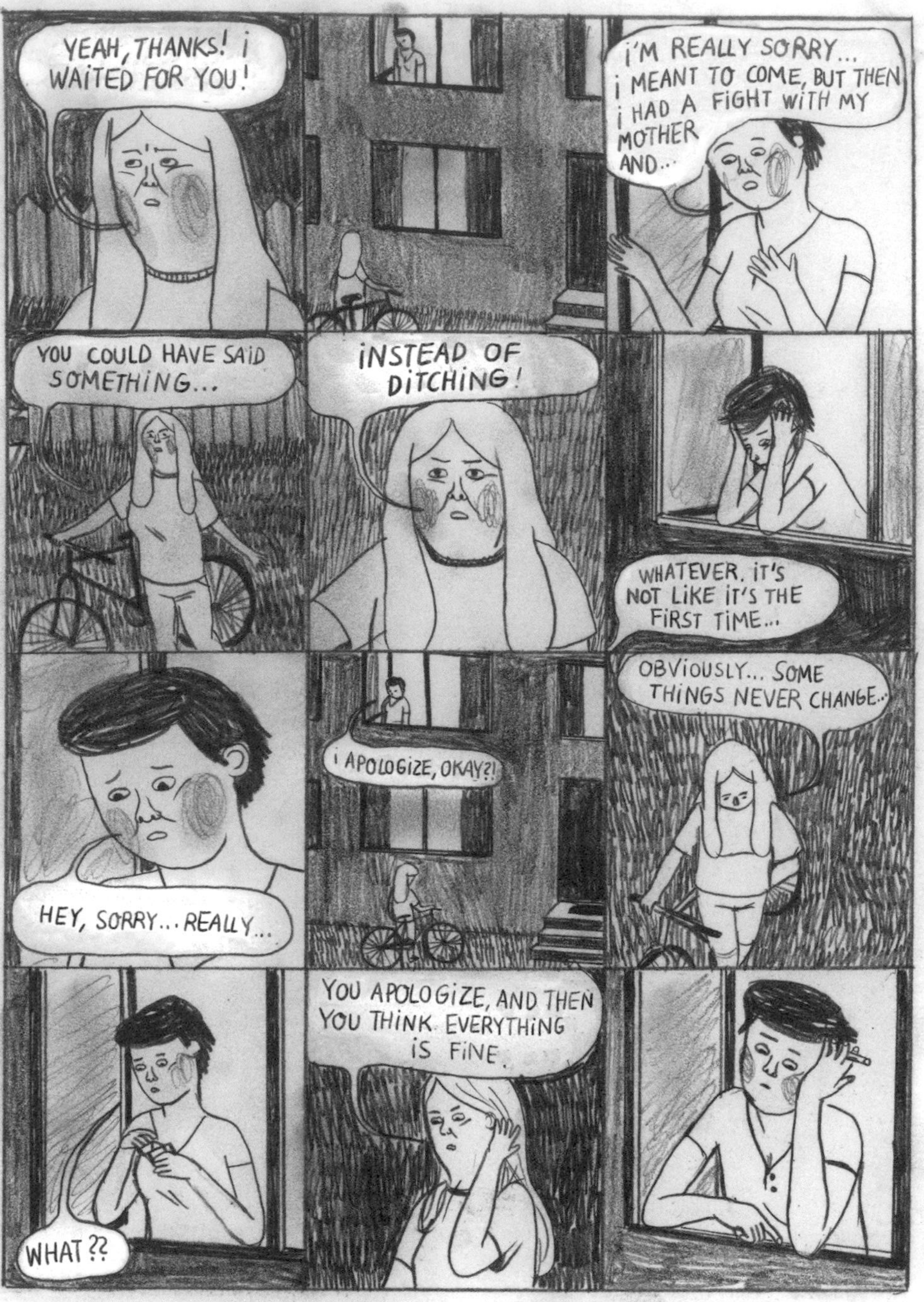
YEAH, THANKS! i WAITED FOR YOU!
i'M REALLY SORRY... i MEANT TO COME, BUT THEN i HAD A FIGHT WITH MY MOTHER AND...
YOU COULD HAVE SAID SOMETHING...
iNSTEAD OF DITCHING!
WHATEVER. IT'S NOT LIKE IT'S THE FIRST TIME...
HEY, SORRY... REALLY...
i APOLOGIZE, OKAY?!
OBVIOUSLY... SOME THINGS NEVER CHANGE...
WHAT??
YOU APOLOGIZE, AND THEN YOU THINK EVERYTHING IS FINE.

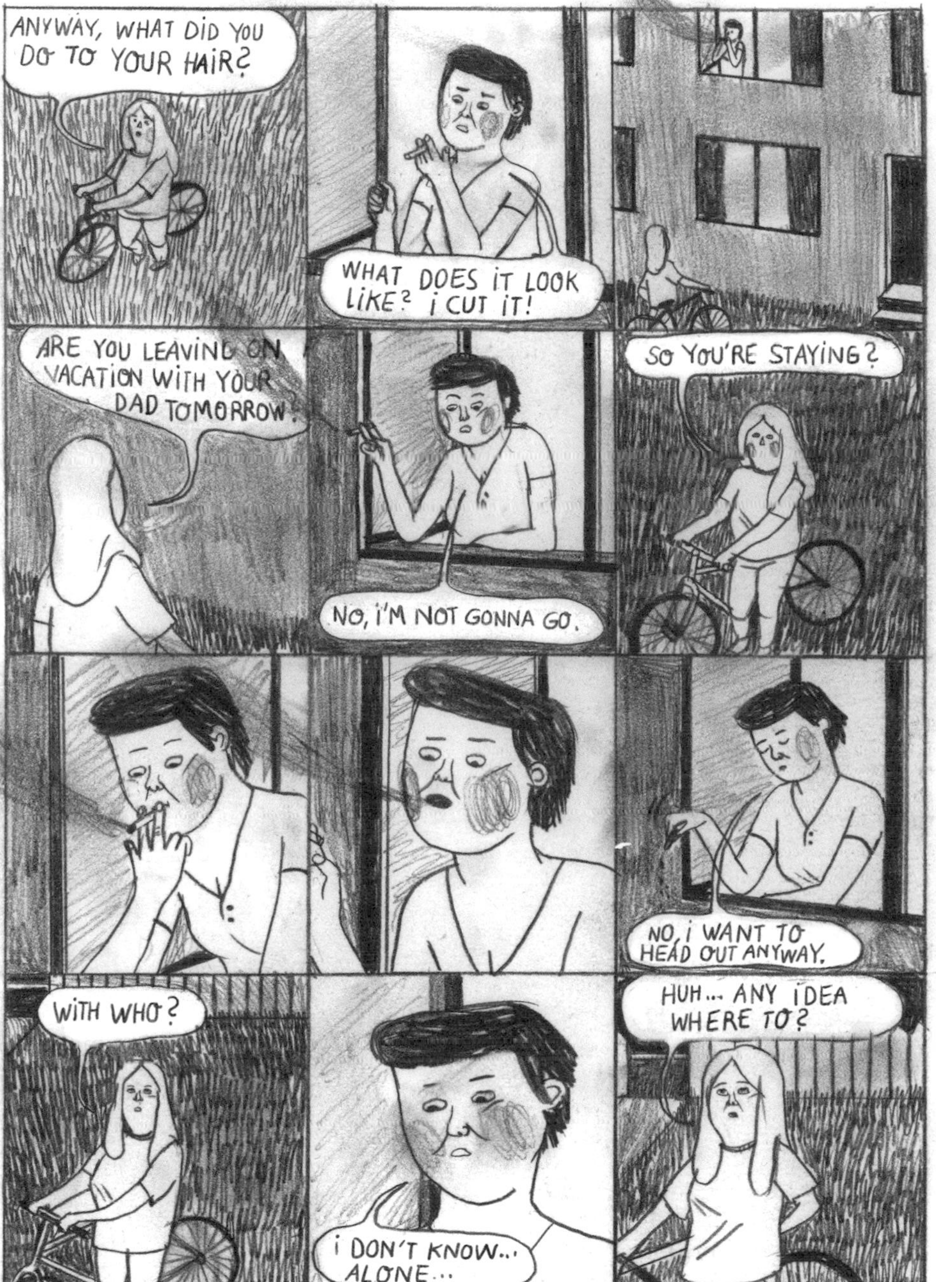
ANYWAY, WHAT DID YOU DO TO YOUR HAIR?
WHAT DOES IT LOOK LIKE? I CUT IT!
ARE YOU LEAVING ON VACATION WITH YOUR DAD TOMORROW?
NO, I'M NOT GONNA GO.
SO YOU'RE STAYING?
NO, I WANT TO HEAD OUT ANYWAY.
WITH WHO?
I DON'T KNOW... ALONE...
HUH... ANY IDEA WHERE TO?

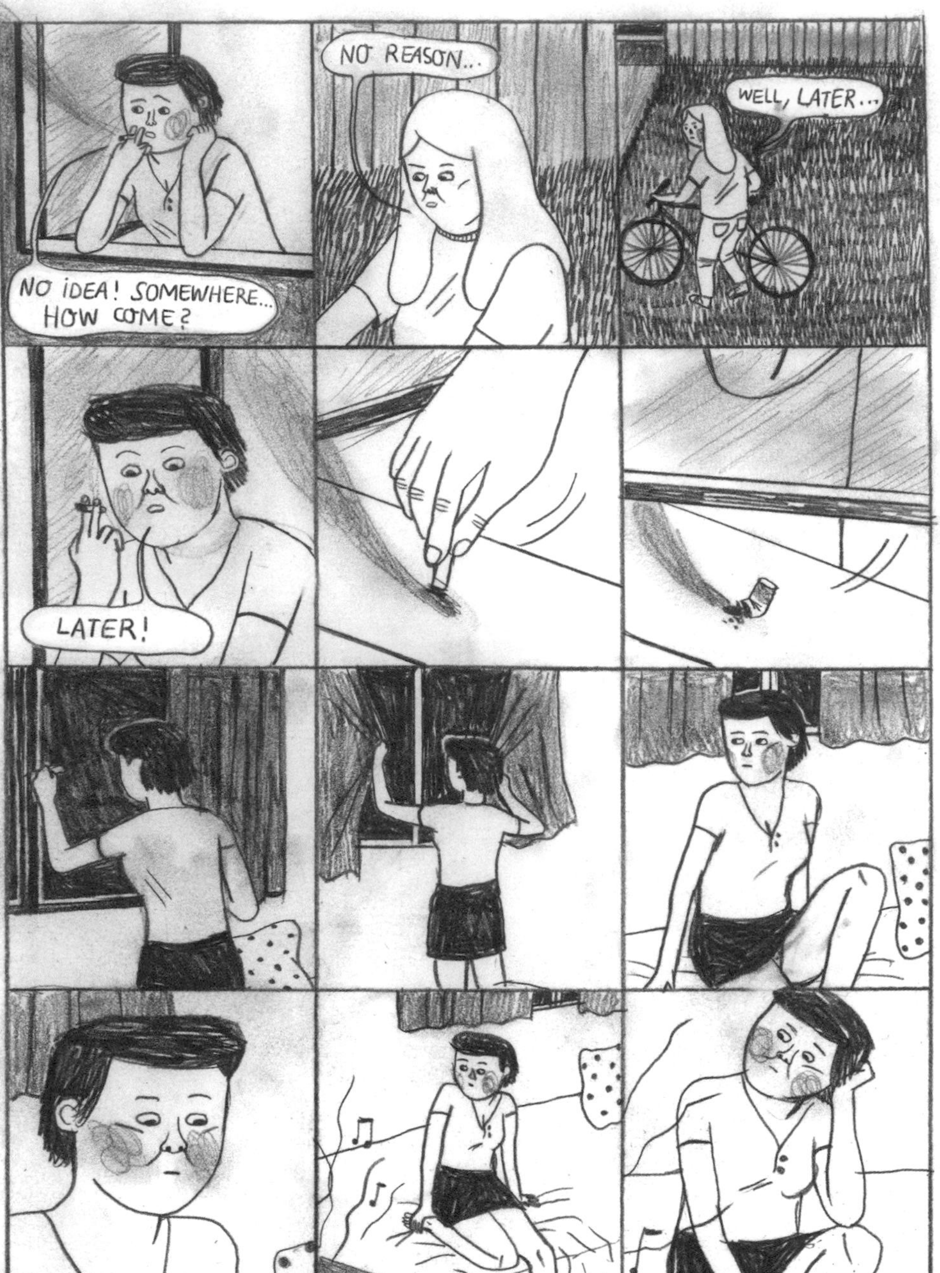

NO IDEA! SOMEWHERE... HOW COME?
NO REASON...
WELL, LATER...
LATER!

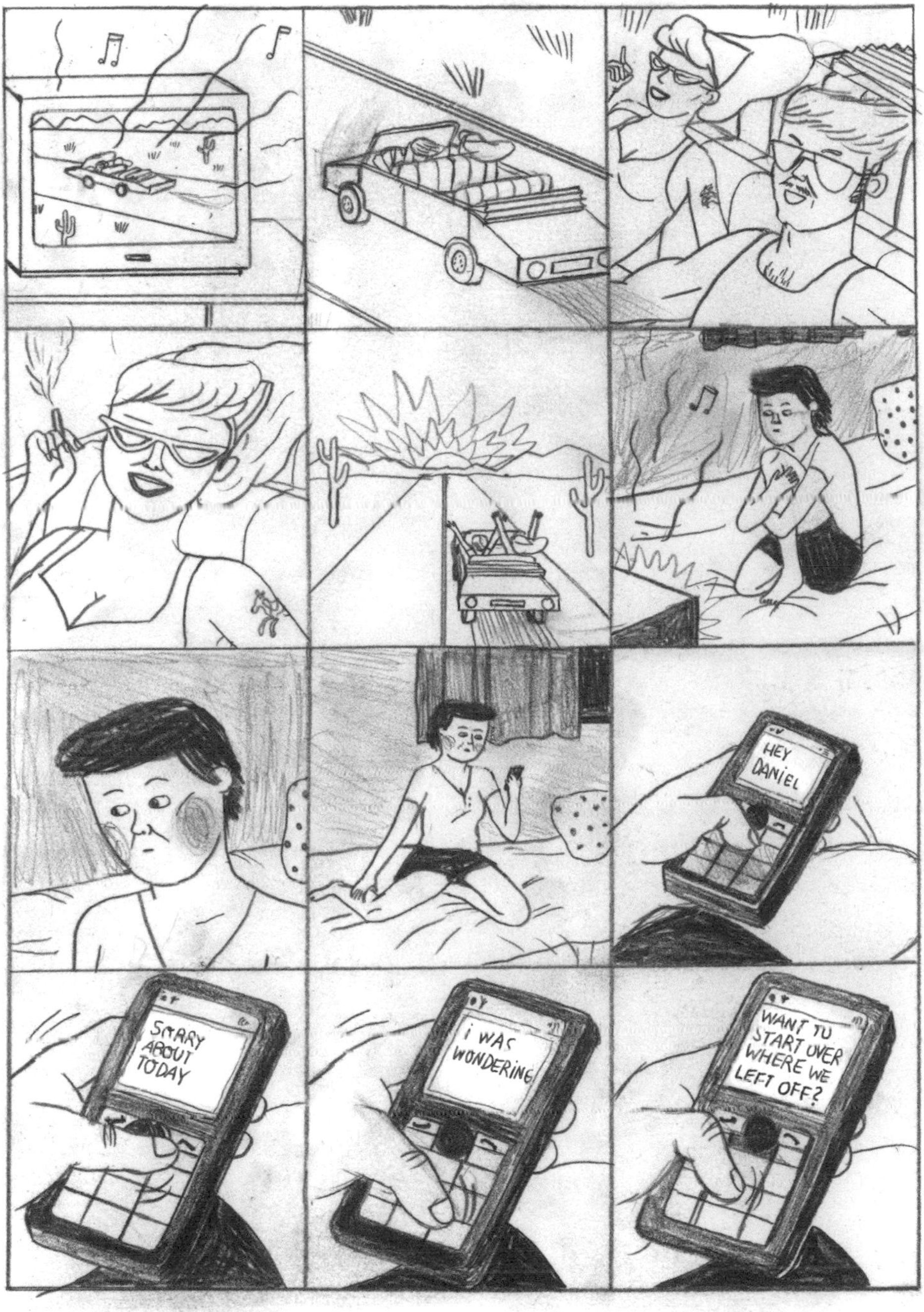
HEY DANIEL
SORRY ABOUT TODAY
i WAS WONDERING
WANT TU START OVER WHERE WE LEFT OFF?

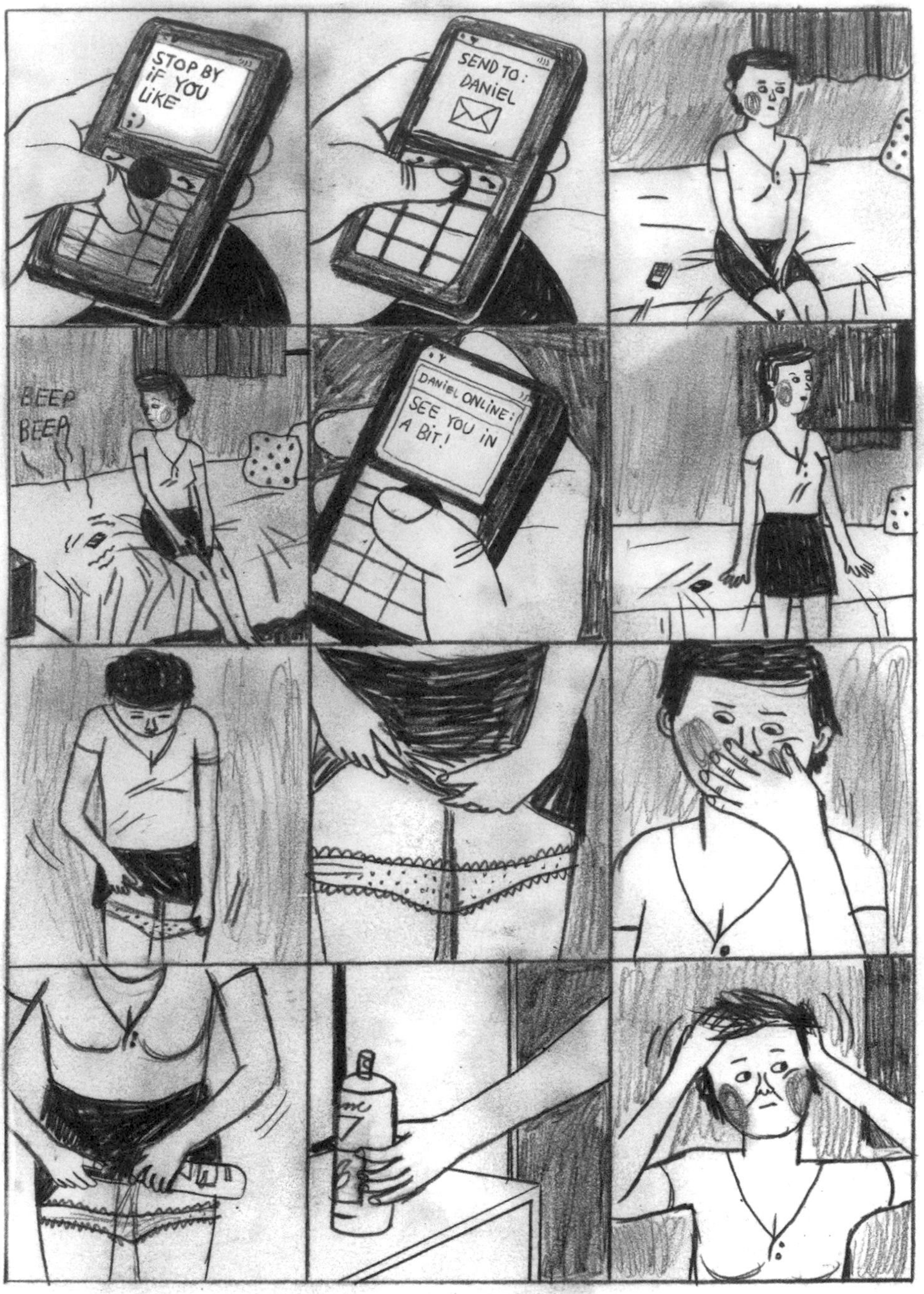
STOP BY IF YOU LIKE ;)
SEND TO: DANIEL
BEEP BEEP
DANIEL ONLINE: SEE YOU IN A BIT!

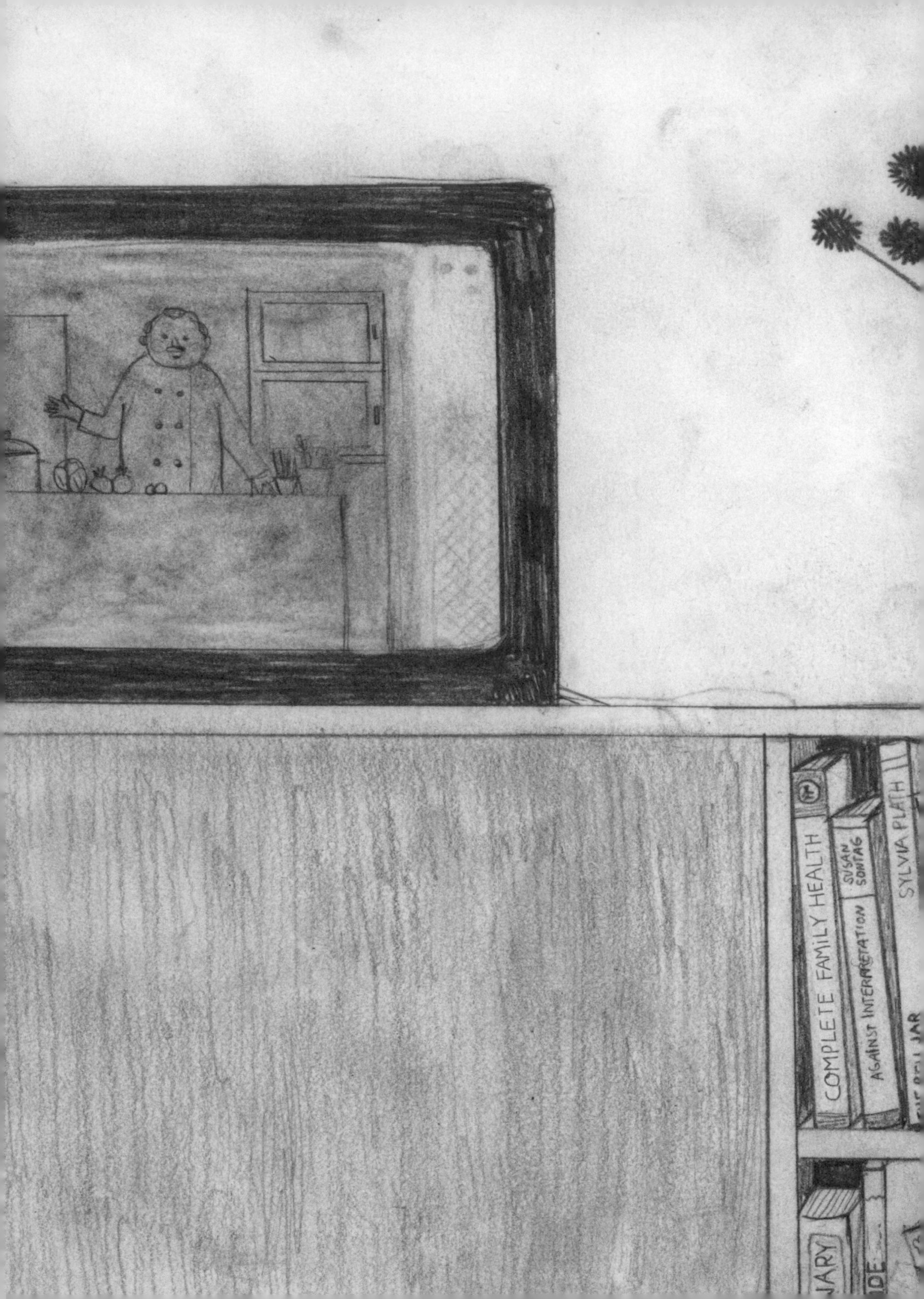
COMPLETE FAMILY HEALTH
SUSAN SONTAG
AGAINST INTERPRETATION
SYLVIA PLATH

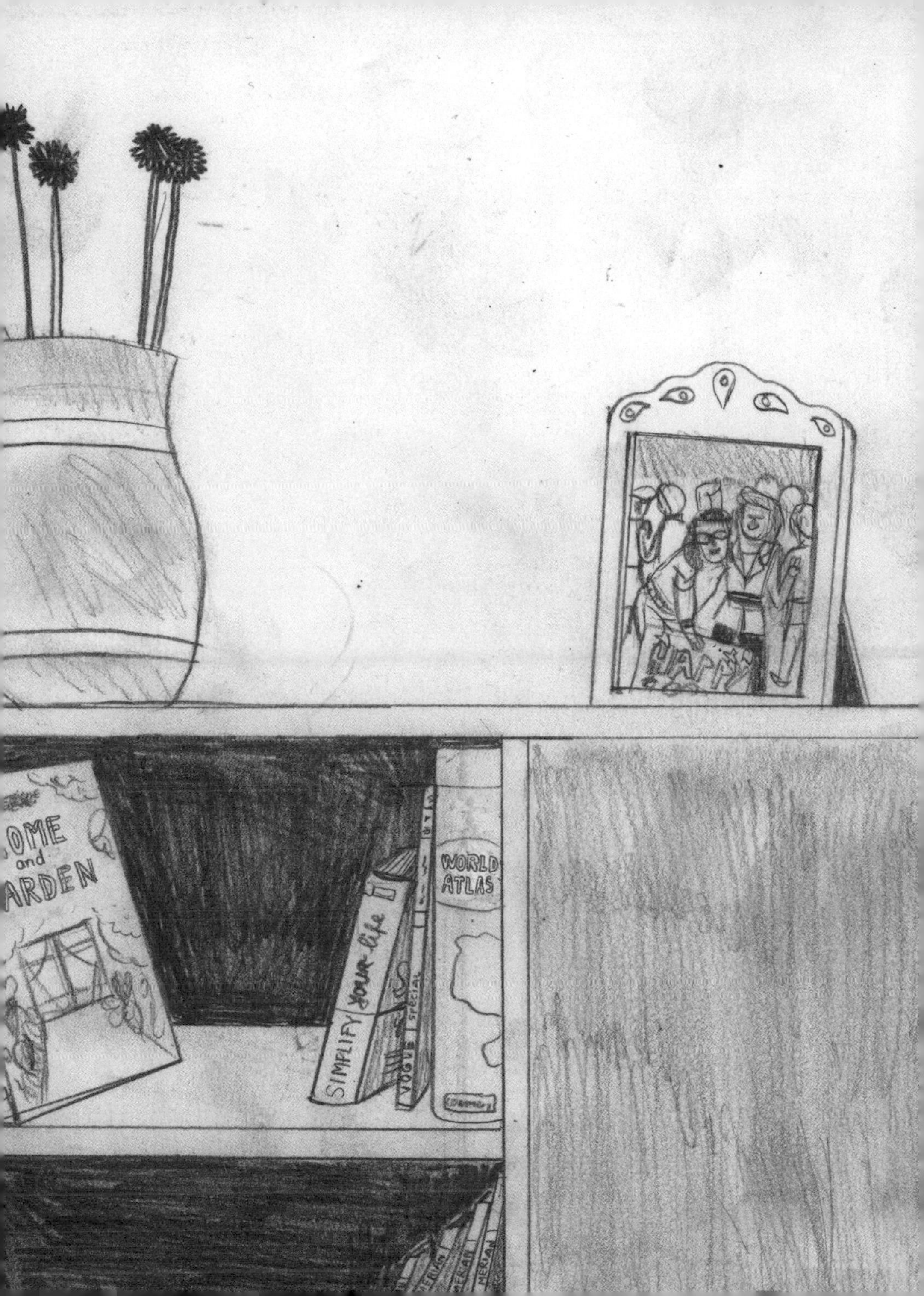
OME
and
ARDEN
SIMPLIFY your life
VOGUE
SPECIAL
WORLD
ATLAS
MERIAN
MERIAN
MERIAN

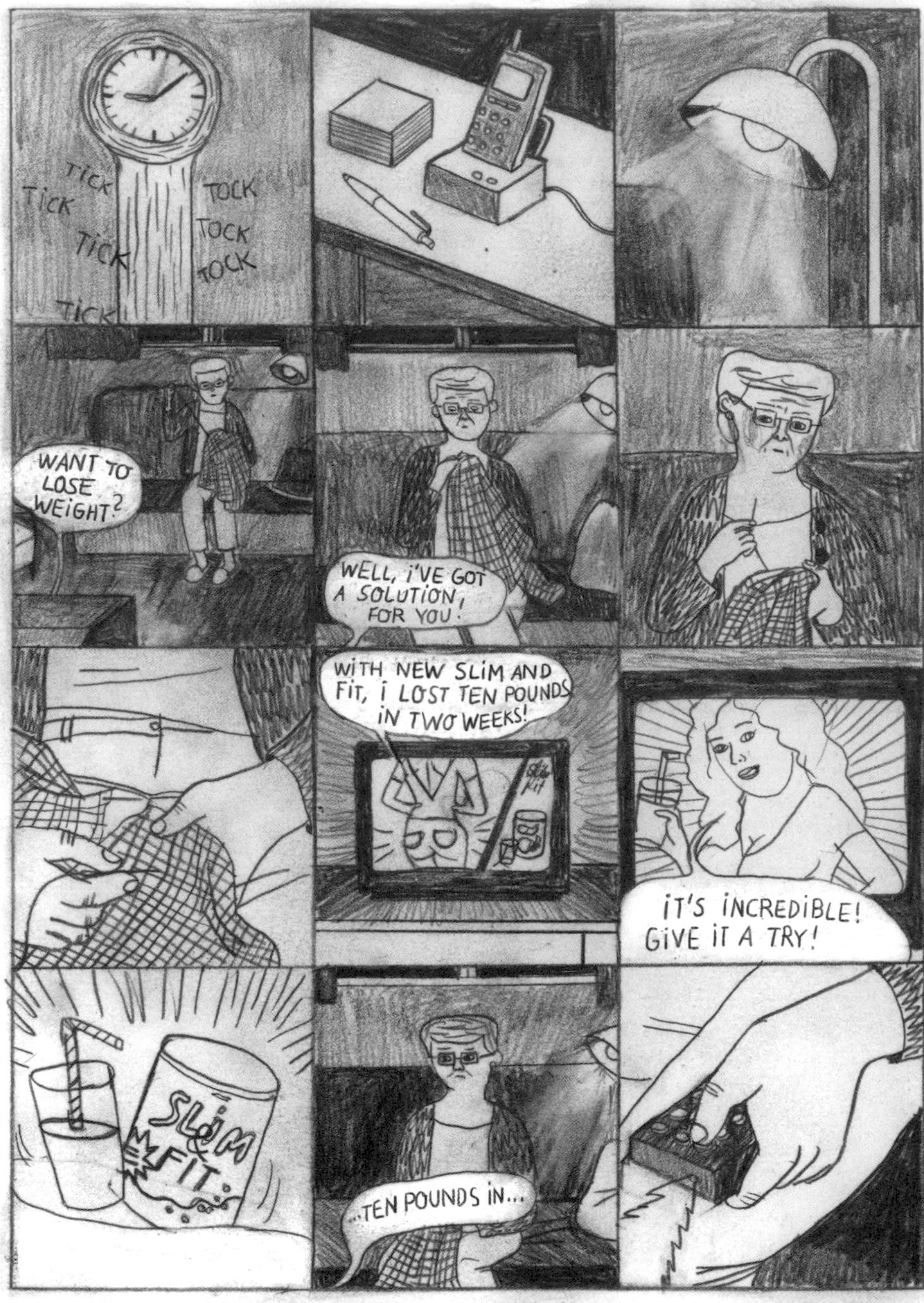
TICK
TICK
TICK
TICK
TOCK
TOCK
TOCK
WANT TO LOSE WEIGHT?
WELL, I'VE GOT A SOLUTION, FOR YOU.
WITH NEW SLIM AND FIT, I LOST TEN POUNDS IN TWO WEEKS!
IT'S INCREDIBLE! GIVE IT A TRY!
SLIM & FIT
...TEN POUNDS IN...

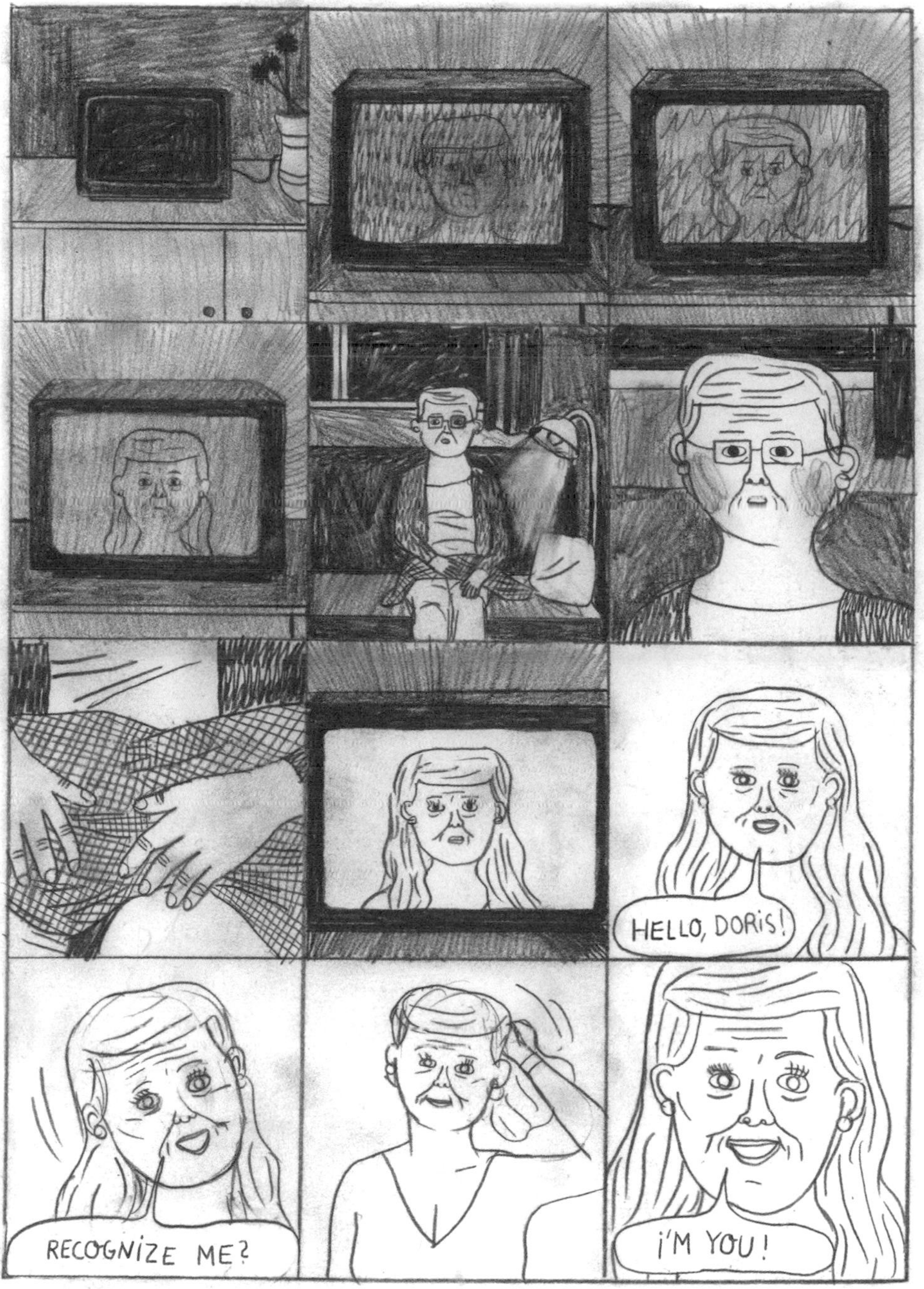
HELLO, DORIS!
RECOGNIZE ME?
I'M YOU!

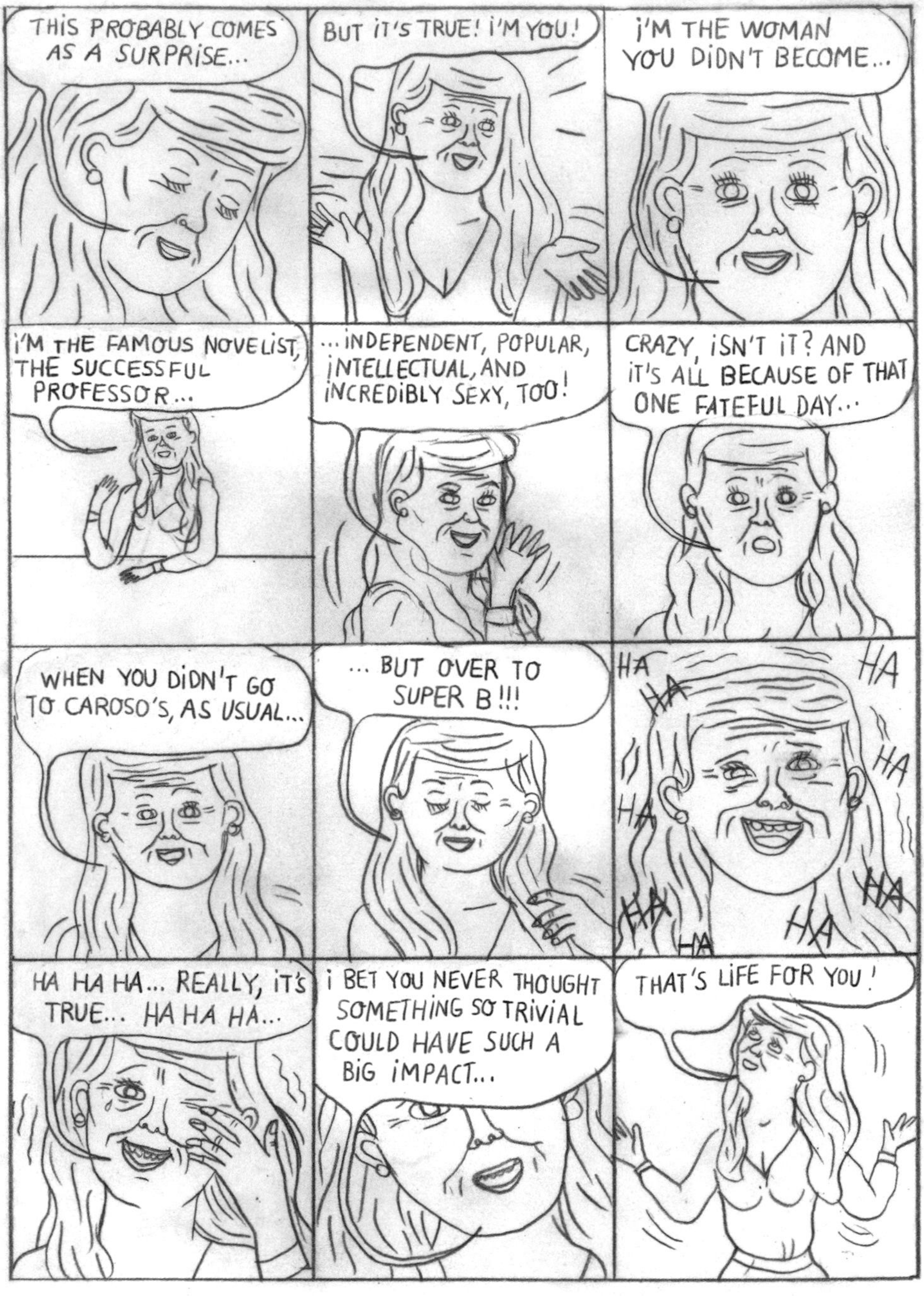
THIS PROBABLY COMES AS A SURPRISE...
BUT IT'S TRUE! I'M YOU!
I'M THE WOMAN YOU DIDN'T BECOME...
I'M THE FAMOUS NOVELIST, THE SUCCESSFUL PROFESSOR...
...INDEPENDENT, POPULAR, INTELLECTUAL, AND INCREDIBLY SEXY, TOO!
CRAZY, ISN'T IT? AND IT'S ALL BECAUSE OF THAT ONE FATEFUL DAY...
WHEN YOU DIDN'T GO TO CAROSO'S, AS USUAL...
... BUT OVER TO SUPER B!!!
HA HA HA HA HA HA HA HA HA HA
HA HA HA... REALLY, IT'S TRUE... HA HA HA...
I BET YOU NEVER THOUGHT SOMETHING SO TRIVIAL COULD HAVE SUCH A BIG IMPACT...
THAT'S LIFE FOR YOU!

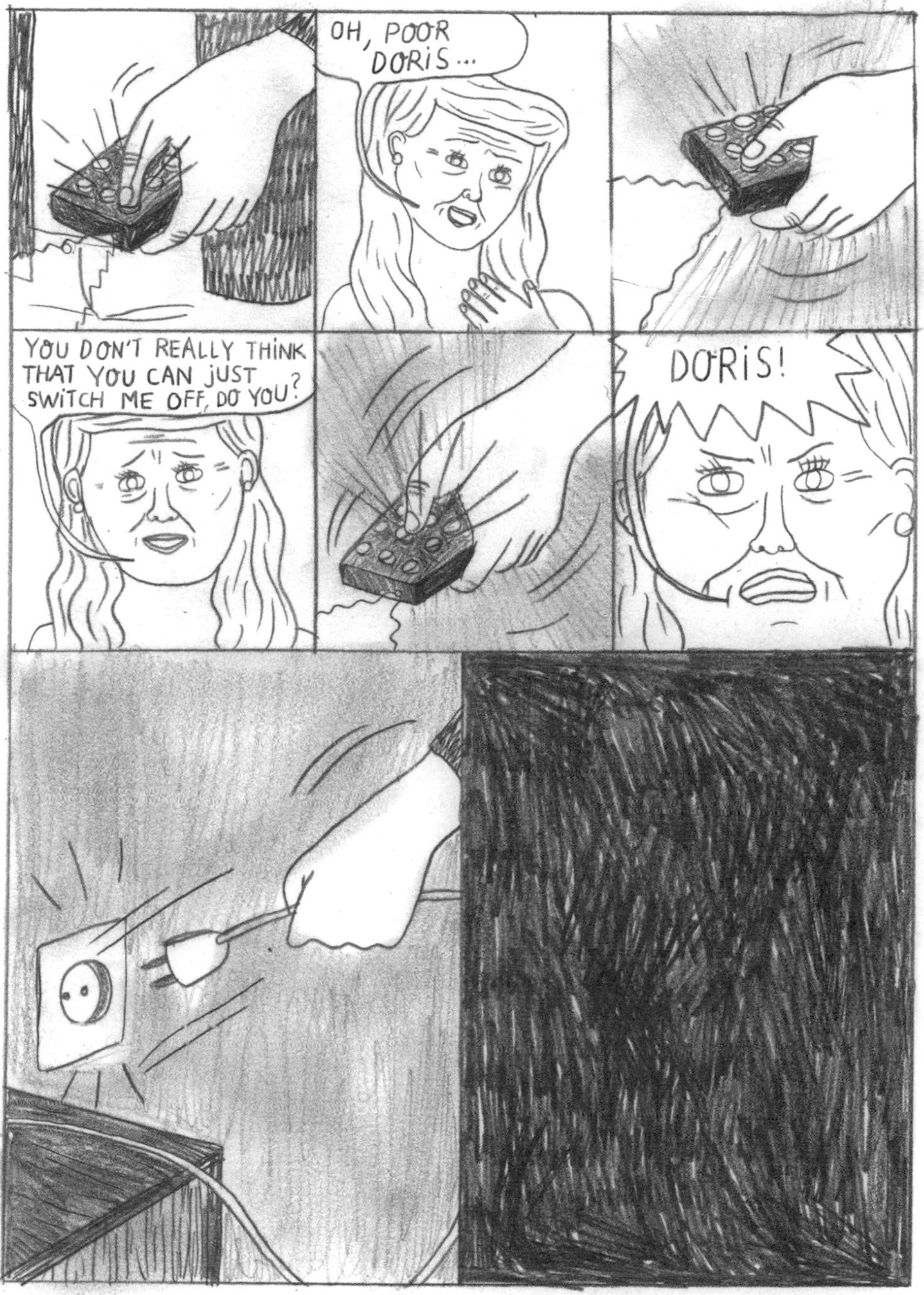
OH, POOR DORiS...
YOU DON'T REALLY THiNK THAT YOU CAN JUST SWiTCH ME OFF, DO YOU?
DORiS!

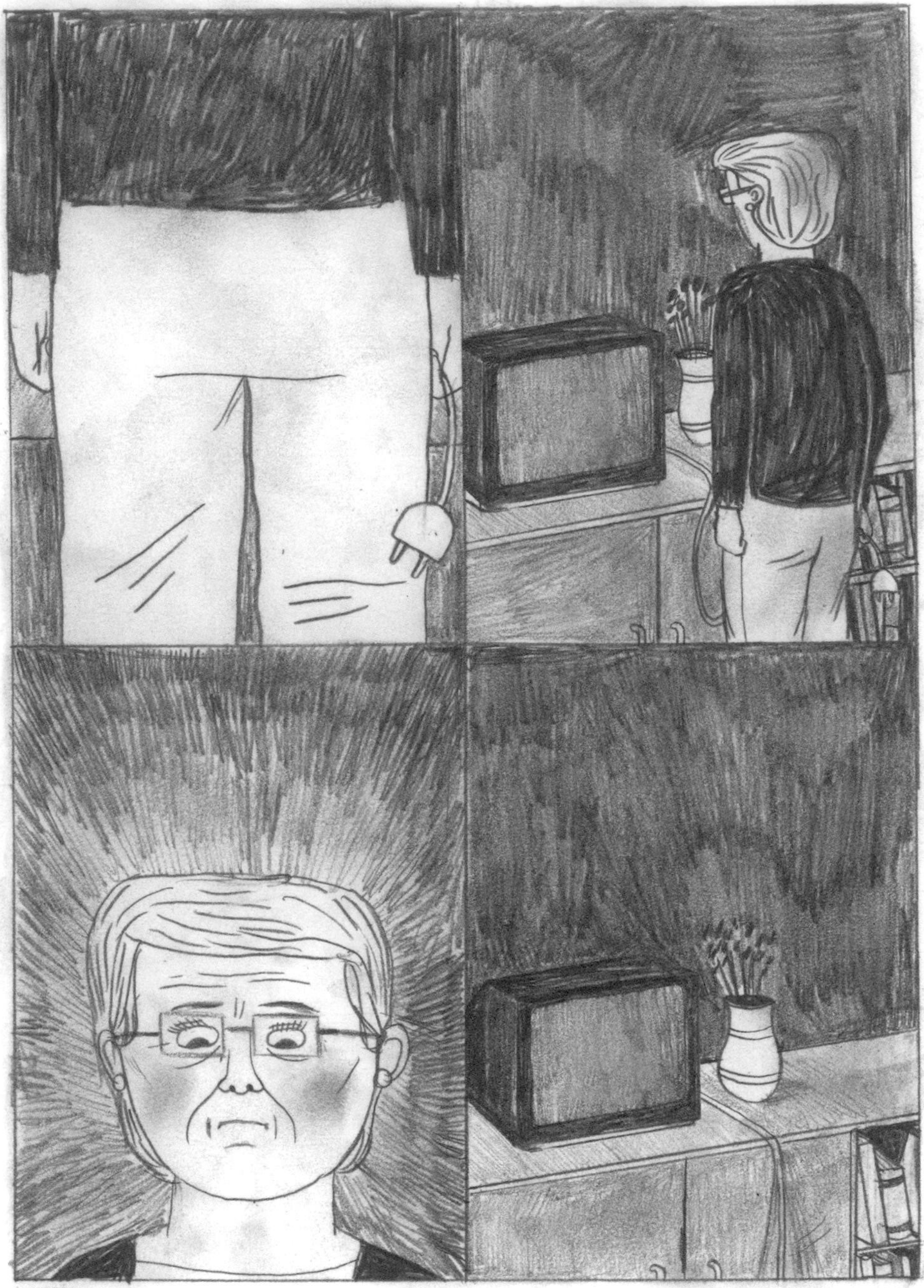

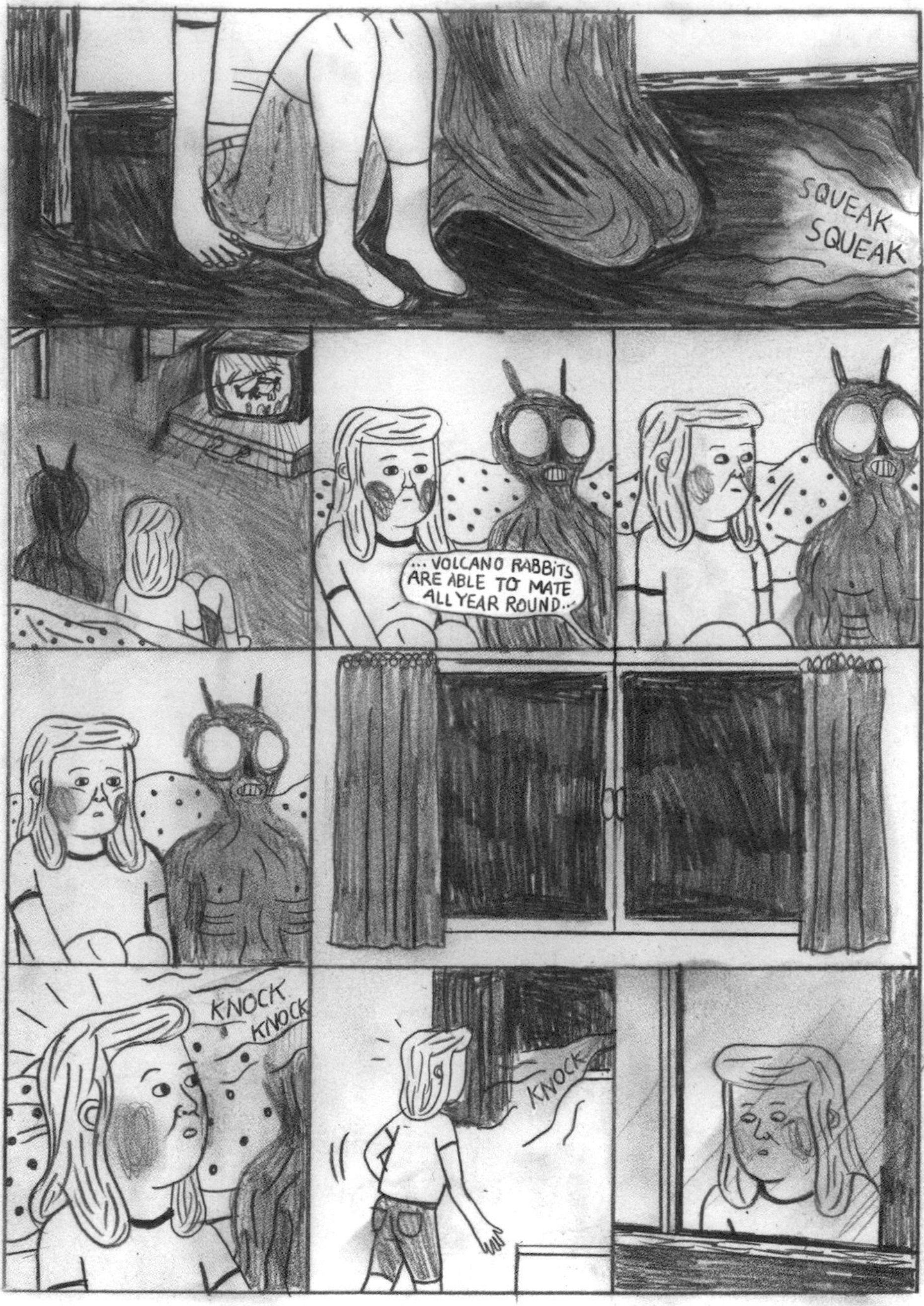
SQUEAK
SQUEAK
... VOLCANO RABBITS ARE ABLE TO MATE ALL YEAR ROUND...
KNOCK
KNOCK
KNOCK

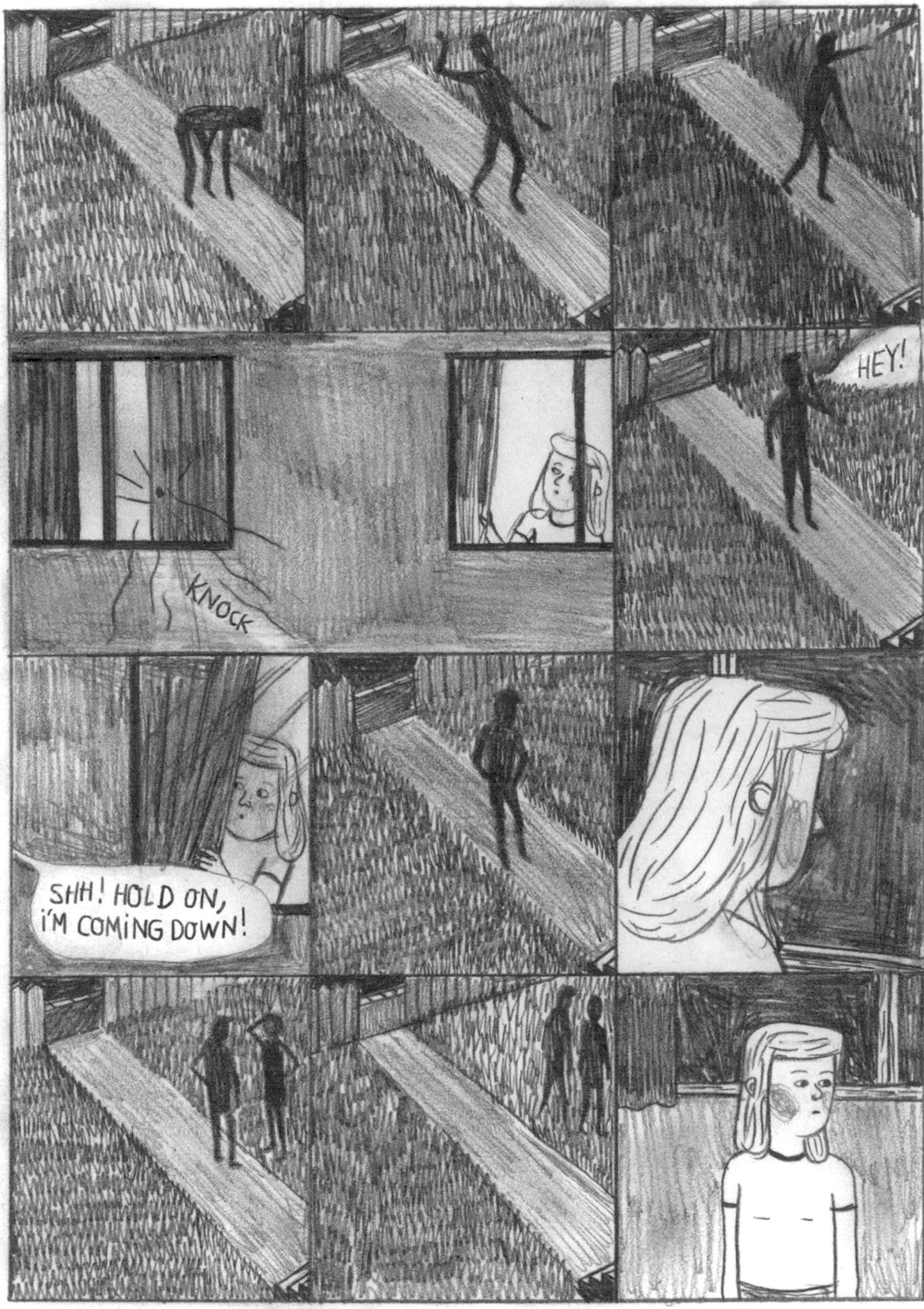
KNOCK
HEY!
SHH! HOLD ON, I'M COMING DOWN!

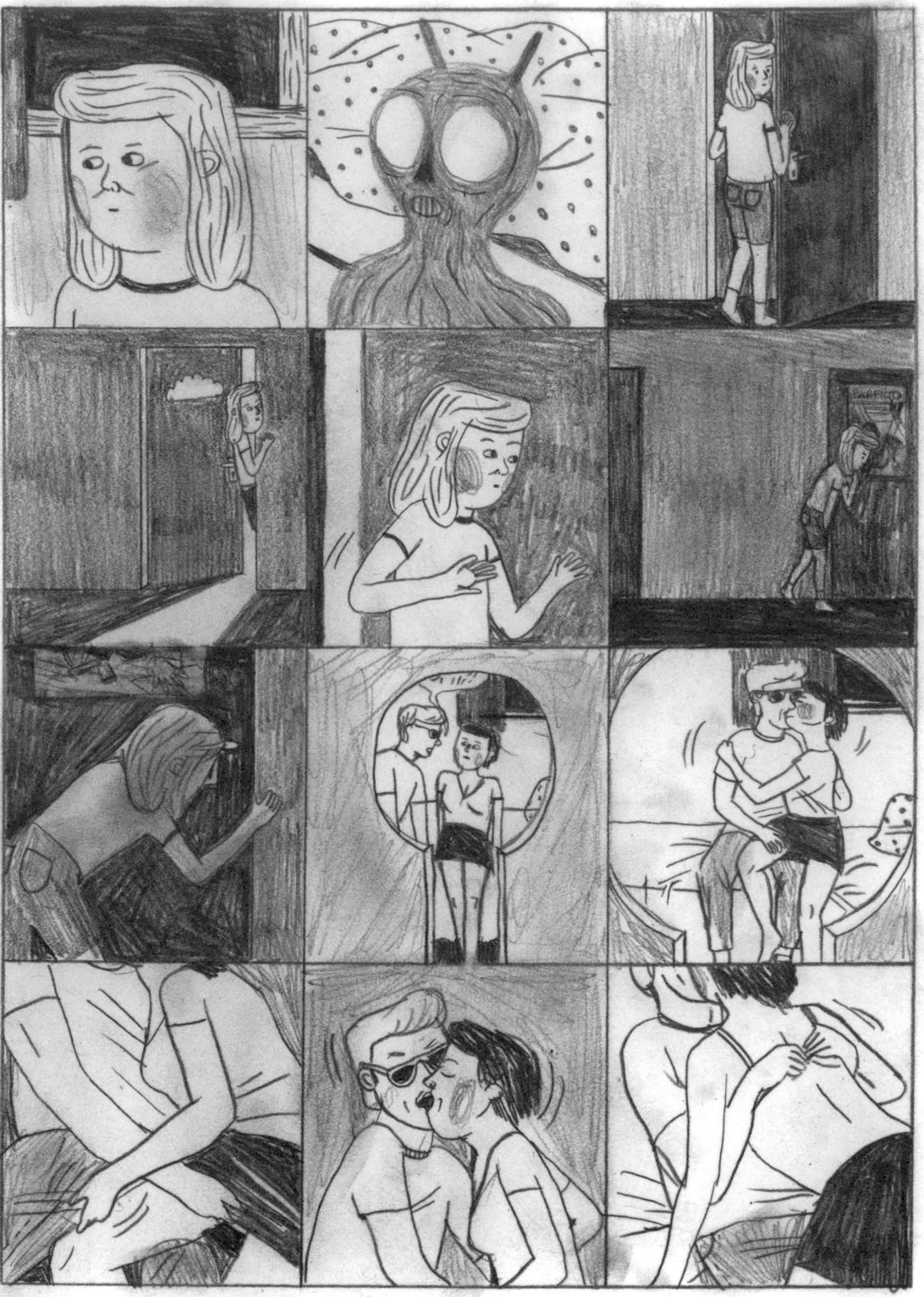

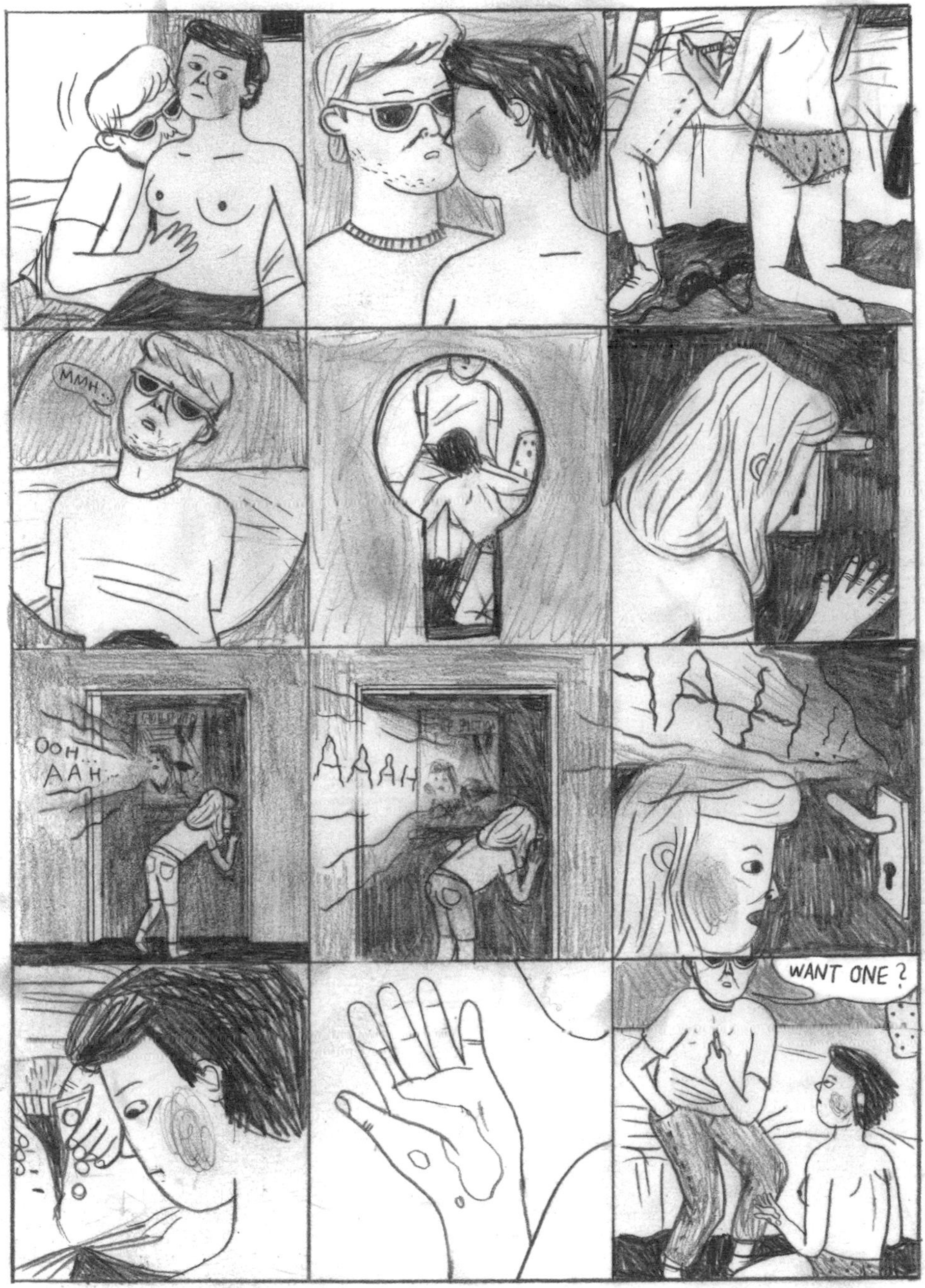
MMH...
OOH... AAH...
AAAH
WANT ONE?

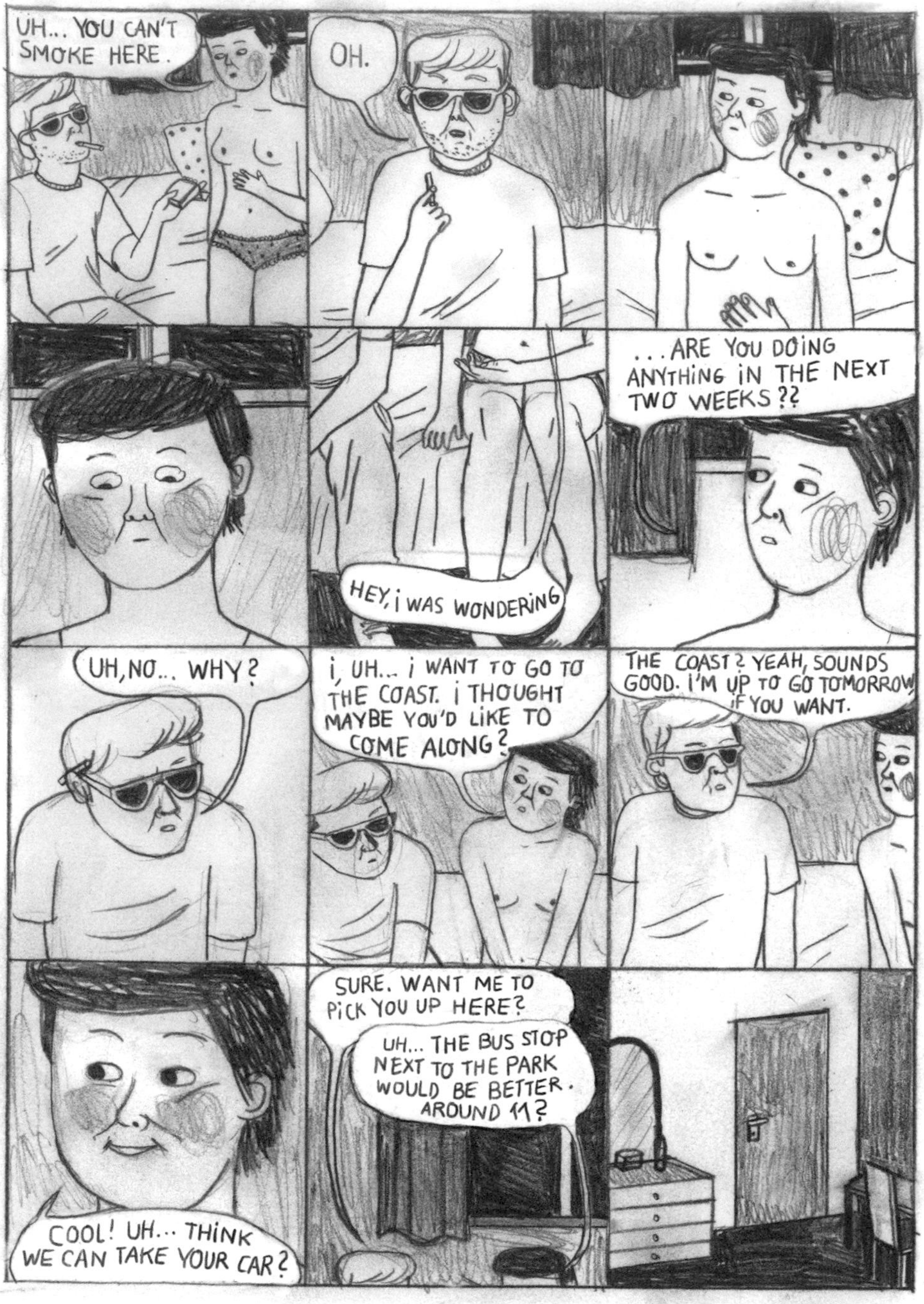
UH... YOU CAN'T SMOKE HERE.
OH.
HEY, i WAS WONDERING
...ARE YOU DOING ANYTHING IN THE NEXT TWO WEEKS??
UH, NO... WHY?
i, UH... i WANT TO GO TO THE COAST. i THOUGHT MAYBE YOU'D LIKE TO COME ALONG?
THE COAST? YEAH, SOUNDS GOOD. I'M UP TO GO TOMORROW IF YOU WANT.
COOL! UH... THINK WE CAN TAKE YOUR CAR?
SURE. WANT ME TO PICK YOU UP HERE?
UH... THE BUS STOP NEXT TO THE PARK WOULD BE BETTER. AROUND 11?

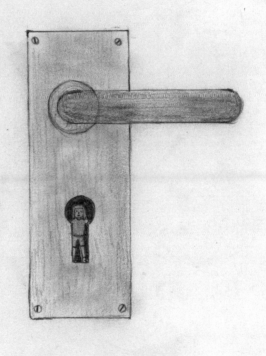

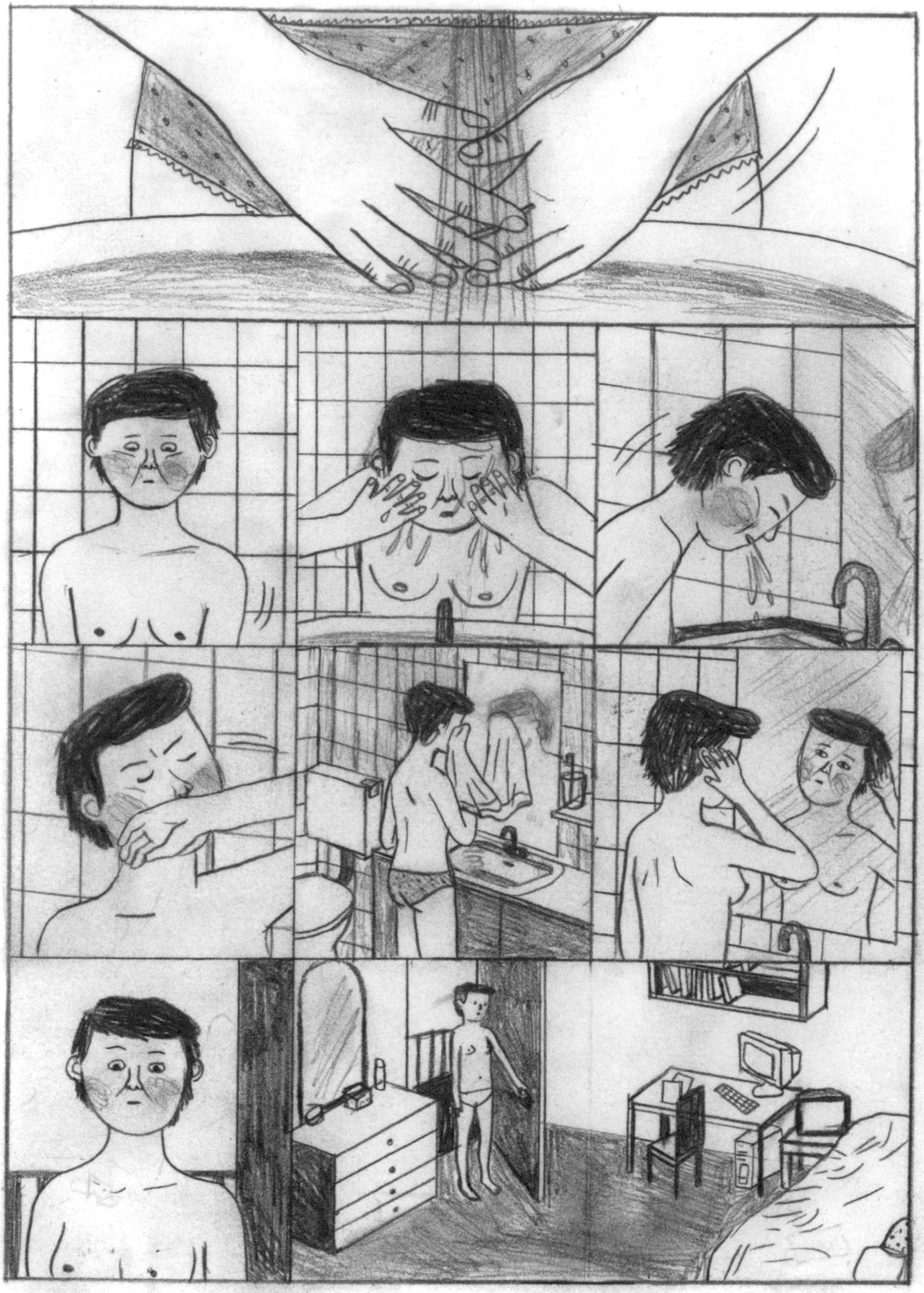

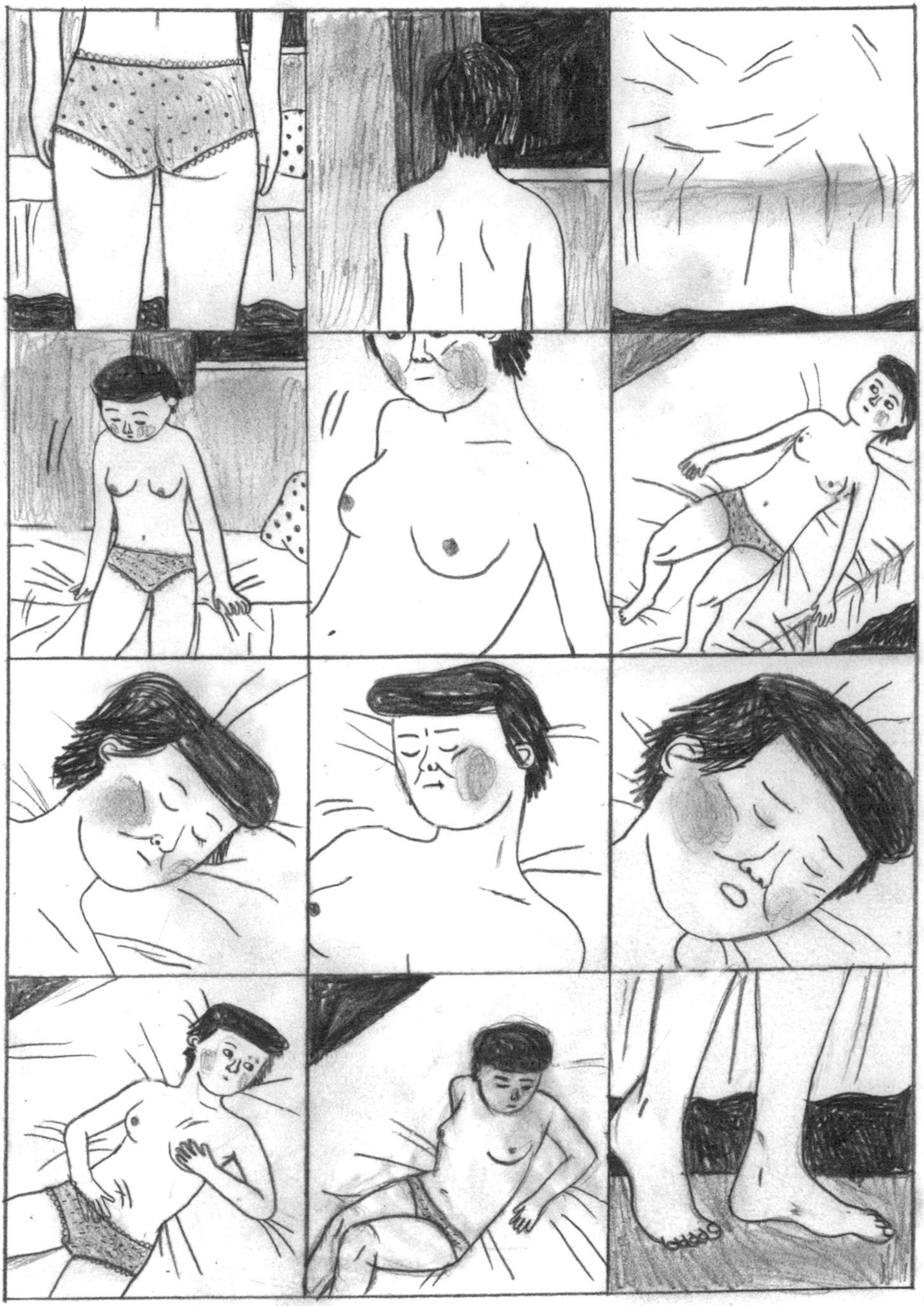

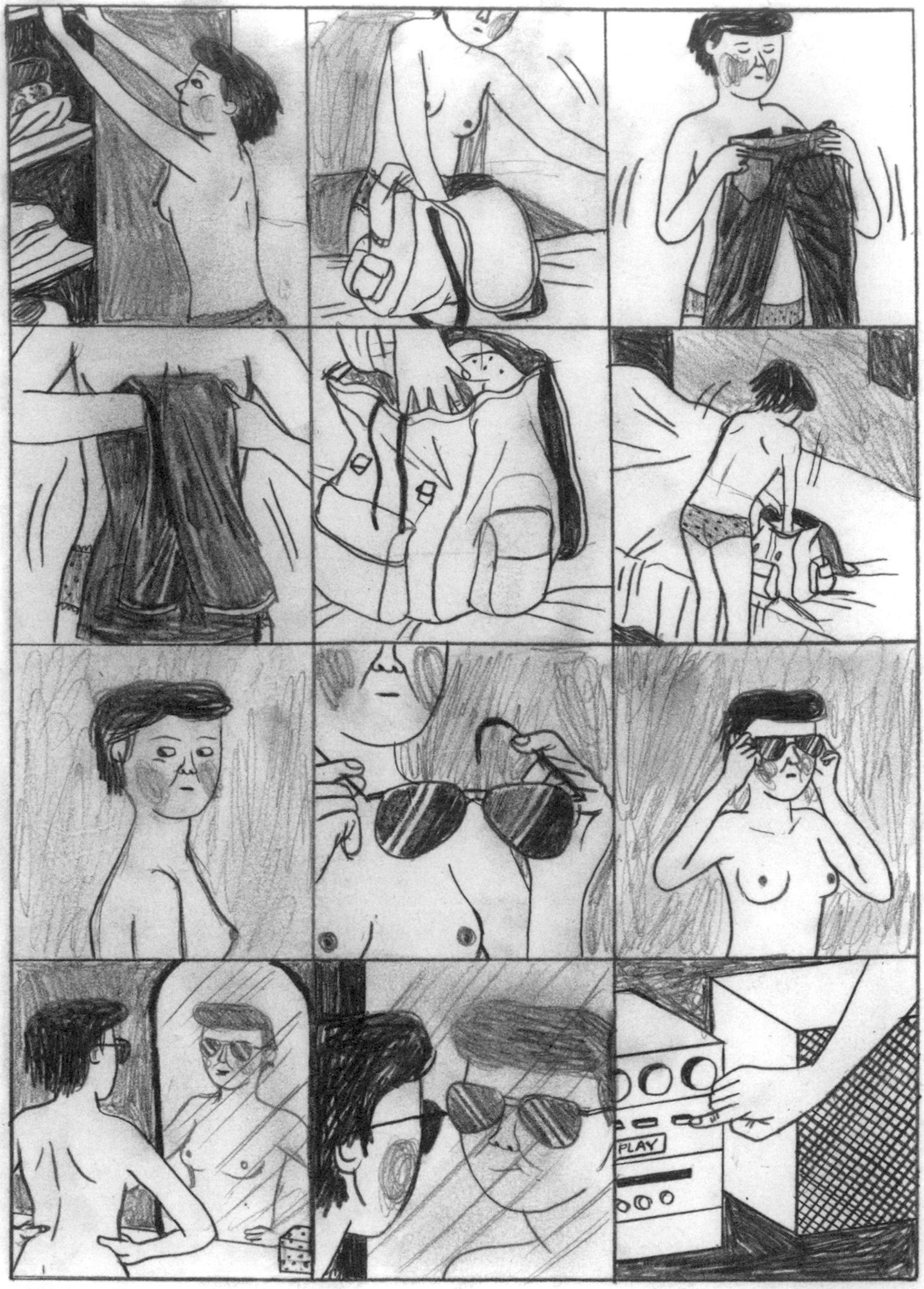
PLAY

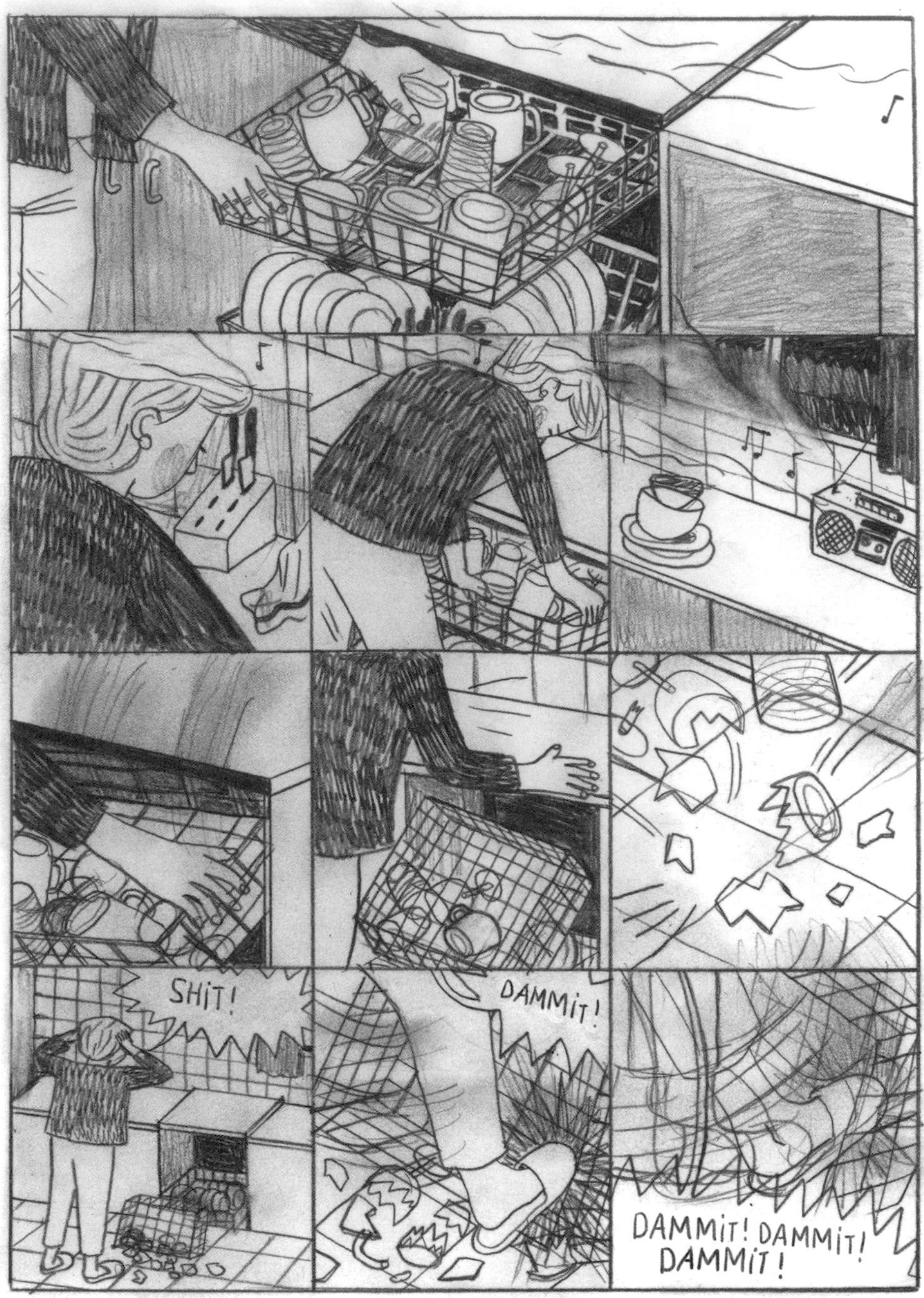
SHIT!
DAMMIT!
DAMMIT! DAMMIT!
DAMMIT!

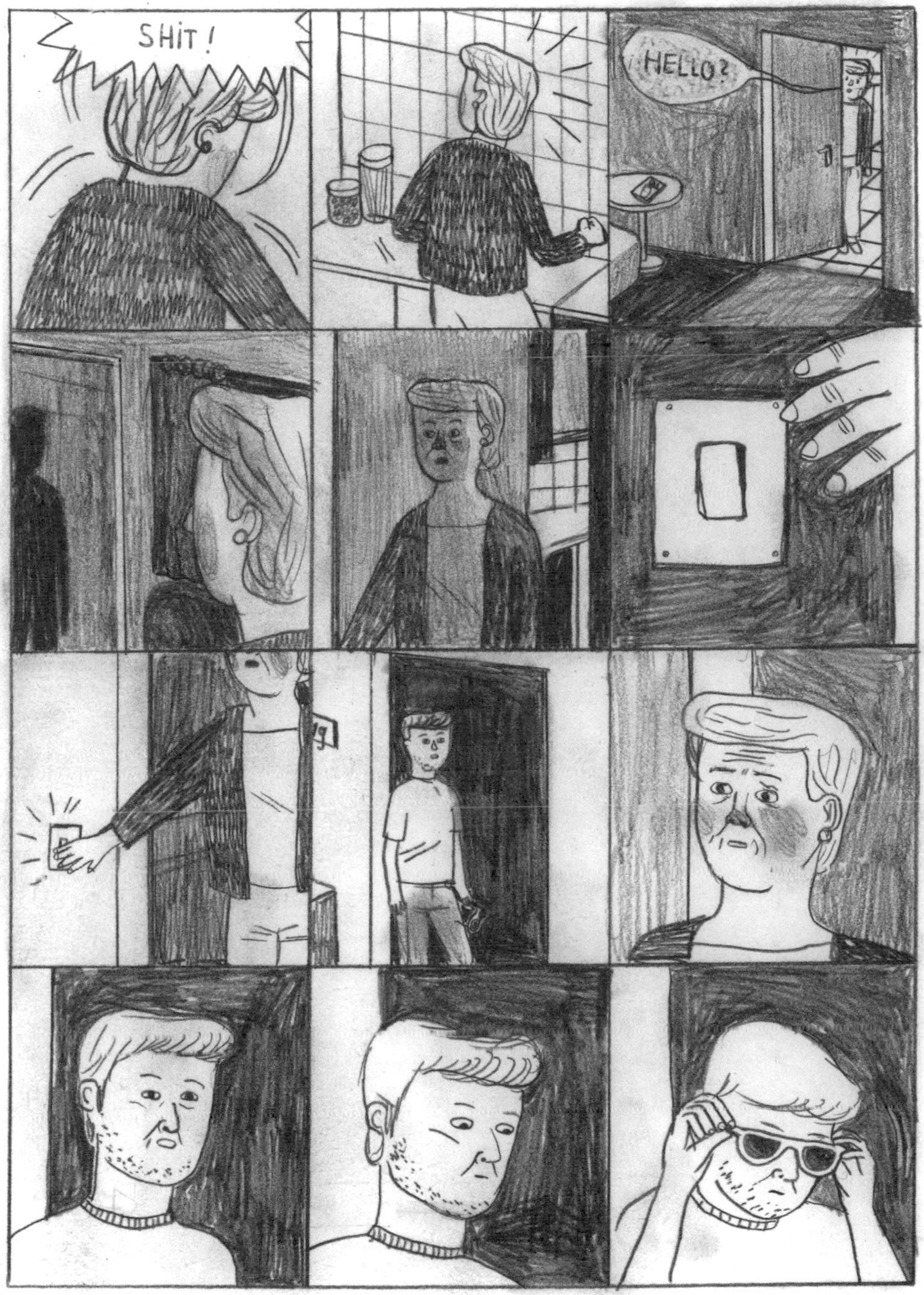
SHIT!
HELLO?

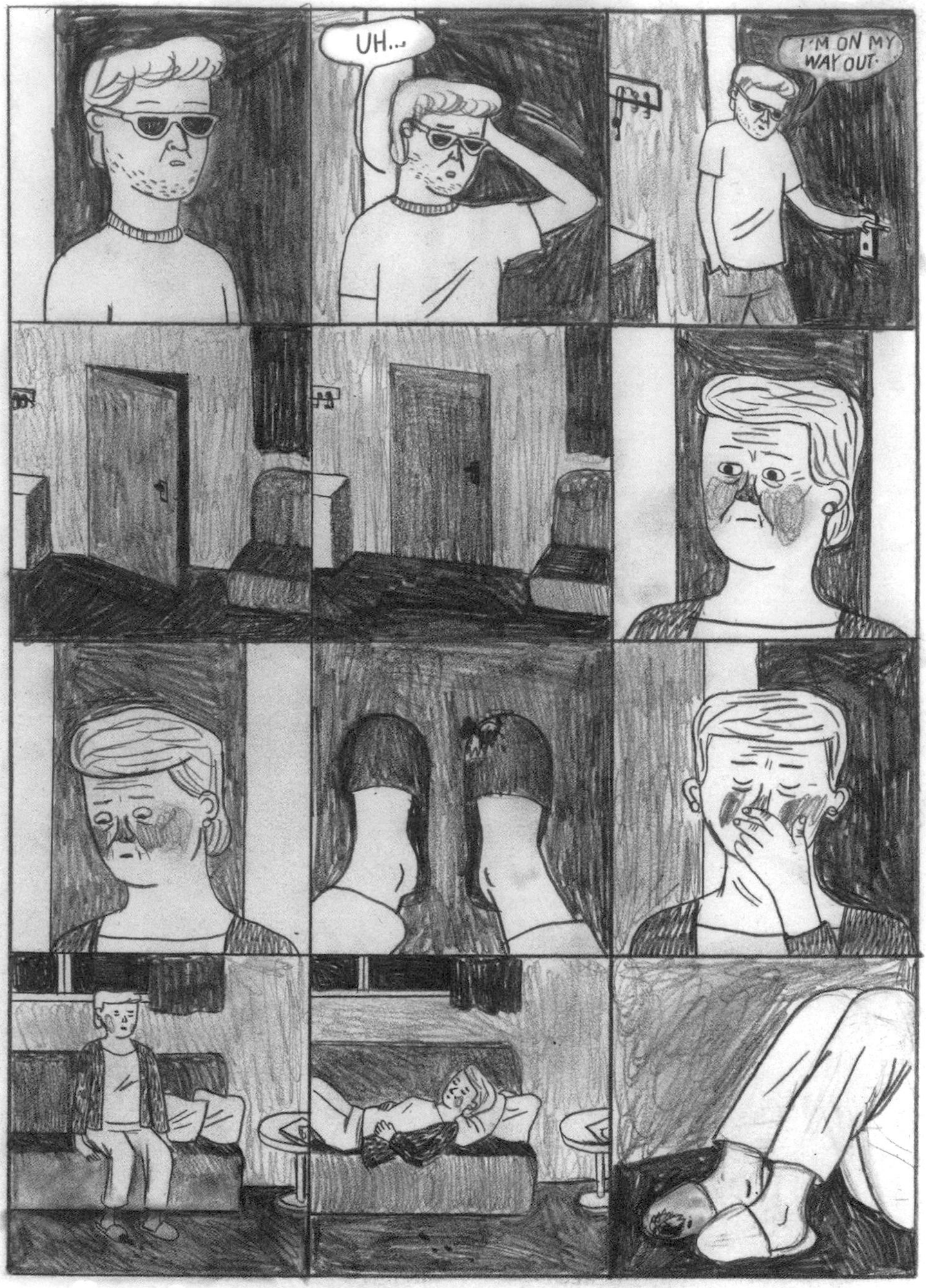
UH...
I'M ON MY WAY OUT.

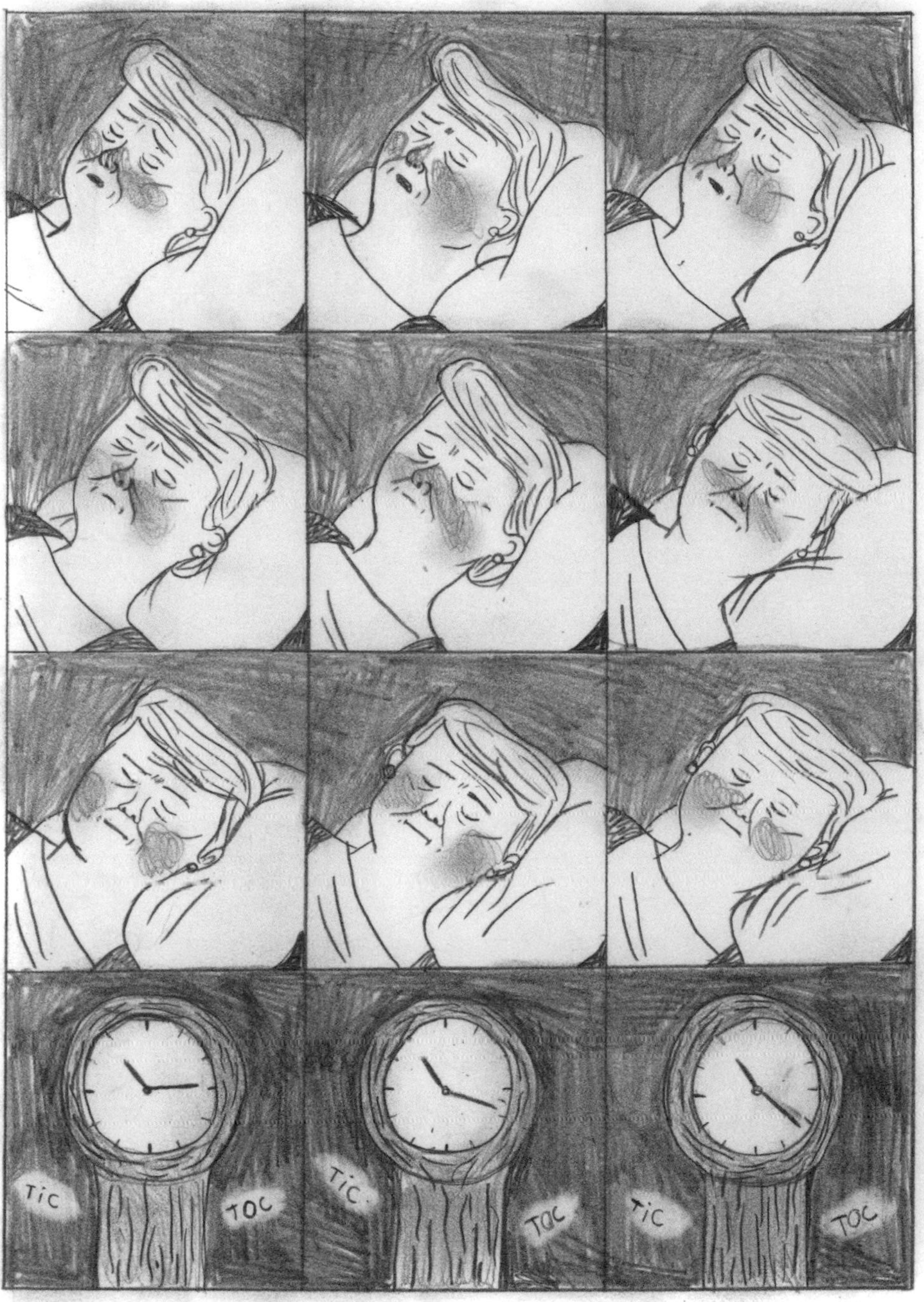

TIC
TOC
TIC
TOC
TIC
TOC

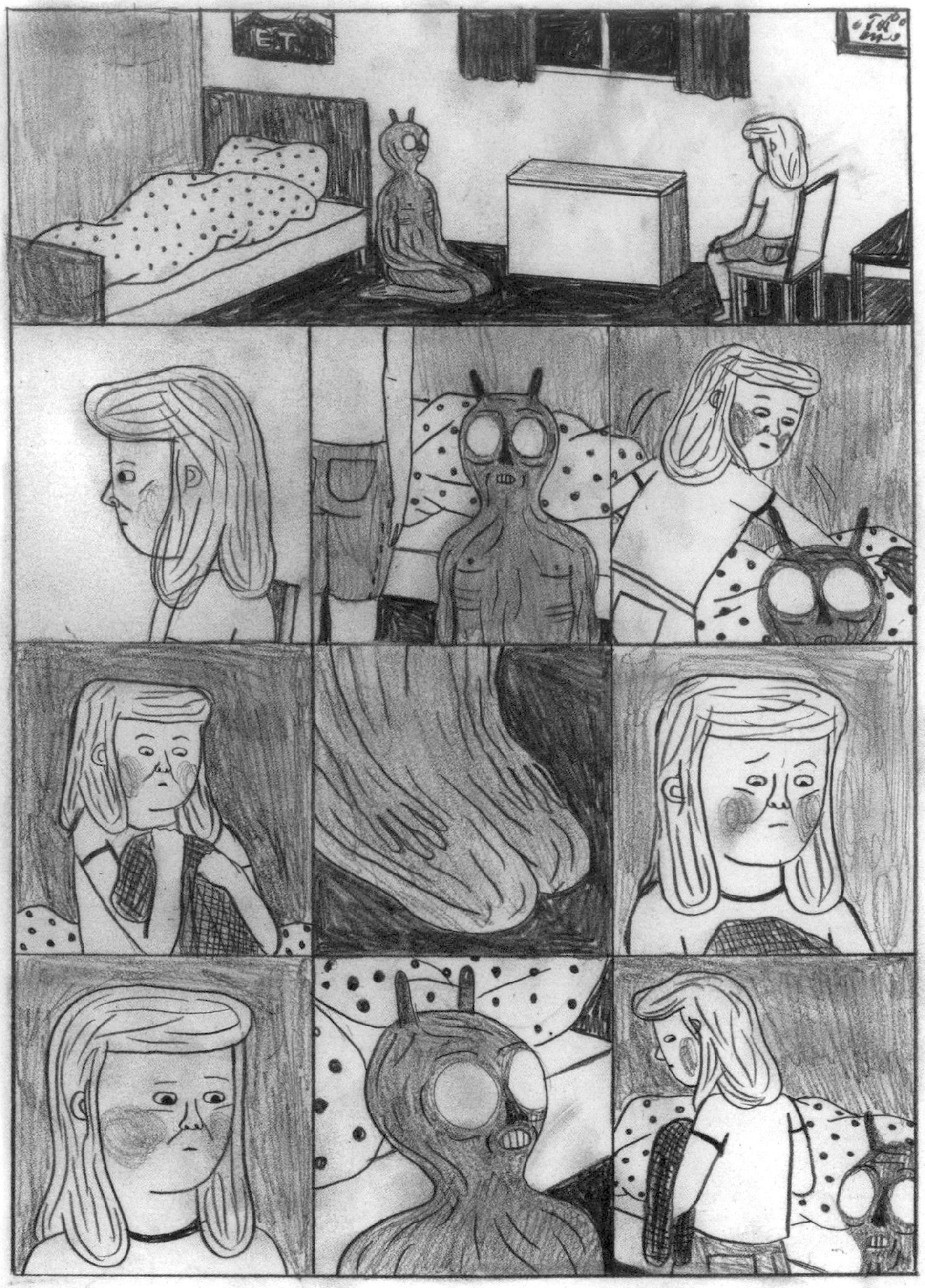
E.T.

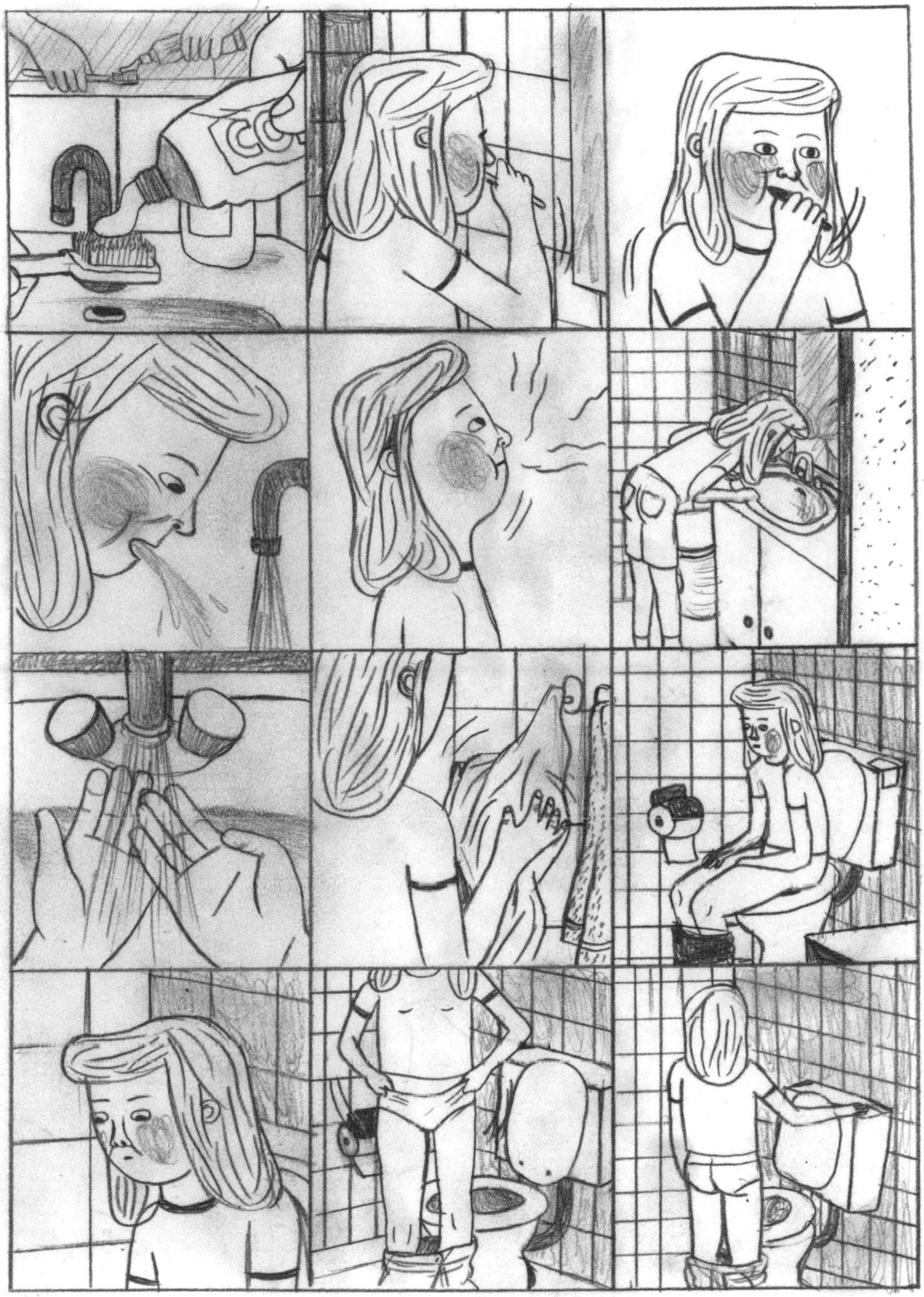

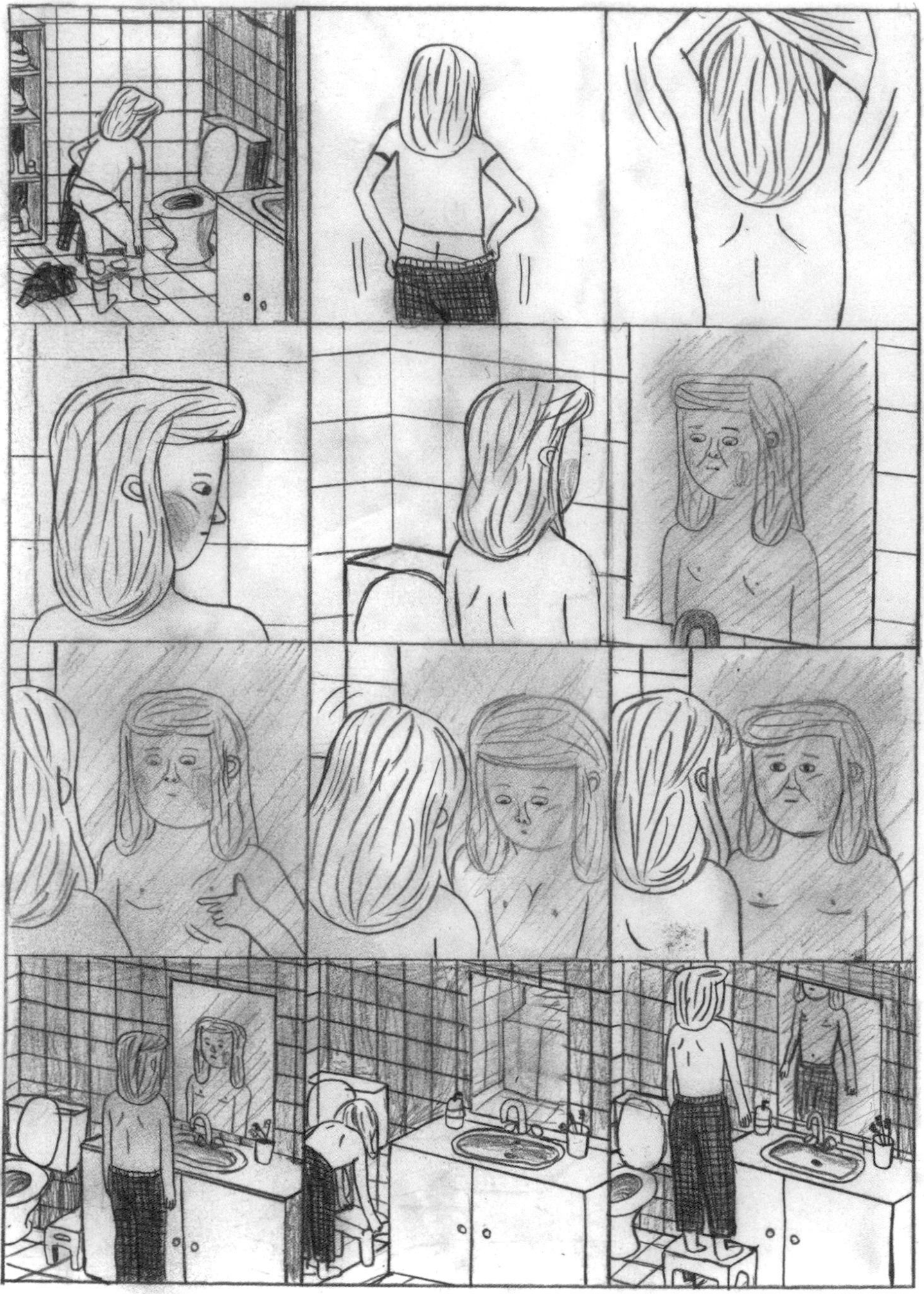

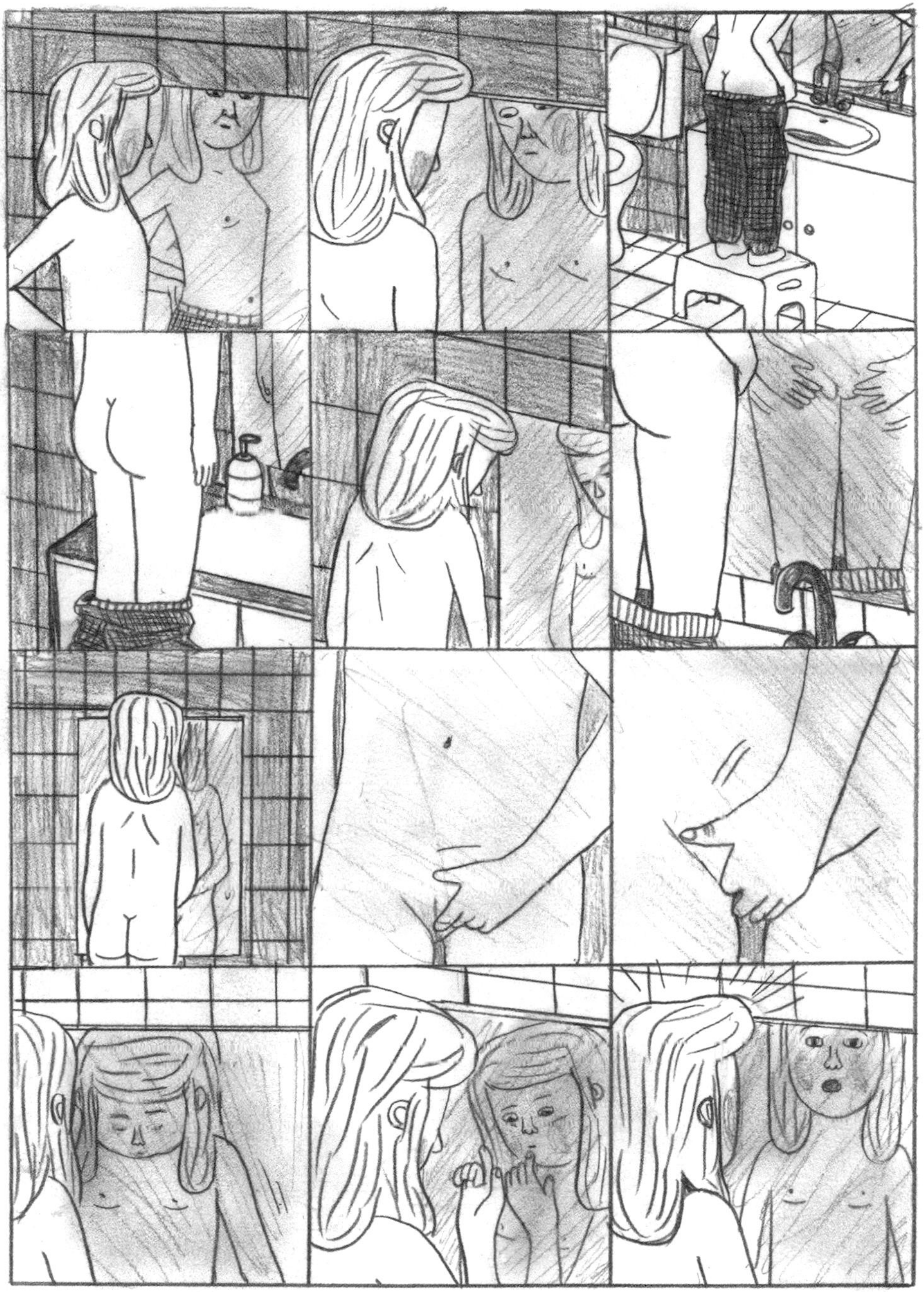

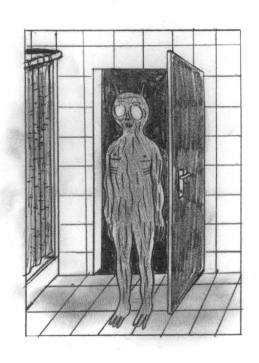

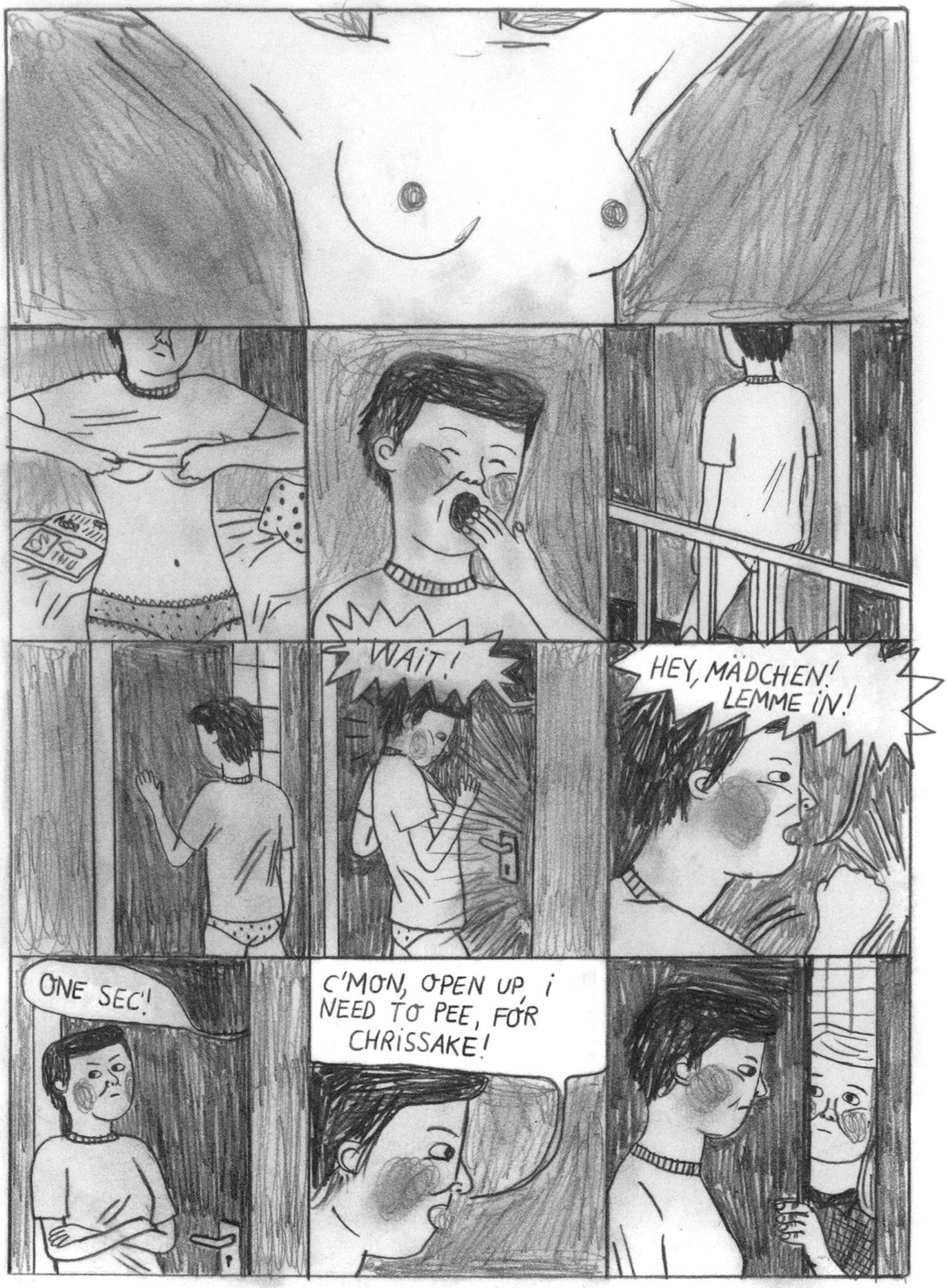
WAIT!
HEY, MÄDCHEN! LEMME IN!
ONE SEC!
C'MON, OPEN UP, I NEED TO PEE, FOR CHRISSAKE!

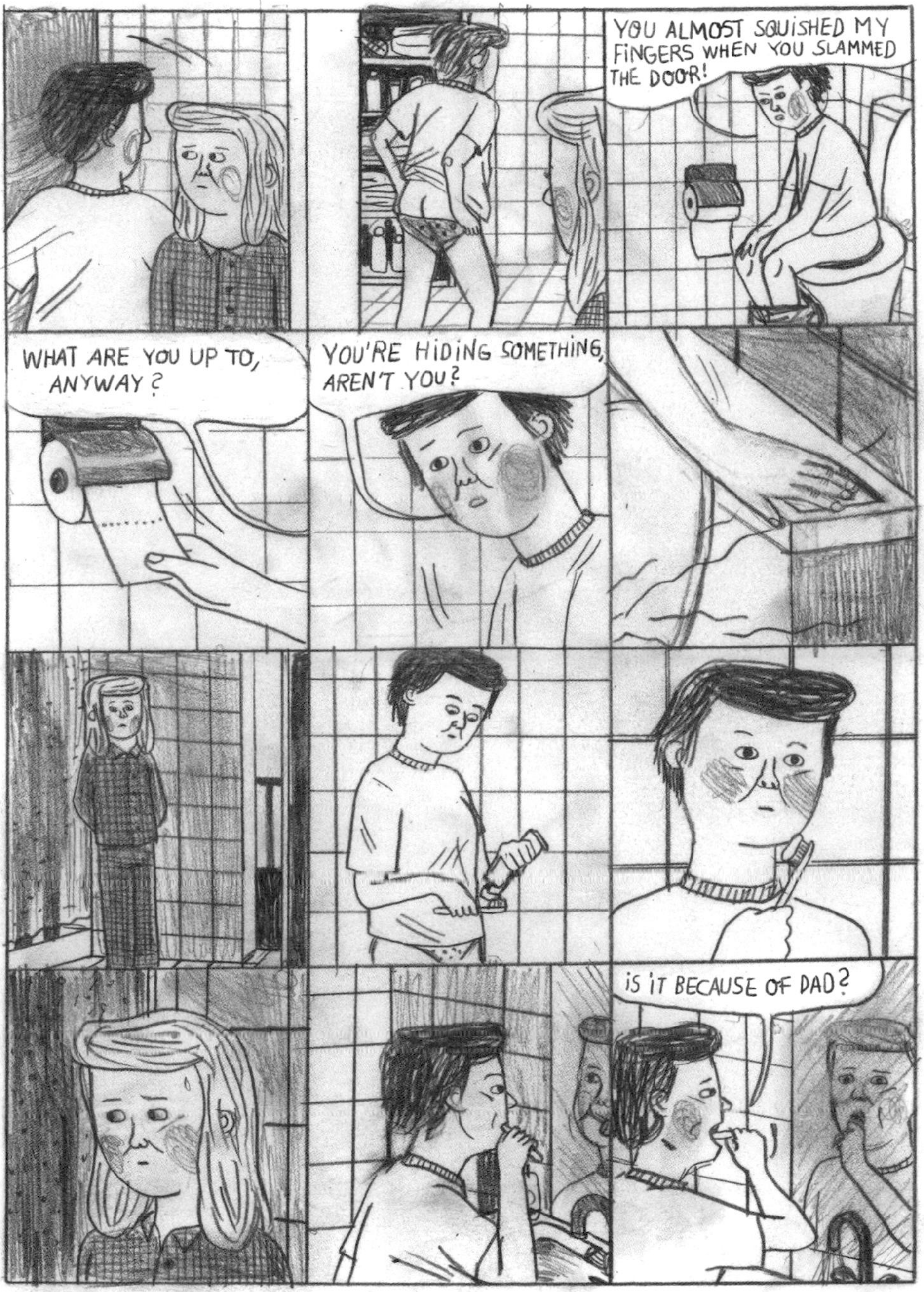
YOU ALMOST SQUISHED MY FINGERS WHEN YOU SLAMMED THE DOOR!
WHAT ARE YOU UP TO, ANYWAY?
YOU'RE HIDING SOMETHING, AREN'T YOU?
IS IT BECAUSE OF DAD?

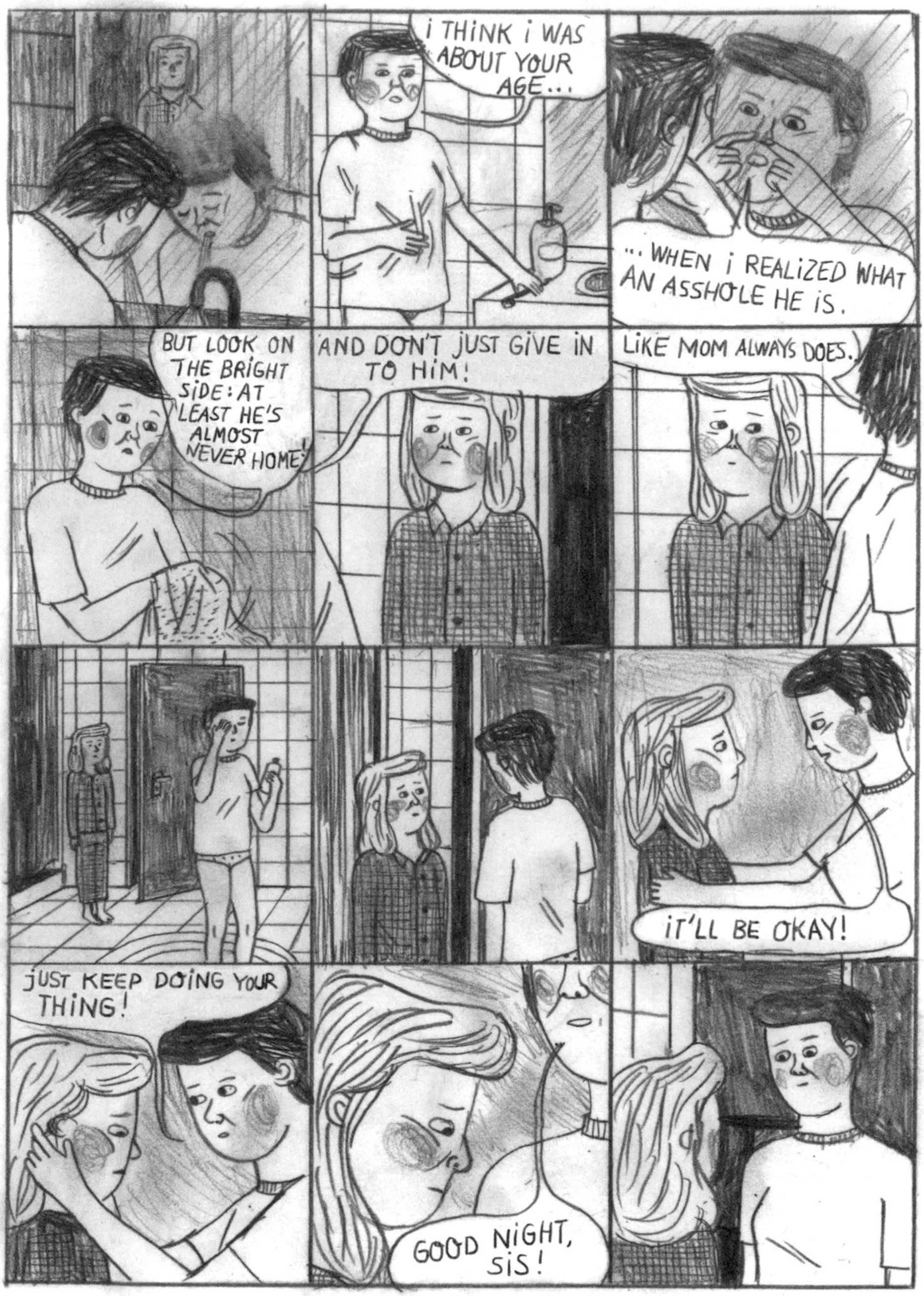
I THINK I WAS ABOUT YOUR AGE...
...WHEN I REALIZED WHAT AN ASSHOLE HE IS.
BUT LOOK ON THE BRIGHT SIDE: AT LEAST HE'S ALMOST NEVER HOME!
AND DON'T JUST GIVE IN TO HIM!
LIKE MOM ALWAYS DOES.
IT'LL BE OKAY!
JUST KEEP DOING YOUR THING!
GOOD NIGHT, SIS!

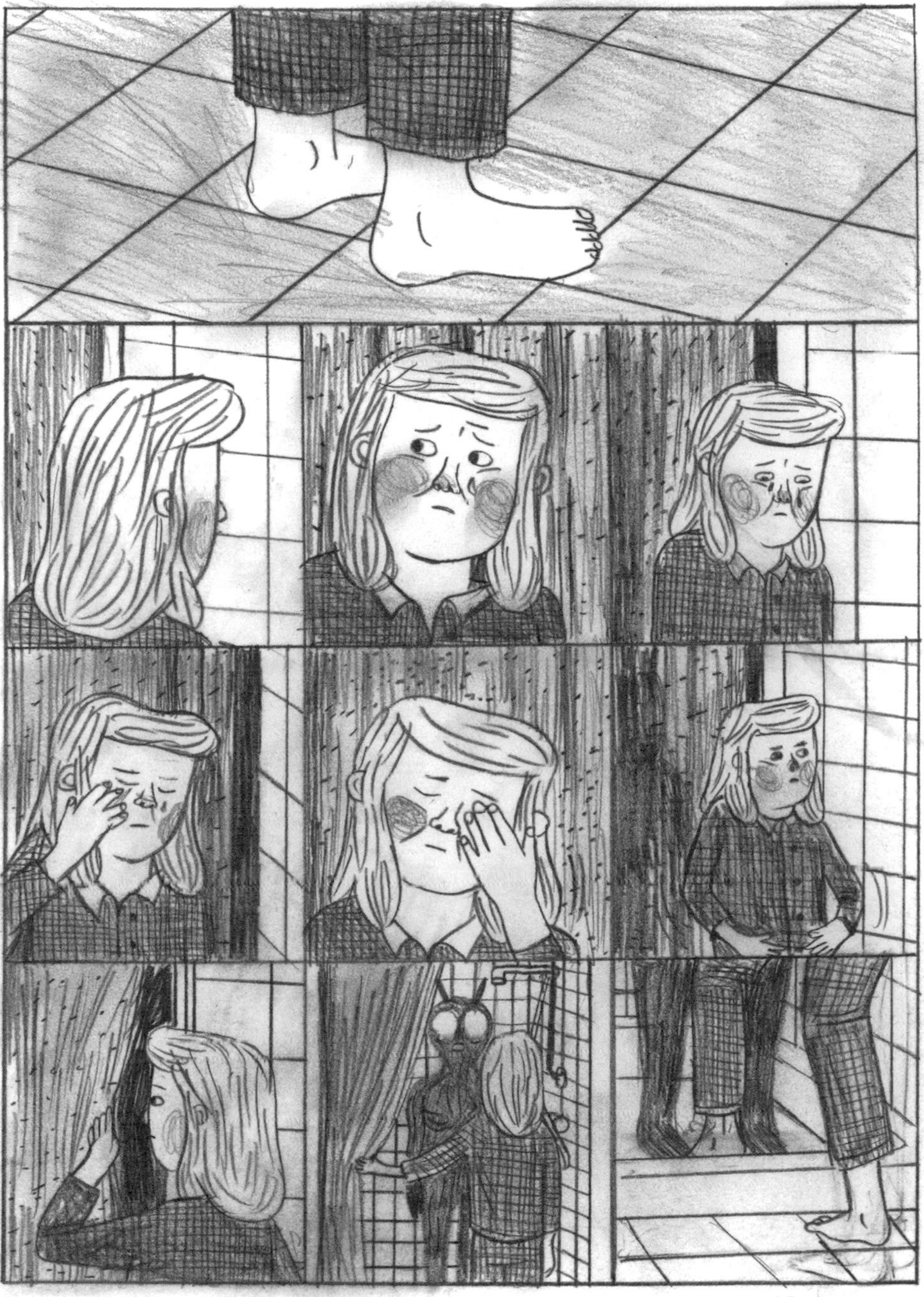

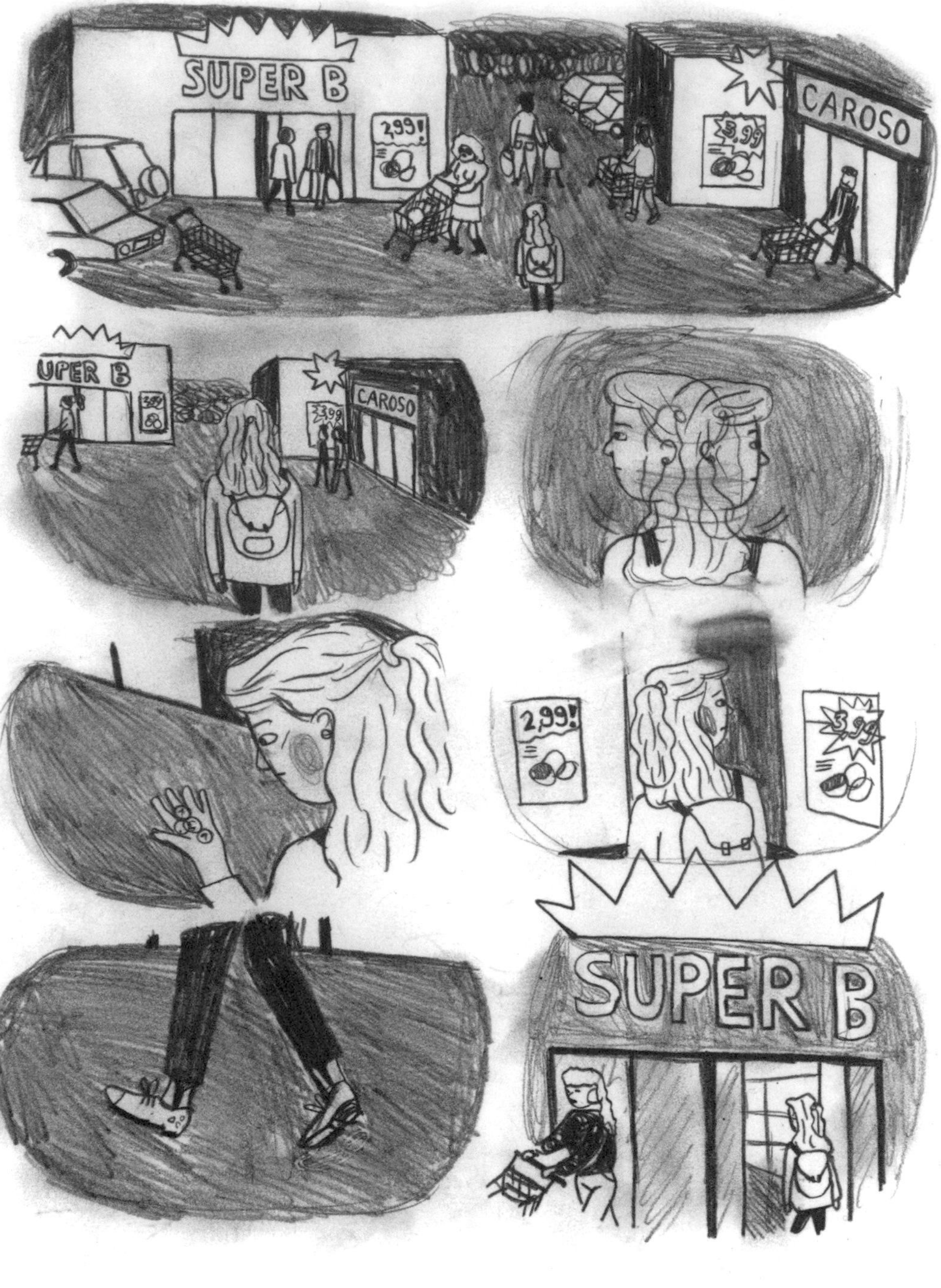
SUPER B
2,99!
3,99
CAROSO
SUPER B
CAROSO
2,99!
3,99
SUPER B

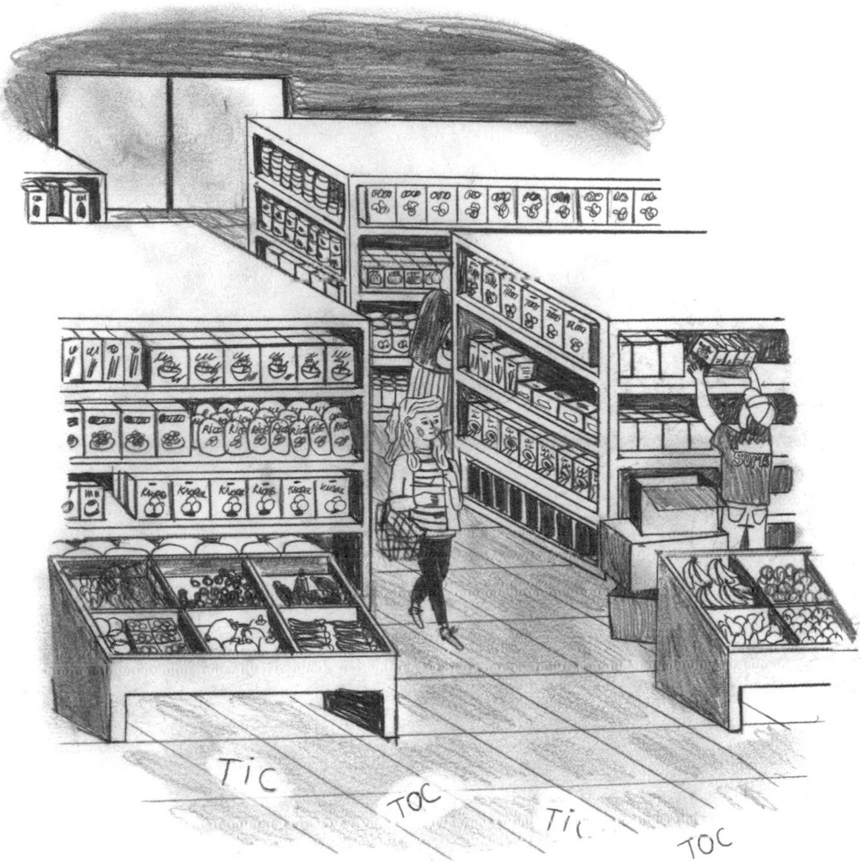
TIC
TOC
TIC
TOC

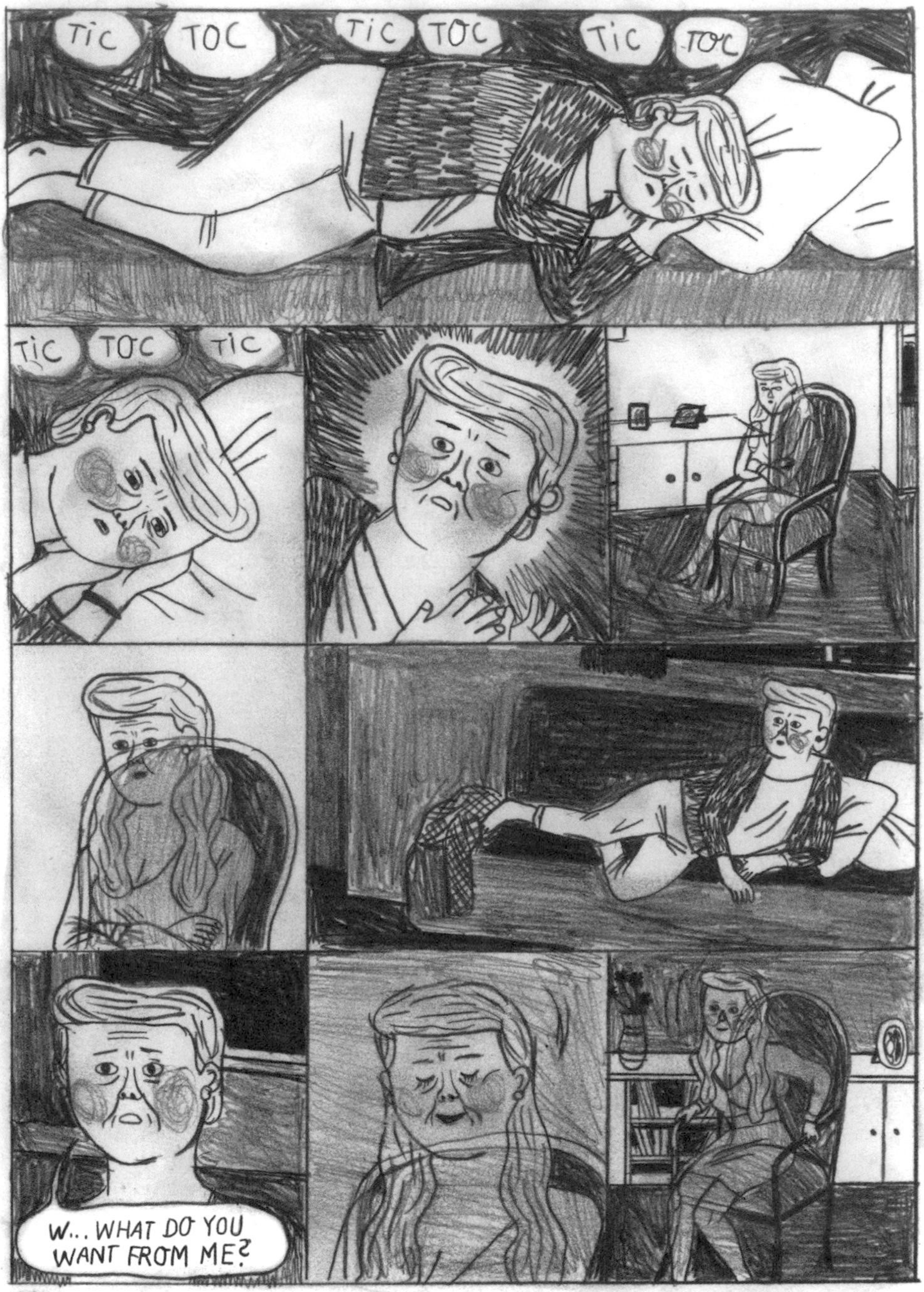
TIC
TOC
TIC
TOC
TIC
TOC
TIC
TOC
TIC
W... WHAT DO YOU WANT FROM ME?

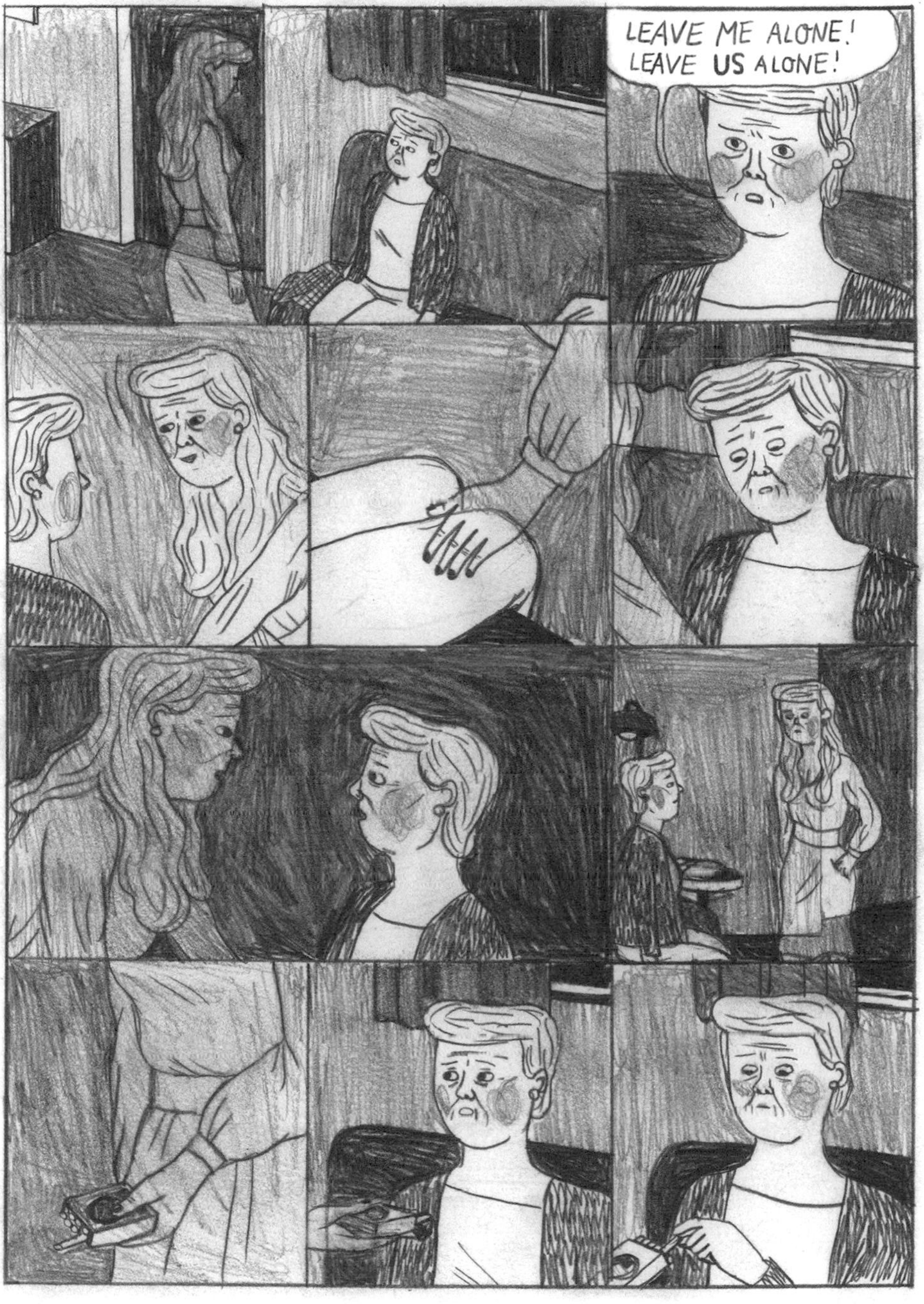
LEAVE ME ALONE!
LEAVE US ALONE!

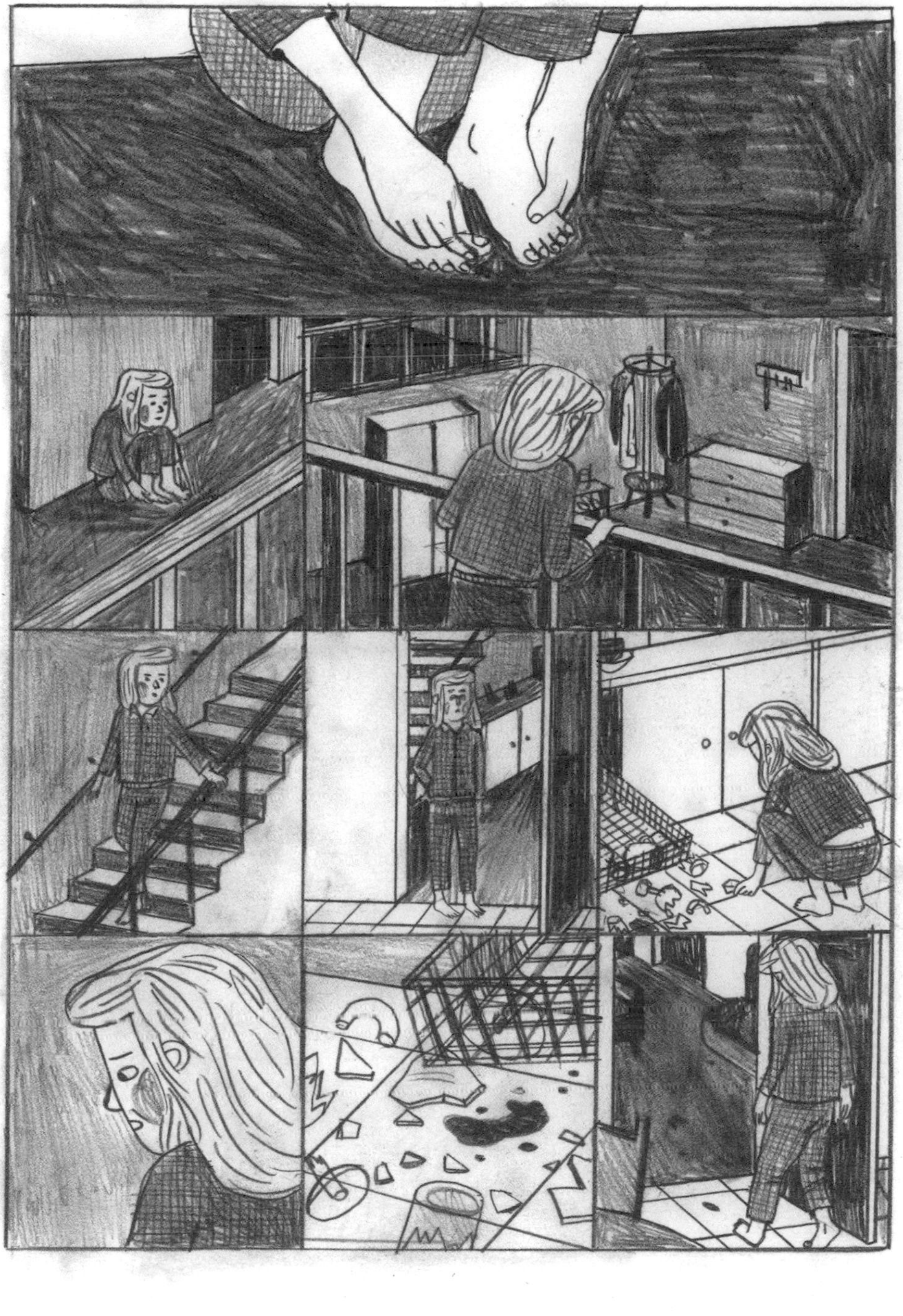

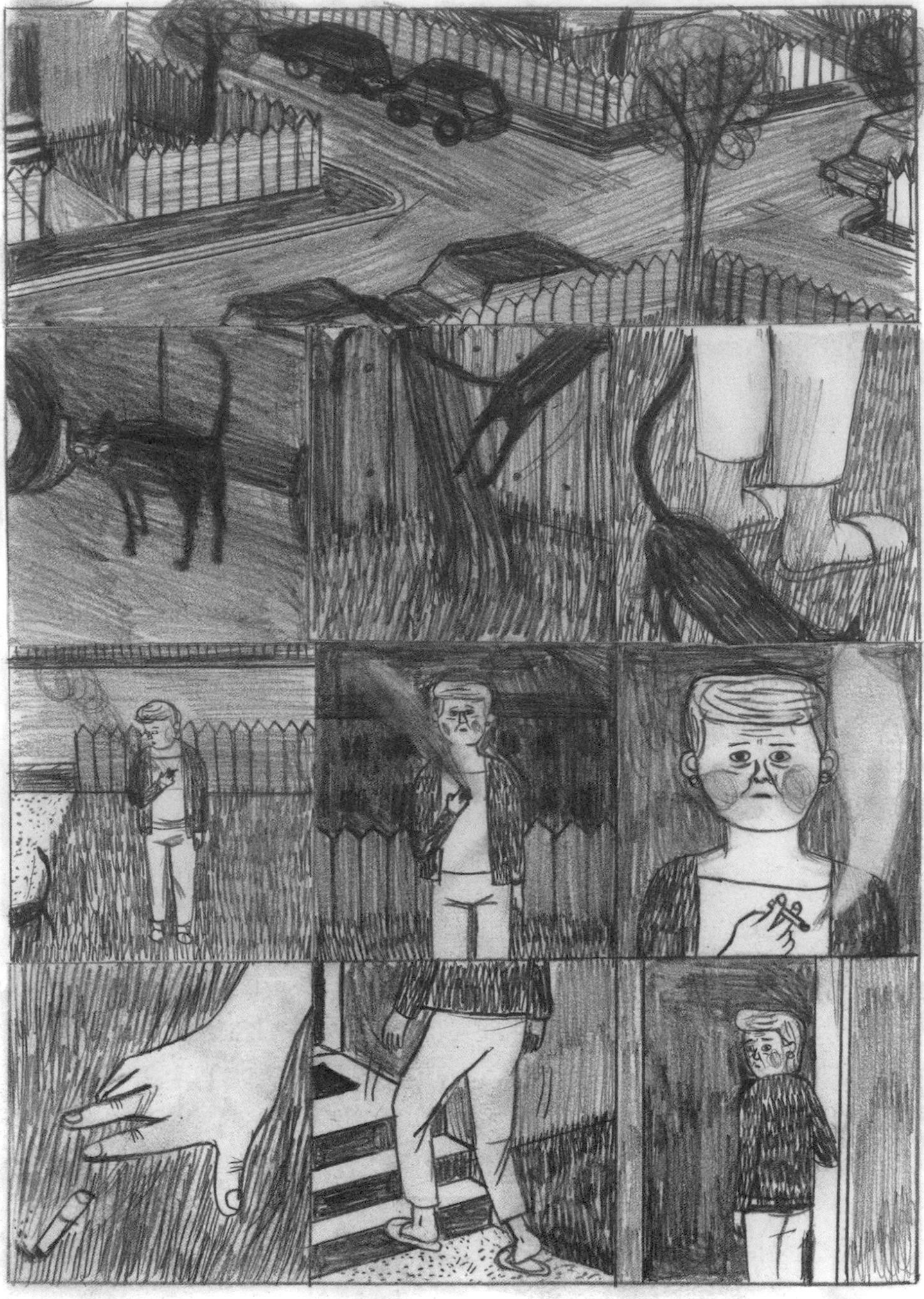

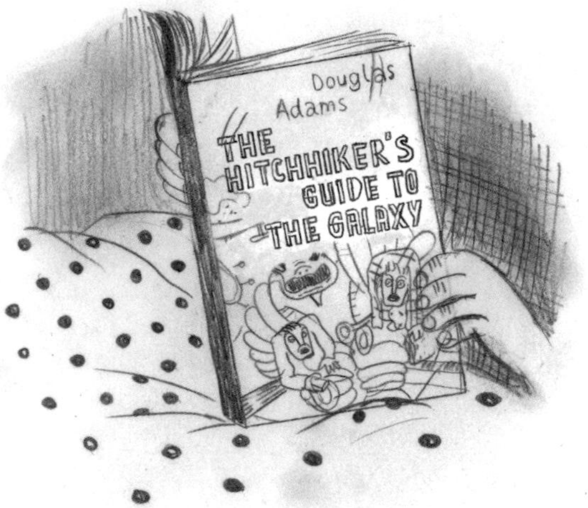
Douglas
Adams
THE
HITCHHIKER'S
GUIDE TO
THE GALAXY

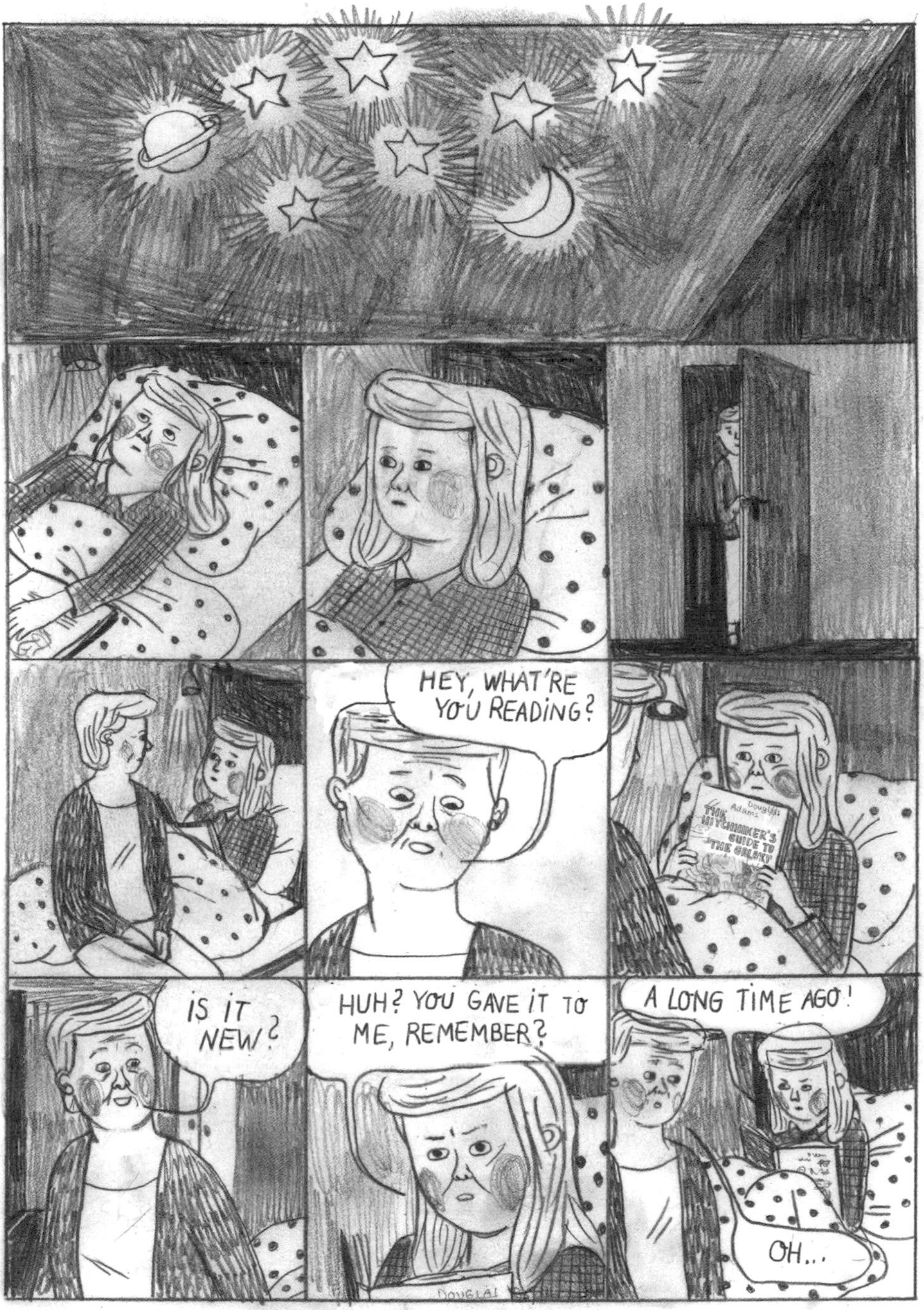
HEY, WHAT'RE YOU READING?
IS IT NEW?
HUH? YOU GAVE IT TO ME, REMEMBER?
A LONG TIME AGO!
OH...

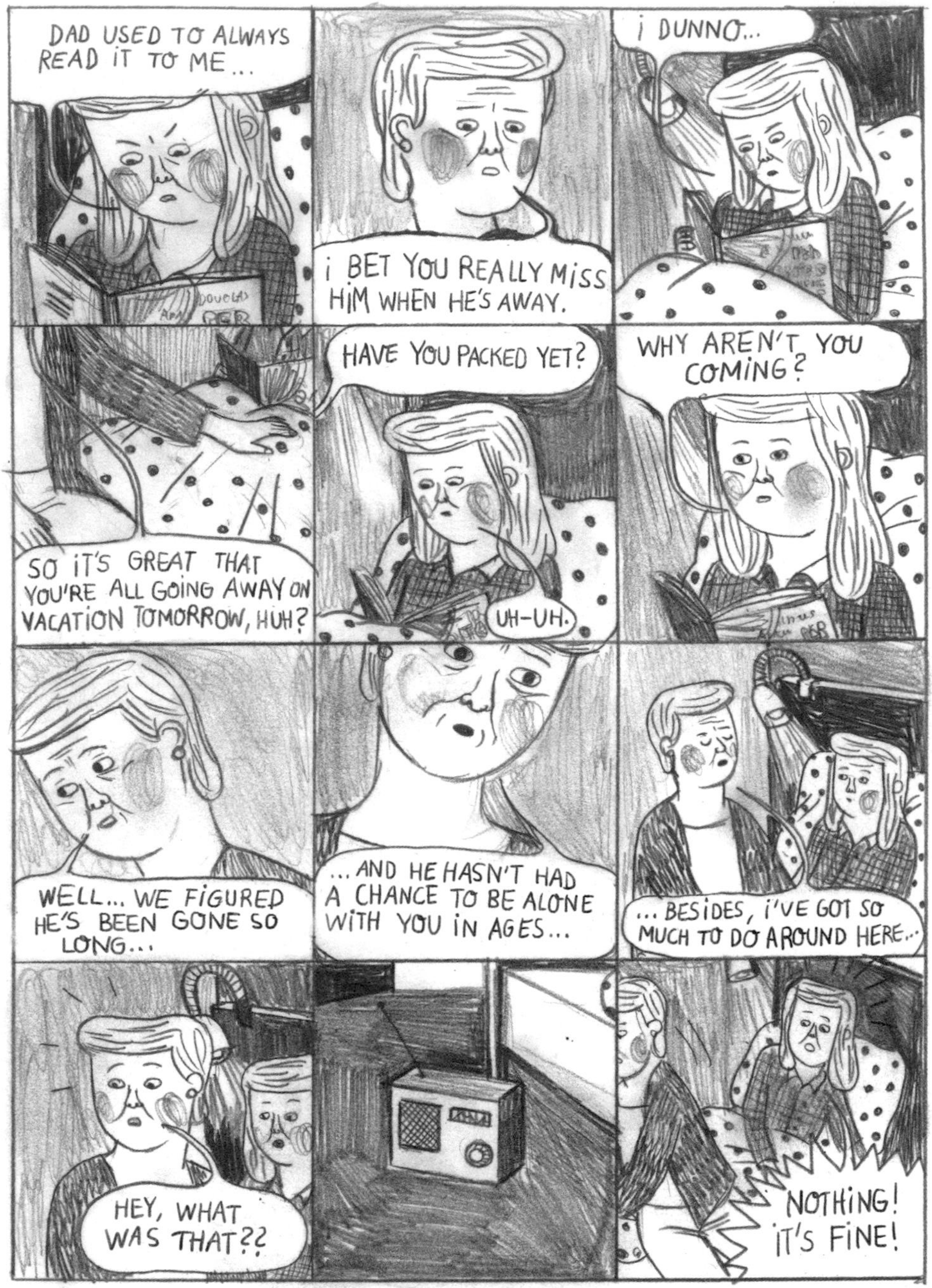
DAD USED TO ALWAYS READ IT TO ME...
I BET YOU REALLY MISS HIM WHEN HE'S AWAY.
I DUNNO...
SO IT'S GREAT THAT YOU'RE ALL GOING AWAY ON VACATION TOMORROW, HUH?
HAVE YOU PACKED YET?
UH-UH.
WHY AREN'T YOU COMING?
WELL... WE FIGURED HE'S BEEN GONE SO LONG...
...AND HE HASN'T HAD A CHANCE TO BE ALONE WITH YOU IN AGES...
...BESIDES, I'VE GOT SO MUCH TO DO AROUND HERE...
HEY, WHAT WAS THAT??
NOTHING! IT'S FINE!

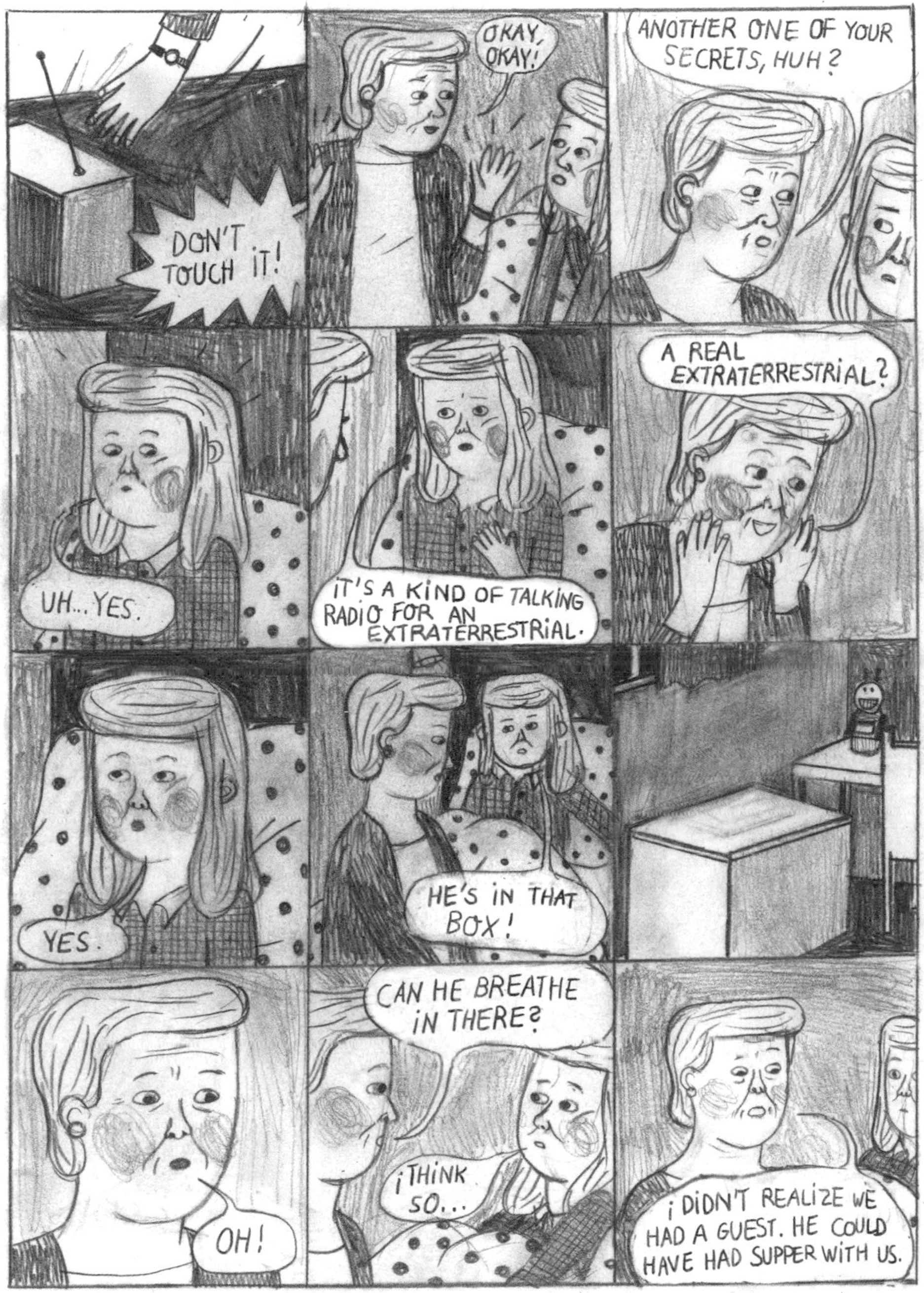
DON'T TOUCH IT!
OKAY, OKAY!
ANOTHER ONE OF YOUR SECRETS, HUH?
UH... YES.
IT'S A KIND OF TALKING RADIO FOR AN EXTRATERRESTRIAL.
A REAL EXTRATERRESTRIAL?
YES.
HE'S IN THAT BOX!
OH!
CAN HE BREATHE IN THERE?
I THINK SO...
I DIDN'T REALIZE WE HAD A GUEST. HE COULD HAVE HAD SUPPER WITH US.

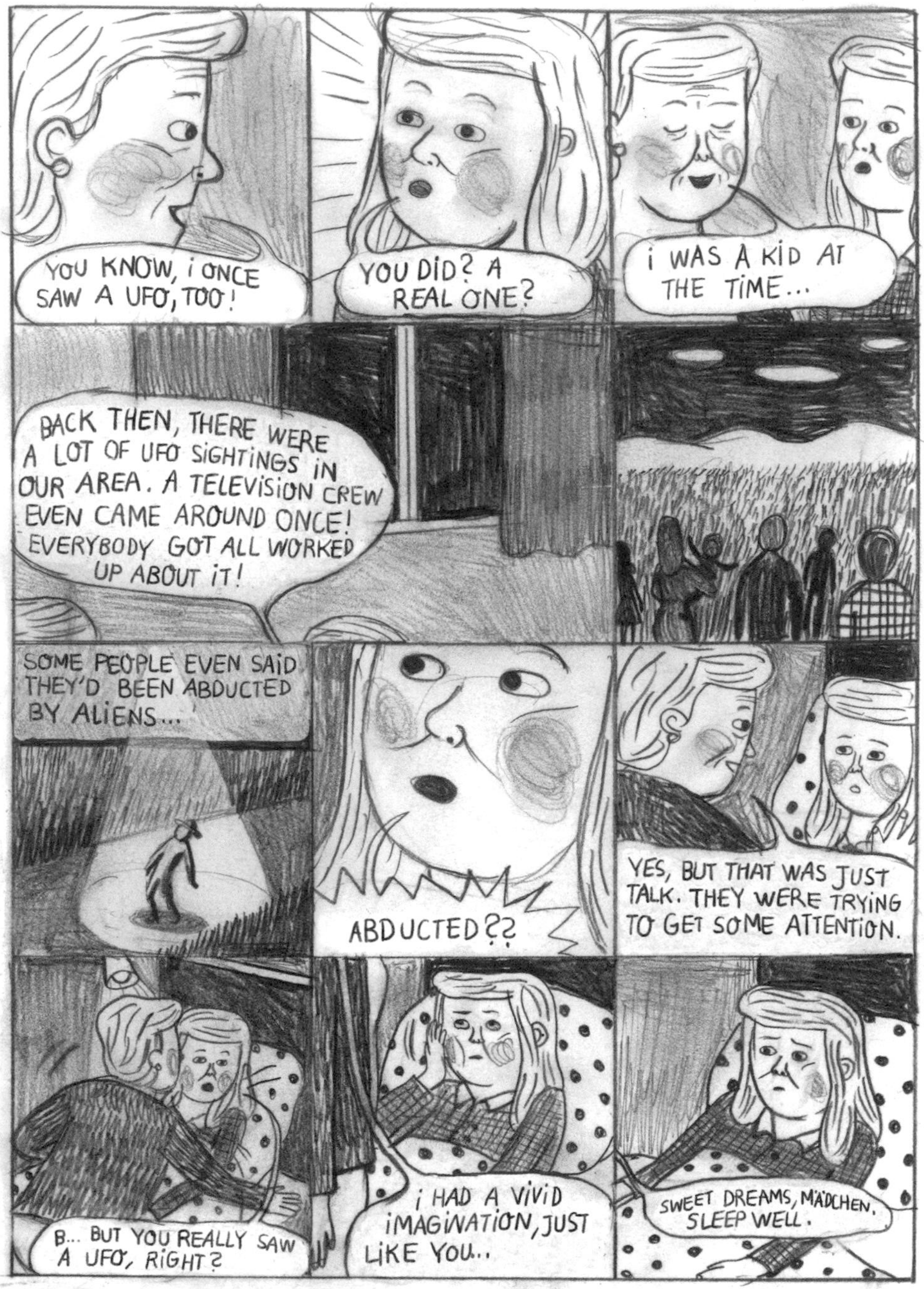
YOU KNOW, I ONCE SAW A UFO, TOO!
YOU DID? A REAL ONE?
I WAS A KID AT THE TIME...
BACK THEN, THERE WERE A LOT OF UFO SIGHTINGS IN OUR AREA. A TELEVISION CREW EVEN CAME AROUND ONCE! EVERYBODY GOT ALL WORKED UP ABOUT IT!
SOME PEOPLE EVEN SAID THEY'D BEEN ABDUCTED BY ALIENS...
ABDUCTED??
YES, BUT THAT WAS JUST TALK. THEY WERE TRYING TO GET SOME ATTENTION.
B... BUT YOU REALLY SAW A UFO, RIGHT?
I HAD A VIVID IMAGINATION, JUST LIKE YOU..
SWEET DREAMS, MÄDCHEN. SLEEP WELL.

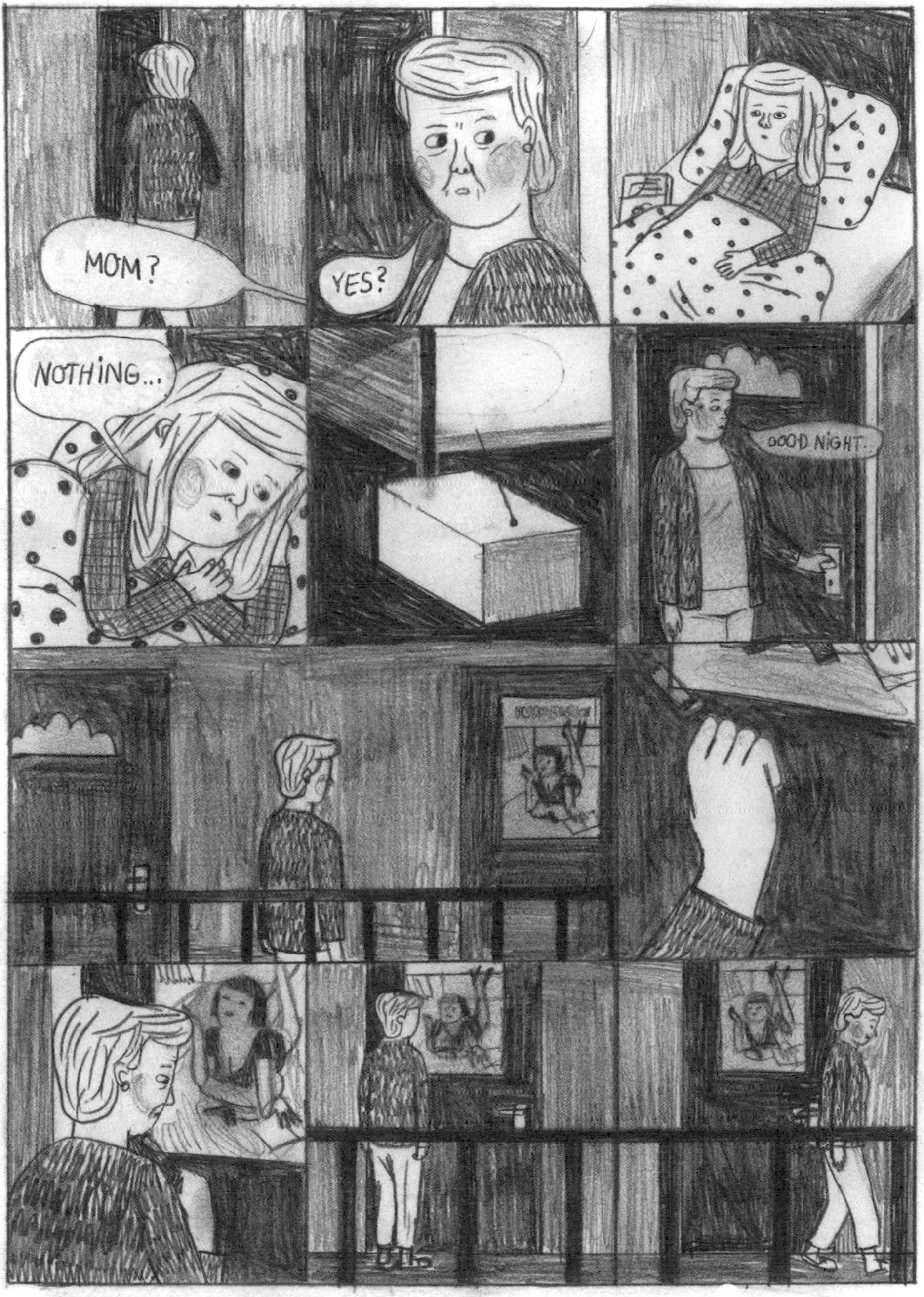
MOM?
YES?
NOTHING...
GOOD NIGHT.

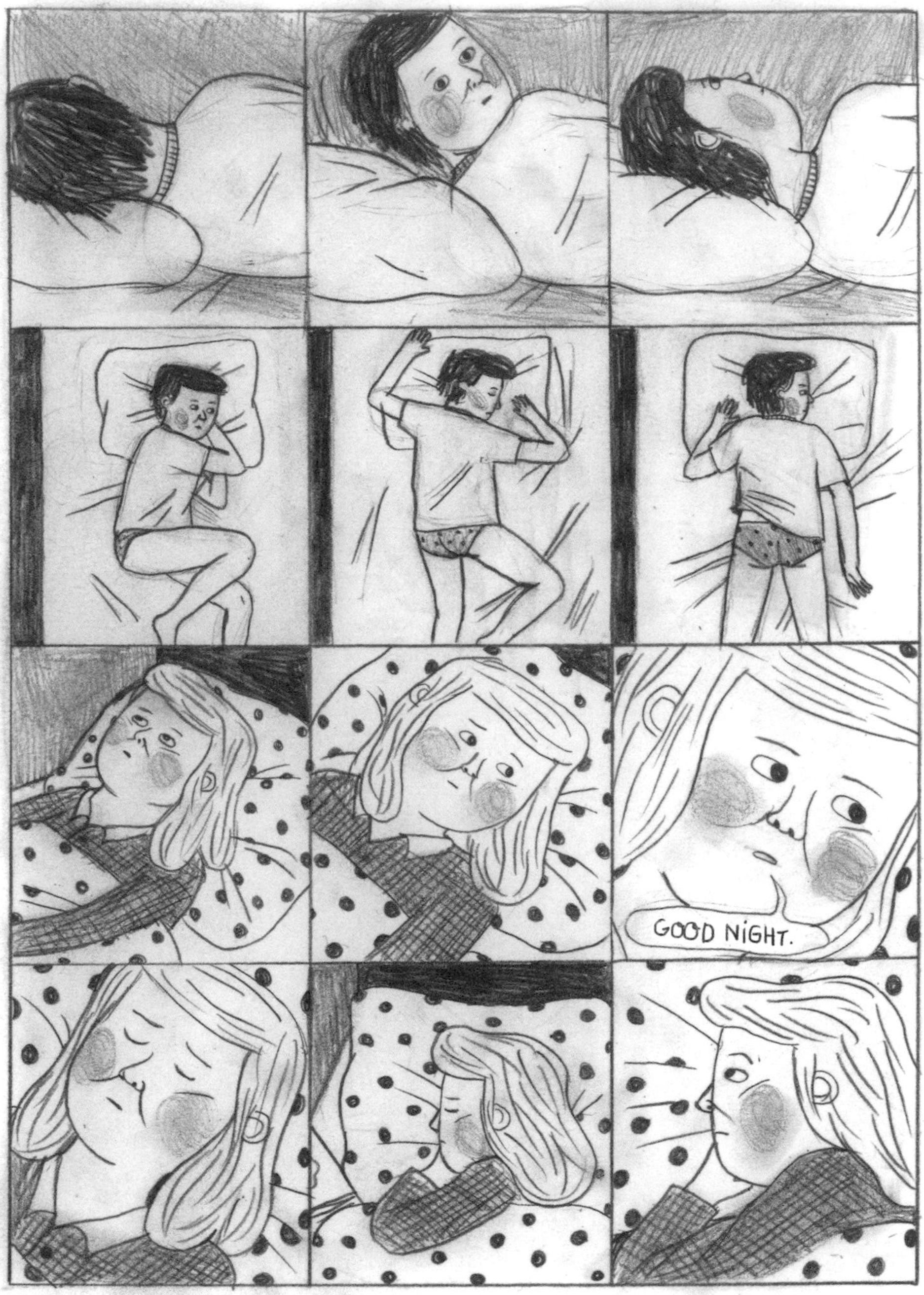
GOOD NIGHT.

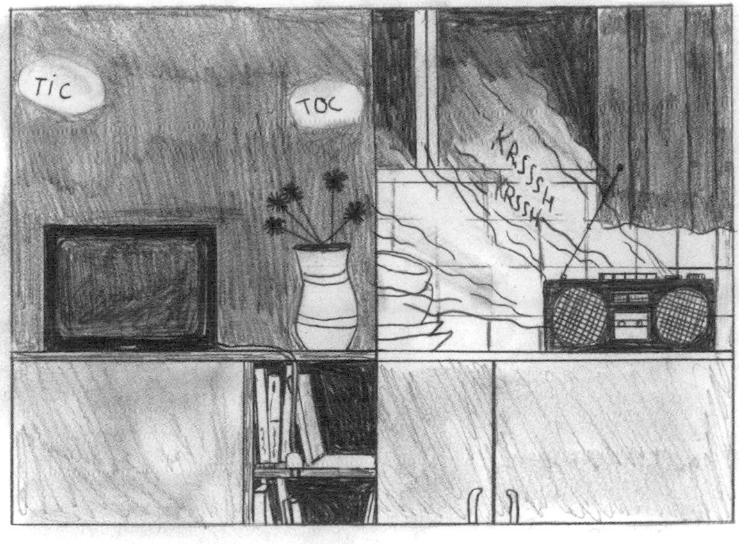
TIC
TOC
KRSSSSH
KRSSH

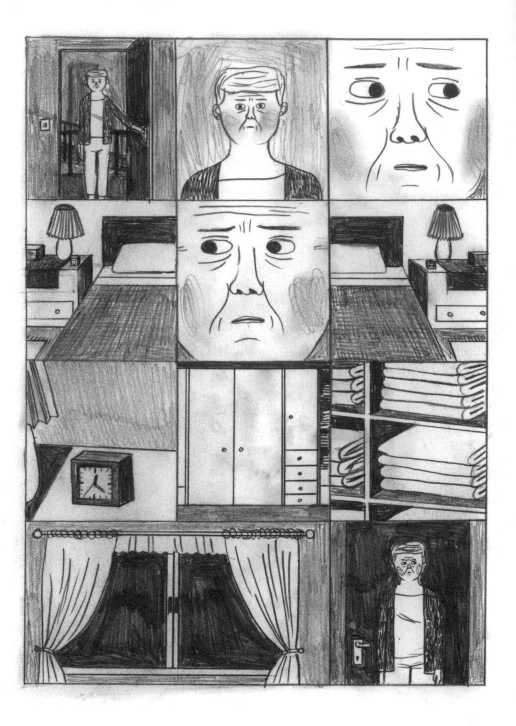

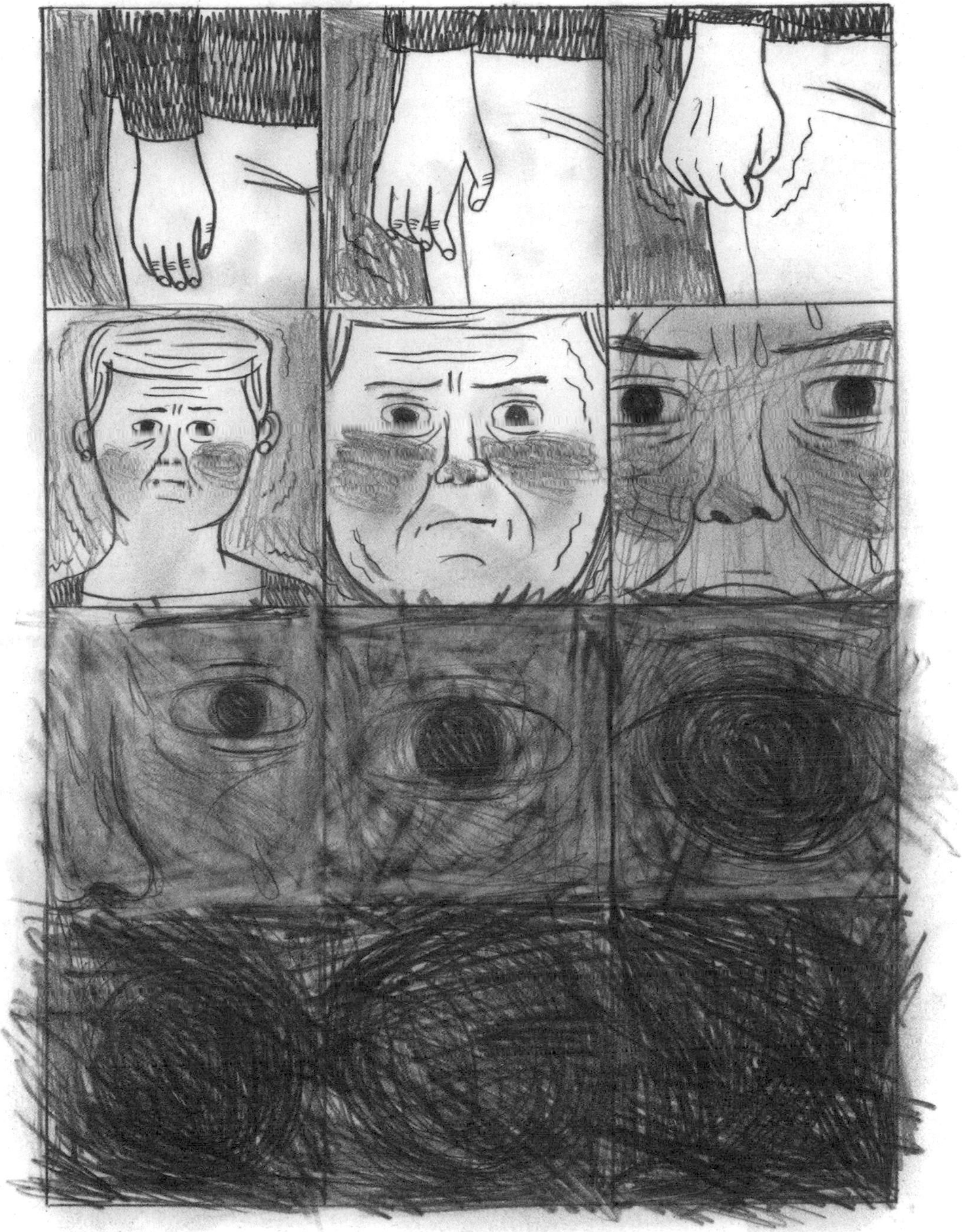

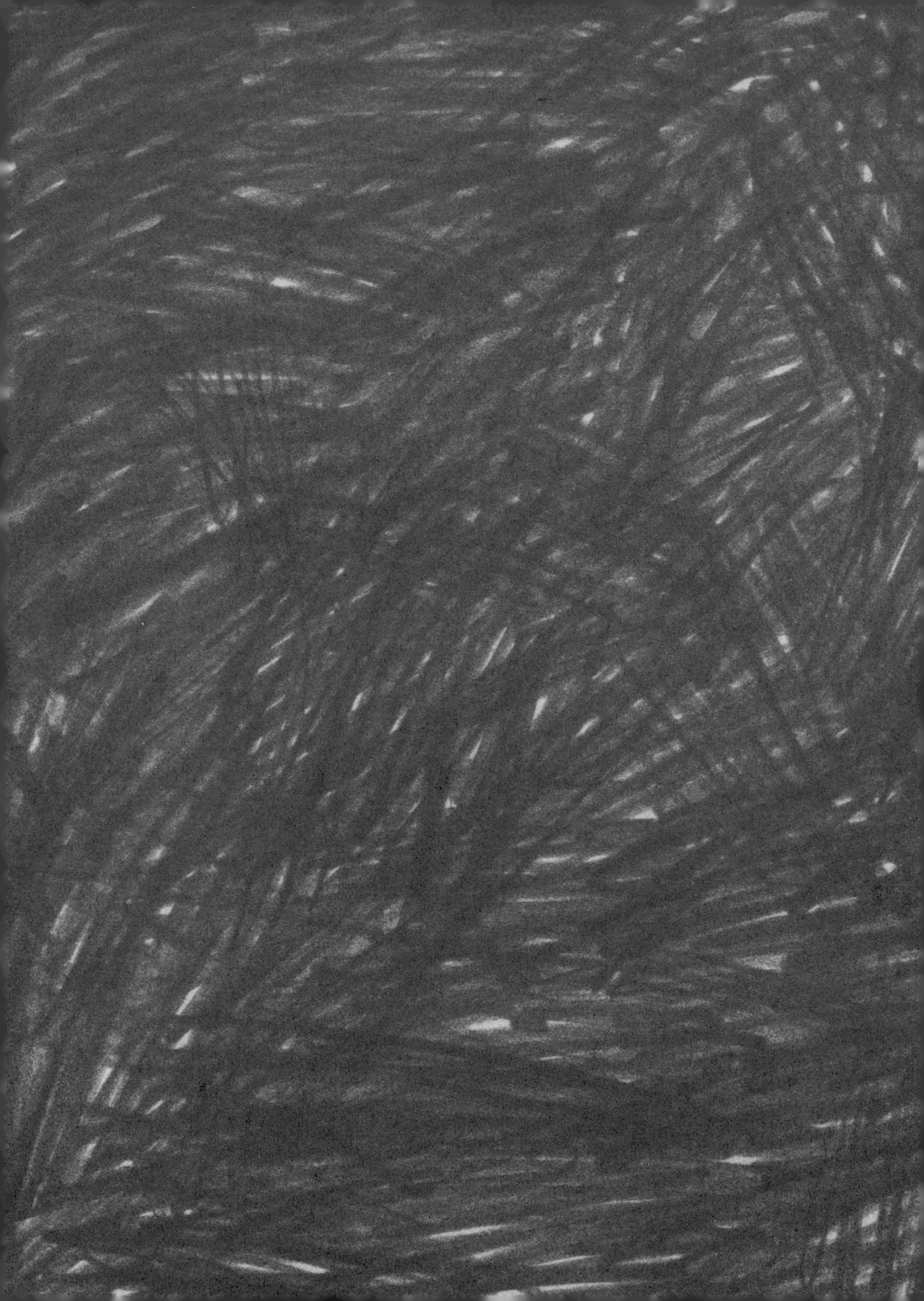

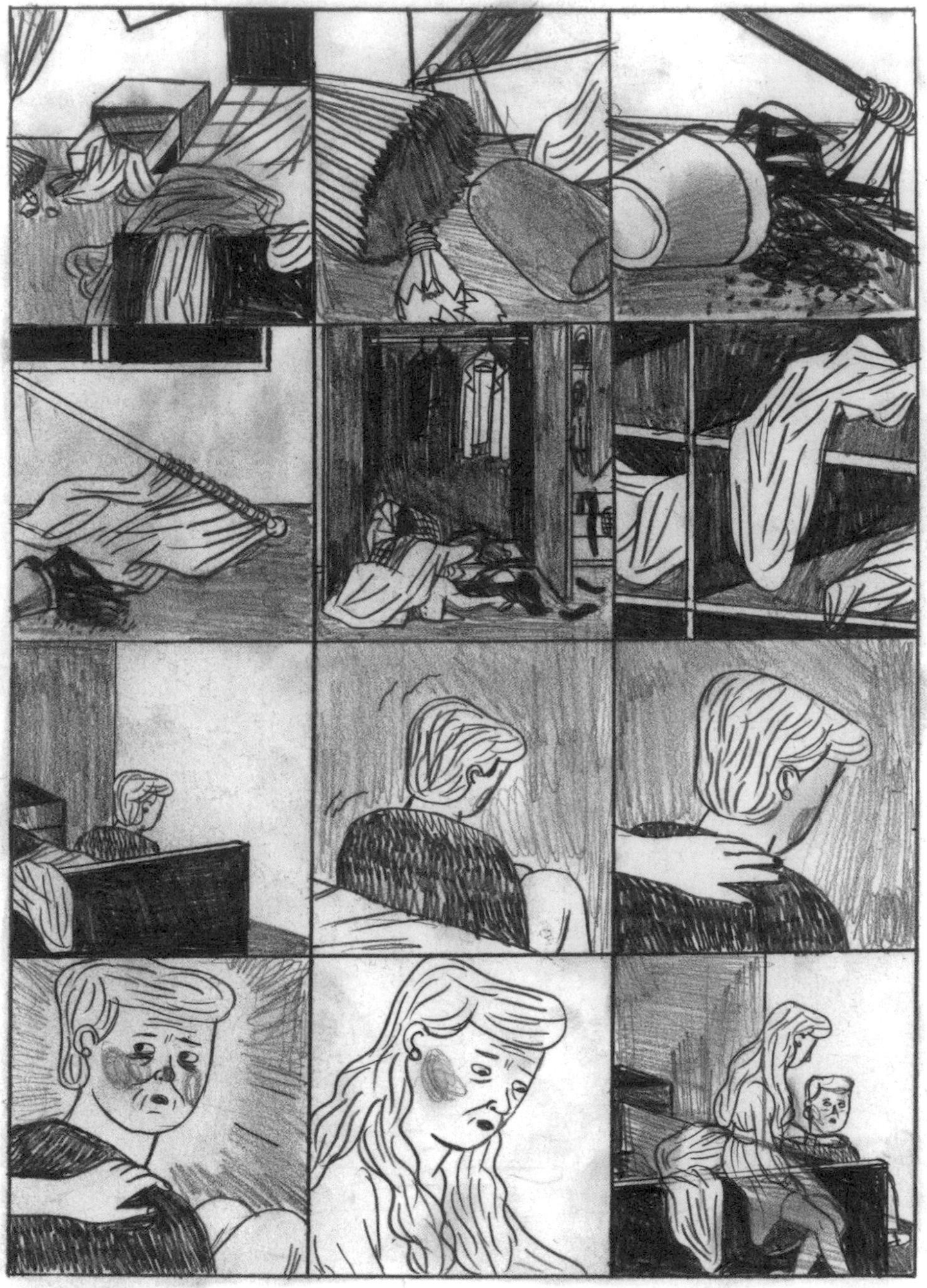

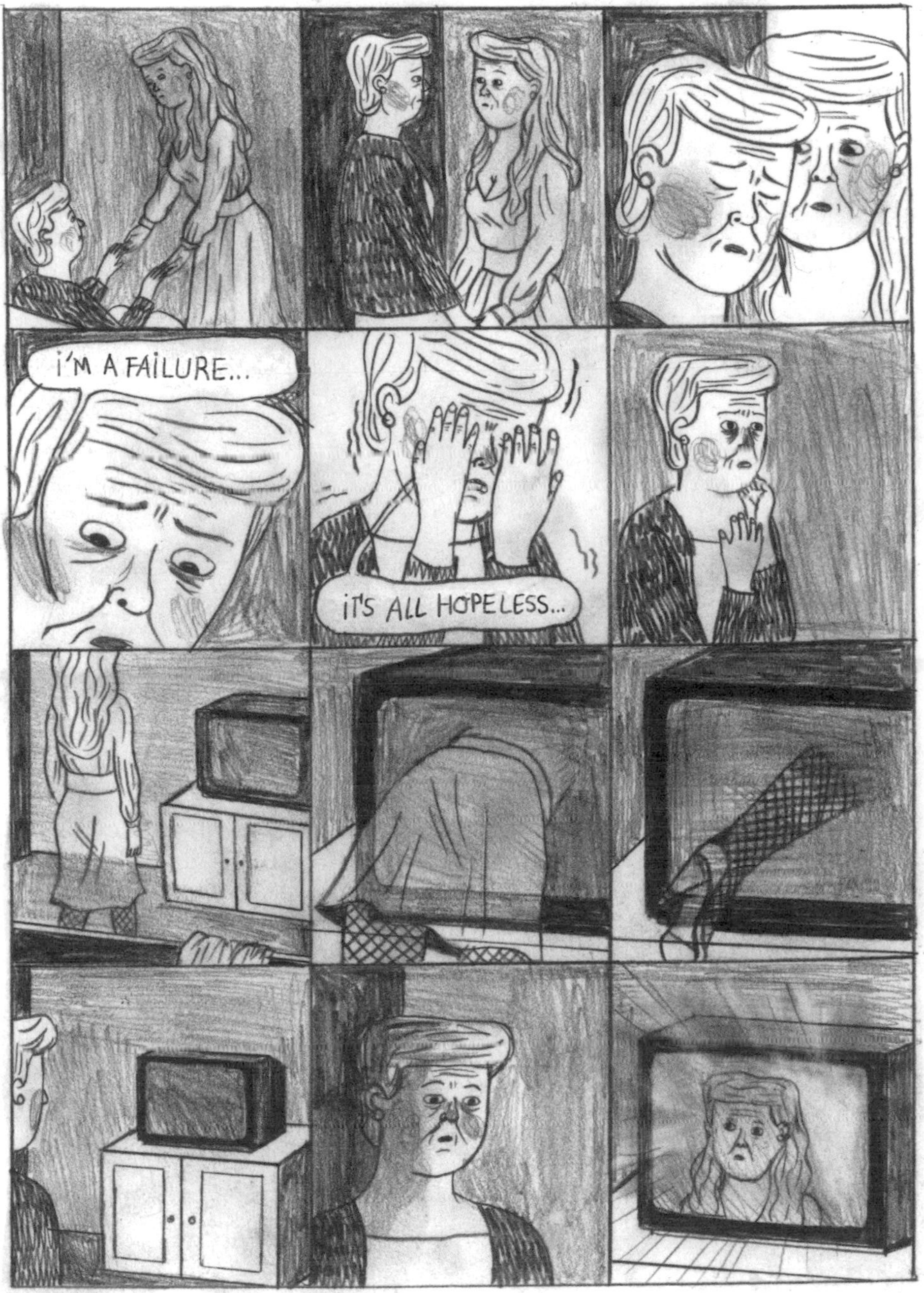
i'M A FAILURE...
iT'S ALL HOPELESS...

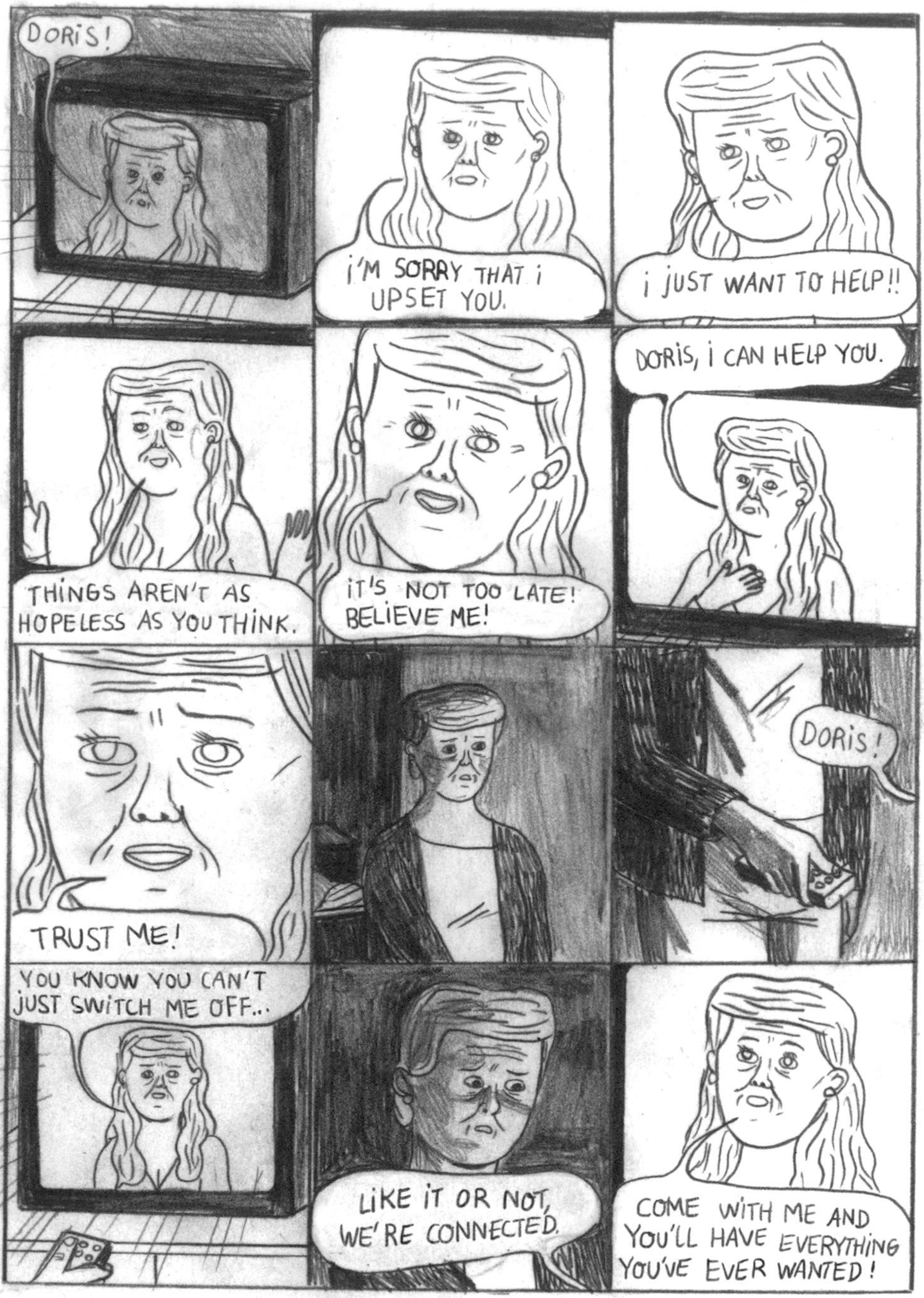
DORIS!
I'M SORRY THAT I UPSET YOU.
I JUST WANT TO HELP!!
THINGS AREN'T AS HOPELESS AS YOU THINK.
IT'S NOT TOO LATE! BELIEVE ME!
DORIS, I CAN HELP YOU.
TRUST ME!
DORIS!
YOU KNOW YOU CAN'T JUST SWITCH ME OFF...
LIKE IT OR NOT, WE'RE CONNECTED.
COME WITH ME AND YOU'LL HAVE EVERYTHING YOU'VE EVER WANTED!

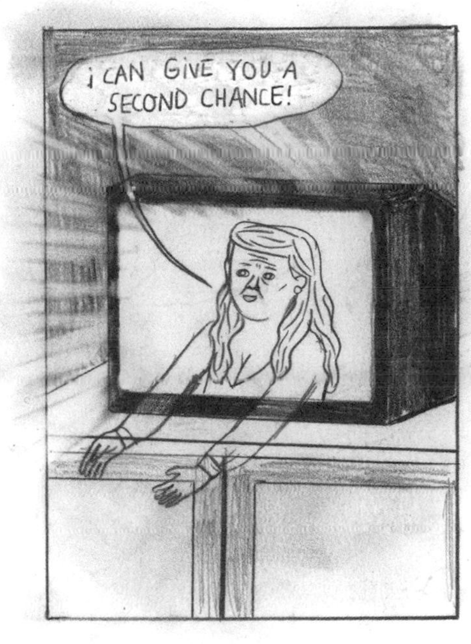
¡CAN GIVE YOU A SECOND CHANCE!

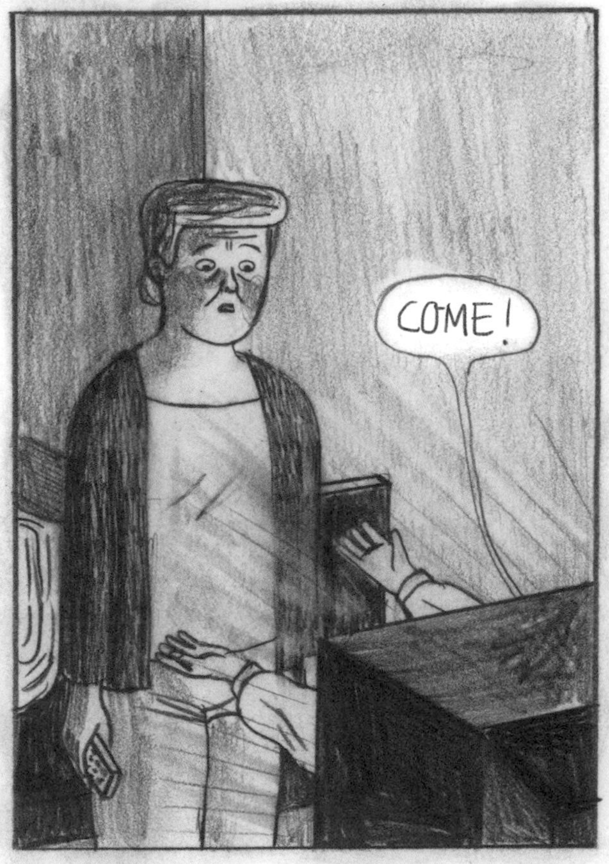
COME!

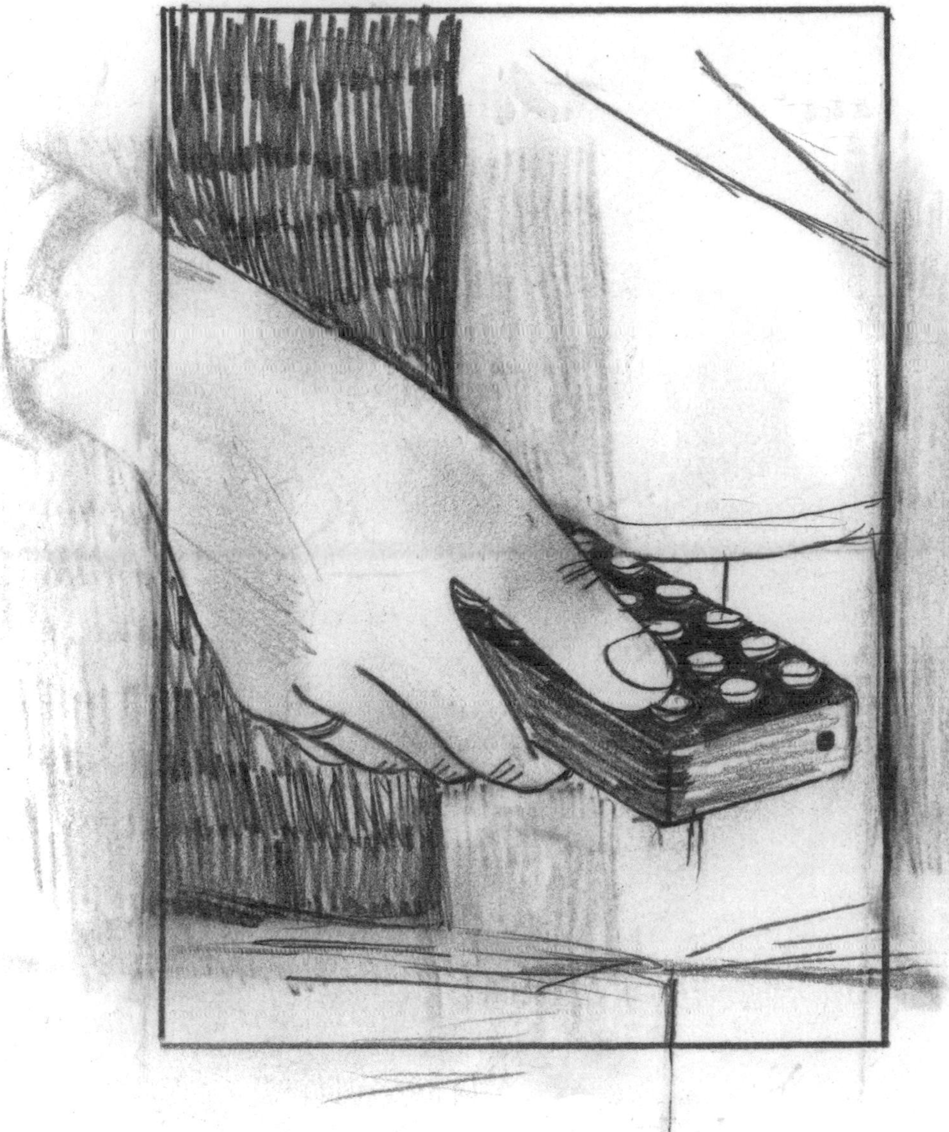

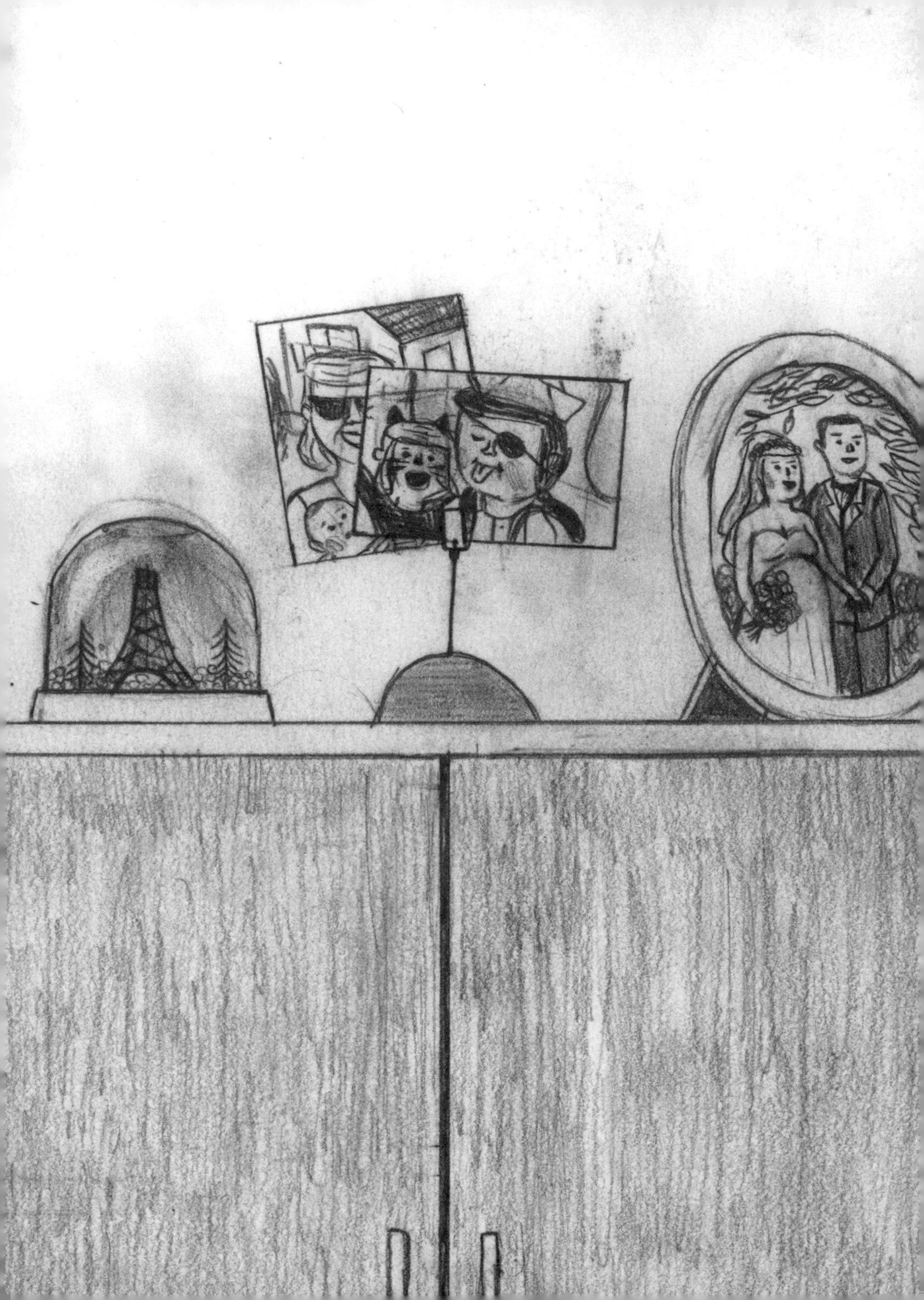

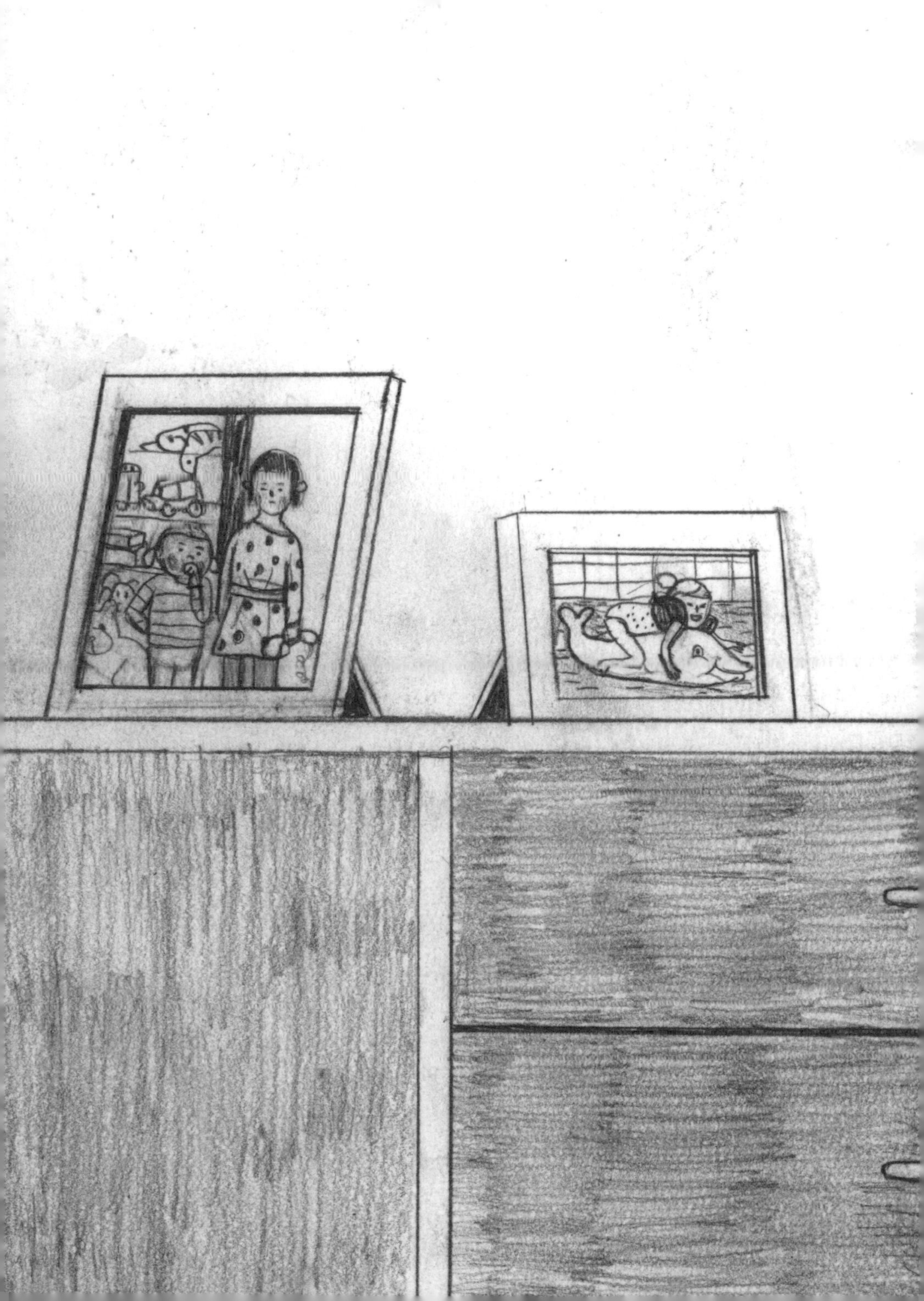

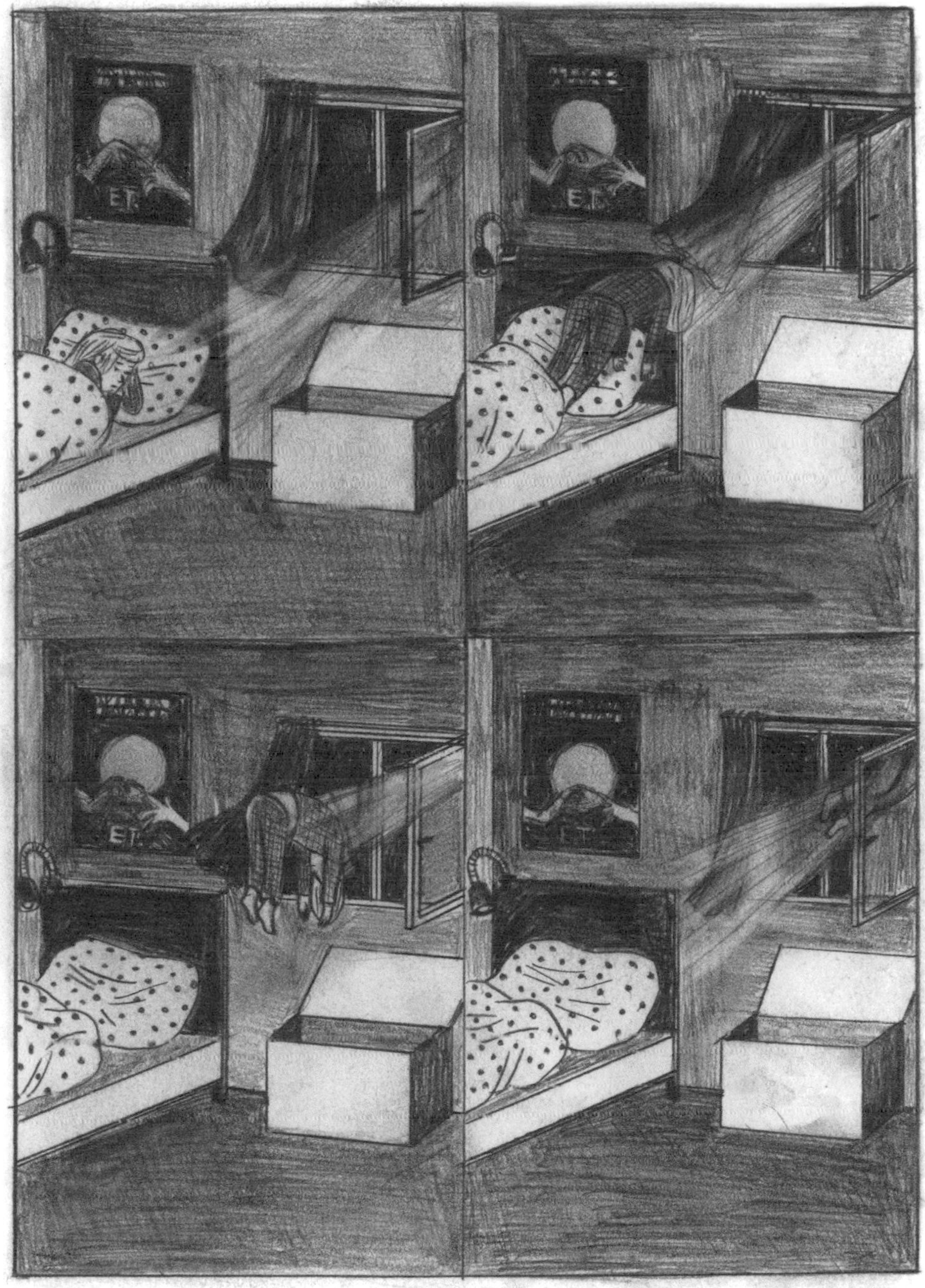
E.T.
E.T.
E.T.

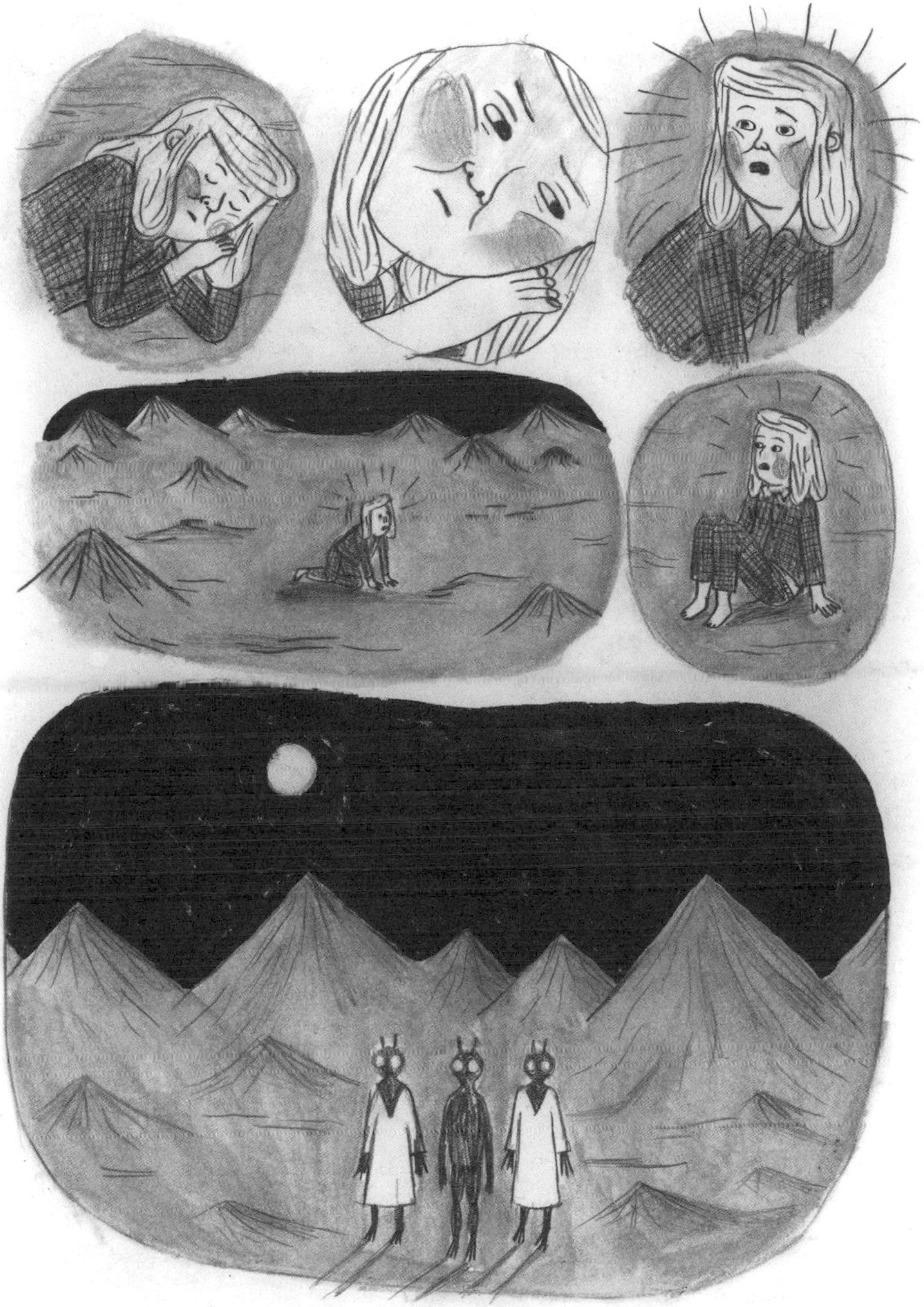

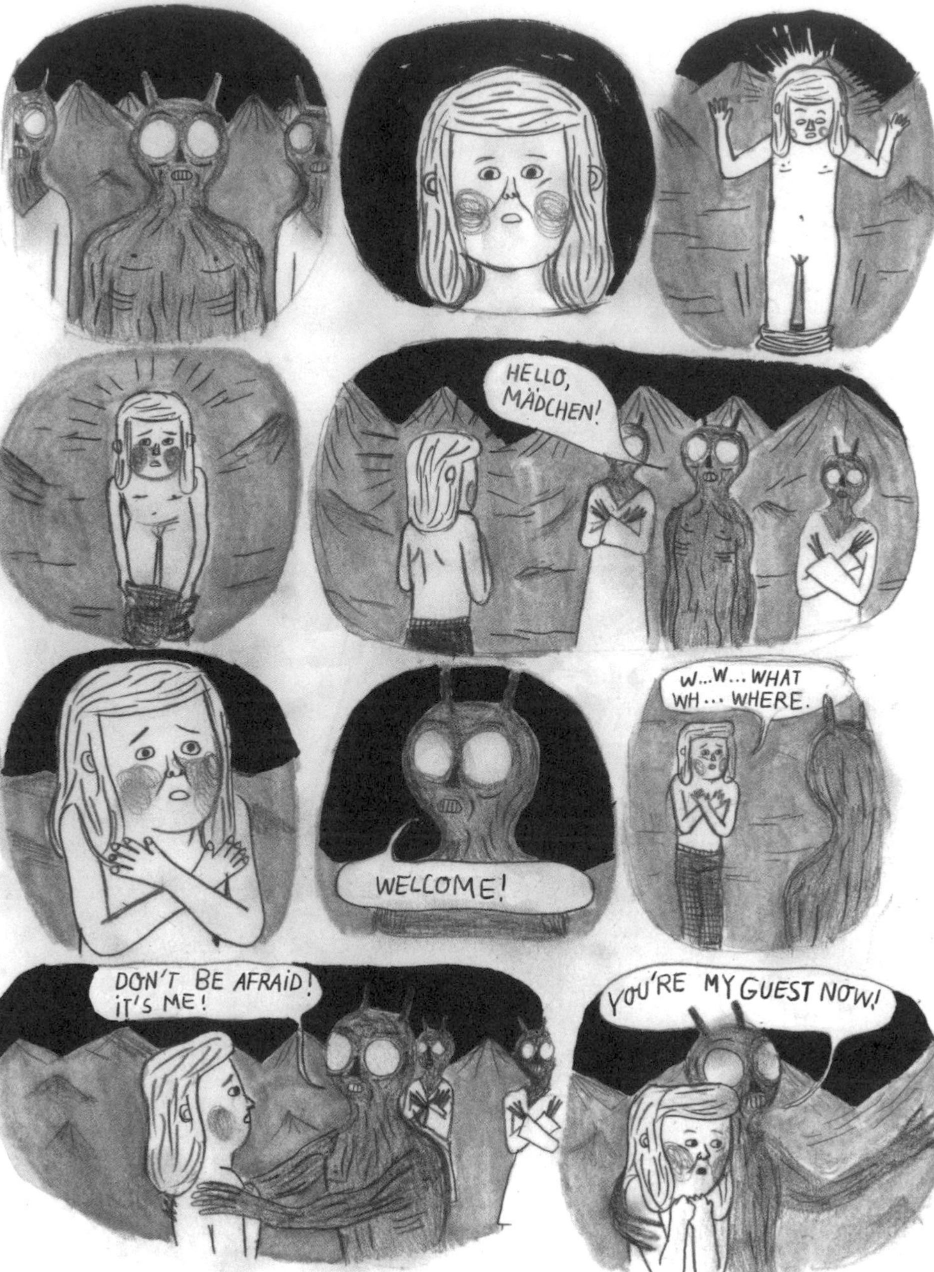
HELLO, MÄDCHEN!
WELCOME!
W...W... WHAT WH... WHERE.
DON'T BE AFRAID! IT'S ME!
YOU'RE MY GUEST NOW!

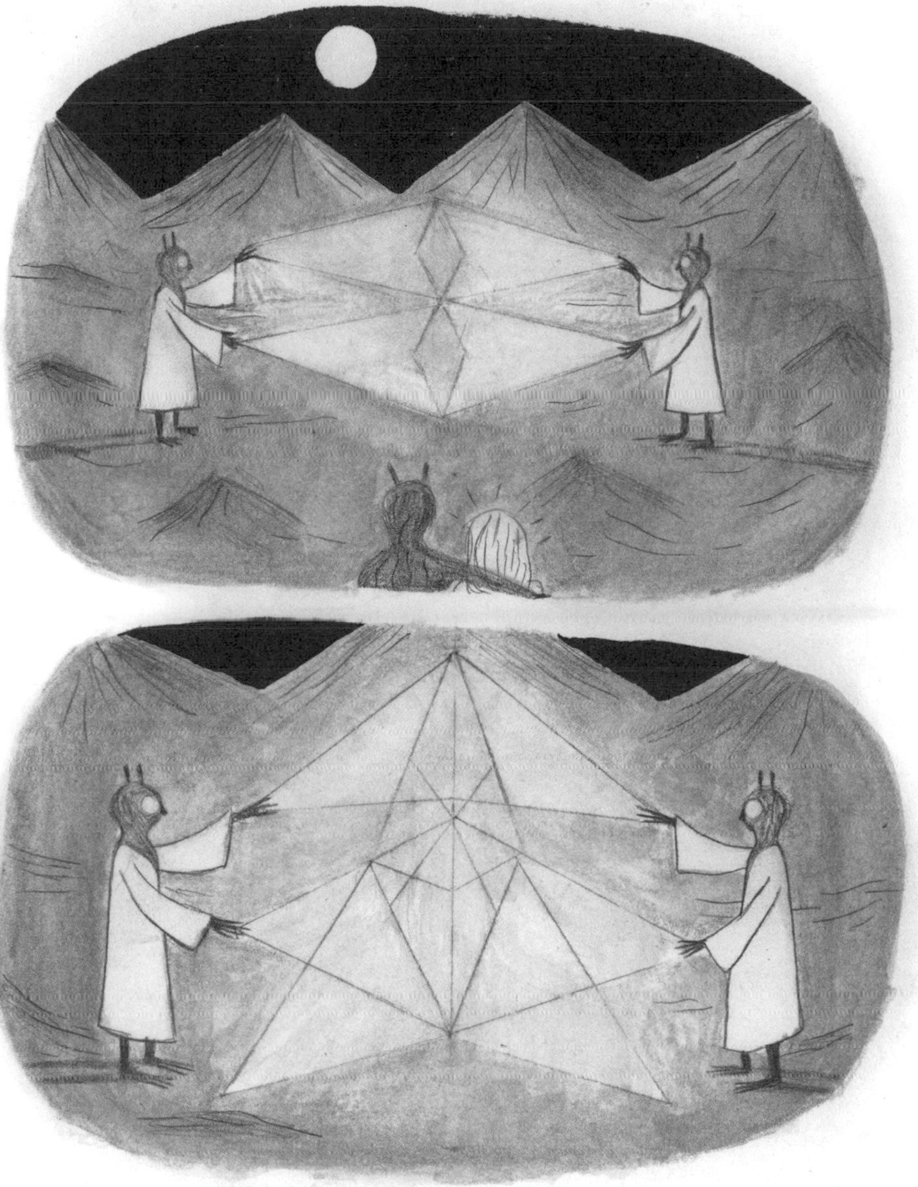

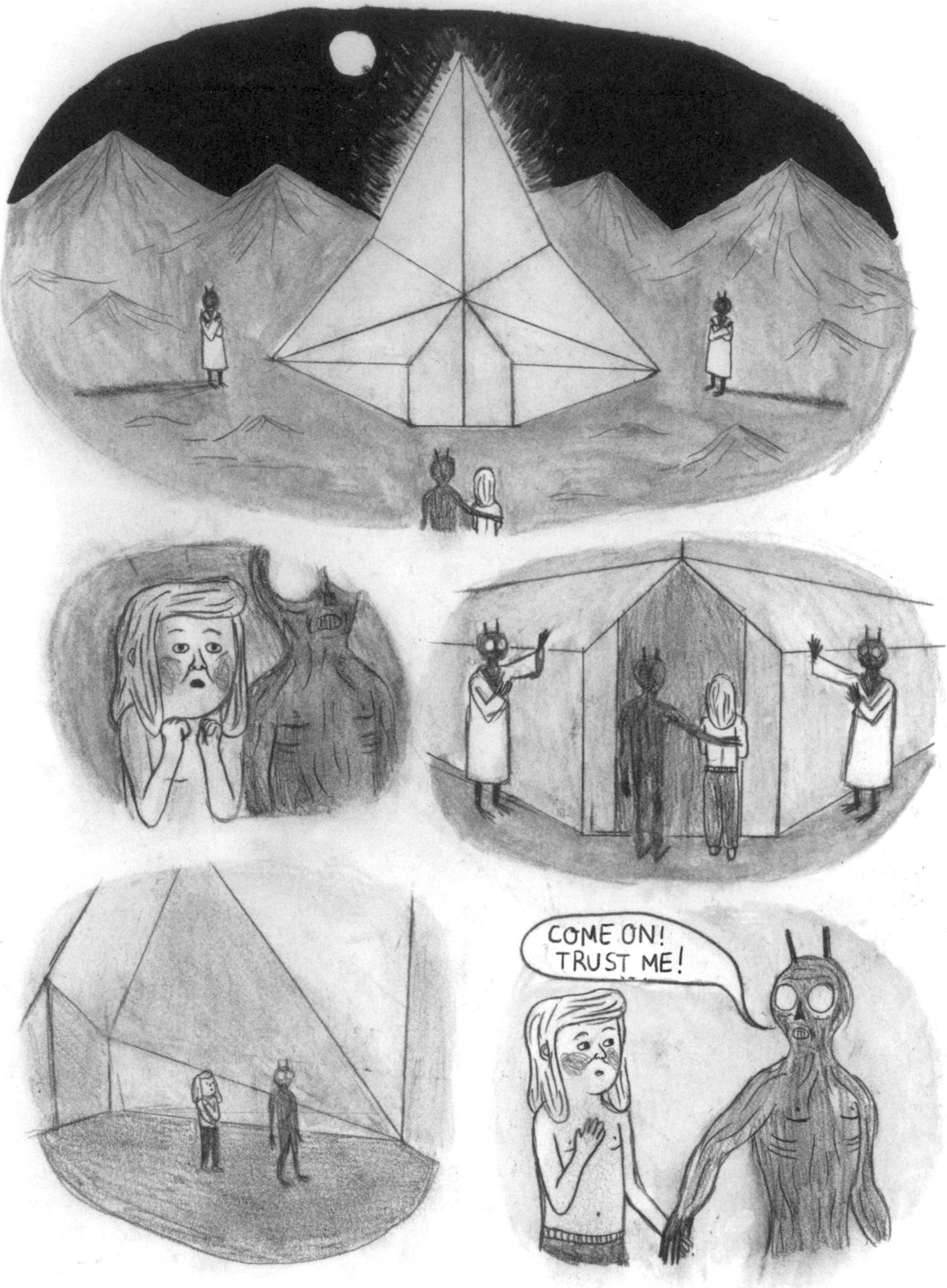
COME ON! TRUST ME!

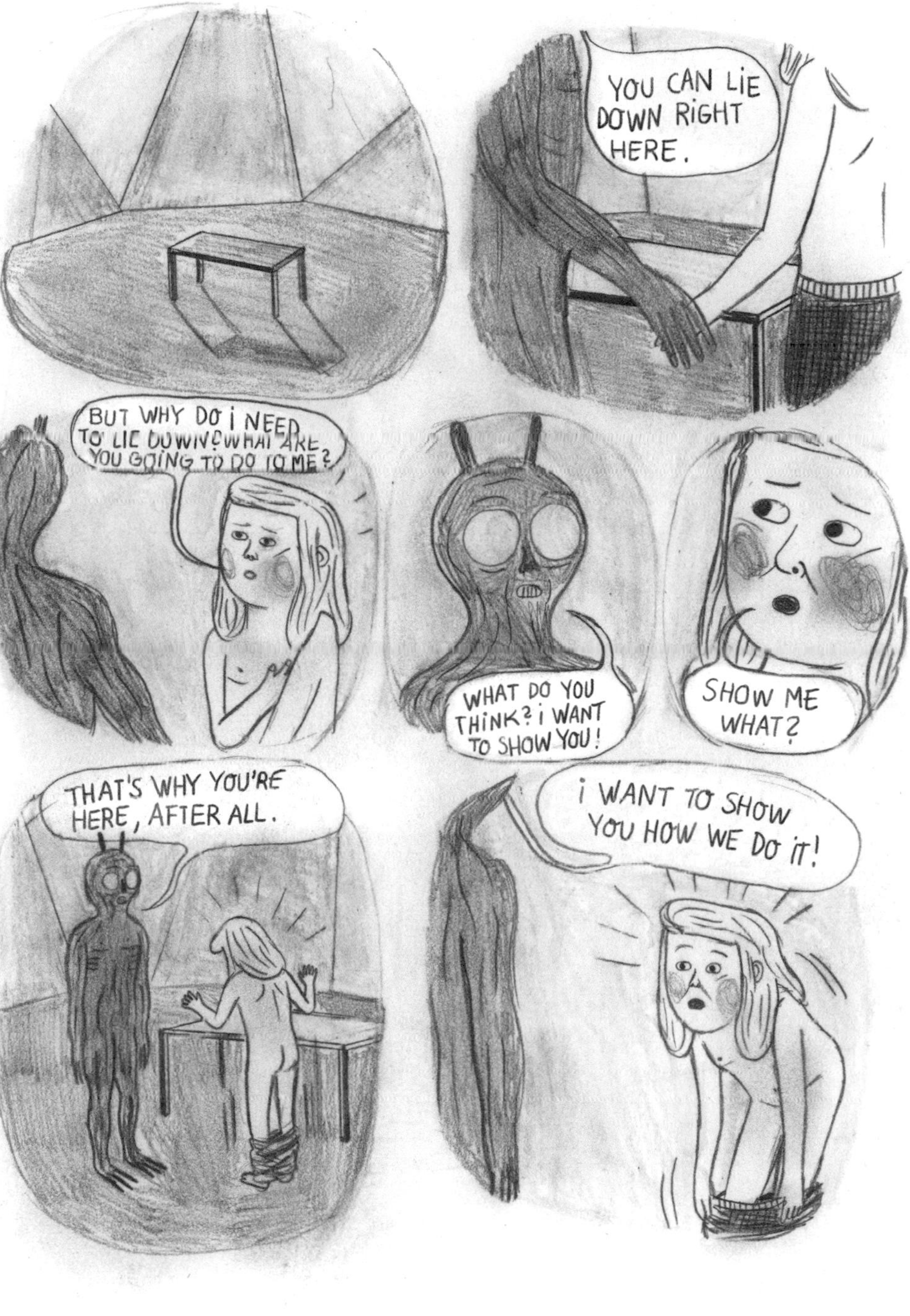
YOU CAN LIE DOWN RIGHT HERE.
BUT WHY DO i NEED TO LIE DOWN? WHAT ARE YOU GOING TO DO TO ME?
WHAT DO YOU THINK? i WANT TO SHOW YOU!
SHOW ME WHAT?
THAT'S WHY YOU'RE HERE, AFTER ALL.
i WANT TO SHOW YOU HOW WE DO iT!

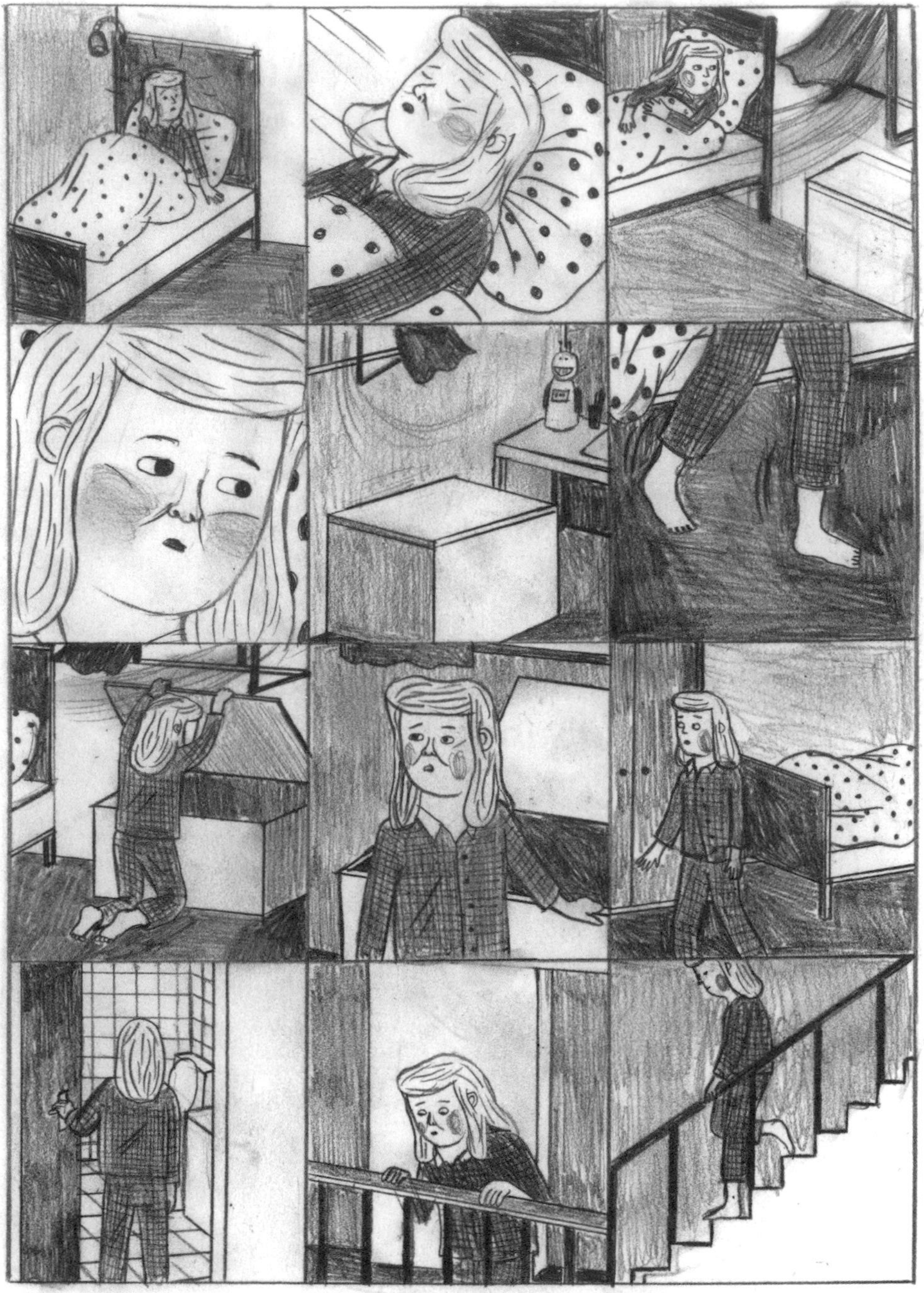

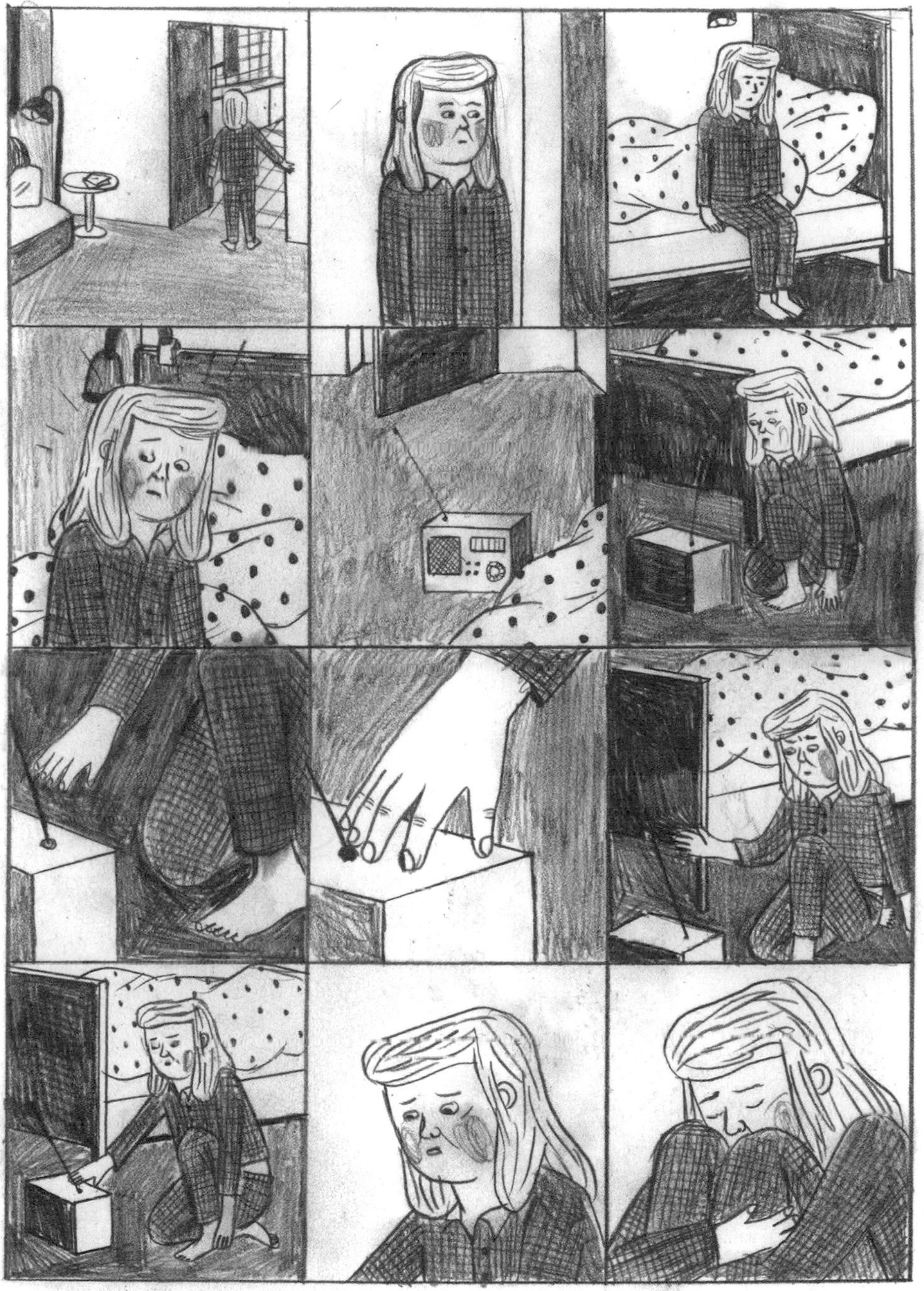

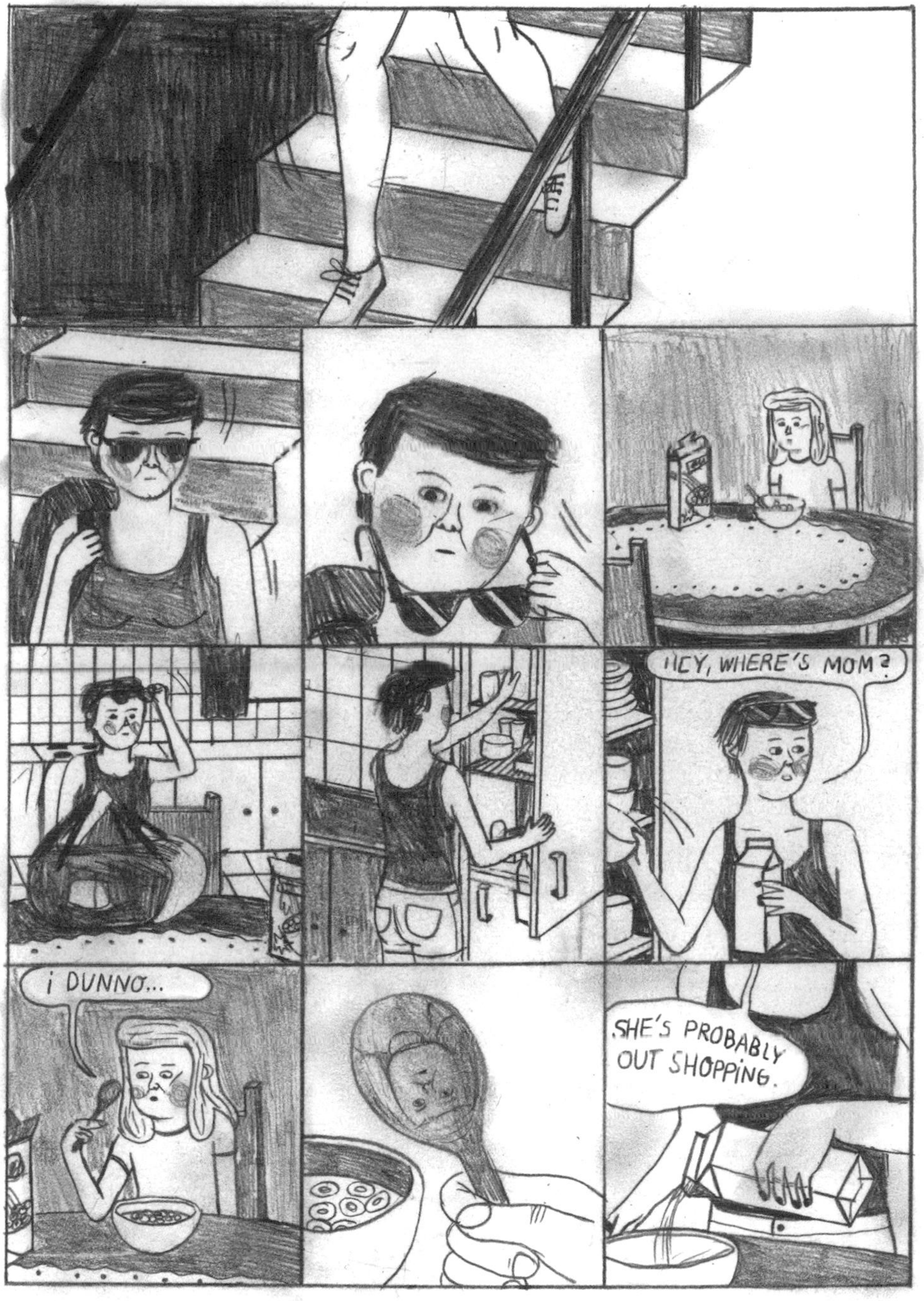
HEY, WHERE'S MOM?
i DUNNO...
SHE'S PROBABLY OUT SHOPPING.

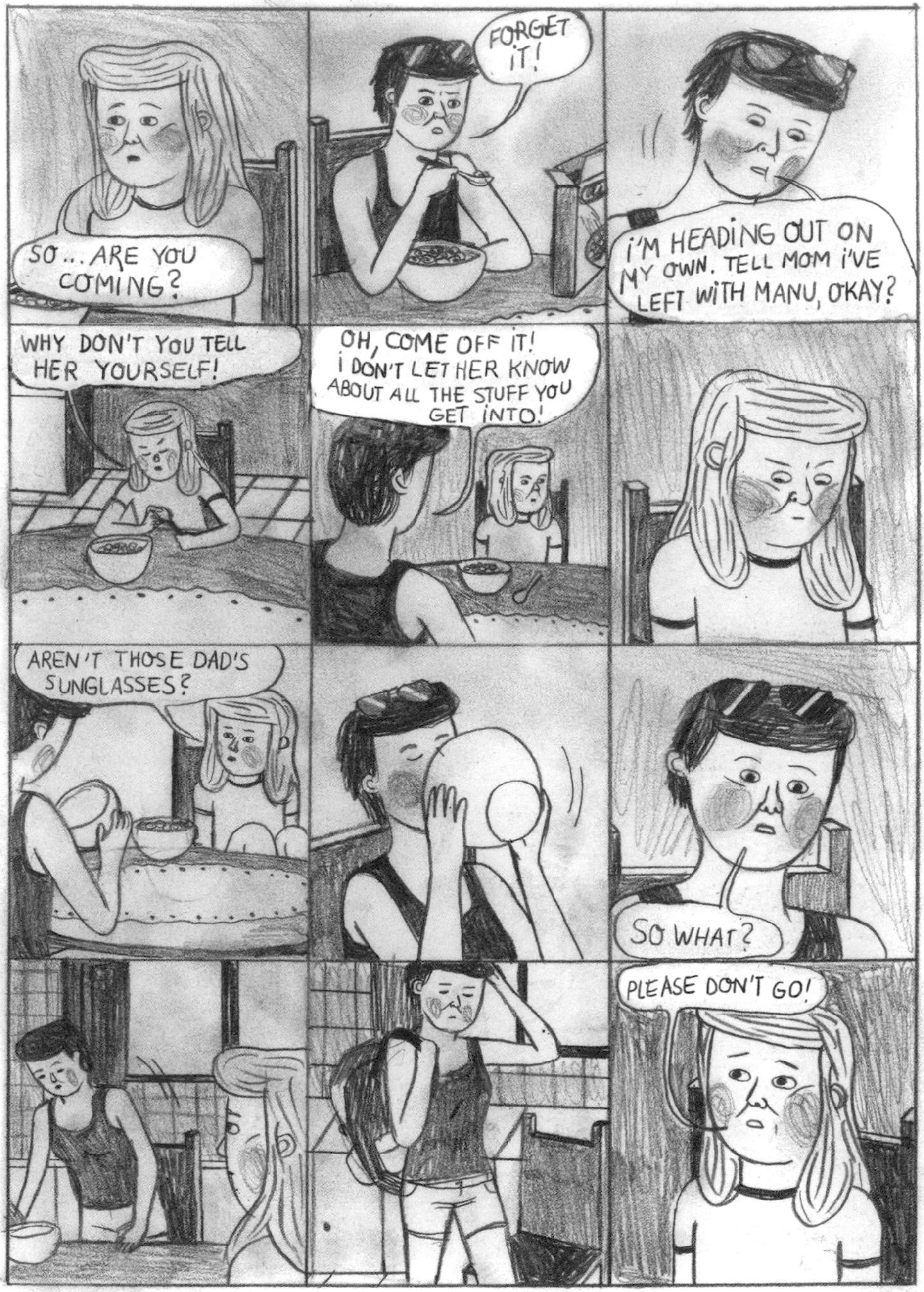
SO... ARE YOU COMING?
FORGET IT!
I'M HEADING OUT ON MY OWN. TELL MOM I'VE LEFT WITH MANU, OKAY?
WHY DON'T YOU TELL HER YOURSELF!
OH, COME OFF IT! I DON'T LET HER KNOW ABOUT ALL THE STUFF YOU GET INTO!
AREN'T THOSE DAD'S SUNGLASSES?
SO WHAT?
PLEASE DON'T GO!

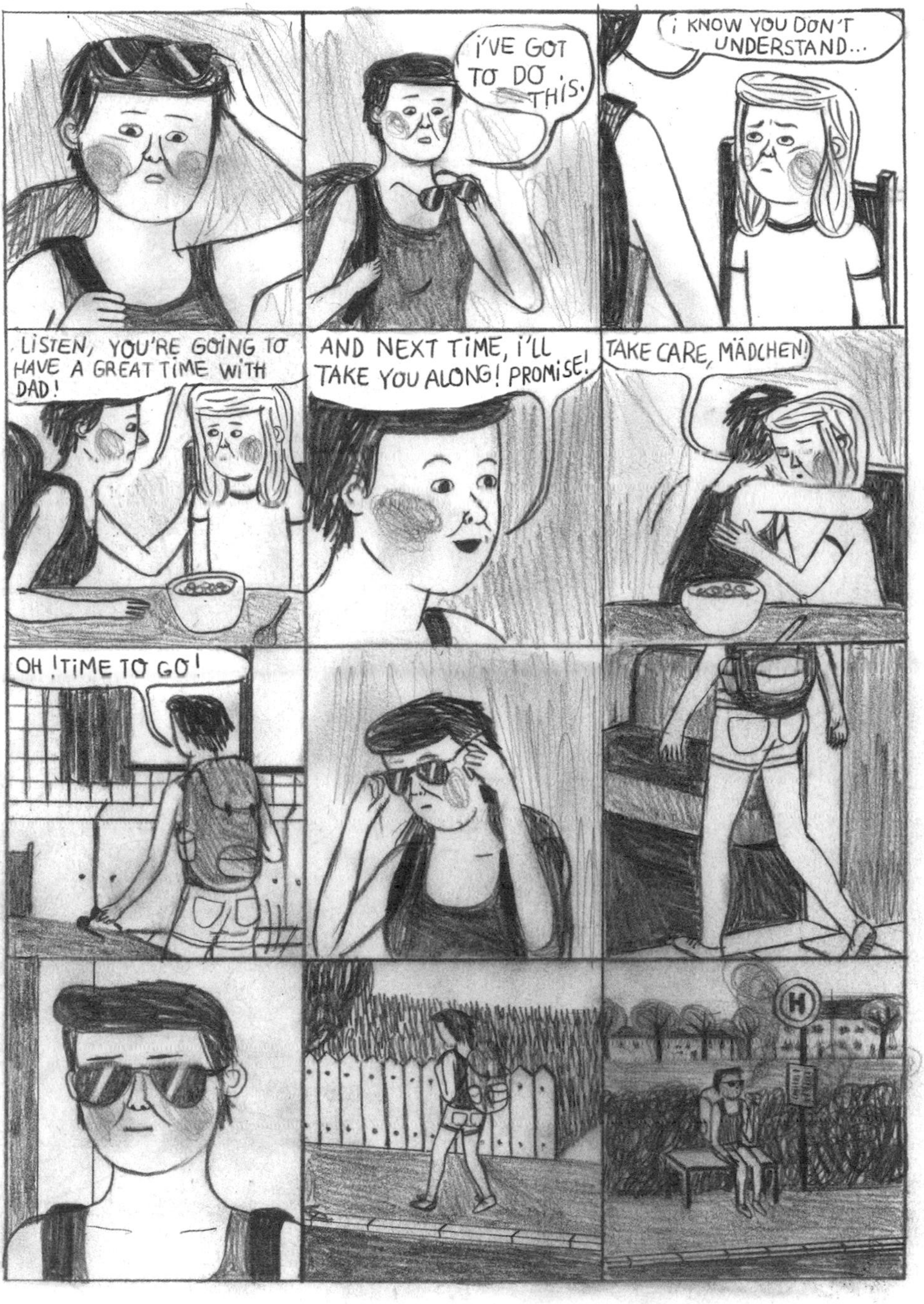
I'VE GOT TO DO THIS.
I KNOW YOU DON'T UNDERSTAND...
LISTEN, YOU'RE GOING TO HAVE A GREAT TIME WITH DAD!
AND NEXT TIME, I'LL TAKE YOU ALONG! PROMISE!
TAKE CARE, MÄDCHEN!
OH! TIME TO GO!
H

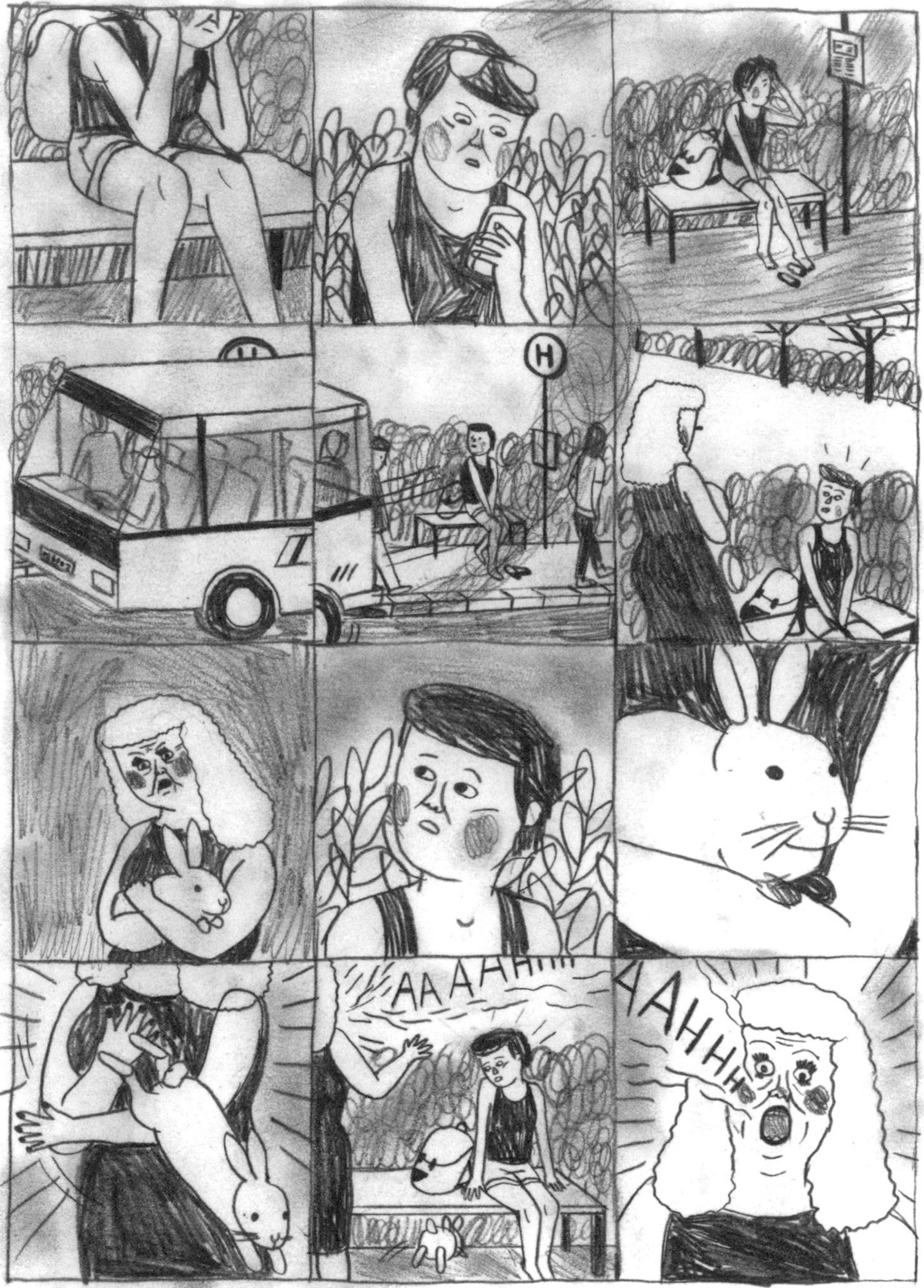
AAAAHH!!!!!
AAHHH

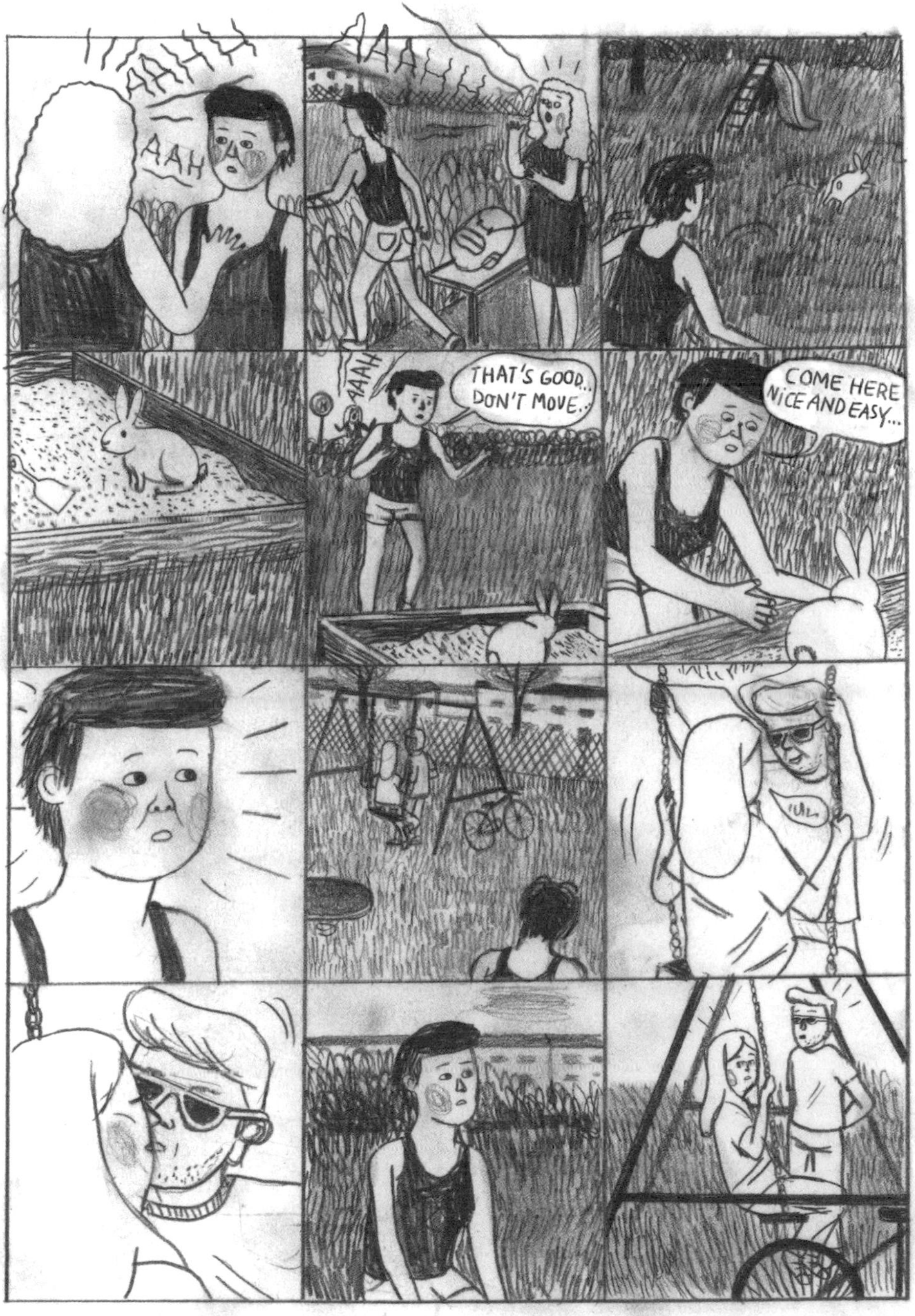
AAHH
AAH
AAAHH
AAAH
THAT'S GOOD... DON'T MOVE...
COME HERE NICE AND EASY...

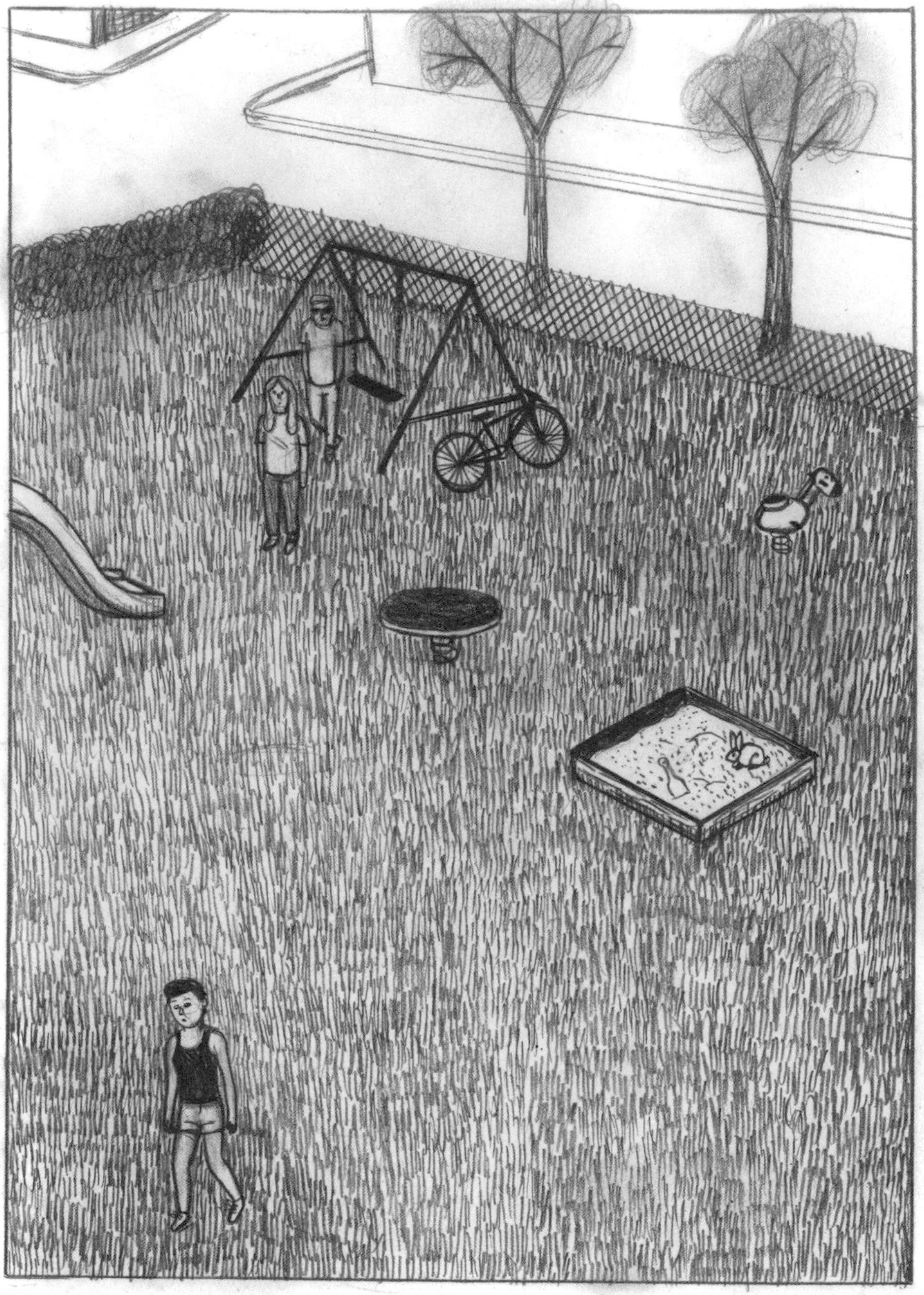

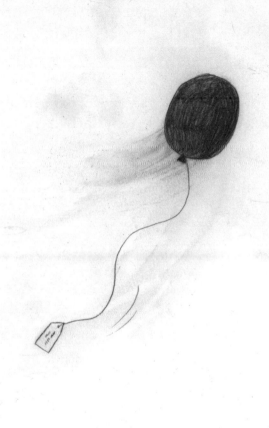

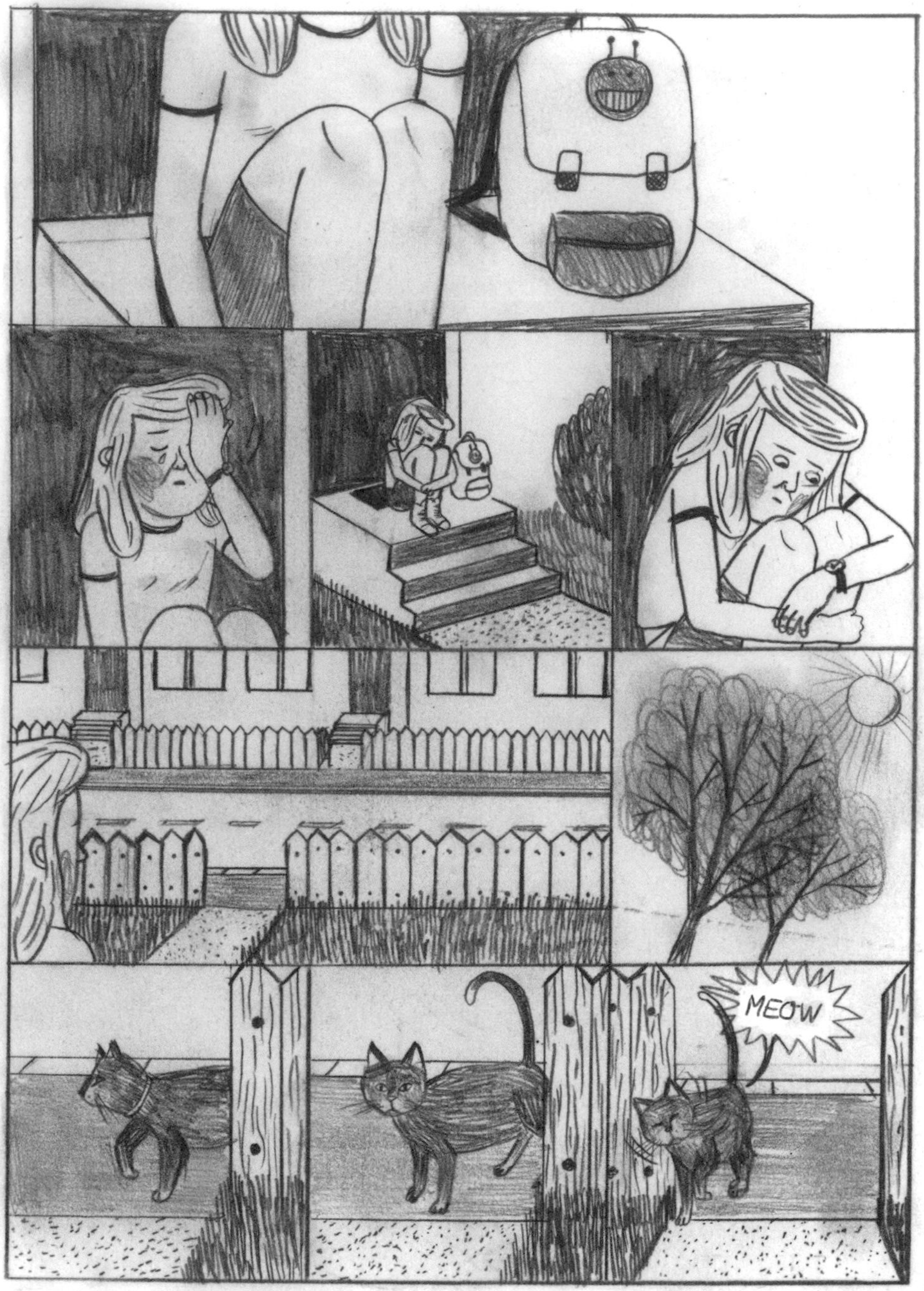
MEOW

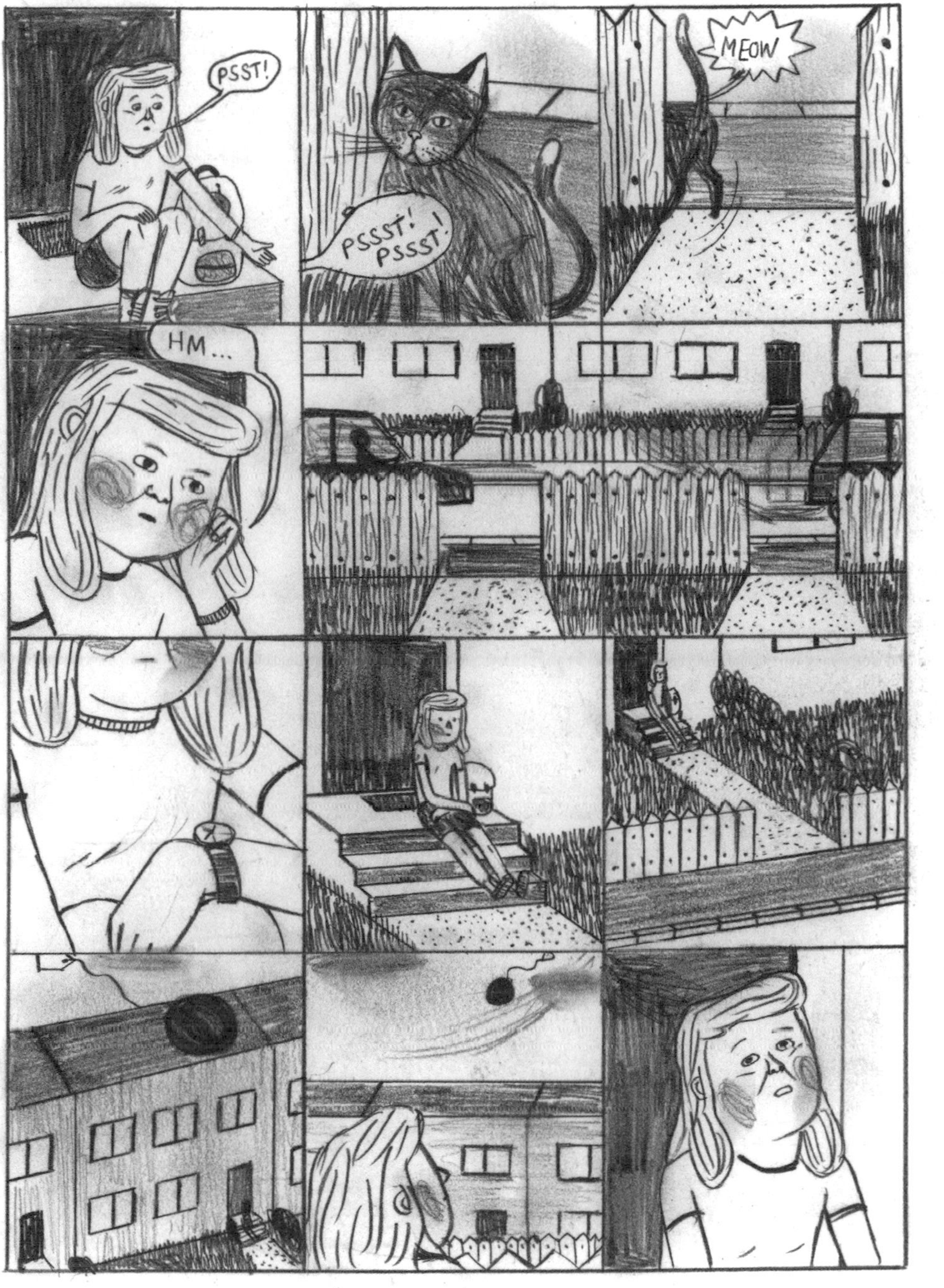
PSST!
PSSST! PSSST!
MEOW
HM...

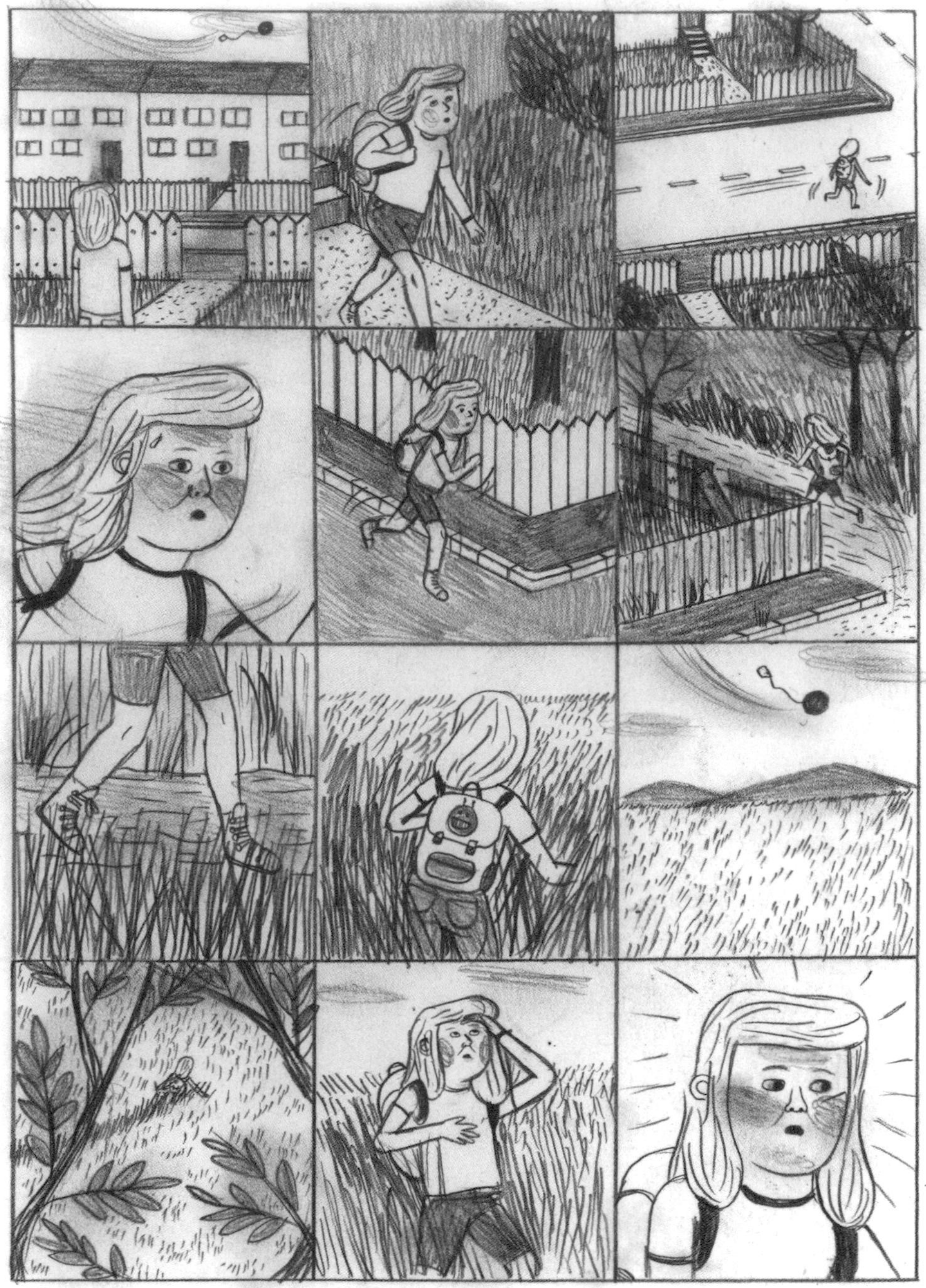

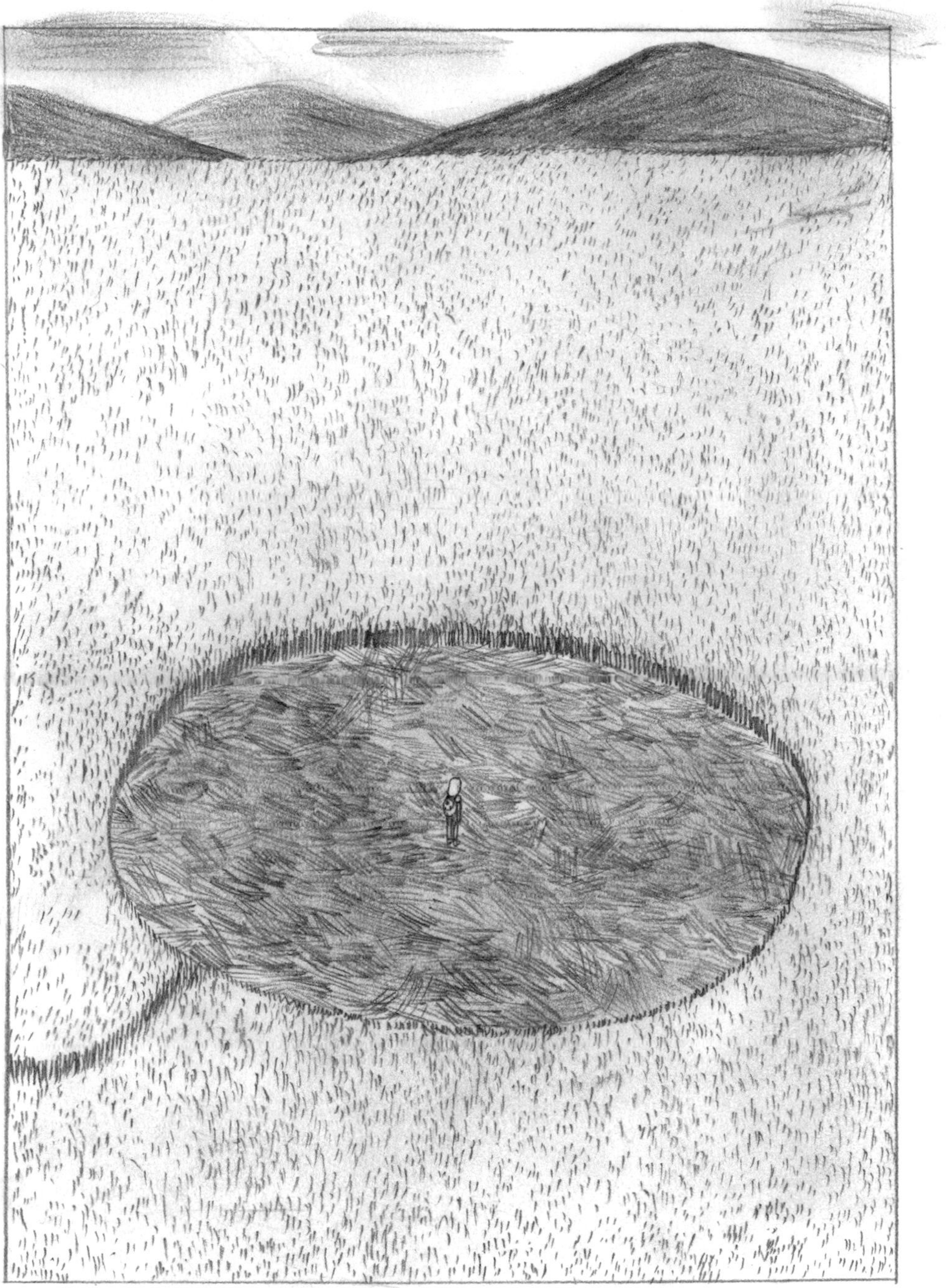

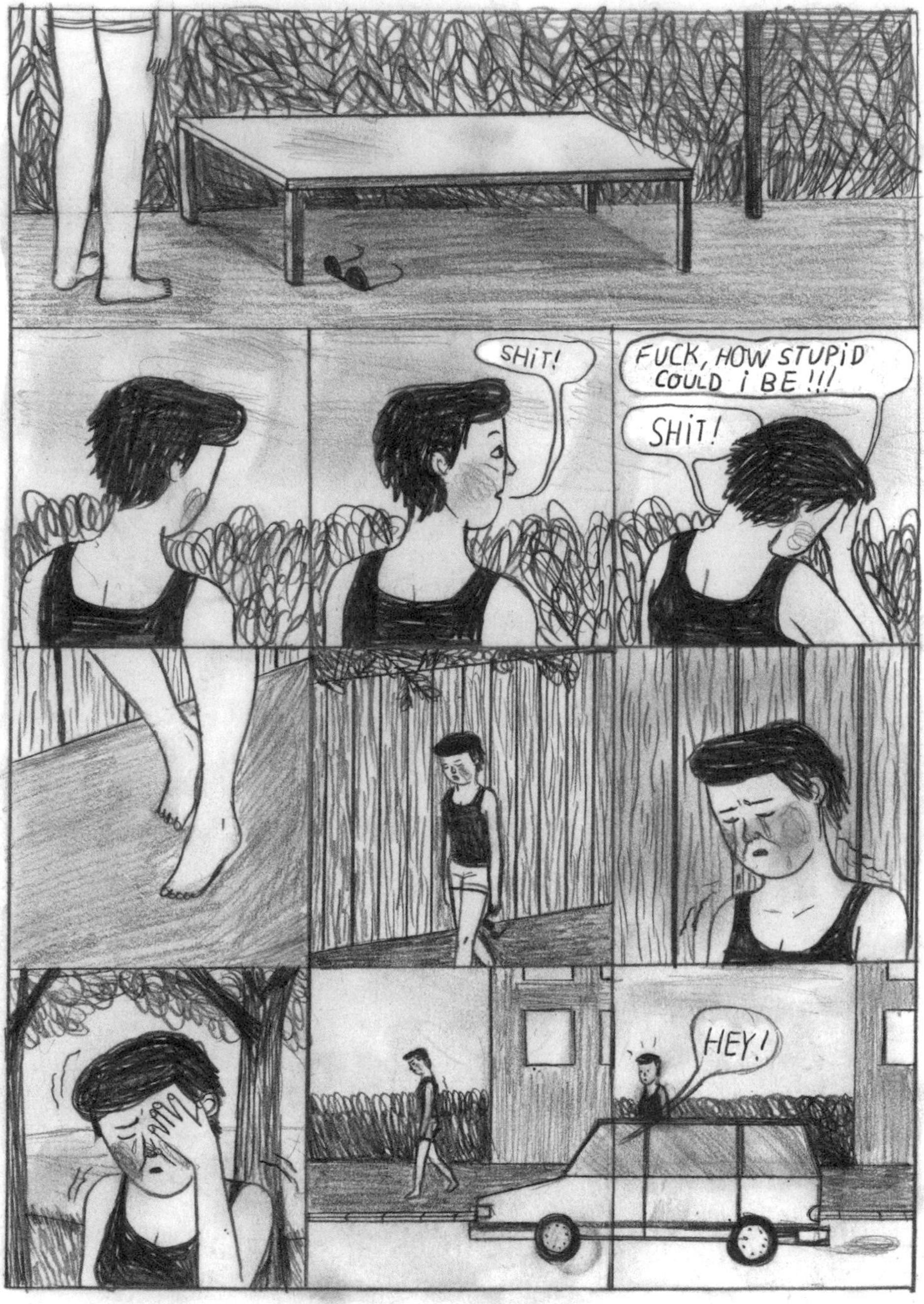
SHIT!
FUCK, HOW STUPID COULD I BE!!!
SHIT!
HEY!

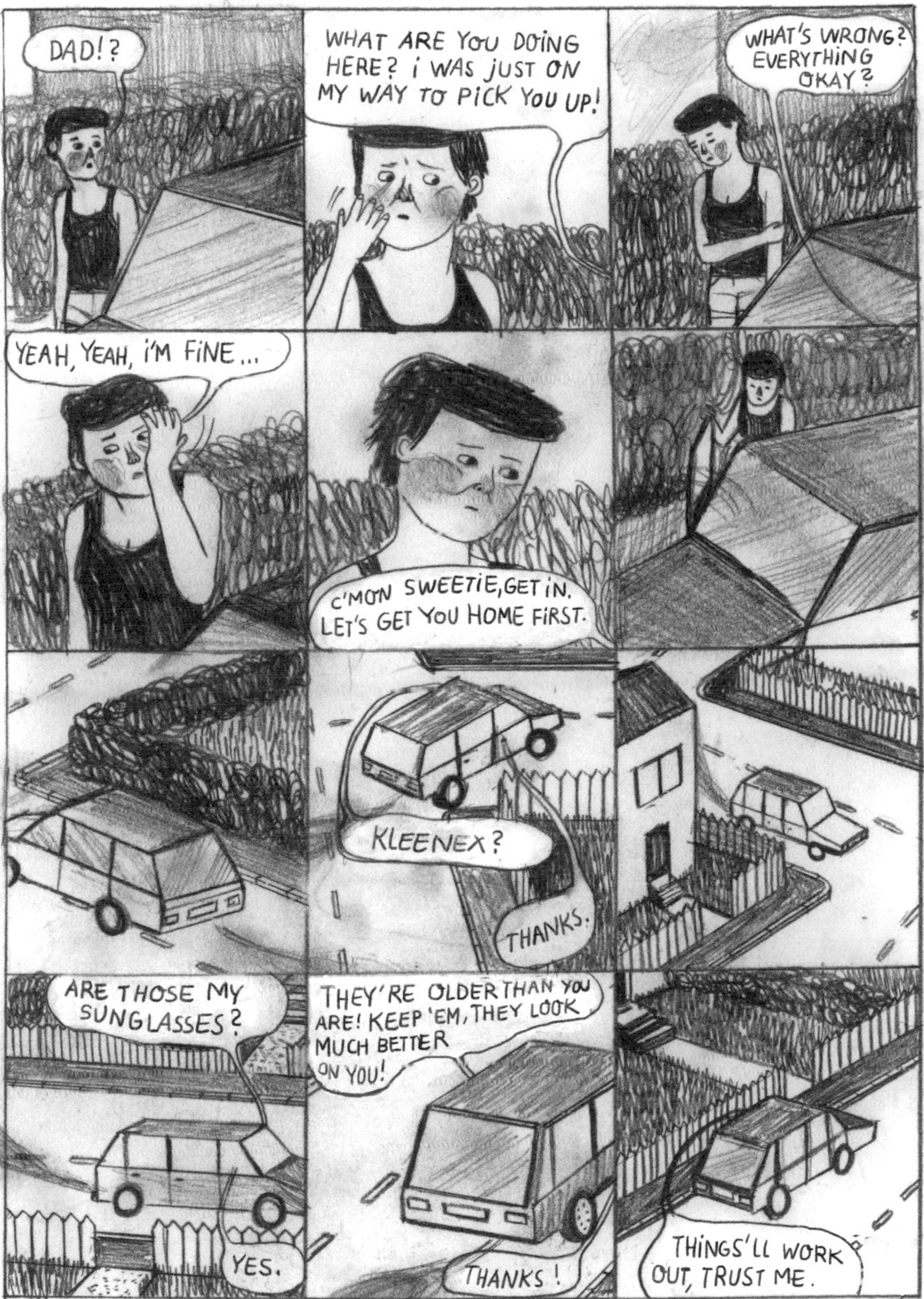
DAD!?
WHAT ARE YOU DOING HERE? i WAS JUST ON MY WAY TO PiCK YOU UP!
WHAT'S WRONG? EVERYTHING OKAY?
YEAH, YEAH, i'M FiNE...
C'MON SWEETiE, GET iN. LET'S GET YOU HOME FiRST.
KLEENEX?
THANKS.
ARE THOSE MY SUNGLASSES?
YES.
THEY'RE OLDER THAN YOU ARE! KEEP 'EM, THEY LOOK MUCH BETTER ON YOU!
THANKS!
THiNGS'LL WORK OUT, TRUST ME.

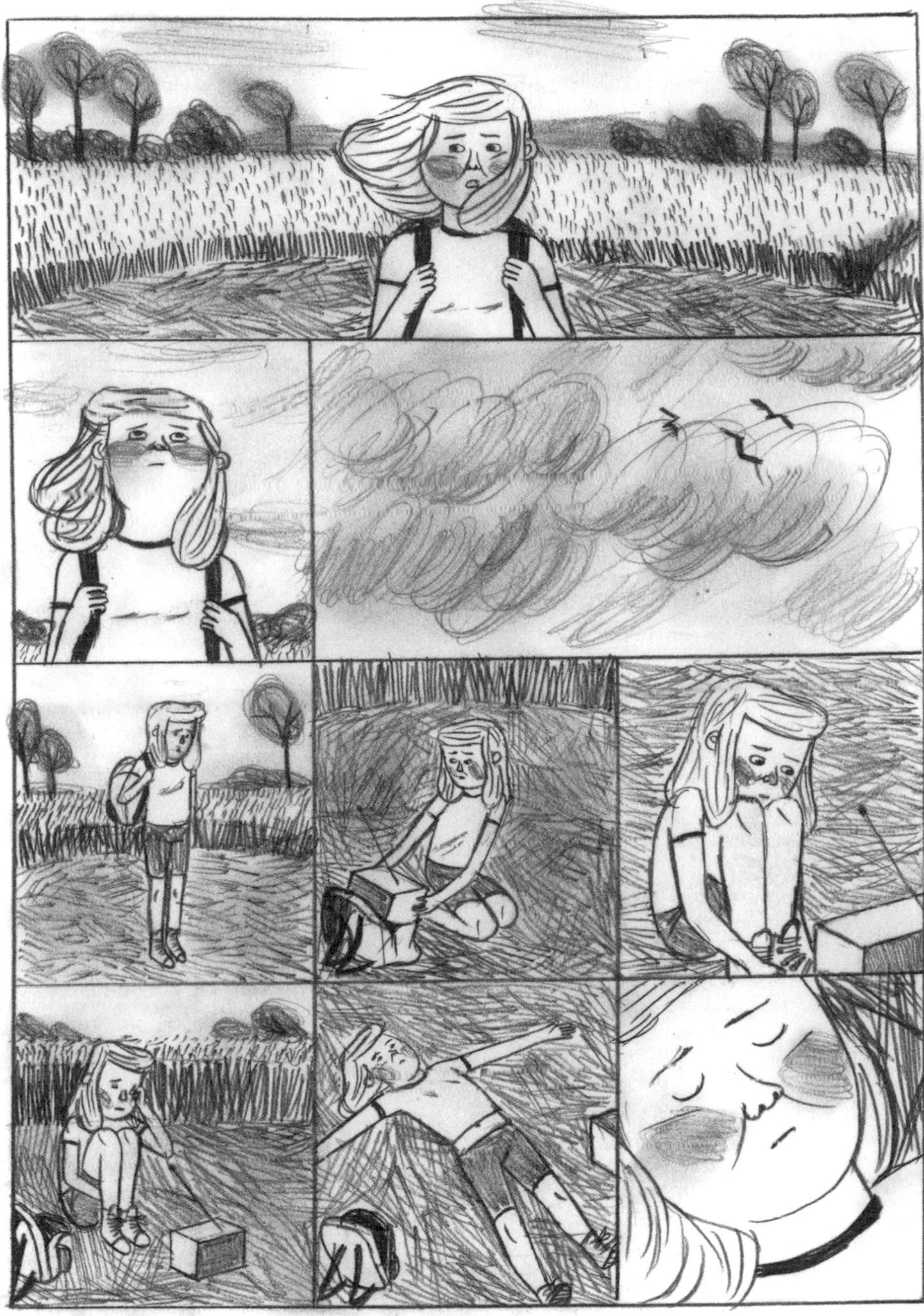

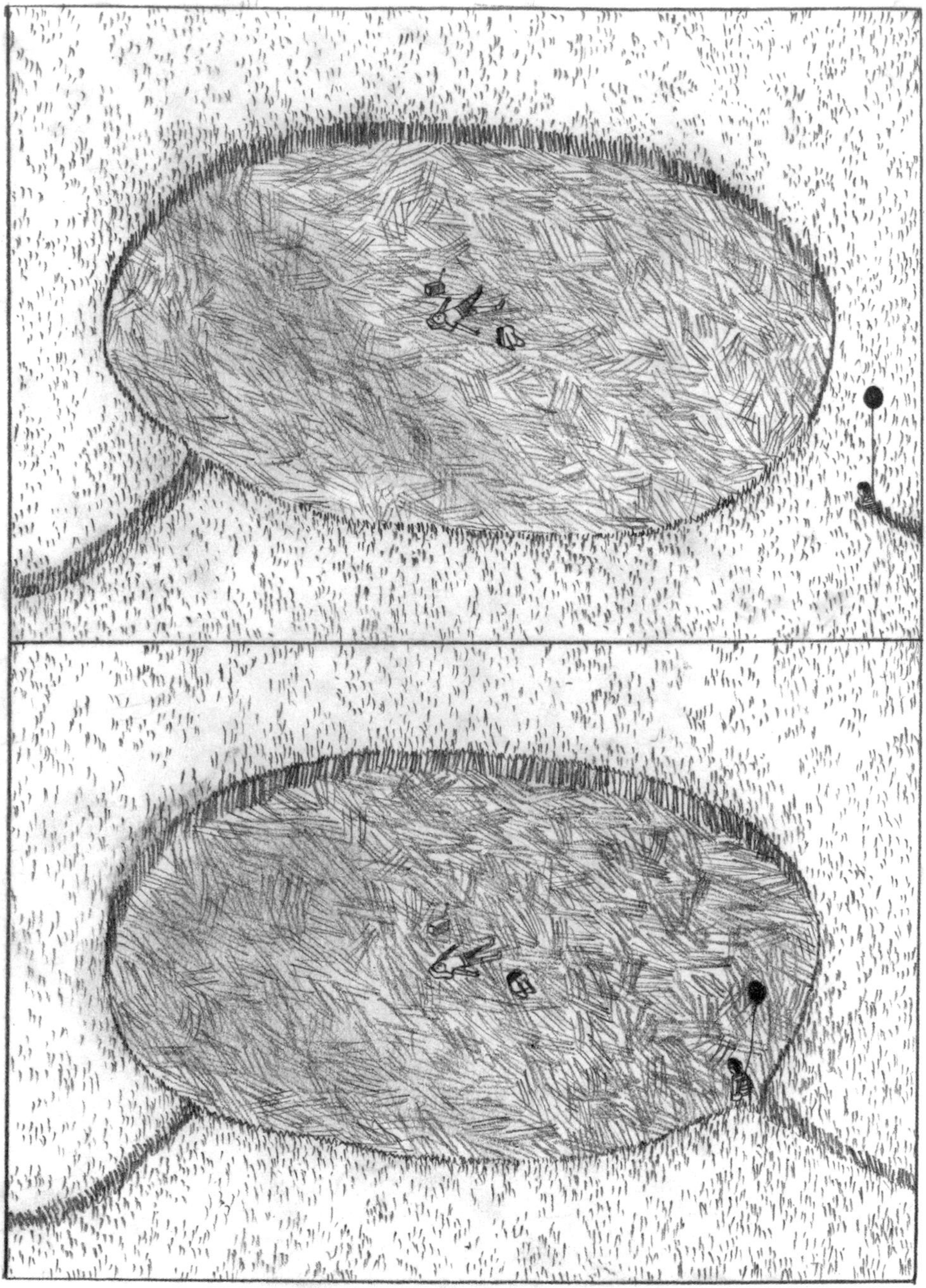

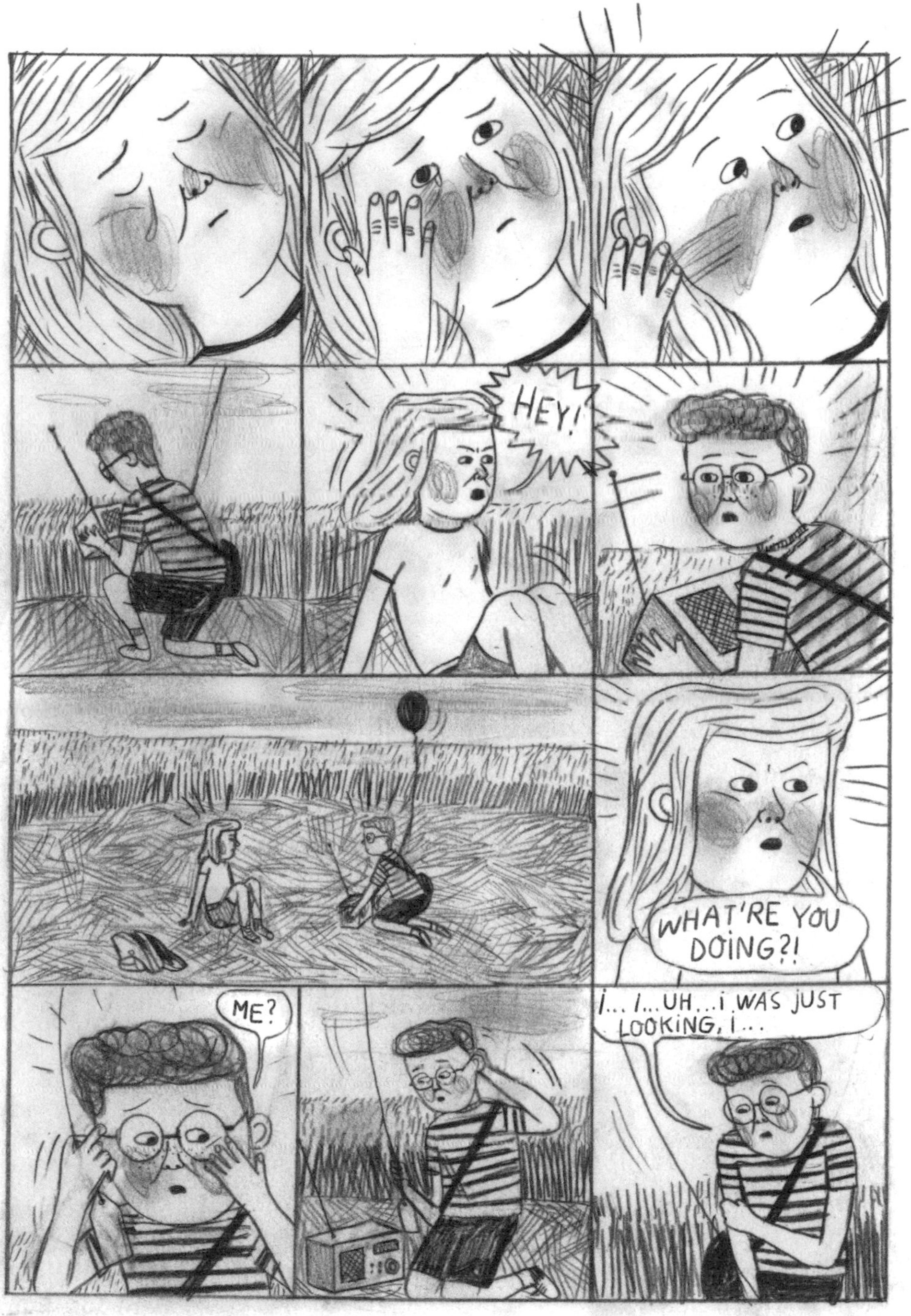
HEY!
WHAT'RE YOU DOING?!
ME?
I... I...UH...I WAS JUST LOOKING, I...

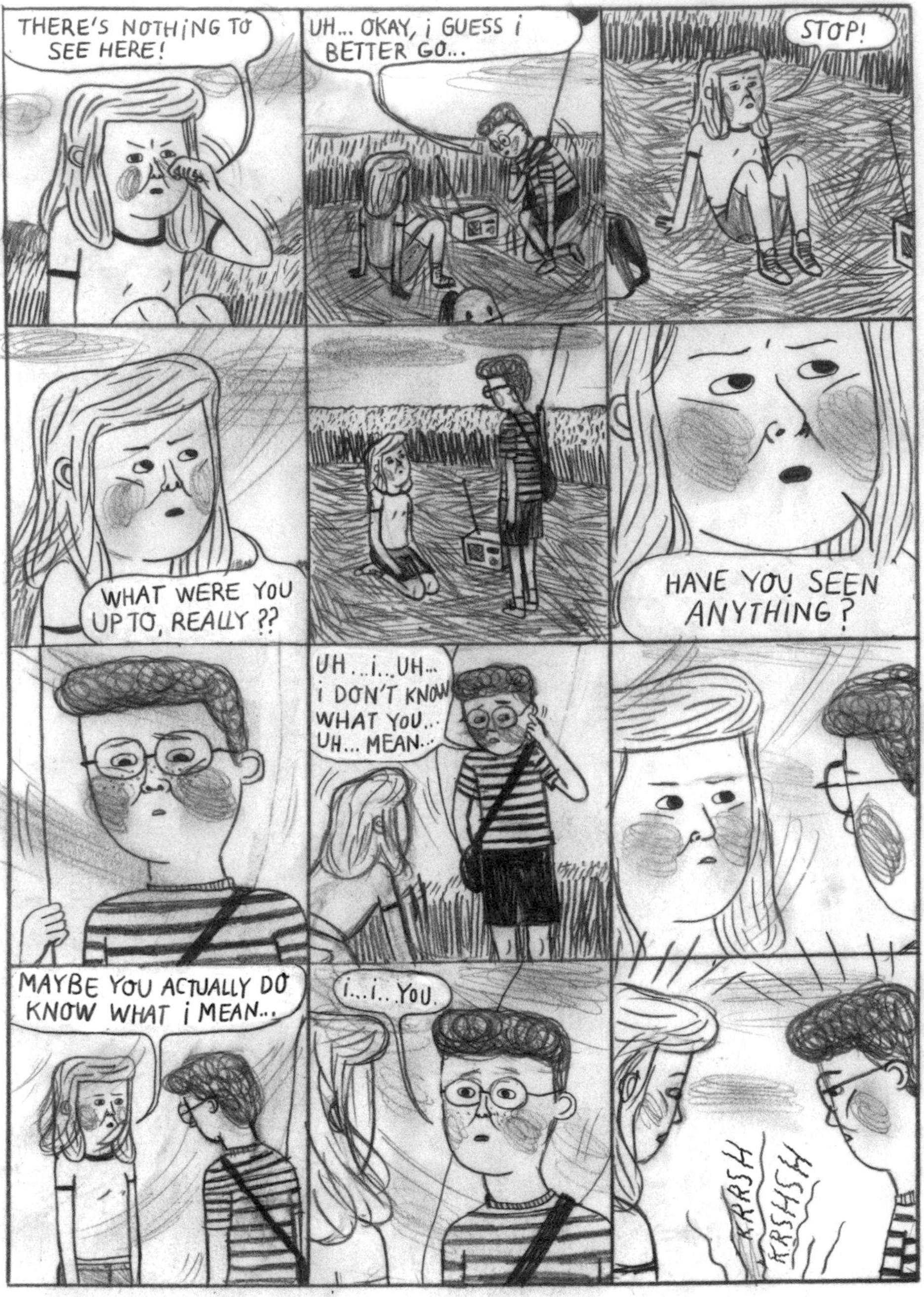
THERE'S NOTHING TO SEE HERE!
UH... OKAY, i GUESS i BETTER GO...
STOP!
WHAT WERE YOU UP TO, REALLY ??
HAVE YOU SEEN ANYTHING?
UH...i...UH... i DON'T KNOW WHAT YOU... UH... MEAN...
MAYBE YOU ACTUALLY DO KNOW WHAT i MEAN...
i...i... YOU.
KRRSH
KRSHSH

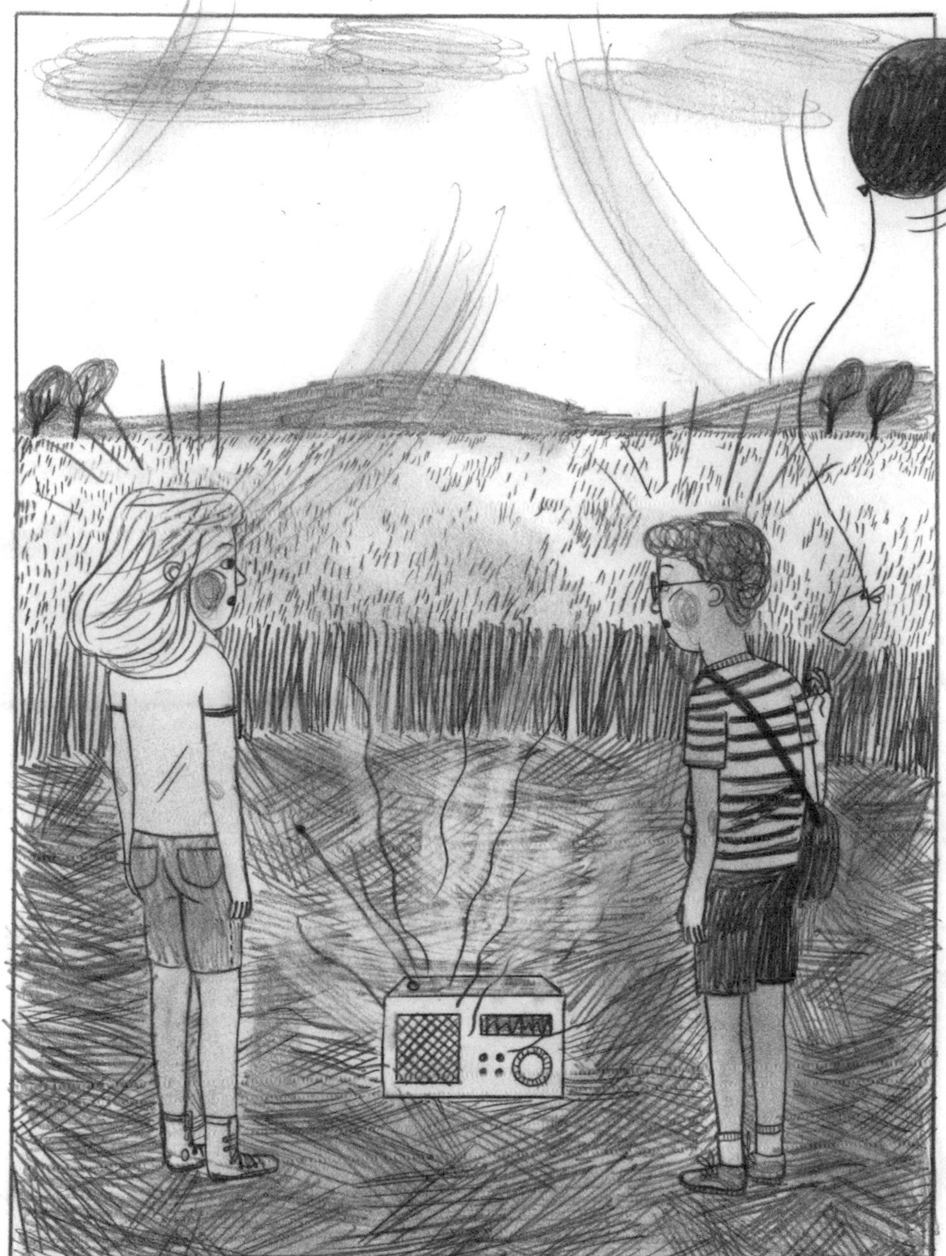

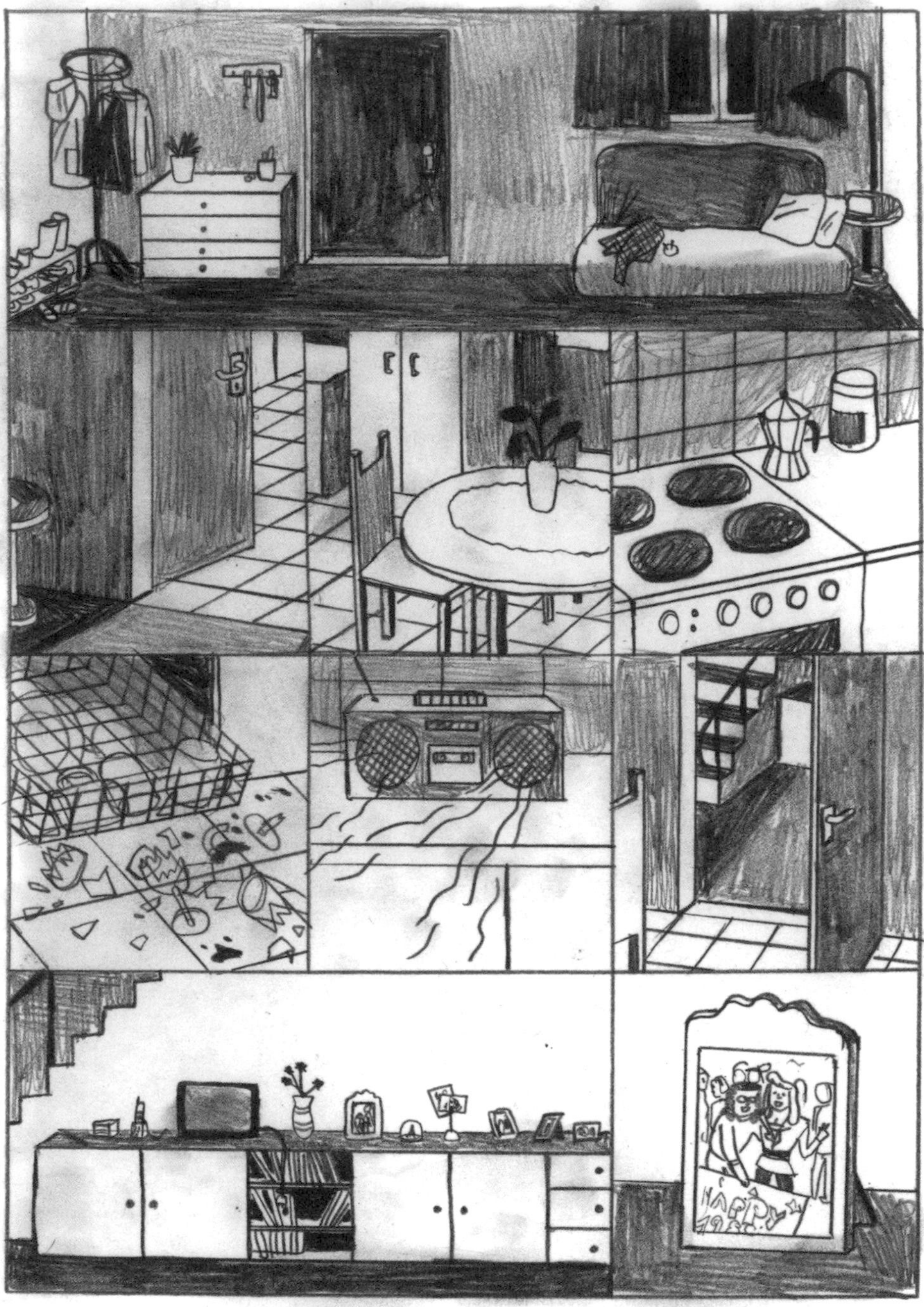
HAPPY

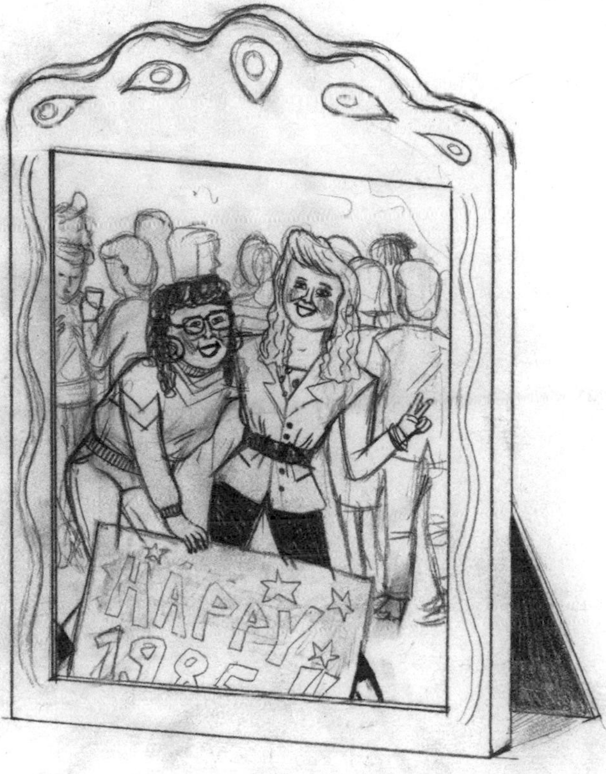
HAPPY

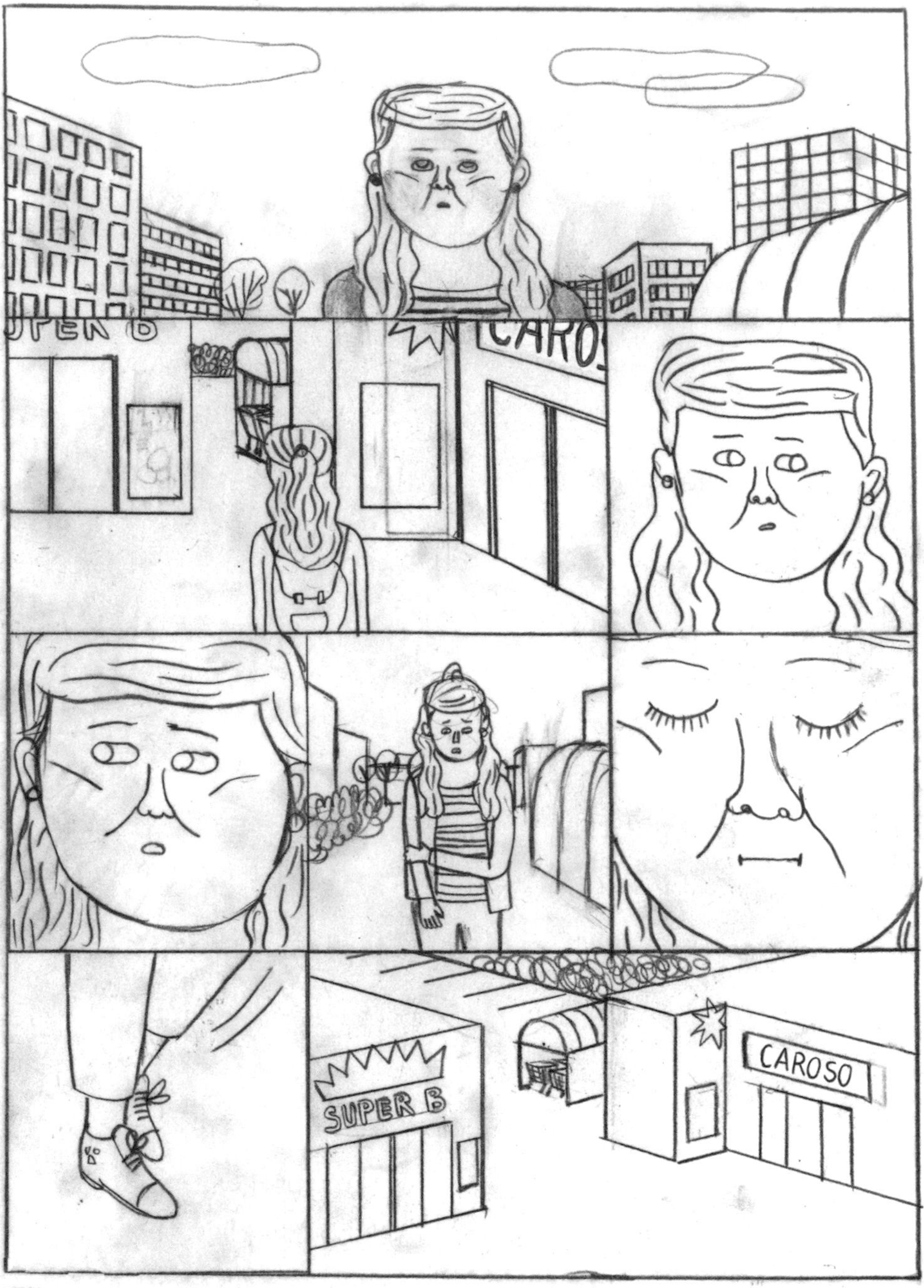
SUPER B
CAROSO

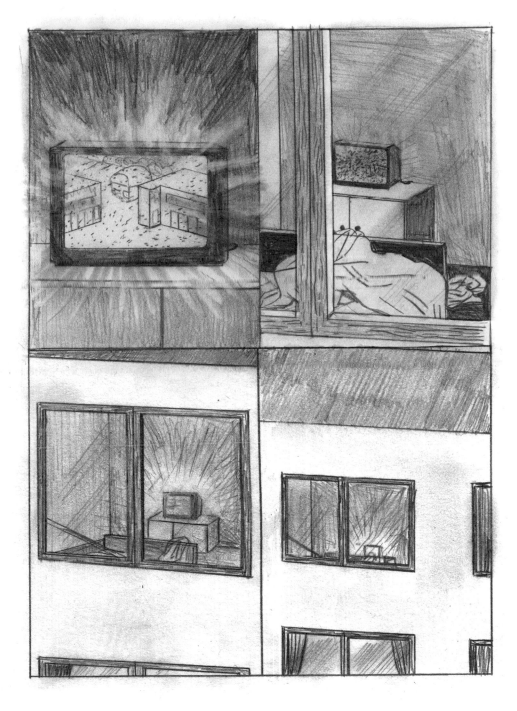

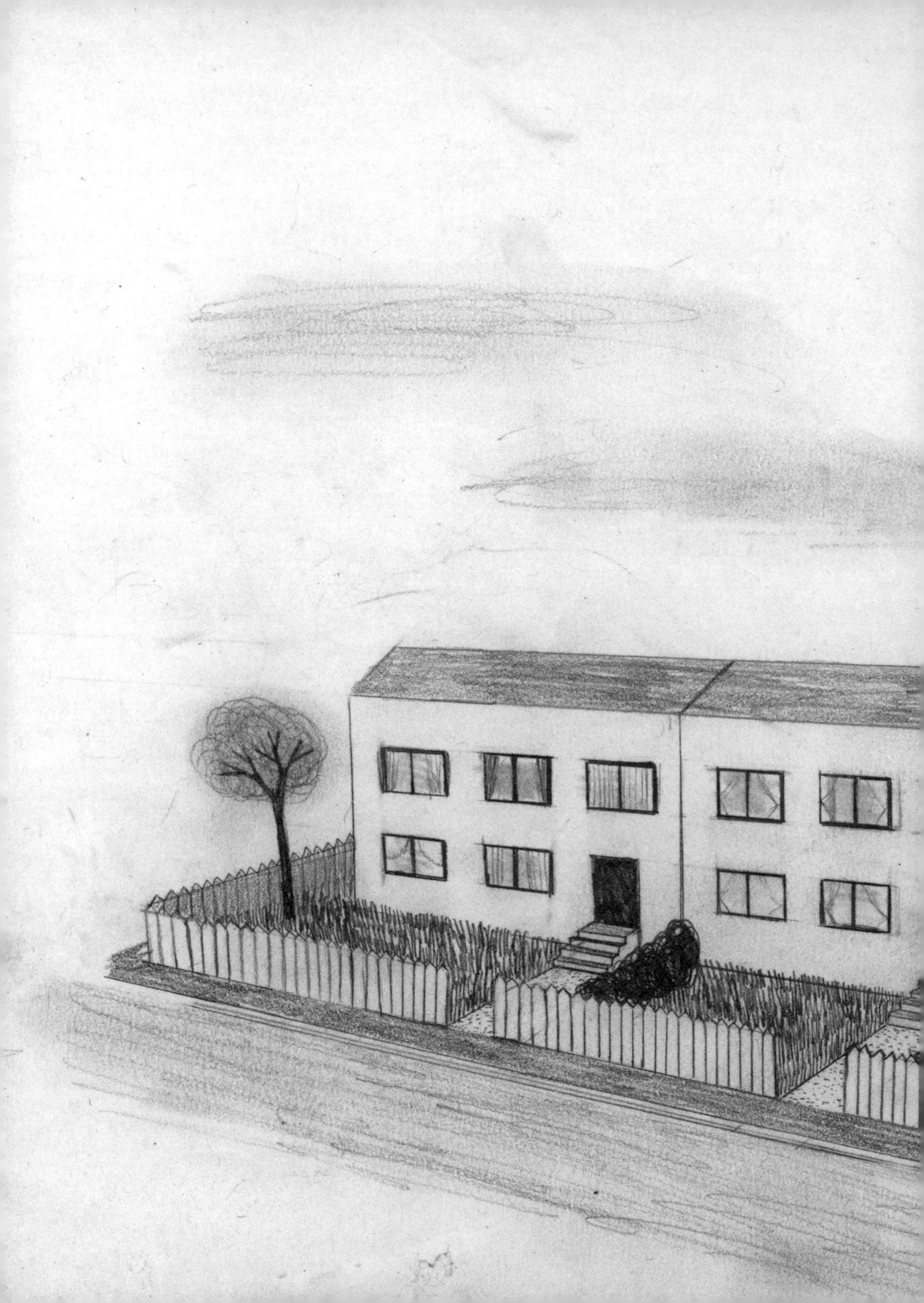

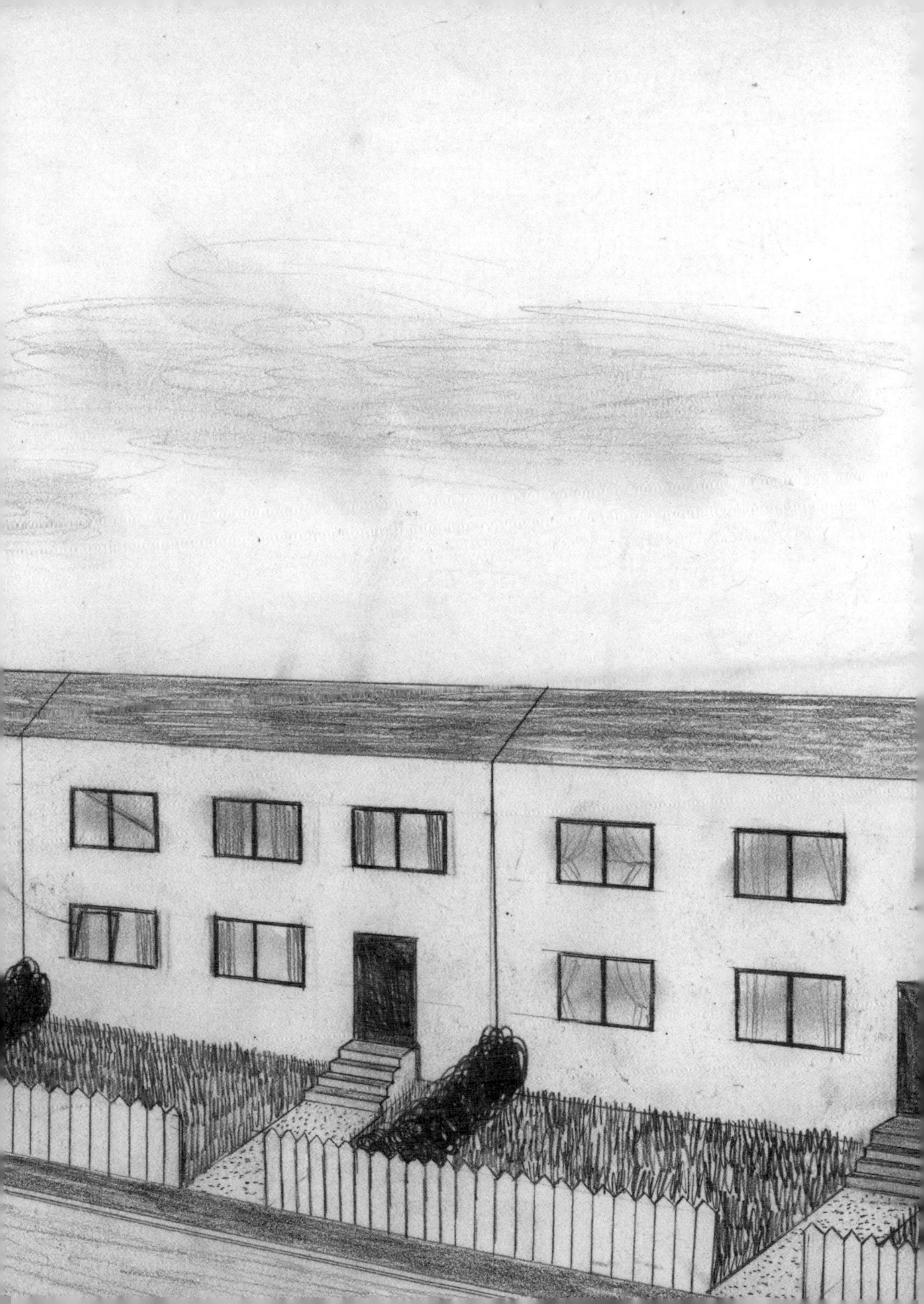

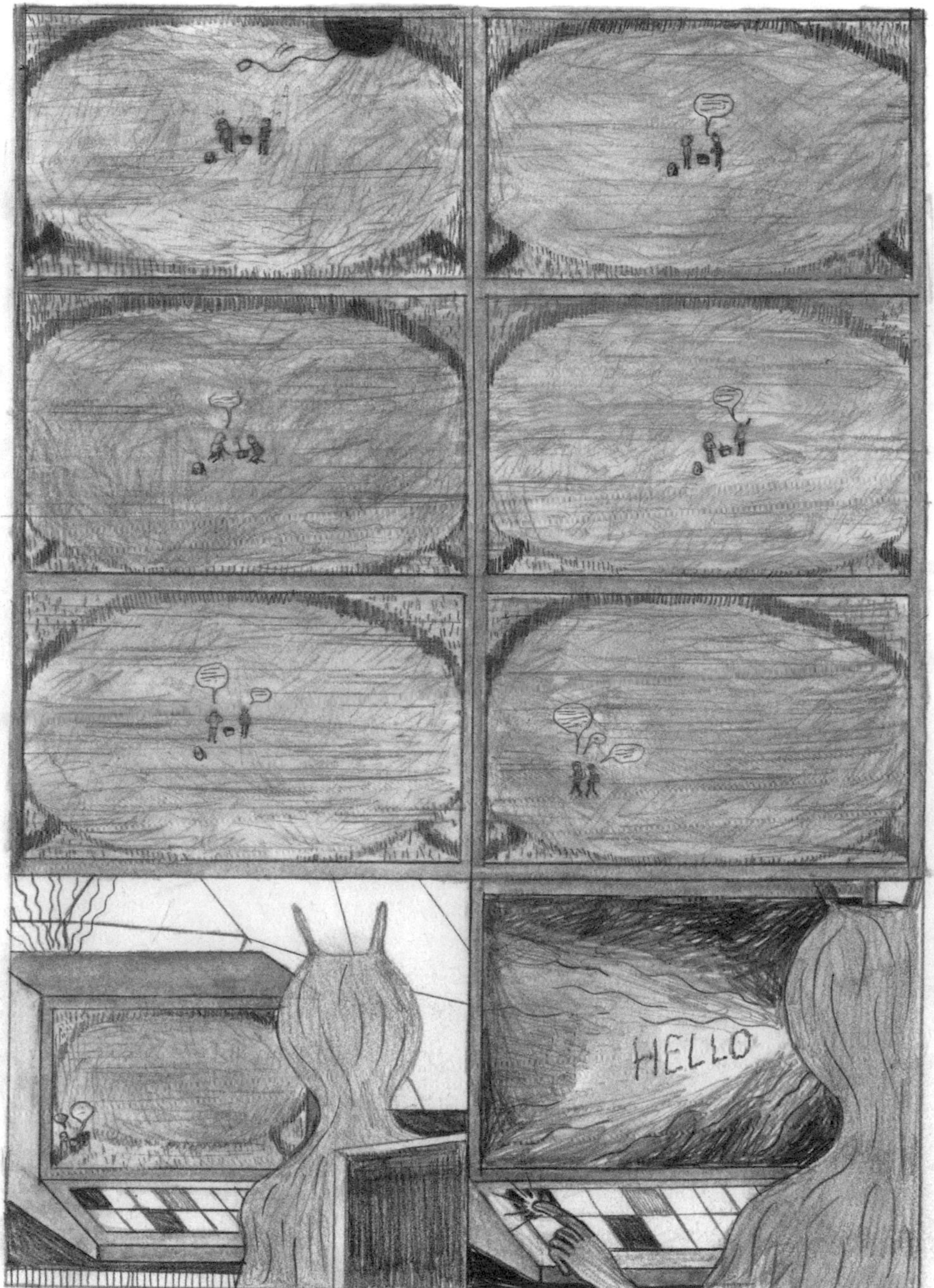
HELLO

[redacted]

THANKS TO
MOM, DAD, SEBASTIAN,
HENDRIK, GABRIELE, KAI, ULLI,
ISABEL, INES, AND
ALL THE OTHER SUPER ILLUS,
GOETHESTRASSE 75,
LAURA,
EVA M. SCHUBART,
YOLANDA,
MÄDCHEN, SISTER AND DORIS,
AND E.T.

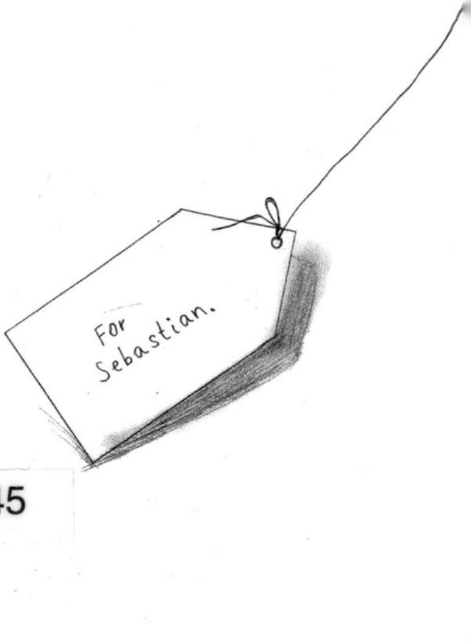
For Sebastian.